*Ethics, Exegesis and Philosophy*

The reputation and influence of Emmanuel Levinas (1906–95) have grown powerfully in recent years. Well known in France in his lifetime, he has since his death become widely regarded as a major European moral philosopher profoundly shaped by his Jewish background. A pupil of Husserl and Heidegger, Levinas pioneered new forms of exegesis with his postmodern readings of the Talmud, and as an ethicist brought together religious and non-religious, Jewish and non-Jewish traditions of contemporary thought.

Richard A. Cohen has written a book which uses Levinas's work as its base but goes on to explore broader questions of interpretation in the context of text-based ethical thinking. Levinas's reorientation of philosophy is considered in critical contrast to alternative contemporary approaches such as those found in modern science, psychology, Nietzsche, Freud, Husserl, Heidegger, Sartre, Merleau-Ponty, Derrida and Ricoeur. Cohen explores a manner of philosophizing which he terms "ethical exegesis."

RICHARD A. COHEN, trained in philosophy, is Professor of Religious Studies and the Isaac Swift Distinguished Professor of Judaic Studies at the University of North Carolina at Charlotte. He is the author of *Elevations: The Height of the Good in Rosenzweig and Levinas* (1994) and editor of *Face to Face with Levinas* (1986). Professor Cohen has translated four books by Emmanuel Levinas and has published many articles on contemporary continental philosophy.

# ETHICS, EXEGESIS AND PHILOSOPHY

*Interpretation after Levinas*

RICHARD A. COHEN

PUBLISHED BY THE PRESS SYNDICATE OF THE UNIVERSITY OF CAMBRIDGE
The Pitt Building, Trumpington Street, Cambridge, United Kingdom

CAMBRIDGE UNIVERSITY PRESS
The Edinburgh Building, Cambridge CB2 2RU, UK
40 West 20th Street, New York NY 10011-4211, USA
10 Stamford Road, Oakleigh, VIC 3166, Australia
Ruiz de Alarcón 13, 28014 Madrid, Spain
Dock House, The Waterfront, Cape Town 8001, South Africa

http://www.cambridge.org

First published 2001

Printed in the United Kingdom at the University Press, Cambridge

*Typeface* Baskerville 11/12.5pt     *System* Poltype ® [VN]

*A catalogue record for this book is available from the British Library*

*Library of Congress cataloguing in publication data*

Cohen, Richard A., 1950–
Ethics, exegesis, and philosophy: interpretation after Levinas / Richard A. Cohen
p.   cm.
Includes bibliographical references and index.
ISBN 0 521 80158 3 (hardback)
1. Levinas, Emmanuel.   2. Levinas, Emmanuel – Ethics.   I. Title.
B2430.L484 C64 2001
194 – dc21      01–045501

ISBN 0 521 80158 3 hardback

*Dedicated with love to my parents, Bette Gordon Cohen
and Sidney S. Cohen,
and with gratitude to
Emmanuel Levinas
— my teachers.*

It was taught on Tannaite authority by Rabbi Shimon ben Yochai: "If *you are my witness, says the Lord, then I am God* [Isaiah 43:12], and if you are not my witness, then, as it were, it is as if I am not the Lord."

*Pesikta de Rav Kahana* 12:6

I do not ask the wounded person how he feels . . . I myself become the wounded person.

Walt Whitman, *Leaves of Grass*

# Contents

# Introduction: philosophy as ethical exegesis

> But it belongs to the very essence of language, which consists in continually undoing its phrase by the foreword or the exegesis, in unsaying the said, in attempting to restate without ceremonies what has already been ill understood in the inevitable ceremonial in which the said delights.
>
> Emmanuel Levinas, *Totality and Infinity*[1]

Parents, teachers and religious leaders have always taught morality to their charges, to their sons and daughters, to school children, and to ordinary people. Emmanuel Levinas (1906–95), the Lithuanian-born French Jewish philosopher, does something different, something perhaps more difficult. He teaches morality to the intellectual elite, to those who all too often, and all too proudly, have become our new "cultured despisers of religion," thinking themselves too intelligent, too sophisticated, too cultured for the common imperatives and well-known limitations of "ordinary" morality. Whether they dismiss the authority of morality as "self-incurred immaturity," "bourgeois superstructure," "grammatical error," "infantile internalization," "mass delusion," "physiological weakness," or some other derisive reduction, Levinas aims to show them – at the highest levels of intellect and spirit – that morality is a matter for adults, intelligent adults included.

Levinas will show that nothing is more serious than morality. For at stake in morality is our highest individual and collective

[1] Emmanuel Levinas, *Totality and Infinity*, trans. Alphonso Lingis (Pittsburgh: Duquesne University Press, 1964), p. 30.

vocation, the very humanity of the human. His writings are difficult, then, not because morality is difficult. Everyone already knows the moral imperatives and knows that they run counter to our instincts and inclinations. Rather, Levinas's writings are difficult because the readers they seek have become difficult. They have become ensnared in the labyrinth of knowledge, both true and false, advanced and elementary, forgetful, however, of the genuine roots of our common humanity.

Levinas's first two book-length works in philosophy were both published in 1947: *Time and the Other* and *Existence and Existents*. Products of the phenomenological school of Edmund Husserl, they present original and distinctive theses that challenge the then dominant readings of phenomenology articulated by Heidegger in Germany and Jean-Paul Sartre in France. They challenge Husserl's own phenomenology too. Nonetheless, these books are but the first steps, and as such appear – retrospectively – as schematic beginnings, when compared to his later, more mature philosophy. This philosophy appears in Levinas's two great works of ethical metaphysics: *Totality and Infinity*, published in 1961, and *Otherwise than Being or Beyond Essence*, published in 1974. Each by itself, and both together, represent major contributions to Western philosophy. Chapter 5 of the present volume will present their chief theses and elaborate the relationship holding these two volumes together. Both works present Levinas's nuanced, ethical re-vision of Western philosophy, and more particularly his challenge to the philosophies of Spinoza, Kant, Hegel, Nietzsche, Husserl, Heidegger, Sartre, Merleau-Ponty and Derrida. Together they form the backbone of Levinas's philosophy, including his so-called "Jewish" writings.

Unlike many thinkers of modernity, Levinas does not separate philosophy from religion or religion from philosophy. Neither does he bind them together, one at the expense of the other. To maintain their integrity Levinas will insist that philosophy rethink its origins. He will insist that in acknowledging the limits of knowledge, which has been philosophy's obsession throughout the modern period, philosophy also recognize something greater than knowledge, a dimension or excellence more compelling than knowing but at the very root of knowing itself. Levinas will point knowledge to its own moral responsibilities and obligations. To be sure, this dimension and its demands will strike a militantly epistemological philosophy as unjustified, excessive, indeed, as "religious."

But Levinas will also insist that religion is alien to mythology and ideology. As a philosopher, he will reject the intrusion of "proof texts" and "religious experience," no less than any philosopher – in contrast to the sophist – would reject the intrusion of opinion, personal narrative, violence, power. As a philosopher, he will not rely on the prior agreement, the common consent of a particular community of religious faithful. This route, the shared ethos and history of a particular group, perhaps attractive and even necessary for a certain pedagogy, ends by suppressing the universal experience of humanity and the universal knowledge of science, hence it ends by divorcing religion from its proper intellectual heights. Religious thought, and certainly Jewish religious thought, is for Levinas no less universal than philosophy's epistemological discipline imposes on genuinely scientific thought. Indeed, philosophical thought, as Levinas conceives it, is universal precisely because it is bound to the universality of religious thought. That is to say, both philosophical and religious thought are universal insofar as both are attached to the universality and humanity of morality and justice. Showing how these connections are made, without sacrificing the particularity of religion or the universality of philosophy, is one of the great attractions of Levinas's work.

All twentieth-century philosophy, aside from positivism, rejects the hegemony of science. This is the very contemporaneity of contemporary thought and the deepest sense of its "postmodernity." The modern period, inaugurated by Spinoza and ended by Bergson, as I shall argue in chapter 1, was the epoch of science and unqualified faith in science. Because he accepts the authority of science without totalizing that authority, Levinas's two most important interlocutors and protagonists are Husserl, staunch defender of science, and Heidegger, staunch opponent of science. Levinas will challenge the Heideggerian turn from science and technology to language and "the question of being." Thus he will also challenge this same turn as found in Heidegger's most faithful and clever disciple in France, Jacques Derrida. Levinas's confrontation with Heidegger – the opposition between ethics and ontology – is the topic of chapter 4.

But Levinas is engaged in deep debate not only with Heidegger, his anti-scientific protagonist, but also with Husserl, his pro-scientific teacher. Husserl, a philosopher's philosopher, not only vigorously defended the ultimacy of science, like the positivists, but he extended its range. He extended its method, naming this enlargement "phenomenology," including phenomena, that is, meanings, within the range of a science that had hitherto limited itself to "objects." So powerful and compelling was this extension of science that phenomenology would become the all-embracing context of all subsequent twentieth-century continental philosophy, and influence all the humanities and social sciences throughout the twentieth century. To see Levinas's intimate appreciation for phenomenology, his appropriation of it, and at the same time his profound and critical deviation from this school of thought, will be the task of both chapters 2 and 3 of the present volume. While Heidegger (and Derrida) breach the confines of phenomenology by way of an aesthetic development of language, Levinas will show that the root of this breach derives from the higher demands of ethics, whose compelling say – its obligations – cannot, without violence and injustice, be suppressed within the play of what is said, however delicate.

The importance of Levinas's philosophy lies, then, in its "argument" about *what is most important.* And in our day, where the sweet songs of sophism are daily heard in the lecture halls, one could even say that the importance of Levinas's philosophy lies in its defense of the very importance – not to mention the existence – of importance. Like Matthew Arnold, Levinas will not argue that "only one thing is needful." His is not, to be sure, a narrow-minded or sectarian thought. But he will argue that the very force of *importance* or *seriousness* derives most fundamentally neither from the search for truth nor from a scintillating play of lights. Nietzsche had already grasped this lesson, but rather than recoil he embraced its nihilist consequences, attacking seriousness as such (which he called "the spirit of gravity," and characterized as a physiological condition – sickness, weakness, bad nutrition). But contrary to Nietzsche, philosophy has always favored the intellectual life conceived as a quest for knowledge. Philosophy has always conceived itself as the search for truth, and it has always proposed that no greater quest exists for humankind, individually if not collectively. Furthermore, philosophy has proven itself, made good on its many self-congratulatory paeans.

Philosophy's greatest results have come in what was traditionally called "natural philosophy," what we today simply call "science": mathematics, physics, chemistry, and biology. The Periodic Table puts to rest the concocted mythologies of alchemy. No one but an intellectual ostrich would dispute the success of philosophy conceived on the model of knowledge. It is a success that validates philosophy's quest for truth, for knowledge in the strong sense, for the universal, for an accurate and coherent account of the real. But already at its very origins, two and one half millennia ago, Socrates – Plato's Socrates – challenged the hegemony of knowledge of the *real*. For Socrates, more important than knowledge of the real would be knowledge of the *good*. The good was not only *more important* than the true, but the true itself would rest on the good. Socrates, however, remained wedded to the hegemony of knowledge, for he wanted above all to *know* the good. Once again, even if the object of his most serious inquiries – justice, love, piety – was different, one would *first* have to *know*.

Levinas, in contrast, challenges the hegemony of knowledge. Knowledge, by itself, as has become nearly transparent today, is incapable of determining worth, value, or purpose. It knows, to be sure, but it cannot rank importance. Its object is "difference" not excellence. No knowledge is more or less urgent than any other. In truth, then, contrary to its own paeans, knowledge cannot defend even its own priority. Instead, as a sort of displacement, a masking of its indifference, it reduces everything else to knowledge, until there is nothing else but itself or ignorance. Knowledge, by itself, thus remains indifferent to the very humanity of the human. This latter, the humanity of the human, Levinas finds not in knowledge, but in ethics. More important than epistemology would be ethics: the demands of morality and justice.

The unique contribution of Levinas, however, is not simply to declare that ethics is more important than knowledge, but to show knowledge, in all its nuances, its own shortcomings, and to show those shortcomings in a manner faithful to the very priority of ethics itself. Hume and Kant had both seen the limitations of knowledge but, one in habit and custom and the other in a moral repetition of knowledge, had succumbed to its hegemony nonetheless. In defending ethics *ethically*, insisting on an excellence rather than yet another truth or untruth, Levinas surpasses the entire enterprise of philosophy hitherto conceived. Herein lies his importance, his genuine postmodernity.

Kant, in particular, had shown that knowledge could not stand by itself, that it was incapable of fully knowing its own knowing. In the dialectical "paralogisms" and "antinomies" of his *Critique of Pure Reason*, Kant had shown once and for all that knowledge had its limits. He had also understood that two routes lay open beyond knowledge: ethics and aesthetics, the will and the imagination. But when Kant tried, in his *Critique of Practical Reason*, to present an ethics operating otherwise than knowledge, he once again reverted to the very terms and structures he had ostensibly surpassed in his first *Critique*. That is to say, Kant understood ethics in terms of an adherence to universal law, in terms of a respect not for the other person, but rather for the rationality of the other person as a law-abiding agent. Thus Kant saw the Promised Land, but did not enter. Unlike Levinas he did not grasp ethics ethically.

Ethics operates otherwise than epistemology and is not first subject to its restraints. It is not the law in the other person that a moral agent respects, but the very otherness of the other person, the other's morality, that is, the other's mortality, the other's suffering. Otherness is not abstract like moral law but concrete, in the very flesh of the other, the other's mortality, aging, degradation, suffering. This will be shown in chapter 8: the link between mortality, suffering, and evil. Morality is not based in freedom, as Kant thought, still constrained by the model of freedom of thought, but is based rather in a more profound *obedience*. Levinas, like Emil Fackenheim, challenges the fundamental Kantian dichotomy between "autonomy" and "heteronomy," a dichotomy so influential for all modern thought. Heteronomy, in contrast to an unhampered and pure freedom of choice, would represent the non-moral *par excellence*: external coercion depriving the agency of freedom, hence depriving human actions of their moral quality. Levinas, rooted in the wisdom of an older and profound Jewish tradition – commenting, no doubt, on the "we will do and we will hearken" said by the Jewish people at Mount Sinai – understands that moral choice depends on a more complicated and intimate structure than the Kantian opposition between inner freedom and external coercion. The human is neither wholly free nor wholly determined. Pure freedom and pure necessity are mental constructs, products of intellectual abstraction, alien to the structure of morality. In chapter 6 we will examine the intimate structure of a moral consciousness, the "maternal psyche."

Morality, for Levinas, is always a "difficult freedom," at once bound and free. He does not in the least suggest by this phrase that the skies must open for some self-proclaimed "moral" commandments to burst forth to order humans to do what is right. Rather, it is the other person who commands the self. Moral command comes to the self by way of the other person. Before self-consciousness, the other is in the self, gets to the self, and hence the self is maternal – pregnant with the other – before it is egoist. Or, rather, that being-for-the-other is deeper, more truly oneself, than being-for-oneself. But the idea as well as the reality of being-for-oneself is a subtle, seductive temptation, practically and intellectually, in any account of human agency. In chapter 9, we will examine Ricoeur's attack on Levinas, and his alternative, his defense – in *Oneself as Another* (1990) – of moral agency *qua* self-esteem. We will show, in a close examination of the deepest recesses of moral agency, the *transcendence* rather than the *immanence* of the priority of the other. The other suffers, I must act. The other is mortal, I must help. Yes, in helping the other the self is rising to its proper height, to its responsibility, but it rises to its proper height in response to the other's plight. "The other's material needs are my spiritual needs," Levinas is fond of saying, citing Rabbi Israel Salanter, founder of the Mussar movement in eighteenth-century Eastern Europe. Or, a more frequent citation, from Dostoyevsky's *Brothers Karamazov*: "We are all guilty of all and for all humanity before all, and I more than others." Moral agency, in a word, while entirely on my shoulders, does not originate in myself. My responsibility emerges as a response to the other person, to the other person who in coming first ordains the self as a moral agent.

Moral agency thus arises in a complicated social dialectic comprising two distinct terms and two distinct relations: (1) the obligating other, (2) the responsible self, (3) the priority of the other, and (4) the service of the self. Not one of these is reducible to the other. The self is responsible for the other. The self is and increasingly becomes (or fails to become) its "brother's keeper." Such is the moral self. It is neither an ontological nor an aesthetic event but an ethical event. It is to point to this "height," this "excellence," this greater "urgency," the moral priority of the other person and the "better self" that responds to the other, that constitutes the positive *work* of Levinas's philosophy and the wedge with which he criticizes the hegemony of epistemology or the seduction of aesthetics. Levinas is not arguing in the name of the real or the beautiful (or the "different"), but for what is better than being, or, as in the title of his second *magnum opus*, for what is "otherwise than being or beyond essence." "To be or not to be," Levinas asks, "is that the question? Is it the first and final question?" He answers "No," for the *more urgent* question has to do with one's "right to be." This Levinas calls "the question *par excellence* or the question of philosophy. Not 'Why being rather than nothing?', but how being justifies itself."[2]

The force of Levinas's thought is thus a moral force, and this precisely is its excellence and its urgency. Pursuing the close analyses of consciousness opened up by the phenomenological method, taking advantage of its careful descriptive method, and no less attentive to the manner in which language contributes to signification, Levinas tracks down the moment of rupture, transcendence, "the trace of the other," the peculiar inversion and interplay of activity and passivity by which a "better" claims priority over "being" and the prescriptive overloads the nominative. Against Husserl, who makes consciousness the starting point of meaning, and Heidegger, who makes one's own mortality the launching point of individuation and the opening onto the ultimate "issue of being," for Levinas it is the *other's* mortality and the other's signifying that count first and most. The other – mortal and

---

[2] Emmanuel Levinas, "Ethics as First Philosophy," trans. S. Hand and M. Temple, in Séan Hand, ed. *The Levinas Reader* (Oxford: Blackwell, 1989), p. 86.

aging – suffers, therefore I am commanded in my singularity. And so commanded, the self is ordered to its singular responsibility for the other all the way, right up to my own possible death for the other. Such, for Levinas, is the nobility, the dignity of the human. That one can be called upon to die for the other would be the ultimate structure of a responsible self. Thus, for Levinas, the self is not first for itself and then for the other, as if morality were some removable gloss or changeable role. Rather, the self first rises to its true humanity, to its irreplaceable singularity, as – to borrow an ancient biblical term – an *election*. One is chosen before one chooses. One is oneself when and insofar as one is for-the-other, for-the-other-before-oneself. The true self is the moral self. It is a heightening, arising in obligations and responsibilities to and for the other person, the one in need of help. Such is the ethical structure of morality.

But what about justice? If I am for-the-other, the other who faces, who needs help, what about the others, the others not present, absent others? A striking feature of Levinas's philosophy is the derivation of justice from morality, and hence the dependency of justice on morality. A moral self, giving everything to the other, would at the same time – in the name of morality – neglect all others. Morality, by itself, would engender injustice. To give all to one is to deprive others. But in this dilemma Levinas sees not the failure of morality, a flaw in its infinite demands, but rather the very link tying justice to morality. Justice, far from being imposed from outside, arbitrarily, by the State, say, or by miraculous Commandments, is required to *rectify* morality. The force of justice is the rectification of morality. If the self is to be good to the other without producing injustice it must also be good to others, hence it must come to treat others equally. Perhaps in a "Garden of Eden" (the Bible's peculiar version of what philosophers would later call "state of nature" myths), where there are only two persons, one could be moral and just at the same time. In society, however, the society in which we live, in our "unredeemed" world, one must be both moral and just, balancing the infinite demands of morality with the equities demanded by justice.

But to have the equality demanded by justice, one must have knowledge. One must have just balances and equitable distribution. Indeed, in a society of scarcity one must also maximize resources, increase crops, manufacture goods, and so on. Thus knowledge, instead of making itself ruler, serves justice. In this way, Levinas's ethical philosophy teaches the *significance* of signification, the *rationale* for the rational. It is not merely an account of science and knowledge, but their justification. Knowledge, science, intellect, truth, would all serve justice, a justice that itself serves morality. This also means that the state – where justice is institutionalized, in legislation, in courts, in social programs, with police and army – is itself beholden to justice and hence also to morality. Thus Levinas will oppose Machiavellian politics and the entire twentieth-century experience of statism from Stalin to Nationalist Socialism. The state is neither the creator nor the final arbiter of justice. True enough, the state maintains justice, but it does so for the sake of morality. The aim of statecraft, then, is thus neither sheer survival nor brute aggrandizement, but justice – the maximization of morality. Thus, too, one can and must judge the state – morally. Politics would have an aim, would be free of sophism and nihilism. The ultimate aim of politics, as of ethics, is a society where morality and justice do not contradict one another, where giving all to one deprives no one else. Such would be the good society of plenty, in contrast to the present society of scarcity. In the Western religious tradition this goal is known as the "messianic age" or the "kingdom of God on earth." This religious language expresses a humility, our ignorance of how exactly to get from where we are, the struggle of good and evil, justice at war with injustice, morality and justice fighting selfishness and cynicism, to where we aim to go, to morality and justice in harmony. Aiming in the direction of the good, through concrete actions that help the other before oneself, and creating the lasting institutions of a just society – these are the heights of human life, the very "humanity of the human," as Levinas calls it. And these are the tasks of our time, as individuals and as collectivities, linked to long ethico-religious traditions. What are the repercussions for philosophy? In contrast to a philosophy of ethics, what would be an ethical philosophy?

What can philosophy as ethical exegesis mean? Will philosophy have to be good? Why does this question sound so infantile, so unprofessional? Are we proud of our sophistication or our cynicism? Do they not both in some way reflect the suspicions cast on the integrity of philosophy by Marx, Nietzsche, and Freud? Is it always naïve to be straightforward, upright? Do we still have any idea what it would be like to be wise, beyond being knowledgeable? And is not philosophy a quest for wisdom? Ethics, so Levinas teaches, cuts us to the quick, to the very core of our being, deeper than all our knowledge, our erudition, even our good sense. And certainly it cuts deeper than our vanities, our pleasures, or our economic resources. And what is his argument? In the end it is quite simple: it is better to be good than anything else. It is better to help others than to help ourselves. Nothing in the world is more precious than serving others. I am my brother's keeper. Love thy neighbor is oneself.

But did not such a strange adventure mark the very start of philosophy? Was it not, after all, to seek the good that Socrates ended his studies of the natural sciences, and sought wisdom? Levinas will remind us that Socrates – and hence philosophy – was beholden to the highest, to the form of all forms, the "good beyond being". And taking a contrary case, did not even Spinoza – he who was scientist through and through – still think of philosophy as the route to love, to beatitude? Does an ethical philosophy have the audacity to restrict philosophy's free experimental style, its questioning mode? Certainly, if inspiration and elevation are restrictions. Do we need to be reminded that philosophy has never been free, and never dreamed of being free, free to think anything and everything? Only today is such "freedom" a temptation. It is what Levinas calls "the temptation of temptation,"[3] an unattached thought and life, attached only to its unattachment. This is "freedom" as an open-mindedness closed to everything but open-mindedness. But a totally free freedom would be far less than philosophy, indeed the very opponent of philosophy: opinion, myth, fantasy, speculation, rhetoric, politics. Wisdom has always known that this so-called freedom is never really free, but only the illusion of freedom. Ethical exegesis, then, would be philosophy conscious of the true stature of the good. One finds it already in

[3] Emmanuel Levinas, *Nine Talmudic Readings*, trans. Annette Aronowicz (Bloomington: Indiana University Press, 1990); "The Temptation of Temptations," pp. 30–50.

Plato, where an explosive infinity of dialogue forever prevents the contentment that comes with the formation of a totality of knowledge. Plato is a world. His is like the world of the Talmud, whose vastness Jews call an "ocean," and which Levinas, overly modest, somewhere calls a world "at least as large as the world of Plato."

In our time, philosophy has seen through to the limits of its own longstanding epistemological bias. Philosophy as the self-standing search for truth, as the internal search for the limits of human understanding, as the self-critique of pure reason, as the complete phenomenology of mind, has finally reached its conclusion. Without success. Knowledge cannot, despite its best efforts (Spinoza, Hume, Kant, Hegel), and without sleight of hand, pull itself up by its own bootstraps, that is to say, ground itself. Or if it does, it's only a boot, a part, and not the whole it intended to be. An all-inclusive, comprehensive, self-grounded System of Knowledge is not possible. Kierkegaard, Schelling, Stirner, Marx, Nietzsche – these are some of the names of those who spoke from outside a system that could have no outside. And has not Gödel, in our own time, shown the impossibility of a self-enclosed axiological system in mathematics, alleged first and last bastion of the purest truth? Shakespeare contains less than life, but, like life, more than philosophy. Even phenomenology, the broadest, deepest, most flexible conception of science ever to be conceived, cannot encompass all.

Two alternatives have thus opened up for post-epistemological philosophizing, for the quest for wholeness: the aesthetic and the ethical. And in these alternatives lies the answer to our initial questions about philosophy's temptations, its uncharted freedoms, and its dissatisfaction with the strictures of goodness. Is it so hard to see the why and wherefore of its temptations?

The domain of the aesthetic is not merely made up of painting, sculpture, music, dance, poetry, theatre, film, fashion, and the like. It is not merely art and culture. It is art and culture, to be sure. But it is also athletics, the Olympics, sports, dieting, care of the body, cosmetics, celebrity, and all the realms of the senses in their sensuousness. In its original Greek sense, the aesthetic is not limited to a cult of the beautiful – the "beautiful" was already a restriction of the aesthetic. In its broadest sense, one to which Heidegger reverts, the aesthetic is the *show* of what is. It is no less than the display of what is in its be-ing (verbal). It is publicity, renown, fame, which in Homer's day an Achilles preferred even over life. It is thus *physus*, what we now call "physics" or "nature" – as well as *poesis*, that part of the show made up by creative human making. It is the shining forth of what is, the manifestation of being, the very "manifestation of manifestation," as Levinas will call it, the "epochal" revelation of "earth, sky, gods, mortals," as Heidegger teaches. Or, in yet another register, it is ambiguity, and beyond ambiguity it is multi-vocity, a far-flung differential play of significations signifying significations, as Heidegger's French disciple Derrida would have us believe. In Greek, the term for aesthetics, *aisthesis*, means very simply "perception." The aesthetic is *the spectacle*. Above all, it is the *Visible*.

Is it any wonder, then, that in the novelty of its post-epistemological freedom, freed from the impossible burden of self-grounding knowledge (Hegel's Absolute), philosophy is seduced by and seduces by means of the aesthetic? The realm of the senses is anything if not seductive – tempting, alluring, allusive, multiple, ever on the move, onward, forward, avant-garde. Sirens' calls, rocky coasts, molting selves – adventure! But Levinas will call this freedom for freedom's sake the "temptation of temptation." Attachment to non-attachment, it is immaturity itself – the very denial of maturity. Trying everything, choosing nothing. Always, as Erich Fromm put it, "freedom from," never – God forbid – "freedom for." God forbid "God forbid"! its contradictory motto, a firm, unwavering, unshakable commitment to non-commitment. But its best proponents lack conviction. In the *Genealogy of Morals*, Nietzsche will bravely assert that "a married philosopher belongs in comedy," as if his own very real marriage proposals – to Mathilde Trampedach, Lou Salomé,[4] and who knows to whom else – had not been rejected. Alone, he ended up wedded to his

---

[4] R. J. Holingdale, *Nietzsche: The Man and His Philosophy* (Baton Rouge: Louisiana State University Press, 1965), pp. 116–177. David Allison has recently written a brilliant interpretation of the famous 1882 photograph of Nietzsche, Lou Salomé and Paul Rée (she in a cart with whip; they "pulling" the cart). Contrary to his intentions, however, his analysis only shows once again that Nietzsche never rose above posing (and posing others), while Rée, who looks into the camera, is quite aware of the difference between photograph and reality.

work! Plato's Diotima, who also rejected "earthly children," had higher aspirations.

Ethics, in contrast to aesthetics, has to do with the invisible. Its glory is an entirely different glory. Its light – like the light of the first day of creation, before even the sun – shines in an entirely different way than the mind's light or the spotlight. Morality opens up a deeply private dimension, with vast ramifications for the realm of the visible as well. Think of an anonymous donation of charity. Think of opening a door for someone. Think of volunteer work for the handicapped. Foolishness, madness, naïveté, bourgeois luxury? The world's greatest events have always taken place in the proximity of a face-to-face seen by no one else. No one else need know, ever. Levinas will call it "sacred history," deeper than the history of kings and armies, the history of publicity and material success. These events do not seek the television camera. They cannot be recorded. To be sure, they have a public face, and an important one. Justice is the public face of morality. But the heart and soul of our humanity – morality – is indifferent to publicity.

The good is neither a being nor the be-ing of beings. It is not a show, a display, a manifestation. To be good – to spend an hour of one's own precious time, once a week, reading to a blind person – is both to be and to be beyond being. It is a rip in the manifestation of being, a vocation called from above, a subjection to higher demands than "to be or not to be," the demands of the self. The moral self is essentially utopian in this way – here and there, here as there. In being moral one is at the same time above being – being and above, in a time Levinas will call "diachrony." Levinas will also call this trace of transcendence the "otherwise than being or beyond essence." Not the obliteration of being or essence, for the material world is the concrete realm of goodness, but otherwise and beyond – above. The moral dimension is one of height, elevation, command, but not as geometry or a logarithm that could ever be measured or predicted. Responsibility, not publicity, is the great glory of humanity.

Of course, our aesthetic sensibilities would rather not be hampered, bothered, disturbed, restricted by moral responsibilities and obligations – the aesthetic is precisely this "rather not," this looking the other way, averting the eyes, refusing the other. Surrounded with beauty, one lives in a happy beautiful world – but blind at the same time. There need be nothing wrong with beauty. Rather, it is "idol worship" in the love of beauty, the love of the show above all, which is at fault. To love oneself before others – here lies the formula of all evil. Levinas cites Pascal (*Pensées*, 112): " 'That is my place in the sun.' That is how the usurpation of the whole world began."[5] To see but not be seen, to not be caught, not be responsible – to wear Gyges' ring – this is the aesthetic trick. But no, it is to see and to be seen – to see oneself being seen! – but never to be held accountable, here lies the impulse of aesthetic desire: for the glory of the visible, for triumph and trophy, enthralled by the spectacle and the spectacular. The glory of a kindness done requires no such fanfare. "Sacred history" will never be known: volunteer work, anonymous donations, a hand lent, obligations kept, justice maintained, the widow protected, the orphan nourished, the stranger welcomed – the world's deep and weighty and true history. According to Jewish legend, in each generation the world itself survives only owing to the good deeds of a few righteous but hidden individuals – the so-called "*lamed vovniks*" (the "thirty nine"). The visible held secure by the exigencies and frailties of the invisible. And all the visible, too, must be drawn upward to these higher, invisible heights. For all the visible world is permeated and upheld by a different light, by "sparks," so the mystics would say, whose greatest desire, as it were, is precisely to be so drawn upward.

Philosophy as ethical exegesis – discovering the ethical in the ontological, seeing the lower in the light of the higher, not anthropology but ethics – is attuned to this deeper, weightier, truer history that defies straightforward language and is refractory to the light of publicity. Its commitments are not to visible history alone, the history of historiography, but rather to a more insecure but deeper history, that of the humanity of the human. The human is not a biological or a rational category. Rather, the human emerges when and where morality is at work. Humanity is not a given but an achievement, an accomplishment, an elevation. Moral rectitude and justice are rare enough for philosophy also to miss them.

---

[5] Emmanuel Levinas, *Otherwise than Being or Beyond Essence*, trans. Alphonso Lingis (The Hague: Martinus Nijhoff, 1981), p. vii.

Ethical exegesis is philosophy attentive to responsibilities beyond epistemology, and higher than the aesthetic celebration of the spectacle of be-ing or its language. It is thinking bound to the "difficult freedom" of moral responsibilities and obligations – for fellow humans, for sentient life, and finally for all of creation in all its diversity. And as such it is wisdom, or the quest for wisdom – philosophy.

Just as the aesthetic dimension is not by itself evil (or good), one cannot say that the aesthetic life is false (or true). Like good and evil, truth and falsity are not its standard. They are standards of epistemology. Epistemology need not refrain from judging aesthetics, but neither epistemology nor aesthetics has the right to the last word. Ethics, in contrast, can and must remind us that the aesthetic life is inferior to the moral life. The aesthetic world – however spectacular, grand, or beautiful – is too small a world. When aesthetics takes itself for a world it becomes precious, as in Huysmans, or both precious and precocious, as in Heidegger and Derrida, or fascist, its true moral face. And let there be no doubt, the aesthetic life revolves around the self, is indeed its very cult. And thus it is essentially linked to death or, by dialectical rebound, linked to youth, for the self by itself is a mortal being.

Regarding not the truth but the superiority of morality, of ethical commitment ("either/or") over aesthetic disengagement ("both/and"), Kierkegaard has written penetrating and moving tributes to this wisdom. The great nineteenth-century German Orthodox rabbi and scholar, Samson Raphael Hirsch, in the Jewish tradition, commenting on Proverbs (chapter two, "Wise Men and Fools"), notes that the word that text opposes to "wisdom" (Hebrew: *chochmah*), namely, "foolishness" (Hebrew: *olat*), "is related to *oulai*, 'perhaps,' and *ahfal*, 'darkness'."[6] Again, Levinas's "temptation of temptation," the perhaps, the maybe, the possible, opposed to and by the actual, the here, the now, not the real but the moral "demands of the day." No one would oppose beauty, to be sure, but when self-regard becomes disregard for others – and surely it tends in this direction – then aesthetic desires become evils, hardening rather than softening the heart. There are

---

[6] Samson Raphael Hirsch, *From the Wisdom of Mishlé*, trans. Karin Paritzky (Jerusalem: Feldheim Publishers, 1976), p. 43.

worthier, nobler tasks. Ethical exegesis – penetrating through the spectacle and its display of signs to its human dimension, the dimension of suffering and moral demand – articulates the fragile but overpowering solidarity of a human community on the difficult road of redemption. It will say and say again the rupture of the masks of being demanded by morality and of justice.

Beyond but through morality, ethical exegesis will also dare to suggest, obliquely, to be sure, the glimmer of another exigency – spirit, inspiration, absolution – more intense, higher, brighter, illuminating and not illuminated by the light of sun, moon and stars. Micah 6:8: "For he has told thee, oh humans, what is good, and what the Lord thy God does require of thee, but to do justice and to love mercy and to walk humbly with thy God." Not a "proof text," to be sure, but a confirmation.

The difference putting ethics first makes is of no less consequence than that which, according to Husserl, separates philosophy and psychology. That difference was at once the greatest chasm and yet barely discernible, in that the findings of these two disciplines would be strictly parallel to one another, so parallel that a sentence from one could be transposed word for word into the other, yet their significance would be entirely different. Philosophy – in this case ethics, what I am calling ethical exegesis – would be the absolute source of all meaning, hence the ground of psychology and sociology and all the sciences, social or natural. While not another epistemological grounding of epistemology, ethical exegesis nonetheless still has the pretension to provide the *reason* for philosophy. But "reason" in the sense of "end," "purpose," "aim" – what is most important, most significant. Without returning to pre-modern philosophy, without imposing one arbitrary onto-theo-logy or another, without making a fetish of science or of its drifting, and most especially without the pretended "second innocence" of aesthetic celebration, ethical exegesis – in moral responsibilities and obligations, and in the call to justice built upon these – supplies a reason for philosophy, a reason for knowledge and a reason for living. No doubt this is a very large claim. And in this sense, this is an ambitious book. Very simply: nothing is more significant than serving others. All other significations, in all other registers, derive from this deepest or highest significance.

Thus moral proximity with another, like the present words, is always an introduction. Signification does not rest on grasp or comprehension or any form of complacency, but rather on a heightened sobriety, an availability, the "here I am" of one inter-locutor to another. Ever since Hegel's introduction to *The Phenom-enology of Spirit*, philosophers have been troubled by introductions. How, after all, can the complete system of all knowledge have an introduction? One is perforce already within an absolute system, already introduced to it, even if not yet as fully acquainted with its entirety as one will be after comprehending the system. There is nothing outside the system, no place from which to introduce it that has not already been introduced, even if that introduction is temporarily implicit or presupposed. Levinas's thought works quite differently. Not only is one never fully introduced to it, but also one can never be fully introduced to it. I refer the reader to the citation, taken from the preface to *Totality and Infinity*, at the heading of this introduction: "But it belongs to the very essence of language, which consists in continually undoing its phrase by the foreword or the exegesis, in unsaying the said, in attempting to restate without ceremonies what has already been ill understood in the inevitable ceremonial in which the said delights."

Let us think more about introductions. Not introductions to books, primarily, but the meeting of two people, two flesh and blood people. The two sorts of introductions, however, are related. Although they are not made of flesh and blood literally, books, as a whole and their introductions too, permit a meeting of sorts between author and reader, or perhaps more exactly and modest-ly, a meeting between author-*qua*-book and reader. One person is introduced to another. By reading Kant or Bergson one comes to know Kant or Bergson, without the slightest possibility of meeting them in "real life." With enough insight, one can even say – without guarantees, to be sure – what Kant or Bergson would have thought about questions and issues they themselves never con-sidered! Plato, Aristotle, Descartes, Spinoza, et al., "live" through their writings. We meet them, are introduced to them, in and through their books.

But what about "real" introductions, flesh and blood introduc-tions? In the not so distant past these sorts of introductions were, at certain levels of society and in certain societies, often more formal than they are today. A mutual friend would be asked to introduce someone to someone else. Travelers might carry a letter of introduction. In this way, as in philosophy itself, the familiar would mediate the unfamiliar. Perhaps there would be a purpose behind the introduction, the possibility of business, say, or sport, pleasure, love, or marriage. Today, of course, at least in the Western world, introductions have lost much of their formality. Strangers often introduce themselves. Telephones and electronic mail open us to the most distant and often unanticipated connections, and yet at the same time these same "encounters" have their own privacy and intimacy.

Compared to the creativity and world of meaning within a book, introductions of this sort – the meeting of two people – may seem like the smallest of events. But if this is so, we must also consider why, unlike books but like life's most important occasions – birth, maturity, graduation, marriage, death – they still remain couched in a certain formality. "How do you do?" "Pleased to meet you." A handshake, a slight nod or bow, a smile – a look in the eye. The formalities of introductions, small though they are, mask or palliate (or do both at once) the awkwardness of stranger meeting stranger. These allegedly slight encounters are in fact deep and rich with signification. It is as if their words and gestures were saying: "You are a stranger. I do not know you. Yet I already do know you, for we are both human, and thus both recognize these gestures, this nod, this handshake, this smile, that look, for the solidarity they offer, and for the veritable bond they establish between us." These formalities, however minimal, indicate the depth of a shared humanity – this is the presupposition of introductions.

Philosophers might call introductions "mediations." But the unmediated contact, the proximity of one to another, remains despite them – and conditions everything. Proximity, Levinas will say, is "the condition – or the uncondition" of all signification. Of course, no one expects the common gestures and words of introductions to be scrutinized for their depth, though neither can they be insincere or stilted without causing personal slight. They are indeed "ceremonials," rituals of meetings, the "things one says," "what one does," the lubrication of polite society, the habits of everyday life, good manners, the show of civility. Still, and this is the point, they are not inconsiderable. After all, goodness comes of such gestures. In introductions, where strangers meet and lose a certain degree of strangeness, we are each of us at the front lines and frontiers of an everyday humanism.

Introductions, simple or common as they may seem, can even be life's most important events. Must we be reminded? At some specific moment in time a person is introduced, unawares, to a future wife or husband, a future boyfriend or girlfriend, or best friend, or to one's neighbor, teacher, co-worker. We are introduced or introduce ourselves to everyone we know – except for our parents and siblings. We are at first strangers to all and everyone – except for our parents and siblings. A remarkable point, this last.

We have perhaps not paid sufficient attention to the significance of this lack of introductions within families. The peculiar proximity that occurs in the family cannot simply be dismissed as an outmoded patriarchal or economic or biological heritage, or some other primitive holdover. Rather, the family not only has central ethical importance, as these dismissals recognize well enough but reject, it continues to have a central relevance. Levinas will see in the peculiar proximity of the family ontological significations. He has written extensively about this significance – eros and family – in section four, entitled "Beyond the Face," of *Totality and Infinity*. We speak of "immediate" and "extended" families. But we do not mean an immediacy or an extension that can be accounted for by formal logic. Gender divides in an altogether different way than formal oppositions, species within a genus, or contradictories. As early as 1947, Levinas will make the following radical claim in the name of gender and familial relations: "The difference between the sexes is a formal structure, but one that carves up reality in another sense and conditions the very possibility of reality as multiple, against the unity of being proclaimed by Parmenides."[7] Parmenides' fall would come not from Heraclitus, but from gender! The immediacy of familial relations refers to an intimacy, and to a sharing of this intimacy. It is an intimacy more intimate, to be

---

[7] Emmanuel Levinas, *Time and the Other and Additional Essays*, trans. Richard A. Cohen (Pittsburgh: Duquesne University Press, 1987), p. 85.

sure, than the strangeness of encounters with strangers, but it is also more intimate, at least to begin with, than the familiarity that follows from introductions. The family is more "closely knit," we say, "tighter," more immediate, more oneself, than the relationships we enter into mediated by introductions.

While husbands and wives can remember when they first met, children are never introduced to their parents, or younger siblings to their older siblings. Marriage, for its part, is meant to both transcend and not transcend the memory of an introduction. Thus it too borrows from the model of sons and daughters, and brothers and sisters, to become "one flesh." "Oh were you like a brother to me," pleads the heart-struck Beloved in the Song of Songs (8:1). In the same song we hear the Lover's repeated refrain: "My sister, my bride."[8] Parents, sons, daughters, brothers and sisters, are already one flesh. Sons and daughters and younger siblings cannot remember the origins of these profound relations. And perhaps the less they can remember of origins the *more profound* the relation. They have begun, as it were, prior to their own origins, prior to introductions. One is reminded – as Levinas is often reminded – of Descartes, who in his Third Meditation is dazzled by an infinite *put* into him *prior* to the finitude that is his very foundation. An intimacy more intimate, more immediate than any possible mediation. Something has passed that was never present. One is more vulnerable, more open, than one's ownmost abilities and capacities. One is always already a son or a daughter.

We thus see in filiality – both because of the depth of its vulnerability and the depth of its bonds – "the condition – or uncondition" of proximity, and the basis of all loyalty. Clearly it is more intimate than an encounter or an introduction. It is even more intimate than siblings. It is so intimate, in fact, that the very identity of the son or daughter is inextricably tied up with that of the parent. Levinas will invoke the term "transubstantiation"[9] to characterize this link across the rupture of generations. The child

---

[8] In his commentary to the Bible, *Horeb*, Rabbi Samson Raphael Hirsch (1808–88) interprets the cycle of marital sexual abstinence encoded in Leviticus 18:19 ("Also thou shalt not approach to a woman in the impurity of her menstrual flow, to uncover her nakedness") to provide husband and wife opportunity to be literally like brother and sister to one another.

[9] Levinas, *Totality and Infinity*, p. 271.

is "me, but not myself."[10] In this unique multiplicity, the unity of
Parmenidean being is broken. Since everyone is a son or a daughter, however empirically close or distant be the parents, this means
that the core of human identity is not closed off like a windowless
monad, a substance, fortress for-itself. The struggle for identity
comes later, as all the crises of adolescence testify. Identity is
secondary to non-identity, to a murkier relationship whose
parameters can never be sharply defined. These are certainly
deeper relations than those by which significations are loosely
grouped into a "family resemblance," as Wittgenstein put it, again
borrowing from the source of all relationships. No doubt, too, the
latter depend on the former. Levinas is one of the few philosophers
to have grasped the philosophical importance of this event – the
event of paternity/maternity/filiality. Its significance transcends
biology, psychology, and sociology. Phenomenology was able to
see its way to it, even if it could not capture its full significance.
This is because the full significance of this deep multiplicity in
being comes to light not in ontology, but in ethics.

From this relation – filiality – comes the ontological possibility
of our openness to one another, our vulnerability to one another.
We are born open to others, and for this reason we are social
beings – a "political animal" according to Aristotle. It is not a
matter of indifference to our freedom that we are *born* and not
*caused*, and that of necessity we have parents. Filiality is the paradigm of all vulnerability – Abraham and Isaac: "the binding." It
links all the brothers so central to the Hebrew Bible, and ultimately
the "brotherhood" of humankind. It is so special, indeed, that in
all cultures, everywhere, it is cushioned, as it were, protected, by
far more than manners. It is surrounded by taboo – from the first
society recognizes something sacred in its intimacy, and something
vulnerable. Filiality is inviolable precisely because it is so vulnerable. Its vulnerability is both the price and the prize of our
inter-humanity, our civilization – too valuable to leave unprotec-
ted. We are all brothers, all sisters. From such intimacy comes the
hope of our humanity.

Identities are never untangled within families, cauldrons of

<hr />

[10] Ibid.

intimacy. Open from the start, even adult identities continue more or less to intermingle with other identities. However, it is not a matter of Merleau-Ponty's "flesh of the world," where our semi-permeability is an ontological affair. Rather it is a matter of ethical openness, of moral vulnerability, of an all too demanding contact, where the other's suffering is my suffering. To be a self is a risk, with many dangers, and many rewards. Identities are less discrete than bodies, which are themselves less discrete than things. Fraternity is the product of filiality. It is no accident that God is called "Father," and that humans were created in His "image and likeness." This same core of vulnerability, which links each to each in the possibility of a human community, can also produce an inhuman community, an animal or pagan communion, sinking below the human condition. Drunken participation – Dionysus – in the anonymity of the group mind, or rather the group body, is an abdication of singularity. But it is made possible by the very vulnerability that makes for human solidarity.

The difference between this *aesthetic* eventuality and a truly human community – the humanity of a moral humanity striving for justice – begins in the good manners of gestures as simple as introductions, in welcoming the stranger. That is to say, humanity begins in the kindness of moral relations, in responsibilities and obligations, and in the fairness that comes from the institution of justice. Vulnerability can thus become human solidarity – fraternity – across morality and justice. Levinas will call this vulnerability and openness beneath identity by many names: "proximity," "non-indifference," "dia-chrony," "an-archy," "insomnia," "substitution," "hostage." These relations will be considered throughout the present book (especially in chapter 6, "Maternal body/ maternal psyche"), for they are its topic. In each instance, with a different inflection, Levinas is referring not to a savage or cultured dissolution of the self. He is rather pointing to the piercing responsibilities and obligations that link one human to another, demanding that each be attentive, alert, and awake to the other. It is a high calling. This book is written in the hope and with the aim of saying that we have not become – or ought not to become – too cynical for our better selves. It will insist on a certain ethical naïveté – directness, forthrightness, proximity – higher than all sophistication, just as philosophy once understood itself to be far superior – without riches, without might – than all the sophistication of the sophists.

By means of introductions we leave our families and our tribes to enter into the human fraternity. They are our doorways into the world of humanity, into encounters with strangers, with others who by passing through their portals become less strange, the near, the neighbor, perhaps a friend, perhaps family, always a fellow human being. Introductions are thus our access to our own humanity too. And thus I conceive this book, as such an introduction – to the complex links that bind ethics, exegesis and philosophy, to thoughtfulness, to a reorientation of thinking, but also to myself, to Levinas, to yourself, and to life. Though less immediate, less intimate, less available, than the face-to-face.

# I

*Exceeding phenomenology*

# CHAPTER I

# Bergson and the emergence of an ecological age

Levinas is a contemporary thinker. But what, beyond mere temporal proximity, makes contemporary thought "contemporary"? Surely much of what passes for thinking today not only derives from sources and perspectives from a bygone past, but does little more than reproduce those perspectives in a contemporary idiom, old wine repackaged in "new" flasks. One way, perhaps even the best way, to grasp the radical difference between contemporary thought and all prior thought is to appreciate the intellectual revolution effected by the work of Henri Bergson (1859–1941). Although other names are often paraded – Marx, Nietzsche, Freud – and credited as originators of vast paradigm shifts, in the light of Bergson's achievement the radical nature of their contributions, undeniably original as they are, is dimmed. In form if not in content they carry on a tradition of intellectual abstraction, with all the strains and dangers, real and theoretical, idealist and egoist, which are the price of abstraction. In subtle ways they end up continuing the very heritage they allege to overturn. So, too, there are thinkers who followed Bergson – most obviously Heidegger – who though often credited with a revolution in thought are but continuing a revolution that had already taken place, beneficiaries of it.

Though today his reputation is somewhat eclipsed, we are not the first to recognize the importance of Bergson's accomplishments. Indeed, the depth and revolutionary character of his thought were recognized very early, and perhaps it is only because contemporary thought has adopted Bergson's fundamental point of view – duration (*durée*)[1] – that we have forgotten his originality.

[1] We will have more to say about this term later. That duration is central to Bergson's thought – certainly Bergson's own opinion – is non-controversial. Thus we find ourselves

To jog our memories, and to whet our curiosity, let us recall some of the early kudos. Edouard Le Roy, who was, it is true, Bergson's direct disciple, claimed for the philosophical revolution effected by Bergson equity with those of Kant and Socrates.[2] But discipleship cannot account for Bergson's election to the College of France in 1900, to the French Academy in 1914, and his receiving the Nobel Prize in 1927. America's two leading philosophers at the beginning of the twentieth century, John Dewey and William James, both praised Bergson exceedingly. Dewey, an exemplar of balance and judiciousness, wrote: "No philosophic problem will ever exhibit just the same face and aspect that it presented before Professor Bergson."[3] James, who corresponded with Bergson, met him in Paris, and felt a great affinity for his thought, wrote in 1907 that Bergson's book *Creative Evolution* "is a true miracle in the history of philosophy and as far as the content is concerned it marks . . . [t]he beginning of a new era."[4] A half a century later, in 1959, it was certainly not a function of the exaggerated homage typical of centennial celebrations that led Maurice Merleau-Ponty to speak of "Bergson's great books," singling out a different volume, *Matter and Memory*.[5] In his own inaugural address at the College of France,[6] and on many other occasions, Merleau-Ponty acknowledged the general importance as well as the direct influence of Bergson, as we shall see in more detail later. On the same centennial occasion, Jean Wahl declared ". . . that if one had to name the four great philosophers one could say: Socrates, Plato – taking

---

in agreement with Pierre Trotignon, who also makes this point in "Autre voie, même voix: Levinas and Bergson," in Catherine Chalier and Miguel Abensour, eds., *L'Herne: Emmanuel Levinas* (Paris: Éditions de l'Herne, 1991), p. 287.

[2] Reported by Edouard Morot-Sir in "What Bergson Means to Us Today," in Thomas Hanna, ed., *The Bergsonian Heritage* (New York: Columbia University Press, 1962), p. 37; the reference is most likely to Edouard Le Roy's *The New Philosophy of Henri Bergson* (New York: Henry Holt, 1913).

[3] John Dewey, "Preface," *A Contribution to a Bibliography of Henry Bergson* (New York: Columbia University Press, 1912), p. xii; cited in Robert C. Grogin, *The Bergsonian Controversy in France 1900–1914* (Calgary: The University of Calgary Press, 1988), p. 206.

[4] Cited in Joseph Chiari, *Twentieth Century French Thought: From Bergson to Levi-Strauss* (New York: Gordian Press, 1975), p. 32.    [5] *The Bergsonian Heritage*, p. 137.

[6] See Merleau-Ponty's inaugural lecture of January, 1953, at the College of France: Maurice Merleau-Ponty, *In Praise of Philosophy*, trans. John Wild and James M. Edie (Evanston: Northwestern University Press, 1963), especially his remarks on Bergson, pp. 9–33.

them together, – Descartes, Kant, and Bergson."[7] And if proximity or eulogy had somehow deluded these thinkers – and it exceeds our credulity, our respect for these thinkers, and the argument of this chapter, to believe this was so – then we would still have to account for the no less exalted assessment made by Emmanuel Levinas. In a Paris radio interview of February 1981, Levinas ranked Bergson's doctoral dissertation, *Time and Free Will*, as one of the "four or five . . . finest books in the history of philosophy," alongside Plato, Kant, Hegel and Heidegger.[8] Can this Bergson be the same Bergson who is hardly remembered today, as he was already almost forgotten in pre-World War Two France? What, then, is Bergson's proper place in the spiritual history of the West, that is to say: what did he accomplish?

To anyone familiar with the history of Western philosophy, or with philosophical histories of that history, what is striking about the above claims regarding the who's who of philosophical greatness is not the appearance of such names as Socrates, Plato, Kant, Descartes, Hegel, or Heidegger, who are "regulars" in such estimates, but rather the appearance of Bergson, who is not. It is not that anyone would deny the conceptual rigor, the intellectual penetration, or the literary elegance of Bergson's works. Bergson published relatively little and what he did publish were highly polished and strikingly original works of philosophy. One need only read them to be impressed again and again. Rather, it is that with the exception of Levinas,[9] hardly a leading thinker in the final third of the twentieth century has placed Bergson's philosophical genius at the highest level in the elite pantheon of great thinkers. It seems to me that while Bergson's reputation may have been eclipsed, his sun shines as brightly as ever – and it shines brightly indeed. The object of this first chapter is to show how and why the

---

[7] *The Bergsonian Heritage*, p. 153.
[8] Emmanuel Levinas, *Ethics and Infinity*, trans. Richard A. Cohen (Pittsburgh: Duquesne University Press, 1985), p. 37. The other four books named by Levinas are Plato's *Phaedrus*, Kant's *Critique of Pure Reason*, Hegel's *Phenomenology of Mind*, and Heidegger's *Being and Time*.
[9] Another exception is Gilles Deleuze, author of *Le Bergsonisme* (Paris: Presses Universitaires de France, 1966). Two recent collections of secondary literature published in Great Britain evidence a renewed interest in Bergson: Frederick Burwick and Paul Douglas, eds., *The Crisis in Modernism: Bergson and the Vitalist Controversy* (Cambridge: Cambridge University Press, 1992), and John Mullarkey, ed., *The New Bergson* (Manchester: Manchester University Press, 1999).

estimation of Levinas and his other admirers is right. It is to show in what way contemporary thought is at bottom Bergsonian, and how in Bergson we find the defining character of contemporary thought. In showing this, we will also be showing, though to a more limited degree, the influence of Bergson's thought on the ethical metaphysics of Levinas.

My claim is that the philosophy of Bergson is not only profound and important, but is indeed a philosophy of the highest rank because it represents nothing less than one of the three seminal turning points of Western thought.[10] It represents a turning point that by radically revising both the approach and the findings of epistemology and ontology laid the essential groundwork for a shift in philosophy – certainly not fully pursued by Bergson[11] – from its rationalist *and* empiricist epistemological and ontological orientation, to a better appreciation for the irreducible role of temporality, incarnation, and novelty in the constitution of truth and reality. Bergson lays the groundwork for a shift in thought that integrates humanity and philosophy, morality and science, without sacrificing concepts to subjectivity or subjectivity to concepts.

In order to show how and why Bergson merits standing in the very first rank of philosophers and at the dawn of contemporary thought, we must turn away from the standard philosophical histories of philosophy, especially those influential histories propagated by Hegel and Heidegger. We must turn instead to a lesser known history, that elaborated by the Harvard medievalist Harry Austryn Wolfson (1887–1974). For the latter, the fulcrums of Western thought turn not upon Socrates, Plato, Descartes, Kant, Hegel, Nietzsche or Heidegger, but rather upon two thinkers who

[10] My claim for Bergson's contemporary significance is thus much larger than that of Robert C. Grogin, who while greatly appreciating Bergson's past and present contribution, ends by limiting his importance to the religious sphere. See Grogin, *The Bergsonian Controversy in France 1900–1914*, pp. 206–207.

[11] While it is certainly true that Husserl, Heidegger, Merleau-Ponty, and Levinas "fleshed" out the essential insights of Bergson, particularly his notion of "duration," it seems to me that the young Albert Camus goes too far in attributing a formality or emptiness to Bergson's critique of rationality. Though Camus was admittedly quite powerfully struck by Bergson's critique, he was no less disappointed that Bergson, in his eyes, did not satisfy those expectations with a positive philosophy. See Camus, "The Philosophy of the Century," in Albert Camus, *Youthful Writings*, trans. Ellen C. Kennedy (New York: Random House, 1977), pp. 126–129.

do not appear on the usual lists and who are rarely highlighted even in philosophical histories of philosophy. These two thinkers are Philo of Alexandria (*c.* 20 BCE–50 CE) and Baruch Spinoza (1632–77). The standard histories pass swiftly over the former, and though they usually recognize the greatness of the latter, are content to cast Spinoza in the shadow of Descartes, Kant, Hegel, and sometimes even Leibniz (who is in truth but a variation of Spinoza). Nonetheless, so I will argue, it is by grasping how and why these two thinkers, Philo and Spinoza, are the two major pivots, the two decisive turning points, in the history of Western spirit, that we shall then be able to see how and why Bergson's contribution, like theirs, is of the highest order and at the root of contemporary thought. My thesis is that the originality and profundity of Bergson's work is as radical and revolutionary as that of Philo and Spinoza, and that, as the third and most recent figure in a trinity of momentous turning points that have determined Western spirit, his is nothing less than the core inspiration and guiding spirit of our time.

Wolfson, who saw himself as a historian rather than a philosopher, did not write a history of Western spirit. Rather, his vision of that history appears in the course of two major studies: *The Philosophy of Spinoza*[12] (1934) and *Philo: Foundations of Religious Philosophy in Judaism, Christianity and Islam*[13] (1947). My thesis – that

---

[12] Harry Austryn Wolfson, *The Philosophy of Spinoza*, 2 vols. (Cambridge, MA: Harvard University Press, 1934).

[13] Harry Austryn Wolfson, *Philo: Foundations of Religious Philosophy in Judaism, Christianity and Islam*, 2 vols. (Cambridge, MA: Harvard University Press, 1948). Wolfson's thesis regarding the periodicity of Western spiritual history is also found in his *Philosophy of the Church Fathers* (1956). Both Wolfson's Spinoza and Philo books were published after Lev Shestov's 1929 book, *In Job's Balance: On the Sources of the Eternal Truths*, trans. Camilla Coventry and C. A. Macartney (Athens: Ohio University Press, 1929; originally *Na Vassakh Iova* (Paris: Annales Contemporaines, 1929)). In Shestov's book one already finds a very similar historical thesis to Wolfson's (with no mention of Wolfson) regarding the central roles played by Philo and Spinoza (see *In Job's Balance*, pp. 257–263). One might think that Shestov does not mention Wolfson because he preceded him in this outlook. One might even think that Shestov influenced Wolfson. But neither may be the case. Shestov, who had moved from his native Russia to Paris in 1920, would have had the opportunity – before writing his book – to read four articles by Wolfson on Spinoza, which were printed in the first four volumes of the *Chronicon Spinozanum*, in 1922, 1923, 1926 and 1927. These four articles make up the main body of Wolfson's Spinoza book, published years later in 1934. Though my own inclination is to think that it was Shestov who learned from Wolfson, I leave it to Shestov and Wolfson scholars to sort out this question of influence.

Bergson's philosophy of duration, incarnation and novelty is of the highest rank because it represents a third, no less decisive, turning point – is thus both a supplement to Wolfson's original thesis and, as we shall see, requires that we revise it. Thus, to appreciate Bergson and the character of contemporary thought, we must first turn to Wolfson.[14]

To a certain extent Wolfson's account follows well-beaten paths. Like standard narratives of the Western heritage, he divides Occidental history into three periods: the ancient, the medieval and the modern. His story deviates, however, as we have indicated, by placing Philo and Spinoza at the two great turning points in this tri-part history. Philo stands between the ancient and medieval periods. He is the first medieval, and the entire medieval period is in some sense "Philonic." Spinoza stands between the medieval and modern periods. He is the first modern, and all of subsequent modernity is in some sense "Spinozist." Standard philosophical histories, in contrast, begin the medieval period later, usually with neo-Platonism, and begin the modern period earlier, with Machiavelli, Francis Bacon, or more usually Descartes.

To grasp how and why pride of place must be accorded to Philo and Spinoza, however, we must first understand the principal question or issue that in Wolfson's estimation drives Western history and marks its specific character. Here Wolfson is, if not completely original, radical and comprehensive. In contrast to the philosophical histories of the West elaborated by Hegel and Heidegger, which in typical post-Renaissance fashion present a narrative revolving around the epistemological conflict inaugurated by the difference between Parmenides and Heraclitus, that is, between the relative weight and roles assigned to *being* and *becoming* in the constitution of truth, what defines and drives Western spiritual history for Wolfson is the larger and more complex question of the proper relation between *reason* (stretched between being and becoming) and *revelation*. That is to say, what is central

---

[14] We can speculate that Levinas's assessment may have been influenced by Wolfson, insofar as already in 1937 Levinas had published a review of Wolfson's *The Philosophy of Spinoza* in the *Revue des études juive* ("Spinoza, philosophe médiéval," January–June issue, pp. 114–119). As far as I know, Levinas never mentions Wolfson after this review.

and decisive for Wolfson is not the being–becoming debate, which so stimulated Greek thought (and Hegel and Heidegger), but rather the Athens–Jerusalem encounter, which is the genuine stimulus of Western spirit.[15] Not being and becoming, but rather reason and revelation would thus stand as the two genuine absolutes whose contention – within and between one another – would define Western spiritual development. In comparison to this genuine encounter between Athens and Jerusalem, the encounter between being and becoming can finally be seen for what it is, a relative and local Greek affair (even if like Jerusalem, it has universal import). The concrete accommodations worked out between these two comprehensive and fundamentally different worldviews – Reason and Revelation, worked out by and through individuals, beliefs, literatures, peoples, traditions, institutions, cultures, and philosophies, would thus constitute nothing less than the most profound meaning of the history of Western spirit. Indeed, meaning itself, the meaningful as such, would be the bone of contention between these two contending worldviews, each insisting – for itself and in the face of the other – on its own absolute rights. Nothing, and not even "nothing," would escape this battle of giants (or this battle between David and Goliath).

The logical permutations of possible relations between the spheres of reason and revelation are four: (1) their separation, (2) the domination of revelation over reason, (3) the domination of reason over revelation, and (4) their harmony. Wolfson, however, identifies only three of these four possibilities in his actual history. The ancient period is that epoch defined by the separation of reason and revelation. Even today, then, the separation of reason and revelation, one oblivious to the other, would represent an "ancient" pattern of thought and culture. The medieval period, inaugurated by Philo, is that epoch defined by the harmony – or

---

[15] Wolfson was certainly not alone in highlighting the centrality of the Athens–Jerusalem question. One thinks, perhaps in the first instance, of his contemporary, University of Chicago scholar Leo Strauss (1899–1973), who also wrote extensively on Spinoza, whom he considered "the most extreme, certainly of the modern critics of revelation, not necessarily in his thought but certainly in the expression of his thought," "Progress and Return," in Leo Strauss, *Jewish Philosophy and the Crisis of Modernity: Essays and Lectures in Modern Jewish Thought*, ed. Kenneth Hart Green (Albany: State University of New York Press, 1997), p. 130.

harmonization – of reason and revelation. And thus, again, such a harmonization expressed today would be "medieval" or "Philonic" in character. The modern period, finally, which for Wolfson is our period, inaugurated by Spinoza, is that epoch defined by the domination of reason over revelation. Thus, again, the "man of reason" today, he or she who understands – whether explicitly or implicitly – religion, art, politics, indeed everything, in terms of science, is a "modern," and in this sense a "Spinozist."

Notice that nothing has been said about a "contemporary" period. Without challenging Wolfson's underlying principle of signification, that is, the primacy of the Athens–Jerusalem encounter over the Parmenides–Heraclitus debate, my thesis requires a twofold revision of his account. First, my claim is that Bergson inaugurates a fourth period, our epoch, which, following philosophical convention, I am calling the "contemporary" period. Second and more specifically, my claim is that the contemporary period inaugurated by Bergson represents the genuine harmonization of reason and revelation, or, more accurately, that it represents the first steps and the prospect of the harmonization of reason and revelation.

Thus I must also disagree with Wolfson's characterization of the medieval period as being defined by the harmony that I am attributing to the contemporary period. Instead I will argue that the medieval period, in direct opposition to the modern period, represents the domination of revelation over reason. Thus we must re-evaluate and revise Wolfson's understanding of what was accomplished by Spinoza in relation to medieval thought. For Wolfson, who supports the harmonization of reason and revelation (as do I, and as does Levinas), the modern period represents a disturbing upset of a medieval harmony. In the modern period reason no longer accepts a complementary place alongside revelation but aims rather to subjugate and rule it. And there is no doubt that Spinoza and modernity do represent the effort of reason to dominate revelation. What I challenge, however, in the name of Bergson, is the claim that what the modern period overcame was a harmonization of reason and revelation. What upsets Wolfson is the modern destruction of that harmonization. My claim is that that harmonization never existed. Indeed, it is precisely because Wolfson did not appreciate what Bergson had accomplished that he was led to mistake the medieval accommodation of reason and revelation for a harmonization and, furthermore, to mistake the modern period for our own.[16] In the face of Bergson's well-argued philosophical defense of the irreducible status of duration, incarnation, and novelty, however, it becomes evident that the medieval period was defined not by harmonization but rather by the domination of revelation over reason. Thus the modern and the medieval epochs stand in converse relation to one another, but neither represents the harmony of the Athens–Jerusalem encounter.

That the medievals saw themselves as harmonizing reason and revelation in no way upsets the above thesis. Spinoza, too, after all, makes the same claim for his own thought, a thought that is so obviously biased in favor of reason against revelation. Indeed, it is precisely because neither the modern nor the medieval represent harmony, but are both forms of domination, converse forms, that we can understand the fierce intensity and the harsh rhetoric of their life and death struggle. Thus we see partisans of both periods attempting to persuade their antagonists that their interests have been satisfied – the medievalist argues for the reasonableness of the medieval period, its higher intellect; the modern argues for the faithfulness of the modern period, its deism. At the same time these partisans, unaware of or seeking to minimize their one-sidedness,

[16] Such an attachment and bias is of course hardly surprising coming from a Jew, especially a Jew of Wolfson's deep *Jewish* learning. Jews have long considered the material and spiritual flourishing of the Jewish communities of eleventh- through thirteenth-century Moorish Spain to have been the "Golden Age" of Judaism, as it is called. In a short article entitled "Hebraism and Western Philosophy in H. A. Wolfson's Theory of History" (English translation in *Immanuel*, vol. 14, Fall 1982, pp. 77–85), Professor Warren Zev Harvey (Hebrew University of Jerusalem) points out that in a youthful essay of 1912, entitled "Maimonides and Halevi, A Study in Typical Jewish Attitudes towards Greek Philosophy in the Middle Ages" (reprinted in Wolfson, *Studies in the History of Philosophy and Religion* (Cambridge, MA: Harvard University Press, 1973–77), vol. II, pp. 120–160), Wolfson had not yet settled into his later estimation of the medieval period as the harmonization of reason and revelation. Oddly enough, instead of understanding it as harmonization, or even as the victory of Hebraism, as I argue, the young Wolfson saw in medieval philosophy the victory of Hellenization. I would argue that both of these mistaken views, Wolfson's mature view that medieval Jewish thought represents a harmonization of reason and revelation, and his youthful view that it represents the domination of reason over revelation, result from his lack of appreciation for Bergson's philosophical contribution.

are each truly deceived themselves. Spinoza, for instance, will speak viciously against Maimonides,[17] one of the greatest of the medieval synthesizers, and yet appropriate a religious gloss for his own scientism. In turn, in our own time, we see certain medieval-ists, who are in truth disdainful of the theories of modern science, claim for their own theological constructions a scientific status (as in the case of "Creationism").

Spinoza saw better than Wolfson that the reason allegedly harmonized with revelation in the medieval epoch was in fact reason subjugated to revelation, that is to say, reason teleologically glossed. Such reason was not, as he writes against the medievals, a reason "superior" to scientific reason, but rather an ignorance inferior to scientific reason.[18] A non-teleological reason, reason reduced to logical ground, efficient causality and deductive impli-cation, which for Spinoza (in his rationalist one-sidedness) are the only genuine or scientific forms reason can take, finds any inner accommodation with revelation intolerable. The alleged medieval accommodation was not, then, as Wolfson thought, based on a genuine harmonization, but rather was based on a harmonization of revelation with reason teleologically glossed, that is, revelation's reason. The modern period, in turn, is precisely defined by the insistence by reason that teleology is the province solely of revel-ation, that it has no truth value, and the concomitant positive claim that non-teleological reason is alone genuine reason.

In view of the above twofold revision of Wolfson, we can now properly grasp the significance of Bergson's overcoming of the modern period. It represents an unprecedented harmonization,

[17] In chapter seven of the *Tractatus Theologico-Politicus* Spinoza writes of Maimonides and his method: "[H]e assumes that it is legitimate for us to explain away and distort the words of Scripture to accord with our preconceived opinions, to deny its literal meaning and change it into something else even when it is perfectly plain and absolutely clear. Such license, apart from being diametrically opposed to the proofs advanced in this chapter and elsewhere, must strike everyone as excessive and rash . . . Thus this method of Maimonides is plainly of no value . . . Therefore we can dismiss Maimonides' view as harmful, unprofitable and absurd." Baruch Spinoza, *Tractatus Theologico-Politicus*, trans. Samuel Shirley (Leiden: E. J. Brill, 1991), pp. 158–159. Spinoza is no less harsh on almost all other rabbinical exegetes.

[18] Spinoza, ibid., ch. V: "And if they claim for themselves some supra-rational faculty, this is the merest fiction and far inferior to reason" (trans. Shirley, p. 123). Ch. VI: "For whatever is contrary to Nature is contrary to reason, and whatever is contrary to reason is absurd, and should therefore be rejected" (trans. Shirley, p. 134).

or, more precisely, it represents a thought that does not harmonize reason and revelation, as if each could be itself independent of the other, but begins with their integral unity (and hence also their reinterpretation). Just as Philo is the first medieval because he brought reason and revelation together by making reason the handmaid of revelation, and Spinoza is the first modern because he reversed this relation, making revelation the handmaiden of reason, Bergson is the first contemporary, and our epoch is Bergsonian, because he brings reason and revelation into harmony, or rather, again, he begins with their integral unity. It is thus by not beginning abstractly – either above (spiritualism) or below (materialism) the concrete – but "in the midst," with duration, incarnation, and novelty, by not reducing and sacrificing these notions to rationalist constructions of matter and spirit (or idea), that one is a contemporary.

Because it is central to the concerns of this entire book, let us look once again, but even more closely this time, at the modern–contemporary turning point. What did Spinoza accomplish that Bergson overcomes? But to answer this question we must first ask another: What did Philo accomplish that Spinoza opposed? What Philo did, specifically, is to bring reason and revelation together by means of allegory. The revelation of the Bible would henceforth be interpreted, to the limits of human understanding and inventiveness, as an allegory of reason. The Bible would be reason cut to the measure of human imagination. While Philo's allegories often seem forced and far-fetched today, the complex and sophisticated philosophies of Maimonides and Aquinas, at the highpoint of medieval thought, remain no less bound to like biblical parameters. When Maimonides, for instance, in his *Guide for the Perplexed*, follows Aristotle and reason by prizing active intellect above imagination, he will at the same time remain loyal to Philo and revelation by presenting this hierarchy as (or as if it were) a gloss on the story of Adam's fall. It is precisely this framing, this loyalty to the Bible, that irks Spinoza and modernity. It will be derided as parochial, particular, prejudicial, "positive" religion in contrast to the "natural" universality of reason. Spinoza rebels without compromise against the yoke of medievalism, and thus scorns any biblical scaffolding for truth. In his hands, that is to say, within the architecture of a new conception of reason, this scaffold becomes no more than an empty shell, dead letters appropriate perhaps for political purposes, to keep the masses deceived in their ignorance, but of no intrinsic value to the knowing few, who are scientists and hence modern to the core. This uncompromising scientific singlemindedness is no less at the basis of Spinoza's sharp critique of Descartes, whose unresolved dualisms are for Spinoza indications not of the complexity and profundity of the Athens–Jerusalem question, but rather only of an incompletely modern thought.

What transforms the revelatory biblical narrative, the medieval allegory, from authoritative parameter to prudential but ultimately empty and antiquated shell to be discarded, is an altered, thoroughly modern, conception of reason. Knowledge would henceforth be knowledge of necessary efficient causality, coupled with knowing as necessary deductive implication, supplemented by a philosophical knowledge required to logically ground necessity itself in a fully consistent and comprehensive worldview (as in Spinoza's *Ethics*). This new and modern conception of reason – reason stripped of final, formal, and material causality – is fatal to Aristotelian reason, and hence fatal to the Philonic correlation of (Aristotelian) reason and revelation through allegory. The medieval compromise is now unmasked for what it always was: the surreptitious victory of revelation over a reason bridled by the restraints of revelation from the start. Hence the vituperative sting of Spinoza's polemic against the Bible and revelation, against Maimonides and the medieval spirit, is at bottom an attack by modern science against both the medieval spirit and, harbored by that spirit, the ancient Greek teleological notion of reason. Spinoza inaugurates modernity not by augmenting medieval reason but by narrowing it, perhaps even by a shift in paradigm, but in any event by unseating teleological reason – which had served Philo – in favor of mathematical rationality.

In the final chapter, entitled "What is New in Spinoza," of his great work on Spinoza, Wolfson distinguishes four dimensions, four "acts of daring,"[19] by means of which Spinoza overturns the

---

[19] Wolfson, *Spinoza*, p. 332.

medieval worldview and replaces it with a modern one. In each case two incommensurable realms, the divine and the mundane, one above the other, are reduced to one realm of uniform and homogenous nature.[20] In each case the "higher" is eliminated and reduced to the "lower." (1) "By declaring that God has the attribute of extension as well as of thought, Spinoza has thus removed the break in the principle of the homogeneity of nature. This is his first act of daring."[21] (2) "By denying design and purpose in God Spinoza has thus removed the break in the principle of the uniformity of the laws of nature. This is his second act of daring."[22] (3) "Spinoza's insistence upon the complete inseparability of soul from body has thus removed another break in the homogeneity of nature. This is his third act of daring."[23] (4) "Spinoza's insistence upon the elimination of freedom of the will from human actions has thus removed another break in the uniformity of the laws of nature. This is his fourth act of daring."[24] Thus Spinoza, and hence modernity, redefines reason and reality.

Spinoza's "acts of daring" all reflect two closely related and novel dimensions of sense constitutive of the modern worldview: homogeneity and uniformity. Homogenization reverses the dualism and orientation of the hierarchical perspective shared by all parties of the ancient and medieval epochs alike. Prior to the modern epoch, a lower realm – called "creation" in the Judeo-Christian tradition and "nature" (*physus*) in the Greco-Roman tradition – was distinguished from and grasped in terms of a higher realm – named "God," "Creator," "gods," "Olympus" (or, returning to Spinoza's four acts of daring: "intellection," "purpose," "soul," "will"). Spinoza *homogenizes* these two realms by reducing the higher to the lower. While in a certain sense the medieval period was no less reductionist, insofar as ultimately everything was divine and only the divine was real, its reduction was mitigated by the insuperable dualism of Creator and Created, or Divine and

---

[20] Alexandre Koyré, in his famous study, *From the Closed World to the Infinite Universe* (Baltimore: Johns Hopkins Press, 1957), also describes this modern displacement, occurring in the sixteenth and seventeenth centuries, of ancient and medieval dualisms, "the replacement of the Aristotelian conception of space – a differentiated set of inner worldly places – by that of Euclidean geometry – an essentially infinite and homogenous extension" (p. viii).     [21] Wolfson, *Spinoza*, p. 333.     [22] Ibid., p. 335.
[23] Ibid., p. 336.     [24] Ibid., p. 339.

Mortal, distinguished in terms (at least for the philosophers and theologians) of Perfection and Imperfection. Spinoza's homogenization, in contrast, reduces the non-scientific to the purely illusory, even if the majority of humankind in its ignorance refuse to deny it (and while the knowing minority, too, cannot make it go away). Homogenization, in any event, has the initial effect of eliminating the higher realm, reducing "spirit," say, to "matter," but it also has the ultimate effect, as Sade and Nietzsche were quick to emphasize, of leveling all hierarchic schemes of rank, and thus of eliminating the notion of rank altogether.

It is not as simple as saying that Spinoza naturalizes spirit. Rather, in keeping with the mechanist model of physics dominant in early modern science, he mechanizes spirit, and beyond that, he mathematizes it (*more geometrico ordone*).[25] Materialists, like de la Mettrie in France, make clear in a language and thought perhaps simpler, but following the basic contours of Spinoza's, that "man is a machine." Man is a machine not only because the human is an integral part of nature (Spinoza's point), but more profoundly because that nature of which the human is an integral part is itself a machine – or, for Spinoza, an order of precise mathematical character. The human is reduced to being a cog in a larger mechanical order (materialist) or a proportionality of forces in a causal-deductive order (idealist). Like the medievals, who saw the will of God in all things, Spinoza reduces everything to order. But unlike the medievals, he reduces all order not to will, which, at least from the human perspective, retains an ineradicable dimension of the novel and unpredictable, but to the necessary *uniformity* of efficient causality in extension and the necessity of deductive implication in intellection. For Spinoza as for modern science, reality is a *mathesis universalis*.

Based on this new interpretation of reality as ordered uniformity, and of ordered uniformity as ironclad causal necessity and

---

[25] In his 1911 article, "Philosophical Intuition," included as chapter four of Henri Bergson, *The Creative Mind*, trans. Maabelle L. Andison (New York: Philosophical Library, 1946), Bergson calls attention, regarding the form of Spinoza's *Ethics*, to "the formidable array of theorems with the close network of definition, corollaries and scholia, and that complication of machinery, that power to crush which causes the beginner, in the presence of the *Ethics*, to be struck with admiration and terror as though he were before a battleship of the Dreadnought class" (p. 113).

strict deductive implication, Spinoza's four "acts of daring" can all be seen as both following from and carrying out the homogenization or leveling of higher and lower. That is to say, they both reflect and derive from the scientific conception of a *uni-verse*. Returning to the four acts of daring, we can now say that intellection is the mirror of extension, freedom is nothing other than necessity, soul is conflated with body, and purpose is banished altogether from science to politics. Spinoza, scientist to the end, homogenizes higher and lower by reducing everything to the uniformity of universal and necessary relations. This reduction occurs despite, or rather in full view of, his *metaphysical* account of the universe as substance, a substance he must distinguish – in a manner never fully convincing – from its two known "modes," thought and extension (which, it is interesting to note, Spinoza once called "duration" and "quantity," reminding us of Bergson, and further distinguished, again reminding us of Bergson, from "time" and "measure" respectively).[26] Thus Spinoza reduces revelation to an unsavory figment of the imagination.

Philo and Spinoza bring together Athens and Jerusalem, but both do so by means of subordination. The medieval world is based ultimately, as we have said, on the *will* of God. In the final account it is a theo-logical world, a world of providence and miracle, however open or opaque. The modern world, in contrast, guided by the ideal of *mathesis universalis*, is based ultimately not on will (divine or human) but on necessary *causality*, whether material or deductive. In the final account it is a knowable world, either completely necessary or, as one thinks today, statistically probable.

Bergson's approach is entirely different. While Bergson also brings Athens and Jerusalem together, he does so without subordinating and hence reducing one to the other. His work of criticism, then, is to show – in all registers of signification – that modern rationality is itself a distortion of reality. But he does not do this in the name of some old-fashioned revelation either, some declaration of faith bound to the Bible directly or allegorically like the medievals. Instead he claims for *intuition* a philosophical dignity, that is to say,

[26] See Letter #12, April 20, 1663, in Baruch Spinoza, *The Letters*, trans. Samuel Shirley (Indianapolis: Hackett Publishing Co., 1995), pp, 101–107.

he claims to intuit a deeper reality beneath both rational constructions and revelatory declarations. And in this deeper reality, furthermore, Bergson discovers the source point, or the meeting point, or the primal origin, of both reason and revelation.

To have intuited a ground in which what is called revelation would be integrally linked to reason, and vice versa, to have intuited the link binding will and cause, freedom and necessity, is of necessity to reconceive both terms. Bergson achieves this reconceptualization, which undermines – as abstract – both the idea of strict necessity and the idea of unbridled freedom, by joining and hence transforming will and causality by means of a philosophical interpretation of the biologically derived notion of *growth*.[27] Perhaps influenced by the more general impact of Darwin's theory of evolution, Bergson's logic depends neither on that of a disembodied Mind nor on that of a Transcendent Will. It is rather the logic of the bio-logical. Reality, so Bergson teaches, must no longer be conceived in terms of inorganic matter, conceptually reconstructed from elements taken from one periodic table or another, joined together by uniform forces, as it was by modern rationalism. Nor can the real be conceived in terms of a free human will or in terms of a projection of a projected primal family, however extended, as it had been imagined in ancient mythology and cosmology, and in absolutized form in biblical and medieval theology as well. Rather, having cleared his way by means of precise arguments showing the *aporia* of both necessity and freedom traditionally conceived, Bergson positively presents, through descriptions based on intuition, both *physus* and will, reality and desire, order and inspiration, joined in the unity of an organic development determined by cumulative progress and inner growth. In contrast to the theo-logical and onto-logical constructs of earlier epochs, then, Bergson launches what we can properly call an *eco-logical* epoch: the world grasped as an integral develop-

---

[27] "The empirical experience upon which truth rests, is no longer mathematical, but biological, conforming with the fluctuations of life apprehended by consciousness," writes Joseph Chiari of the revolution effected by Bergson (*Twentieth Century French Thought*, p. 27). Professor Henri Gouhier also makes this point – "Philosophy is science in the manner of mathematics according to Descartes, and in the manner of biology according to Bergson" – in his magisterial introduction to Henri Bergson, *Oeuvres* (Paris: Presses Universitaires de France, 1963), p. xii.

ing interrelationship of spirit and matter, mind and body, change and stability.

This is the reality we have named with the irreducible terms "incarnation" (the integral unity of mind–body), "duration" (the temporal inter-penetration of past–present–future), and "novelty" (the one-way cumulative directionality of time). These are the founding "principles" of contemporary thought. What is important is that in contrast to all Cartesian philosophies, Bergson does not show the unity of mind and body, spirit and matter, etc., as if they were first separate and then brought into relation, as if so-called "secondary" qualities could be added to "primary" qualities. By means of eloquent and persuasive argumentation, Bergson shows that such an approach inevitably leads to aporia and therefore must fail. Instead, then, by means of a purified intuition, now philosophically legitimized by the failure of rationalism, Bergson *begins* with the inseparable inner unity, the inextricable or dynamic intertwining – in a word, the integrity – of what previous thought had separated. Intuition, then, would be a vision of the inner character of reality. Because it would require that the inquirer enter into the interior sense, as it were, of the phenomenon under study, it would in this sense be a kind of hermeneutic. From this point of view, Bergson can then also explain how and why previous thought, in every case "analytical" and "objectifying," whether calling itself "empirical" or "rational," had been, quite naturally, oriented – despite itself – by action rather than truth, by a physics rather than a metaphysics. Thus rationality, as disguised instrumental reason, had separated what from the start is joined. It was therefore as a philosopher in the strictest sense, a seeker of truth, and hence in the name of contemplative epistemological interests, that Bergson criticizes and undermines previous rationality for the distortions it produced for the sake of self-preservative action. Later, as we shall see in the following chapters, Bergson's German contemporary Edmund Husserl, will found an entire and new science of phenomenology, making a method of Bergson's purified intuitive-descriptive approach, and he will likewise accuse both common sense and the natural sciences of realist prejudice.

For his part, Bergson's originality lies in conceiving reality in its

original integral unity as "creative evolution." His thought requires that one grasp humanity and world not in the mediated
terms of a scientific reconstruction, which for Bergson is a second-
order explanation motivated by the unacknowledged instrumental
interests of action, but rather in the deeper phenomenological
immediacy Bergson sought under the names "philosophy" and
"metaphysics." Bracketing out (to use a phenomenological expression for what was already Bergson's approach) the unacknowledged influence of practical interests, the immediate is discovered
by intuition to be structured as a *durée* and *zoë*, i.e., duration and
vitality. Enduring and vital, the real would be originally manifest
as an "*élan vital*," the living, cumulating energy that drives and
discriminates all entities and each entity in its own way.

The real would be a function neither of causal sequence nor
logical deduction, but a stream of vital energy, growing and in
each instance novel because growing on its own prior growth.
Bergson's fundamental distinction, running through his entire
philosophy, would be between a "static" quantification, the object
of an objectifying thought, and a "dynamic" inter-penetration,
visible to the empathetic intuition of the philosopher. In this way,
instead of grounding the fluid on the static, as had previous
thought, Bergson would ground the static on the dynamic, perma-
nence upon movement, quantity upon quality, representation
upon life. This fundamental distinction – between static analytical
construction and dynamic integral duration – pervades all of
Bergson's philosophy: whether it is characterized in terms of
discontinuity and continuity, spatialized time and duration, representation and memory, or closed and open society, it is the central
theme and thread linking all his writings, from *Time and Free Will*,
*Matter and Memory*, and *Creative Evolution* to *The Two Sources of
Morality and Religion*. In every instance Bergson shifts from a static
conceptual compartmentalization produced by instrumental reason and serving the limited goals of action, to the detached –
"disinterested" – philosophical intuition of an immediate reality,
grasped in terms of (1) interpenetrating flow, (2) cumulative
growth, and (3) unpredictable future.

From the beginning to the end of his thought, then, by means of
an integral organic model, Bergson overcomes the dualisms and

reductions that plagued prior philosophy and haunted theology hitherto. By means of crisp arguments, uncovering the irresolvable aporia of past philosophical distinctions, coupled with lucid intuitions, descriptively articulated, into a new integral ground, his is a new beginning – a beginning at the source. "It is movement," he writes, "that we must accustom ourselves to look upon as simplest and clearest, immobility being only the extreme limit of the slowing down of movement, a limit reached only, perhaps, in thought and never realized in nature."[28] Henceforth the philosopher would have to be attentive to what had been previously called mind and matter not as alien objects, but as the stream of their own now self-conscious self-constitution, indeed, as their own ongoing creative self-constitution, i.e., as *élan vital*.

One might be tempted, nevertheless, to think that the Hegelian dialectic had already elaborated the conception of an integral developmental movement and unity that I am crediting to Bergsonian thought. But this would be mistaken. It is true that Hegel *homogenizes* a certain dualism that runs through philosophy and theology up to Kant, bringing the "other" (the "unknowable" as such) into the purview of the "same" (the Concept). But upon closer inspection, one sees that what Hegel means by the famous "negation of negation" remains bound to the very representational logic it strives to (and claims to) overcome. Not only does the "negation of negation" blindly fail to appreciate the originary positivity of that which is prior to representational thought, but precisely because of this failure the alleged "movement" it proposes is in truth but a calculus, a reconstruction of movement but not movement itself.[29] It is precisely this "static" thought that Bergson exposes and undermines. Rather than overcome dualism, it reproduces, but now in an even more disguised form, as a calculus, precisely the discontinuity it claims to overcome. Hence its claims – overblown and pompous, to be sure – are secretly rhetorical, in the bad sense of being an empty or political rhetoric, akin to advertising. It is no accident, for instance, that Hegel

---

[28] Henri Bergson, *An Introduction to Metaphysics*, trans. T. E. Hulme (Indianapolis: Bobbs-Merrill, 1955), p. 43.

[29] The later Schelling's "positive" philosophy, with which he attacked Hegel's idealism and all idealism, was intended to be positive in this sense.

attaches a "Preface" to his *Phenomenology of Spirit*, even while admitting that such a preface is not only unnecessary, but superfluous.[30] Per impossibile, something is missing from Hegel's Absolute, and that something is what Bergson will call movement, mobility, vitality. It was, after all, precisely to preserve the truth of judgment from the inevitability of certain aporia that Kant, creating the distinction Hegel claims to overcome, was forced to distinguish noumena from phenomena. It is precisely to preserve the same propositional truth, now called the "Concept," that Hegel conflates Kant's distinction. Hegel, in a word, is as loyal to abstract thought as is Kant, but his abstraction, which may seem concrete in relation to Kant, only becomes visible from the genuinely concrete – the "living" or "vital" – perspective of Bergson.

The unacknowledged loyalty to the rationalist tradition of modern thought, hidden in the novelty of the "positivity" allegedly found by means of double negation – and the artificiality of the high-handed rhetorical claims, made on behalf of this ostensively new positivity, to "surpass" the aporia of "simple" affirmations and negations – is surely what so irked Schopenhauer in his angry polemics against the legerdemain of Hegelian thought.[31] But we must agree with the content, if not entirely with the tone, of Schopenhauer's anti-Hegelianism, though we cannot follow him in his (or, for that matter in Nietzsche's) *speculative* return to Kant.[32] By interpreting the stilted activity of negation as genuine movement, even though negativity remains bound to classical logic, and interpreting the world and history in terms of this allegedly new

[30] In the second sentence of his preface, Hegel writes: "In the case of a philosophical work, however, such an explanation [a preface] seems not only superfluous but, in view of the nature of the subject-matter, even inappropriate and misleading." G. W. F. Hegel, *Phenomenology of Spirit*, trans. A. V. Miller (Oxford: Oxford University Press, 1979), p. 1.

[31] See, e.g., Arthur Schopenhauer, *The Fourfold Root of the Principle of Sufficient Reason*, trans. E. F. J. Payne (La Salle, IL: Open Court Publishing Company, 1974), pp. 165–166: "Thus they [the 'professors of philosophy'] needed the place and name of *reason* (*Vernunft*) for an invented and fabricated, or more correctly and honestly, a wholly fictitious, faculty that would help them out of the straits to which Kant had reduced them . . . For this last step, of course, only the audacity of an impudent scribbler of nonsense like Hegel was bold enough. And so it is tomfoolery of this sort which . . ."

[32] On Nietzsche's appropriation of Schopenhauer's speculative Kantianism, see George Santayana, *The German Mind: A Philosophical Diagnosis* (originally published as *Egoism in German Philosophy*) (New York: Apollo Edition, 1968), chapter eleven, "Nietzsche and Schopenhauer," pp. 114–122.

movement, which is in truth only judgmental activity rhetorically (or "speculatively") glossed, Hegel constructs a simulacrum or an artificial version of the genuine movement found in the organic model Bergson later introduces. The charge of artifice will also be Bergson's complaint against Spencerian mechanism.

Nor, turning to another possible precursor, should we think that the respect for the biological that some commentators have found in Aristotle's notion of finality, and the movement it implies,[33] captured what Bergson would later express. Bergson does not argue, in contrast to Aristotle, that all things tend according to and toward a *telos*, an end, but rather that they manifest, indeed are manifestations of, an internal finality, if one may use this expression, an "impulsion" rather than an aspiration. The interpenetrating qualities and cumulative movement Bergson sees in duration, memory, and life ceaselessly grow not because they approach ever more closely to a pre-set goal, but because they ever increasingly build upon themselves, constantly grow upon their own growth, and do so unpredictably, hence "creatively." "Life," Bergson writes in *Creative Evolution*, "transcends finality . . . It is essentially a current sent through matter, drawing from it what it can. There has not, therefore, properly speaking, been any project or plan."[34] The tendency in all things – Bergson's *élan vital* – unfolds, grows, builds upon itself, but it does so unpredictably, creatively, rather than aiming deliberately at a pre-established goal.

Because the integral unity of Bergson's conception of movement is driven through neither a mechanical nor a final causality, but internally, feeding upon itself, it works quite otherwise than do the unitary visions of either Hegel or Aristotle. If the *élan vital* may be said to be progressive, it is not because it is mechanically or logically driven forward or hypnotically drawn upward, both by predictable order. Rather, it is because Bergson notices that, in the cosmic scheme of things, with the emergence of conscious memory

---

[33] For a biological reading of Aristotle, see Marjorie Grene, *A Portrait of Aristotle* (London: Faber & Faber, 1963). Perhaps Grene's reading reflects rather than offers an alternative to Bergson. The same might be said of John Herman Randall, Jr., as well.

[34] Henri Bergson, *Creative Evolution*, trans. Arthur Mitchel (New York: Random House, 1944), p. 289.

in human life not only is there an accumulation of the past, as there is with inorganic matter and lower forms of organic life, each after their own fashion, but there also arises the new possibility, by means of deliberate reflection, of an awareness of the accumulation. This awareness – "laborious, and even painful"[35] to achieve – is philosophy. Hence, with human reflection, there is opened the possibility of a doubling of the progressive development of all things with a progressively developing awareness of that development. In a word, Bergson's famous intuition,[36] by going against the grain of simple or direct development – that is to say, in the case of the human, by going against the ingrained habit of practical or utilitarian concerns[37] – opens the possibility of a pure or philosophical awareness of instinct and common sense, and hence represents *élan vital* become conscious of itself. In calling the movement of the *élan vital* progressive, Bergson admits no more, then, and no less either, than his preference for the philosophical life.

The true heir to Bergson is neither Aristotle nor Hegel before him, but the masters of the phenomenological school after him. If, as Camus thought,[38] the critical power of Bergson's thought raised enormous intellectual expectations, but ones that Bergson himself did not satisfy, then surely it is phenomenology that did satisfy them. And of all the phenomenologists who came to flesh out and extend Bergson's intuitions, probably the closest of Bergson's heirs is the French phenomenologist, Merleau-Ponty. It is no mere coincidence, then, that Merleau-Ponty succeeded to Bergson's chair of Modern Philosophy at the College of France.[39] Later, in chapter 3, we will also see in what way and to what extent Levinas had anticipated, already in 1940, Merleau-Ponty's central

---

[35] Bergson, *An Introduction to Metaphysics*, p. 45.

[36] Though it is beyond the scope of this chapter to elaborate the precise manner in which Bergsonian "intuition" and "intellect" surpass and function otherwise than faith and reason, traditionally conceived, there can be no doubt that both of the latter must be thoroughly reconceived – with a view to their integration – within the Bergsonian model.

[37] Bergson, *An Introduction to Metaphysics*, p. 39: "To try to fit a concept on an object is simply to ask what we can do with the object, and what it can do for us."

[38] See note 11 above.

[39] Prior to Merleau-Ponty's election in 1953, two professors held Bergson's chair at the College of France: Edouard Le Roy (1870–1954), cited at the beginning of this article, who substituted for Bergson from 1914 to 1921, at which point he was elected in his own right, and Louis Lavelle (1883–1951), elected in 1941. Étienne Gilson, a neo-Thomist, held the chair of the History of Medieval Philosophy from 1932 to 1950.

Bergsonian insight – incarnate thought, the "intertwining," "flesh." So, too, we will also see the continued influence of Bergson on Levinas – not only his central notion of a vital integral unity, or incarnation, but also, more specifically, his elaboration of this integral unity in terms of the inner-temporality of duration and its concomitant creative novelty.

But let us briefly take a further look at Merleau-Ponty's filial Bergsonianism. We have already heard his praise for *Matter and Memory*. That Merleau-Ponty singles out this text comes as no surprise, since it is on the plane of perception so dear to Merleau-Ponty that Bergson repudiates the dualisms of both materialism and idealism, and offers a third alternative, the sense of which Merleau-Ponty's entire work is devoted to extending. The whole of Merleau-Ponty's extraordinary posthumous work, *The Visible and the Invisible*,[40] published in 1964, is a working out, an elaboration and a development of fundamental Bergsonian themes: the intertwining of sense and significance, mind and body, spirit and matter. Thus Merleau-Ponty's "phenomenological" method owes as much to Bergson (and to some extent also to Levinas, as we shall see) as to Husserl, whom Merleau-Ponty criticizes and revises for Bergsonian reasons. The Husserlian "intuition of essences" serves Merleau-Ponty not to alter or deepen but to refine Bergson's earlier intuitive approach – and for the considerable development and articulation of Bergsonian themes due to this refinement we must be grateful indeed.[41]

In many instances, one can hardly distinguish Merleau-Ponty's thought from Bergson's. When, in *Matter and Memory*, Bergson declares that his "problem is no less than that of the union of soul and body," and resolves it, against materialism and idealism (which Merleau-Ponty will call "empiricism" and "intellectualism"), with the following discovery: "It is in very truth within matter that pure perception places us, and it is really into spirit that

---

[40] Maurice Merleau-Ponty, *The Visible and the Invisible*, ed. Claude Lefort, trans. Alphonso Lingis (Evanston: Northwestern University Press, 1968).

[41] Merleau-Ponty writes, for example: "The return to the immediate data, the deepening of experience on the spot, are certainly the hallmark of philosophy by opposition to naive cognitions. But the past and the present, the essence and the fact, space and time, are not *given* in the same sense, and none of them is given in the sense of coincidence." Ibid., p. 124.

we penetrate by means of memory,"[42] this citation could be placed verbatim into the most central positive sections of either of Merleau-Ponty's two major works, the *Phenomenology of Perception*[43] or *The Visible and the Invisible*, without disruption or discontinuity to their philosophical arguments and themes (or style, for that matter). If one were to read the following, without the textual references being supplied: "our perception being a part of things, things participate in the nature of our perception," who could tell, without checking, whether the words were Bergson's or Merleau-Ponty's? They are Bergson's.[44] "Every focus is always a focus on something which presents itself as to be focused upon" – Merleau-Ponty.[45] "Perceiving is pinning one's faith, at a stroke, in a whole future of experiences, and doing so in a present which never strictly guarantees the future" – Merleau-Ponty.[46] "But we must not confound the data of the senses, which perceive the movement, with the artifice of the mind, which recomposes it. The senses, left to themselves, present to us the real movement, between two real halts, as a solid and undivided whole" – Bergson.[47] For Levinas, too, the origin of sense lies in the intertwining of passivity and activity, but unlike Merleau-Ponty, who follows Heidegger's path even while revising it, for Levinas this originary intertwining is the function of an *ethical* encounter and not of a merely ontological relation.

Of course, Merleau-Ponty – who like Bergson believes not only in the inter-penetration of past and present, but in the genuinely *creative* character of reality, its unpredictable futurity – will give up Bergson's optimism that the ongoing amplification of matter, memory and life, must be understood as a progressive creative *evolution*.[48] And we are inclined to wonder whether Bergson did not

---

[42] Henri Bergson, *Matter and Memory*, trans. Nancy Margaret Paul and W. Scott Palmer (New York: Doubleday & Co., 1959), p. 174.

[43] Maurice Merleau-Ponty, *Phenomenology of Perception*, trans. Colin Smith (London: Routledge & Kegan Paul, 1962).     [44] Bergson, *Matter and Memory*, p. 176.

[45] Merleau-Ponty, *Phenomenology of Perception*, p. 264.     [46] Ibid., p. 297.

[47] Bergson, *Matter and Memory*, p. 184.

[48] Merleau-Ponty will also accuse Bergson of not having developed a theory of history (see *The Bergsonian Heritage*, p. 142), but I think on this question Émile Bréhier is more to the point, finding a philosophy of history in Bergson's philosophy of religion elaborated in *The Two Sources of Morality and Religion* (1932); see Émile Bréhier, *The History of Philosophy, Volume VII: Contemporary Philosophy Since 1850*, trans. Wade Baskin (Chicago: University of Chicago Press, 1973), p. 128.

succumb, despite his intentions, to an Aristotelian notion of finality when he interpreted cumulative growth as progressive growth. Though Merleau-Ponty will support the philosophical life of self-consciousness, of conscious awareness of the interactive intertwining character of sense and significance, and will even propose a politics consistent with such self-awareness, he will not follow the thrust of Bergson's later work, which projected his own hopeful – and even cosmic – evaluation of this awareness as a developmental progress onto the universe at large. Who is right and who is wrong regarding a large question such as this, how far or how broadly the intertwining of sensibility and significance can be taken, is not a matter for this chapter to decide. Levinas, however, for his part, as we shall shortly see in detail, will understand the primordial intertwining of sense and sensibility in ethical rather than ontological or cosmic terms.

The point of this chapter, however, is not to show that Merleau-Ponty alone is Bergson's heir, though he is probably Bergson's most faithful and original successor. The point, rather, is much broader. It is to show that the integral and dynamic unity of mind and body, matter and spirit, past, present and future – elaborated by Bergson in many writings, utilizing notions of growth and creative evolution, borrowed from and reflecting the biosphere – inaugurates a new epoch of the Western spirit, our epoch. In contrast to antiquity where reason and revelation stood apart, or the medieval epoch inaugurated by Philo where reason served as handmaid to revelation, or the modern period inaugurated by Spinoza where revelation served as handmaid to reason, the contemporary period inaugurated by Bergson is one in which reason and revelation are reconceived starting from a new zero point, the integral unity of sense and sensibility. In contrast, then, to the prejudices of ancient ontology, medieval theology, and modern epistemology, the contemporary period can properly lay claim to the title *ecology*, where spirit and matter, mind and body, sense and significance – all the old irreconcilable dualisms – are understood in terms of their inner, dynamic, integral unity. Bergsonian intuition will demand that in the name of truth one must enter into the "object" of thought as a "subject" of thought; it thus demands of thinking what we could call a "substitution," the ongoing effort to put oneself in the place of what is other, seeing from that other's point of view, as it were.

Because they accept and further elaborate this fundamental intuition lying beneath and determining the rationality of reason, Levinas, Husserl, Heidegger, Merleau-Ponty, and many others, from the phenomenological school especially, but from elsewhere as well, are Bergson's heirs and contemporaries. But because he sees that the original meaning of "substitution" must be an ethical rather than a purely epistemological meaning, Levinas, unlike these other thinkers, and unlike Bergson himself, will show how thinking exceeds ontology in ethics.

# CHAPTER 2

# *Science, phenomenology, intuition, and philosophy*

It was the new science of phenomenology, elaborated by Edmund Husserl, imposing a more stringent method onto Bergsonian intuition and vastly expanding its fields of investigation, which advanced and determined subsequent contemporary thought on the European continent in the twentieth century. Yet Husserl's phenomenology is a method little known outside of professional philosophy and the social sciences. One can make an analogy with contemporary physics. Though very few people actually understand or could rehearse the equations of Einstein, everyone is aware that his discoveries have altered the map of science. Similarly, the phenomenology of Edmund Husserl is barely known by name outside of academia, and in truth is less known by actual acquaintance even there. Nonetheless, Husserl's phenomenology represents one of the great advances of human thought, and has already been quite influential across the humanities and social sciences, because it exploits the fertile philosophical territory opened up by Bergson. Rich as it has been in itself, and fertile as has been its direct influence, Husserl's phenomenology has also served as the motherlode for nearly all of the major continental philosophies of the twentieth century, from Heidegger's ontology to Sartre's existentialism to Claude Levi-Strauss's structuralism to Jacques Derrida's deconstruction.

Levinas, too, was schooled in Husserl's phenomenology. His attachment to phenomenology is both personal and philosophical. After five years at the University of Strasbourg, at the ripe age of twenty-two Levinas traveled to Freiburg to study under Husserl (and under Heidegger) for the 1928–29 academic year. Within two years he had completed his doctoral dissertation on Husserl's phenomenology, published as the prize-winning book, *The Theory of Intuition in Husserl's Phenomenology* (1930). This book has been in print ever since, and was the first of Levinas's books to be translated into English (1973). Focused on one of Husserl's central works, *Ideas Pertaining to a Pure Phenomenology and to a Phenomenological Philosophy*, volume I (1913), it will be the primary topic of this chapter.

The dissertation was, however, just a beginning. One year later, in 1931, Levinas co-translated an expanded version of the influential lectures Husserl gave in Paris in February of 1920, published as *Cartesian Meditations* (1931). As it turned out, Levinas's French translation had far more impact than Husserl's own German original, which was not published until 1950, posthumously. From the late 1920s to the early 1980s Levinas authored numerous articles on phenomenology (recently published, in 1998, in English translation in a collection entitled *Discovering Existence with Husserl*[1]). This volume in English includes those articles on Husserl that Levinas had himself published in an earlier French collection entitled *En découvrant l'éxistence avec Husserl et Heidegger* [*Discovering Existence with Husserl and Heidegger*] (1949; 2nd edition, 1967), a volume that also included studies of Heidegger's "phenomenological ontology." Though in the course of his long intellectual career Levinas developed his own ethical metaphysics, turning from Husserlian phenomenology to an ethical exegetical approach, he nonetheless remained at the same time and to the end a self-declared phenomenologist. "Phenomenology," Levinas declared in an interview of the early 1980s, "represented the second [after Bergson], but undoubtedly most important, philosophical influence on my thinking. Indeed, from the point of view of philosophical method and discipline, I remain to this day a phenomenologist."[2]

Martin Heidegger, to whom we will turn in greater detail in chapter 4, is another even better known case in point, establishing

[1] Emmanuel Levinas, *Discovering Existence with Husserl*, ed. and trans. Richard A. Cohen and Michael B. Smith (Evanston: Northwestern University Press, 1998).
[2] "Dialogue with Emmanuel Levinas," ed. and trans. Richard Kearney, in Richard A. Cohen, ed., *Face to Face with Levinas* (Albany: State University of New York Press, 1986), p. 14.

the depth and fertility of Husserl's phenomenology. Heidegger, after all, was Husserl's student and sometimes editor, his hand-chosen successor at Freiburg. His monumental work *Being and Time* (1927), which altered the course of continental philosophy and irrevocably established the philosophical credentials of phenomenology, first appeared as a volume of Husserl's *Yearbook for Phenomenology and Phenomenological Research*. It is "Dedicated to Edmund Husserl in friendship and admiration," and expresses gratitude to Husserl for "freely turning over his unpublished investigations." Having shown in *Being and Time* the central importance of time and history for human being and thought, in 1928 Heidegger compiled and published Husserl's groundbreaking 1905 lectures on time and consciousness, *The Phenomenology of Internal Time-Consciousness*.[3] Like Levinas after him, Heidegger also moved away from phenomenology, first to ontology and then, after his "turn" (*Kehre*) in his later writings (Richardson's "Heidegger II"[4]), to *poesis*. His debt to Husserl's phenomenology nonetheless initiated his beginnings and colors much of his subsequent thought. His appropriation of phenomenology also influenced Levinas (who, however, far from becoming a "Heideggerian," is – as we shall see in chapter 4 and elsewhere – his most trenchant critic and protagonist). In the same interview cited above, Levinas will say: "[I]f it was Husserl who opened up for me the radical possibilities of a phenomenological analysis of knowledge, it was Heidegger who first gave these possibilities a positive and concrete grounding in our everyday existence . . . in *time*, in our temporal and historical existence."[5]

Regarding Husserl's influence, one cannot overlook Jean-Paul Sartre, perhaps the most "famous" of twentieth-century philosophers, known for "existentialism," all the rage in Paris in the 1940s and 1950s, and afterwards in America in certain bohemian and academic circles. It was as early as 1932, after having read (through the recommendation of the important French political philosopher Raymond Aron, who also studied phenomenology)

---

[3] Edmund Husserl, *The Phenomenology of Internal Time-Consciousness*, ed. Martin Heidegger, trans. James S. Churchill (Bloomington: Indiana University Press, 1964).

[4] See William J. Richardson, S. J., *Heidegger: Through Phenomenology to Thought* (The Hague: Martinus Nijhoff, 1967).     [5] Cohen, ed., *Face to Face with Levinas*, p. 16.

Levinas's *The Theory of Intuition in Husserl's Phenomenology*, that Sartre
went to Berlin to study phenomenology. Sartre's own philosophical career began shortly afterwards in 1936–37, with the publication of an article entitled "The Transcendence of the Ego." Here
Sartre argues for an account of human subjectivity that is in truth
but a rationalist and truncated version of Husserl's notion of
"intentionality," that is, consciousness as the meaning-giving link
to the world. Sartre's idiosyncratic reading of Husserl in this article
found its full fruition, as we know, in the bible of existentialism,
*Being and Nothingness*, published in 1943 (under the Vichy Government of France), and subtitled "An Essay on Phenomenological
Ontology." One can see in Sartre's famous doctrine of human
"freedom," then, a (no doubt Hegelian) simplification and exaggeration of a tendency – consciousness as meaning bestowing – of
Husserl's phenomenology.

Maurice Merleau-Ponty (disciple, as we have seen, of Bergson),
is a no less original, and certainly a far more profound, thinker
than Sartre who is steeped in phenomenology, indeed more faithfully than Sartre, Heidegger or Levinas. He made intense studies
at the Husserl Archive in Louvain both before and after the war.
How deeply he drank from the Husserlian sources can be seen in
his own groundbreaking phenomenological investigation, *The Phenomenology of Perception*,[6] published in 1945. The "Preface" to this
book is a veritable introduction to phenomenology and, of course,
to Merleau-Ponty's particular appropriation of it. Though in his
second great work, *The Visible and the Invisible*,[7] published posthumously in 1961 (edited by Claude Lefort), Merleau-Ponty would be
critical of Husserl, his book nonetheless was made possible by
Husserlian phenomenology.

Paul Ricoeur, one of the most versatile and prolific philosophers
of the twentieth century, to whose thought we will turn in chapter
9, also labored at the Louvain archives. During his wartime
internment in a German prisoner-of-war camp, Ricoeur translated into French the basic text explicated by Levinas in *The Theory*

---

[6] Maurice Merleau-Ponty, *The Phenomenology of Perception*, trans. Colin Smith (London:
Routledge & Kegan Paul, 1962).
[7] Maurice Merleau-Ponty, *The Visible and the Invisible*, ed. Claude Lefort, trans. Alphonso
Lingis (Evanston: Northwestern University Press, 1968).

*of Intuition in Husserl's Phenomenology*: Husserl's *Ideas Pertaining to a Pure Phenomenology and to a Phenomenological Philosophy*, volume I.[8] This translation was published in France after the war, in 1950, the same year that also saw the publication of Ricoeur's translation of Husserl's important 1935 defense of the Western scientific spirit, "Philosophy and the Crisis of European Humanity." In the latter text, without specific reference to the immediate political context, Husserl profoundly – but obviously ineffectively – opposes the *Zeitgeist* of the Nazi *Reich* in the name of the universality of science and a scientific humanity. Like Levinas, Ricoeur authored numerous articles on Husserl, which were also translated into English and collected into a volume entitled *Husserl: An Analysis of His Phenomenology*, published in 1967.[9] It is precisely because Ricoeur and Levinas both adhere so closely to Husserl while both opening their thought to a "religious" dimension – call it hermeneutics or exegesis – that we must return later in chapter 9 to clarify and sharpen the differences that separate them.

I conclude this short list of phenomenological illuminati with Jacques Derrida. He too was a diligent though eccentric student of Husserlian phenomenology, even if many of his more literary disciples in American universities and elsewhere overlook or seem to have somehow forgotten it. As early as 1962, Derrida translated and commented upon Husserl's *The Origin of Geometry*[10] (originally published posthumously in 1939). Five years later, in 1967, Derrida launched his philosophical career proper with *Speech and Phenomena*[11] (along with two other books), a microscopic textual reading – most Husserl scholars would say a "misreading" – and critique of the notions of "expression" and "indication" as elaborated in the first of the six phenomenological studies found in Husserl's *Logical*

---

[8] Edmund Husserl, *Idées directrices pour une phénoménologie et une philosophie phénoménologique*, trans. Paul Ricoeur (Paris: Gallimard, 1950). During a visit to his home on the outskirts of Paris (Chatenay), on 13 March, 1999, Ricoeur was kind enough to show me the original of his translation, which is hand written between the lines and in the margins of the German text, somehow available to him in the prisoner-of-war camp.

[9] Paul Ricoeur, *Husserl: An Analysis of His Phenomenology*, trans. Edward G. Ballard and Lester E. Embree (Evanston: Northwestern University Press, 1967).

[10] Jacques Derrida, *Edmund Husserl's "Origin of Geometry": An Introduction*, trans. John P. Leaver (Stony Brook, NY: Nicolas Hays, 1978).

[11] Jacques Derrida, *Speech and Phenomena and Other Essays on Husserl's Theory of Signs*, trans. David B. Allison (Evanston: Northwestern University Press, 1973).

*Investigations*[12] of 1900–01. The central deconstructive notions of "trace" and "differance" derive from this work, the former coming to Derrida via Levinas, and the latter (as well as the notion of "deconstruction" itself) coming via Heidegger. Indeed, it is precisely as the most faithful disciple of Heidegger, that is to say, as one who has prolonged and extended the later "poetic thinking" of Heidegger, hence as both a disciple and a critic of Husserl (and, because of his Heideggerianism, as both a disciple and critic of Levinas), that Derrida has made his distinctive mark in twentieth-century thought.

Phenomenology has indeed been the common source of twentieth-century continental thought. The point is well made, I think, so without commentary I only mention the additional names of Adorno, Fink, Gadamer, Gurwitch, Ingarden, Lyotard, Rotenstreich, Scheler, Schutz, Shestov, and Wahl, among the many other productive thinkers influenced by Husserl. Though truly original and independent thinkers such as Heidegger, Sartre, Merleau-Ponty, and Levinas do not end with Husserl, everyone begins with him. And like Bergson before him, Husserl himself, throughout his long and productive career, characterized his own efforts as perpetually at the beginning.[13] Husserl, like all scientists, could be a perpetual beginner because phenomenology, like all science, is a turn to "the things themselves," a turn to the positivity of evidence. Where the great phenomenologists disagreed with Husserl, and among themselves, would not be about the depth or originality of philosophy, but rather about its starting point, that is

---

[12] Edmund Husserl, *Logical Investigations*, vols. I and II, trans. J. N. Findlay (New York: Humanities Press, 1970).

[13] See, e.g., the 1931 "Author's Preface to the English Edition" of Husserl's *Ideas: General Introduction to Pure Phenomenology*, trans. W. R. Boyce Gibson (New York: Collier Books, 1962), pp. 20–21: "If he [Husserl] has been obliged, on practical grounds, to lower the ideal of the philosopher to that of a downright beginner, he has at least in his old age reached for himself the complete certainty that he should thus call himself a beginner." Husserl is of course not referring to a first start, but rather to the repeatedly difficult task of ridding oneself of presuppositions and naïve habits of thought in order to get to the genuine origin of meaning. Bergson, too, refers to the difficulty of getting to originary thought (and to the constant requirement, in genuine science, to confirm and reconfirm one's discoveries): "The mind has to do violence to itself, has to reverse the direction of the operation by which it habitually thinks, has perpetually to revise, or rather to recast, all its categories." Bergson, *An Introduction to Metaphysics*, trans. T. E. Hulme (Indianapolis: Bobbs-Merrill, 1955), p. 51.

to say, about the origin of signification. For Husserl this source increasingly became the representational intentionality of an absolute *transcendental ego*; for Heidegger it would be *being (Seindes)* as the manifestation of history and the verbality of language; for Sartre it was the unalloyed *freedom* of consciousness projecting meaning; for Merleau-Ponty it would be the *flesh*, the incarnate intertwining of meanings given and meaning giving; while for Levinas it is the inordinate *responsibility* of one for the other.

Regardless, or more likely because, of the weighty differences separating his students from one another and from their teacher, one wants to place Husserl and the phenomenological movement he initiated alongside the great triumvirates of philosophy's most prodigious and creative epochs: ancient Greece, Socrates–Plato–Aristotle; modern rationalism, Descartes–Spinoza–Leibniz; modern empiricism, Locke–Berkeley–Hume; German idealism, Kant–Hegel–Schelling; contemporary phenomenology, Husserl–Heidegger . . . Levinas, Sartre, Merleau-Ponty, Derrida, time will tell. But enough of externals. What is it about Husserl's work, the labor of thought, what root issue is it that yields such philosophical capital and reinvestment? Why, more specifically, with so many rich possibilities of inquiry, so many avenues of research and development, did Levinas select Husserl's theory of *intuition* as the topic of his dissertation (and book) on phenomenology? What consequences does this choice, and the particular analyses that follow from it, have for Levinas's own thought, his ethical metaphysics? These are the questions that guide this chapter.

## SCIENCE, THE WEST, MODERNITY, AND INTUITION

The enormous success of phenomenology should alert us to the fact that Husserl was on to something important, and on to it in an important way. Indeed, what stirs his thinking is the central question of modernity (and hence also of modernity's anemic offspring "postmodernity"): What and how do we really know for sure? Just when science attains its greatest strength, conquering our world and all worlds, the deepest question emerges, and along with it the deepest doubt. Never more certain of the truths of science, we wonder how to certify these certainties. *Are* there any certainties? Epistemology comes to take center stage in all endeavors, from science to politics to art to sports, everywhere ideas, logic, philosophy reign. It is the age of philosophy. Wars are fought over ideas and ideologies. Such is modernity, the most knowledgeable of times, the most ignorant of times. Of course, the dialectic of certainty and doubt lies at the very heart of the idea of science itself, which is precisely the process of relentless self-justification, self-questioning, self-correction. Husserl's question and his quest are thus the very same that vexed philosophers before him and have increasingly come to trouble our entire worldview: an unflinching inquiry concerning the limits of human understanding. Husserl's phenomenology will thus be an inquiry no less rigorous than the rigorous science it aims to understand to its limits. And on the basis of this inquiry, Husserl will demand an expansive reconstruction of science according to its proper limits.

That science represents the essence, the very spiritual destiny of the West, its infinite task of self-comprehension, of this Husserl has no doubt. More than any spiritual adventure hitherto, science has not only changed the world – first Europe, then *the whole world*, indeed in its own way it has *established* one world, one nature, one universe – it is a veritable world, a world with infinite horizons, in its own right.[14] Its infinite tasks and horizons do not merely supplement but rather eclipse alternative claims to knowledge or truth regardless of their age, pedigree or popularity. Nor, really, does science merely eclipse them, leaving alternative claims to knowledge and truth intact but in shadows. Rather, it devastates the fixed stars of all traditions, dowsing them, extinguishing their light. Wherever their remnants survive, in whatever nooks and

---

[14] These are the themes of Husserl's late thinking, especially as found in his Vienna lecture of May 1935, "Philosophy and the Crisis of European Man," found in Edmund Husserl, *Phenomenology and the Crisis of Philosophy*, trans. Quentin Lauer (New York: Harper & Row, 1965), pp. 149–192. E.g., "Scientific culture in accord with ideas of infinity means, then, a revolutionizing of all culture, a revolution that affects man's whole manner of being as a creator of culture. It means also a revolutionizing of historicity, which is now the history of finite humanity's disappearance, to the extent that it grows into a humanity with infinite tasks" (p. 164). The same themes find their developed formulation in a more extensive work, two parts of which were published in 1936, but the whole of which (though still incomplete) was published posthumously in 1954, Edmund Husserl, *The Crisis of European Sciences and Transcendental Phenomenology*, ed. Walter Biemel, trans. David Carr (Evanston: Northwestern University Press, 1970).

pretenses, they all eye science warily, suspicious, fearful, licking wounds. In comparison to the infinite horizons and tasks of genuine knowledge, they are merely "finite," "particular," special pleading. The point can hardly be overstressed, especially since the scientific worldview assumes an invisibility like that of the eyes that see but are not seen. Science emerges and establishes itself not as a dimension within the world, but as a whole new world, a world with its own type of humanity, a scientifically enlightened humanity, a humanity without illusions, humanity living in and for the truth, indeed living the truth. Husserl insists on recognizing and promulgating this power, the power of intellectual probity, the responsibility of self-transparency. He proclaims the veritable rights and privileges of science, and of the higher scientific humanity that he sees as our highest spiritual future.

The "Prolegomena to Pure Logic"[15] of the *Logical Investigations*, published at the turn of the century, stands to this day as an unsurpassed defense of the adamantine purity – the conceptual rigor – of genuine science, seeking out and destroying the slightest intellectual backsliding, the least methodological slack, the hollow ring in all skepticism and relativism. Husserl's philosophical courage and quest aim high, as we shall see, not to break science, as if anything could come of standing against it, nor to be stampeded by it, as if we must be glad for a science running roughshod, but rather to ride herd on it, to steer it, in the end to be more scientific than science itself. Husserl's aim is to save science both from its enemies and from itself by raising it to its proper scientific status.

Before turning to Husserl's response to modern science, let us first highlight a certain fundamental dimension in its triumph, in the triumph of modernity. The reappearance and reassertion of scientific knowledge in the sixteenth century and thereafter, a millennium after its decline in the ruination of its Greco-Roman birthplace and childhood, had not merely been a renaissance like a phoenix rising out of ashes, as if the thousand intervening years had made no impression. Worlds had changed. Born under a pagan sky, science was reborn under a Christian cross. It thus reappears as another chapter in the older struggles and

---

[15] Husserl, *Logical Investigations*, vol. I, pp. 53–266.

accommodations – as we saw in chapter 1 – between Athens and Jerusalem, between reason and revelation, between display, *physus*, the brilliant shield of Achilles, the manifestation of manifestation (which so fascinates and absorbs Heidegger), on the one side, and holiness, *sanctus*, the miraculous light of the Chanukah candelabra, the transcendence of a personal God (to which Levinas is partial, without being parochial), on the other.

With the detachment of a historian, we saw the manner in which Harry Austryn Wolfson grasped the spiritual key to the modern reincarnation of science. With the rise of modern science, he argues, what ends is a millennium-old concordance between Athens and Jerusalem, hammered out first by Philo of Alexander and shattered finally by Benedict de Spinoza. It had been by means of the shared notion of *purpose* – telos – that Athens and Jerusalem had collaborated throughout the medieval period. Greek reason and revealed religion were in agreement regarding the fundamental status of *final causality* (or *Providence*) as an integral dimension of the true and the real. The one world of Nature, whose telos reason grasps, is amenable to the one world of Creation, where God's will reigns and to which religion claims access, for why shouldn't a benevolent God not also be reasonable? *Teleology*, then, the heart of Aristotelian science, was the key and the link, making religion a science and science a religion. Theology would not only be the genuine *logos*, it would be the queen of the sciences. Reason retraces God's footsteps.

Modern science, however, destroys that key and hence destroys that link. Not Descartes exactly, but the Cartesians were the first to declare the truce over, to proclaim the death of final causality. A bold instance of this paradigm shift appears in the celebrated appendix to part one of Spinoza's *Ethics*: "Nature has no fixed goal and . . . all final causes are but figments of the human imagination."[16] Knowledge henceforth would have no use for ends, goals, purposes. Bergson, too, as we saw, rejects the finality of final causes, but unlike Spinoza, and modern science, he does not thereby reject the notion of purpose altogether or reduce it to

---

[16] Baruch Spinoza, *Ethics*, trans. Samuel Shirley (Indianapolis: Hackett Publishing Company, 1992), p. 59. "*Naturam finem nullum sibi praefixum habere, et omnes causas finales nihil nisi humana esse figmenta.*"

ignorant illusion. Rather, he integrates purpose into the cumulative creative growth of the universe, and hence takes it seriously, as part of the immanent growth of a creative reality, even if he thereby rejects its pre-established or transcendent status. For Spinoza and modern science, in contrast, ends, goals, and purposes become nonsense, superstition, mere subjectivity, extra baggage from an ignorant past, weighing down a brighter future. In the name of instrumental truth – the causes of causes of causes . . . – the value of values is devalued, to bankruptcy. To know is to know prior rather than posterior causes, departures rather than destinations, grounds rather than goals, desires rather than the desirable. Efficient causality, sufficient reason, no more, no less, nothing but. Through this narrowing of what counts as reason, religion and science are forced to part company, with science holding a monopoly on truth. Religion would thus become a mortal enemy to science – and not only religion. The infinity of science, truth limited to the infinity of prior causes (and the projection of determinate posterior effects), would at the same time vastly expand the finitude – the untruth – of non-science. Never more strictly knowing, never would there be more ignorance.

In the face of this dramatic shift in epistemology, we know that all the modern critical approaches and reproaches to science have had no essential impact on science itself. Repressing, banning, or burning scientists and scientific treatises, for example, though terrible and fearsome for a time, exposes only the insecurity, narrow-mindedness, and cruelty of a Church (secular or ecclesiastical), not the untruth of science. Ignoring science, on the other hand, does not halt its development but rather reduces one to an ostrich. Nor does science recognize itself in philosophy's condescending "grand style," in a Hegel, for instance, whose official and officious dialectic of the Absolute, full of rhetorical self-congratulations, remains extraneous to the work of genuine science, an absolute obsolete even as its brilliance was applauded in the lecture halls of Berlin. Science judges and is not judged, or so it would posture itself, succeeding, we are thankful, against impostors, but also carried away, to our peril, in a sweeping exaggeration of its significance. No one but a latter-day Luddite would oppose science; what is troubling, however, is its hubris. But how show that its pride is unbridled rather than well earned? How does one at once acknowledge both the success and the limits of science?

What is clear is that no longer in harmony with religion, science now stands on one side, and all too often – and this is what troubles – on the only side, a totality brooking no alternatives. All other spiritual ventures are left to fend for themselves, in the limbo of non-science, reduced to epistemological babble. The result of such a repositioning and displacement of the world outside of science is not hard to discern: fragmentation, meanings detached like atoms, factoids, adrift in space and time. Or pastiches, "systems," instant worldviews, "new age" perspectives which are in fact retrograde to the extreme, built on partial perspectives, for example, simple dualisms such as the masculine and the feminine, or spirit and matter, or love and hate, or else archaic fancies such as astrology, "pyramid power," crystals, mythic kabbalahs, masquerading as wholes only by ignoring vast reaches of truly scientific data. But these inanities – however popular, however misguided – only reflect, as in a dialectical mirror, the hubris of science. Outside of knowledge, outside of scientifically verified truth, everything remains possible, to be sure, but only possible, with nothing more worthwhile than anything else, and perhaps nothing worthwhile at all – and "worth" itself distorted and over-reaching its proper imperative. "Whys and wherefores" can no longer be answered, or even rightly asked. All is adrift, meanings ultimately meaningless. By an odd twist, Beckett, with his exasperating obsession with meaninglessness, would be the anti-prophet *of science*.

That modern science at its very core and throughout is premised on the elimination of value and purpose from the universe, a view which today is swiftly becoming a commonplace, follows from its rigorous positivism: to accept nothing that cannot show itself as empirical evidence, quantifiable data. Only seeing – here and now – is believing. Indeed, more careful even than seeing, only calculating is believing. The presence of the present would lie in its representations, in its calculation, the more precise the better. The impersonal universality of mathematics, and not the benevolent omniscience of divinity, is henceforth the key, the standard, the model, of true science. Again Spinoza's *Ethics* speaks decisively to this point: "They [the religious] made it axiomatic that the judgment of the gods is far beyond man's understanding. Indeed, it is for this reason, and this reason only, that truth might have evaded mankind forever had not Mathematics, which is concerned not with ends but only with the essences and properties of figures, revealed to men a different standard of truth."[17] Mathematics, not compassion, either divine or human, would henceforth be the exclusive standard of the true and the real. And the true and the real henceforth become the be-all and end-all. Of course the Greek natural scientists had already proposed something like this, but they did so as pre-Christians not post-Christians. They were not troubled by the modern predicament, the predicament of a time when Christianity and Judeo-Christian morality can no longer assume triumph, much less triumphalism. What *is* to become of all the moral and spiritual values of revealed religion? How *does* one accommodate rather than capitulate to science? How does one make sense, real sense, of any "and" between science and religion?

Husserl's answer is powerful and threefold, siding with science to the hilt while at the same time respecting the values upon which religion and much else is built: (1) One must not desert or denigrate science, rigorous science, since science alone is the bearer of sound knowledge, universal truth; (2) To know the real scientifically, in its universal truth, one must begin at the beginning, getting to "the things themselves" without the interference of prejudices, without any presuppositions whatsoever; and (3) Knowledge of the real can only be presuppositionless, science can only be pure, if it is based on *intuition* rather than experience. In a word, true science is phenomenological not experiential. It is not science that is the problem, but science falsely conceived, science misunderstanding itself. Phenomenology – intuition, not experience – is the cure, the true science. Now we can begin to see Levinas's reason for focusing on the notion of intuition in phenomenology. It is indeed the key to phenomenology and to the defense and expansion of science that Husserl's phenomenology proposes and carries out. Let us briefly examine Husserl's three claims in turn.

There is hardly a theme dearer to Husserl than the scientific

[17] Ibid., p. 58.

character of philosophy, indeed, the scientific essence of the Western spiritual destiny. It is present right from the start, in the attack on relativism and skepticism in the "Prolegomena," and then, in 1911, in his famous article "Philosophy as Rigorous Science."[18] In the 1930s, in the darkened political climate of Germany, Nazi jackboots clicking on the streets, Husserl devotes himself almost exclusively – as I have indicated above – to this meta-theme of phenomenology, to the greater glory of science, to the scientific essence of "Europe." It occupied lectures (e.g., "Philosophy and the Crisis of European Mankind," "The Crisis of European Sciences and Psychology"), and, from 1934 until his final illness of 1937 and death in 1938, culminated in the massive and unfinished work, *The Crisis of European Sciences and Transcendental Phenomenology*, parts one and two of which were published in 1936 (and the whole of which not until 1954 – too late).

Husserl's argument is stunning. The crisis of Europe is indeed a crisis of science, an undermining of the humanities and social sciences, the annihilation of goals, ends, purposes, by the natural or "exact" sciences. But he is unlike Nietzsche, who denounced science and truth altogether, as "slave" morality, and instead turned to art, "honest lying"; and unlike his predecessor and contemporary Bergson, who made such science superficial, a gloss, and instead turned to an underlying non-rational "*élan vital*"; and certainly most unlike his other far more primitive contemporaries, the Nazis, and also certain Marxists, for whom truth was simply a political tool to be used for reasons of state. Rather, Husserl criticizes the exact sciences in the name of an even broader conception of science, one that would overcome the crisis of modern Europe by delegitimizing the *hegemony* of the exact sciences – their hubris – without thereby in the least delegitimizing science itself. Indeed, to the contrary, Husserl's critique of science is launched in the very name of science. Science would have to be saved from itself by itself! Or, more exactly, science would have to become scientific for the first time. Phenomenology would be science made scientific – "rigorous science."

To see how Husserl criticizes the exact sciences in the name of science we must see the central presupposition that he unmasks in

---

[18] Husserl, "Philosophy as Rigorous Science," trans. Quentin Lauer, in *Phenomenology and the Crisis of Philosophy*, pp. 71–147.

the natural or pre-phenomenological sciences. These sciences fall prey to what Husserl calls the fallacy of "naturalism." They take the real to be equivalent to "nature," and nature to be solely what can be grasped as an object of empirical experience or, more precisely, of measurable sense experience. The exact sciences hegemonize the standard of experiential or empirical "objectivity." "The empiricist," Husserl writes in the *Ideas Pertaining to a Pure Phenomenology and to a Phenomenological Philosophy*, "takes genuine science and experiential science to be identical."[19] *But*, Husserl points out, the very consciousness of the scientist is not itself an *object* of sense experience. Neither consciousness nor ideas can be fully grasped if they are "naturalized," treated as objects, objects of empirical inquiry. Science originates not in objects but in spirit, in consciousness. Or, to put this objection in another way: to know objectively, resorting only to the data of sense experience, cannot itself be known objectively, as the datum of sense experience.

What Husserl points out again and again is that it is but a prejudice, a *presupposition* of the exact sciences that reality is only that which can be known objectively, the object of sense experience. "The essential fault in empiricist argumentation," Husserl continues in the *Ideas Pertaining to a Pure Phenomenology and to a Phenomenological Philosophy*, "consists of identifying or confusing the fundamental demand for a return to the 'things themselves' with the demand for legitimation of all cognition by *experience*."[20] This prejudice is the root cause of the crisis of modernity because it prevents a genuinely scientific treatment of reality as a whole. It substitutes a part of reality, object reality, objects of empirical experience, for the whole of reality, which latter must in truth include consciousness and the data of consciousness, even though they are not, Husserl insists, reducible to objects or objects of sense experience. The pride of science is false so long as science is itself not fully scientific. Paradoxically, then, a widening of science is the cure for its hubris.

This brings Husserl to his third claim, to intuition and descriptive phenomenology as the solution. The cure for science limited to experience of the real through the senses, even and especially

[19] Edmund Husserl, *Ideas Pertaining to a Pure Phenomenology and to a Phenomenological Philosophy; First Book*, trans. F. Kersten (The Hague: Martinus Nijhoff Publishers, 1982), p. 35.
[20] Ibid.

when experience includes (and is perhaps determined by) the objects of mathematical calculation, is to extend reality to phenomena, to *meanings* rather than to *objects* alone. "Object" is only one type of meaning. The meaningful cannot without reduction be reduced to the calculable. Rather than reduce meaning in the name of reality, science – and hence the real, reality legitimized through science – must instead be expanded in the name of meaning. Precisely this extension is effected by means of intuition. "For experience we therefore substitute something more universal: 'intuition.' "[21] Exact science, limited to the real *qua* sensed, and to a notion of "experience" limited in the same way, as object experience, must be supplemented by descriptive science, science open to phenomena *qua* meant. Intuition, not experience, is the true ground of the real.

Science must not merely be supplemented or even broadened by intuition, it must be grounded for the first time. The exact sciences are themselves products of consciousness, and hence find their true origin in the broader horizons opened up by the phenomenological sciences, the sciences of meaning. Thus it is intuition and not experience that is the final, broadest, and presuppositionless standard of truth. "If *'positivism'* is tantamount to an absolutely unprejudiced grounding of all sciences on the 'positive,' that is to say, on what can be seized upon originaliter, then *we* are the genuine positivists," Husserl writes. "In fact, we allow *no* authority to curtail our right to accept all kinds of intuition as equally valuable legitimating sources of cognition – not even the authority of 'modern natural science.' "[22] Thus Husserl will free science not only from non-science, but from what is now revealed for the first time to be its own ideological simulacrum, its own theory of science that it inherited from the modern rationalist period. For the first time science will come to see itself scientifically, in full knowledge of its own origins.

Sense experience, the standard of modern empirical science, to the extent that it gives access to meaning, is itself grounded in consciousness, which Husserl, along with a long philosophical tradition, understands to be the constitutive origin of all meaning.

---

[21] Ibid., p. 37.          [22] Ibid., p. 39.

Consciousness does not invent or create the world, but the meaning of the world nonetheless depends on the synthetic meaning-giving activity – *Sinngebeng* [sense-bestowing] – that consciousness is. Meanings, and consciousness as well, can only be *known scientifically* on the basis of exact descriptions, descriptions articulating the findings of the most carefully fixed and repeatable intuitions into the essential or invariant structures operative in the constitution of meaning. Genuine science, that is to say, presuppositionless or fully transparent science, must be based on carefully delineated and hence repeatable intuitions into meaning. Ultimately, science must also include intuitions into the essential structures of consciousness itself, insofar as consciousness lies at the bottom of all meaningful reality. *Intuition*, then, even more than *experience*, makes for the possibility of genuine science, science as the true account of the whole of reality.

This brings us to the second, major, reason why intuition lies at the heart of the Husserlian project, and hence why Levinas has focused upon it: validity. Science is genuine knowledge not only because it studies the whole of reality, but more importantly because its propositions are based on *evidence*. Evidence, however, as we have seen, cannot be limited to empirical experience, measurable sense experience. Empirical evidence, after all, is simply the modern scientific answer to the ancient problem of securing truth, *episteme*. The aim of science is to secure truth. Science is therefore not grounded in the empirical, the empirical is grounded in science. Stepping back from the empiricist modern answer to the demand for *episteme*, Husserl would have us see that conceiving science more broadly means conceiving that which satisfies its demand for evidence more broadly. More broadly conceived, evidence is what is or what can be given to consciousness. What is or can be given to consciousness is the meaningful. What Husserl wants to do, then, is to grasp scientifically the meaningful without succumbing to any a priori prejudices, whether these prejudices be those of a naïve realism (common sense) or those of a scientific empiricism. Faithfulness to the notion of evidence, then, the notion upon which genuine science is based, opens the scientist to a field of meaning given otherwise than the realist prejudice assumes, whether that prejudice be straightforward or sophisticated. Consciousness, and not sense experience alone, turns out to be at the origin of all meaning. This we have already seen.

In the name of science, however, Husserl must take a further step. To be *science*, knowledge rather than opinion or myth, say, the meaningful must be *verified*. One must be able at the very least to distinguish the illusory from the genuine, apparent meaning from real meaning. More than that, one must be able to distinguish fields of meaning (perception, imagination, memory, emotion, etc.) as well as hierarchies within and between fields of meaning (e.g., perception to imagination, imagination to memory, one memory to another memory, etc.). Extending the *field* of science will not do if the price of this extension is to give up the idea of *science*. A genuine *standard* of truth must remain, a standard to verify the universality and necessity of some propositions rather than others. The tradition of philosophy from Parmenides to Hegel satisfied this demand with more or less sophisticated appeals to *logos*, to relations between ideas. The true rather than the false would be that which conforms to the fundamental requirements of logical thought, to the hard rules of non-contradiction and excluded middle, and later, with Hegel, to the allegedly organic movement of a "dialectical" logic. Modern science, in contrast, appeals to *facts*. But it has done so on the basis of a mathematical prejudice. Husserl, in contrast, given his more rigorous carrying out of the basic principle that genuine science must be presuppositionless, cannot ground science in a logic whose terms and relations must themselves first be grounded scientifically, or in a sense experience whose ultimate meaningfulness is naïvely taken for granted. Unlike Descartes, for instance, he will not sneak a mathematical standard in through an epistemological back door, as it were. Mathematics, too, as we learn from Husserl's earliest studies (see *The Origin of Geometry*), must submit to thoroughgoing philosophical scrutiny. But how can Husserl, who does not limit genuine science to empirical experience, to the measurable, satisfy the basic demand of scientific evidence that it be genuine rather than spurious, true rather than false? To the question of verifiability, the root question of the truth of science, Husserl's answer is once again *intuition*. Intuition is not only the key to widening science to its genuinely presuppositionless subject matter, namely, the meaningful, it is also the key to the scientific determination of that field of meaning.

How can intuition serve to sort out true from false, genuine from spurious, and make distinctions between and within fields of meaning? As early as the *Logical Investigations* Husserl spoke of genuine evidence in terms of *fulfilled* [*erfüllt*] rather than *empty* [*leer*] meanings, that is to say, *intuitively present* meanings rather than meanings that for one reason or another – such as confusion or vagueness – cannot be brought to intuitive presence. Intuition is thus the key to validity, the key to sifting genuine meaning from illusory meaning. What is genuinely meaningful is what can be brought to intuitive presence, that whose meaning can be "fulfilled" in intuition. Henceforth all that will be considered scientifically valid, from higher mathematics to the most mundane everyday experiences, must submit to verification by intuition. Phenomenological science will thus transform the entire world from top to bottom not by changing it one iota, but because for the first time it will reveal its constitutive origins in consciousness.

In the *Ideas Pertaining to a Pure Phenomenology and to a Phenomenological Philosophy*, Levinas's primary text in *The Theory of Intuition in Husserl's Phenomenology*, Husserl develops his conception of intuition in terms of "essential intuition," that is to say, "intuition into essences," direct intellectual insight into *ideal* meaning, into the *ideality* of meaning. Husserl had always thought of an "identically the same" meaning as constituting the core of any legitimate meaning. This core of meaning, identical, the "essence," is that to which the phenomenologist would penetrate. One would not only gain a clear and distinct insight of it but, having achieved this insight, one would be able to return to it again and again in the same way. This means, too, that the phenomenologist would be able to provide – and must provide – directions to other scientifically minded inquirers, so that they too could turn to the same essential meaning in the same way in repeatable acts of intuition that would confirm or correct (expand, contract, alter, adjust, etc.) the original intuition. In *Ideas Pertaining to a Pure Phenomenology and to a Phenomenological Philosophy*, focusing on the idea of intuiting *essence*,

Husserl emphasizes the dual criteria of *clarity* and *distinctness*, lean-ing on a perceptual (to *see* the things themselves) rather than a logical or linguistic model of verification. In the phenomenological sense of these terms, the standard of *clarity* means to *see*, to "see" intellectually, to see meaning "in person"; while the standard of *distinctness* means isolating an essence, the invariant core of a meaning that makes a meaning this meaning and no other. At the core of each and every meaning, then, if it is genuine rather than illusory, lies an essence, which is to say, an ideational invariance, the minimal sense necessary to have this unique meaning – "ideal-ity" – and no other. To verify meaning, to intuit a meaning clearly and distinctly, then, is to have an intellectual vision of its essence.

It is thus contrary to Kant, who sharply distinguishes concep-tuality from sensibility, that in the *Ideas Pertaining to a Pure Phenom-enology and to a Phenomenological Philosophy* Husserl argues that the knower *intuits* essences, intellectually "sees" ideal structures, grasps necessity. We should also note that contrary to the seeming mysti-cism of the highest vision of truth elaborated by Diotima in Plato's *Symposium*, in the Husserlian quest for essence the phenomeno-logist never forgoes or surpasses the use of examples. Indeed, a multiplicity of examples, deliberately generated and varied in what Husserl calls "free fantasy variation," lead the phenomenologist to the one essence, the invariant, that which must remain the same. On this point, that is to say, on the inescapable and indeed positive role of imagination in the determination of strict ideational necess-ity, so opposed to Spinoza's denigration of the imagination as the source of falsity,[23] Levinas highlights an interesting citation from the *Ideas Pertaining to a Pure Phenomenology and to a Phenomenological Philosophy*. "Fiction," Husserl writes, "is the vital element of phe-nomenology as well as all other eidetic sciences."[24] This does not mean, of course, that phenomenology is a literary enterprise, or that truth is fiction. Rather, it means that the creativity involved in imagination, and in such activities as literary production, or in the graphic arts, is inextricably linked to the process of achieving

[23] Spinoza, *Ethics*, II, Prop. 41; V, Prop. 28.
[24] Emmanuel Levinas, *The Theory of Intuition in Husserl's Phenomenology*, 2nd edn., trans. André Orianne (Evanston: Northwestern University Press, 1995) (henceforth: *TIHP*), p. 141; Husserl, *Ideas*, p. 160.

conceptual clarity. Not, to be sure, because truth is invented, but rather and precisely because truth is not fiction. For this reason, too, we do not judge literary "fictions" – stories, novels, poems – on purely formal grounds, but also, if not primarily, in terms of the truths which they bring to life. We will be reminded of this link, of the Husserlian methodology of "free fantasy variation," when elsewhere we turn to Levinas's notion of exegesis.

Intuition of essence validates – clarifies and distinguishes – necessary knowledge, scientific knowledge in the strongest sense. "We can now understand what is meant by the intuition of ideal objects, the intuition of essences or *Eide*," Levinas writes, "i.e., the *eidetic intuition* or Husserl's famous *Wesensschau* [seeing an essence]."[25] Eidetic intuition, Husserl's famous *Wesensschau*, is "seeing" "the thing itself," the unique ideational invariant which fulfills and is constituted through a meaning-complex. The ultimate meaning of the meaning-complex "Statue of Liberty," to take a perceptual instance, finds its fulfillment in a perceptual seeing – eyes open, looking, encircling – the bronze green Statue of Liberty standing majestically in New York harbor.[26] This in no way discounts the complex and multilayered cultural and historical meanings that also give sense to the meaning-complex "Statue of Liberty" ("symbol of freedom," "immigrants' welcome to America," "gift of France," etc.), but rather anchors them in an invariant core of sense. The phenomenologist would then have to unravel the sense of "perceptual seeing," to uncover its distinctive place in the larger frame of other significations as well as the specific structure of signification involved in perception itself, a labor which Merleau-Ponty, for instance, began in his work *The Phenomenology of Perception*. The bottom line of science, then, is appropriate intuition. Ultimately this means intellectual intuition, direct mental "seeing," of essences. For phenomenology, intuition is the epistemological fulcrum upon which all meanings, all fields of meaning, all worlds of meaning, and finally the one meaningful

[25] *TIHP*, p. 105.
[26] For this example I am grateful to the late Professor Aaron Gurwitch, master of phenomenology, whose graduate class on Husserl's *Formal and Transcendental Logic*, given at the New School for Social Research, in New York, I had the privilege of attending in 1973.

universe, are consciously reviewed and validated from the ground up. Intuition both defines the field of phenomenology and is at the same time the meticulous labor of consciously returning all meanings to their original home in consciousness.

It should be clear, then, why in 1930, introducing phenomenology to France virtually for the first time, Levinas chose to focus on the theory of intuition in Husserl's phenomenology. It is the veritable key to the entire phenomenological enterprise. As such, it is for Husserl the key to science, and hence serves as nothing less than the key to the spiritual destiny of Europe, the West, and the future of all humanity.

### LEVINAS ON HUSSERLIAN INTUITION

The order of Levinas's *Theory of Intuition in Husserl's Phenomenology*, which attends especially to Husserl's *Ideas Pertaining to a Pure Phenomenology and to a Phenomenological Philosophy*, follows Husserl's own progression into phenomenology. Chapter one, on "The Naturalistic Theory of Being and the Method of Philosophy," criticizes "naturalism" as a limitation and distortion rather than the definition of genuine science. In this Levinas is following chapter two, "Naturalistic Misinterpretations," of part one of Husserl's *Ideas*, as well as following the far more extensive critique of naturalism Husserl had presented in the "Prologomena to Pure Logic" of the *Logical Investigations*. Chapter two, on "The Phenomenological Theory of Being: The Absolute Existence of Consciousness," shows that the exact sciences, as themselves spiritual products, must be grounded in consciousness, the absolute source of all meaning. This follows chapter one, "The Positing which Belongs to the Natural Attitude and its Exclusion," and chapter two, "Consciousness and Natural Actuality," of part two of the *Ideas*. Chapter three, on "The Phenomenological Theory of Being: The Intentionality of Consciousness," like chapter three, "The Region of Pure Consciousness," of part two of Husserl's *Ideas*, develops this idea, namely, that all meaning derives from consciousness, that its *noesis–noema* correlation is originary and inescapable. Husserl is able to sidestep the endless pitfalls of philosophical speculation regarding the reality of the real by holding to the level of meaning constituted by consciousness. Of course, the "repressed" returns, as it does for Husserl's heirs in the controversies and fundamental differences surrounding the meaning of the term "transcendence" (a question Husserl deals with in chapter four, "The Phenomenological Reduction," of part two, whose fifty-eighth paragraph, it is interesting to note, is entitled "The Transcendency, God, Excluded"[27]).

Levinas is a faithful expositor of Husserl, but he is also a thinker in his own right, even if in *The Theory of Intuition in Husserl's Phenomenology*, written when he was barely twenty-four years old, his originality is not yet in view. Still, in chapter four, on "Theoretical Consciousness," Levinas acknowledges the existence of a certain unresolved ambivalence in Husserl whereby "theory, perception, and judgement"[28] are given an exceptional status, indeed they are given primacy. In the *Logical Investigations*, at least in its first edition, Husserl seems to argue that all forms of intentional consciousness – for example, will, desire, affection – are reducible to objectifying acts. Later, in the *Ideas Pertaining to a Pure Phenomenology and to a Phenomenological Philosophy*, so Levinas argues, Husserl tries but does not fully succeed in overcoming this impoverishment. "The notion of an objectifying act," Levinas writes at the conclusion of this chapter, "is borrowed from the sphere of assertions and therefore taints Husserl's intuitionism with intellectualism."[29] This charge of intellectualism, elaborated and nuanced at great length, will become Levinas's persistent criticism of Husserl. Not, to be sure, because Levinas will in any way support anti-intellectualism, but rather because he sees *above* intellectualism – and justifying it – the higher and more compelling claims of morality and justice. On the positive side, however, in *The Theory of Intuition in Husserl's Phenomenology*, Levinas recognizes that this same intellectualism "prepare[s] the way for the intuitionist theory of truth," because "[f]or the first time, judgment and perception are brought together and put on the same level."[30] Thus Levinas

---

[27] Husserl concludes this short paragraph as follows: "Naturally we extend the phenomenological reduction to include this 'absolute' and 'transcendent' being. It shall remain excluded from the new field of research which is to be provided, since this shall be a field of pure consciousness." *Ideas*, trans. Kersten, p. 134.     [28] *TIHP*, p. 62.
[29] Ibid., p. 63.     [30] Ibid.

shows, with the notion of "intellectual intuition," Husserl's opposition to Kant, for whom judgment and perception, though mutually conditioning one another (to produce objects and objectivity), could never be placed on the same level as they are in Husserl's theory of intuition.

Chapters five on "Intuition," six on "The Intuition of Essences," and seven on "Philosophical Intuition," which make up the bulk of Levinas's book and reveal his emphasis on intuition, elaborate the various roles that intuition must play as the new key to the verification of evidence. Regarding science, intuition is, first of all, the key to clarifying the essence of the exact or natural sciences, with their *noematic* or "object" orientation. Husserl had already demonstrated this regarding basic logical-mathematical terms in the *Logical Investigations*, and does so once again in chapter one, "The Noematic Sense and the Relation to the Object," of part four of the *Ideas*, and Merleau-Ponty was to later demonstrate it, *mutatis mutandis*, regarding perception in *The Phenomenology of Perception*. Second and more broadly, intuition is the key to clarifying essences discovered through potential phenomenological sciences, such as phenomenologies of anthropology, history, sociology, or psychology. These would take up regions of meaning whose orientation is from the first and inescapably *noetic-noematic*, that is, "subject" oriented as well as "object" oriented, even if certain scientistic practitioners succumb to the naturalist fallacy by aping the mathematical model of the exact sciences. Finally and ultimately, intuition is the key to clarifying the essence of the whole of phenomenology itself, in a phenomenology of phenomenology, clarifying the deep structures of absolute consciousness itself, such as temporality, motility, synthesis, and the like. Here Levinas touches on some of the concerns and projects Husserl presented in the concluding chapters of *Ideas*, in chapter two, "Phenomenology of Reason," and chapter three, "The Levels of Universality Pertaining to the Problems of the Theory of Reason," of part four, "Reason and Actuality."

While his reading is for the most part expository, as I have noted, Levinas does not hesitate to point out certain unresolved difficulties in Husserl's work. In chapter seven on "Philosophical

Intuition," for example, Levinas detects "a wavering in Husserl's conception of consciousness," an "indecision," or perhaps an "obscurity,"[31] regarding the transcendence or immanence of its intentional character. On the one hand, the idea of intentionality as "consciousness of . . ." seems to imply the transcendence of the world, that *of* which consciousness is conscious. On the other hand, with his notion of "hyletic data" Husserl also seems to imply that consciousness constitutes meaning independent of the world, in an egological or self-contained sphere of absolute immanence.

Similarly, in the same chapter, Levinas wonders how Husserl's phenomenology will finally resolve the as yet unclarified relation between the egological sphere and the intersubjective sphere. "The reduction to an *ego*, the *egological reduction*," Levinas comments, "can be only a first step toward phenomenology. We must also discover 'others' and the intersubjective world."[32] We are witness here to a Levinas not so much reporting an established desiderata, as prodding the phenomenological movement with the first faint glimmerings of his own itinerary.

Determining these two issues – the significance of transcendence and immanence, and the relation between solipsist egology and intersubjectivity – will have the utmost importance for Levinas's own philosophy, for his later profound commitment to and elaboration of the exceptional ethical role of intersubjectivity in the constitution of meaning. Levinas hints, without supplying details, that Husserl too had been "much preoccupied" with the question of intersubjectivity, specifically with the idea of an analogical perception of others' bodies by means of one's own body. This particular preoccupation does appear not long after the *Ideas Pertaining to a Pure Phenomenology and to a Phenomenological Philosophy*, in the celebrated fifth of Husserl's *Cartesian Meditations*. Levinas concludes chapter seven by mentioning that Husserl has extensive "unpublished works" on intersubjectivity, which, he continues, "have been very influential" (no doubt on Heidegger's *Being and Time*), but which "we are not authorized to use . . . prior to their publication."[33]

---

[31] Ibid., p. 150.    [32] Ibid.    [33] Ibid., 151.

## The question of value

Before moving on to Husserl's influence on Levinas, let us return to two topics treated earlier: the question of value and the questionable Derrida.

First, value. The crisis precipitated by modern science is in large measure that of the exclusion of, and loss of access to, values, ends, goals, purposes. This loss occurs because modern science arises, as we saw, with the reduction of truth to an account of efficient causality. By extending science from experience to intuition, and thereby at once returning science from its naturalistic prejudice to its genuine origins in consciousness, Husserl should be able to retrieve such practical meaning-complexes as "end," "goal," and "purpose," and treat them seriously *within* the framework of genuine science. "Since truth does not belong essentially to judgments but to intuitive intentionality," Levinas writes in chapter seven, "our contact with the world of useful and practical values has a legitimate right to be also considered as truth."[34]

Value can no longer be considered extraneous, even detrimental to science, as it had to be under the regime of naturalism, because a fully expanded science perforce includes a legitimization and examination of the life world wherein consciousness has its beginnings and wherein values play a crucial role. By returning science from a naturalist prejudice to its origin in consciousness's constitution of meaning, values as values can take their rightful place as a legitimate subject of scientific inquiry. This is an important development and growth in reason. It is an important step in the direction of what we have already called "ethical exegesis," a topic we will elaborate at length in chapter 7. Values too would have their own truth, their own sense. "To be in contact with the world of values," Levinas points out, "certainly does not mean to know it theoretically. The existence of a value – its mode of presenting itself to life – does not have the same ontological structure as theoretically represented beings."[35] It is remarkable to find such a formulation already in 1930. The great power of Levinas's thought, and the importance of *ethical exegesis as a new form of philosophy*, depends on recognizing and faithfully carrying out the

34 Ibid., p. 133.    35 Ibid.

implications of the insight that *the value of values is not determined by theory*.

Though in this way phenomenology seems to open the door to a scientific retrieval of an autochthonous sense for goals, values, purposes, Levinas makes us aware that Husserl's own prejudices unfortunately prevented this door from opening as wide as it could have, if indeed it opens at all. What prevents Husserl from realizing the novelty of his own insight? The answer lies in an unexamined tendency, quite natural, to be sure, toward theoretical thought. Husserl limits the meaning of "existence" solely to the constitutive act he calls the "doxic thesis." He then interprets the doxic thesis in terms of theoretical knowing. What follows is that for Husserl all meanings such as "value," "goal," and "purpose," despite their independence from "objects" from the point of view of their having a different intuitional fulfillment, are restricted to a theoretical account when it comes to affirming their existence. Thus, Levinas writes, "Husserl's phenomenology is not free from the theory of knowledge."[36] The modern devaluation of values remains at work in the heart of Husserlian phenomenology. Husserl sees the land where science can be liberated from its theoretical bias, but he does not enter it. Levinas will enter that land, and he will indeed call it Israel, and by "Israel" he will also mean the whole world.

## *The questionable Derrida*

Second, Derrida. Let us return to what seemed earlier like a passing remark about him, in order to see how Levinas's reading of Husserl in 1930 anticipates and defuses (or could have defused) the central methodological and formal principle of deconstruction.[37]

---

[36] Ibid., p. 134.

[37] Let there be no mistake: I am perfectly aware that all statements – the said – are liable to deconstruction, which, to look at the bright side, is certainly one more prod for care in thinking and writing. Nonetheless, I am deliberately using a terminology antithetical to deconstruction to speak about deconstruction. Need it be said that I am an unabashed critic of deconstruction? In an earlier book, *Elevations: The Height of the Good in Rosenzweig and Levinas* (Chicago: University of Chicago Press, 1994), I devoted an entire chapter to a moral critique of "Derrida's (mal)reading of Levinas" (pp. 305–321). One can, and perhaps one has an especial obligation to, criticize any misreading that refuses to recognize criticism and misreading. Criticism and commentary (we will discuss both,

It was mentioned earlier, parenthetically, that most Husserl scholars consider Derrida's 1967 reading in *Speech and Phenomena* of the
first of the six investigations in Husserl's *Logical Investigations* – the
very reading which launched Derrida's own distinctive career, and
through which he established certain notions central to deconstruction – to be a misreading.[38] Very briefly, Derrida radically
criticizes the Husserlian project – science, phenomenological
science – by arguing that the intuitions that are alleged to ground
its truths can in principle *never* be fulfilled because meaning cannot
be fully present to consciousness, fully present even to eidetic
intuition. Meaning, he argues, using Husserl's own testimony, is
necessarily dispersed across both *noetic* and *noematic* temporal slipp-
ages, dispersed across the non-presence of past and future. And if,
per impossibile, meaning could be made fully present, as Husserl
apparently would like, it would still make no sense, since meaning
is only meaningful *because* it is dispersed across absences of past and
future meanings.

Meaning, according to Derrida, is thus always but a "trace,"
constituted not by presence but by absence, not by a vision or a
speech but through the dispersion of a "writing," not an identity
but a differ*a*nce, etc. Meaning is meaningful, to the extent that it is
meaningful at all, not because a sign can ultimately be brought to
an absolute presence in intuition, as Husserl is alleged to have

especially the latter, in chapter 7) are, after all, two of the most non-violent ways in which
communication and instruction between human beings transpires. Criticism is certainly
the preferred method in academia. While academics might bemoan the negativity of too
much criticism, for it often displaces if not destroys the possibility of positive appreciation, too little criticism, in contrast, such as one finds in deconstruction (which mistakes
its a priori smugness for criticism), is far worse.

[38] The anti-Derrida sentiment amongst Husserl scholars is well entrenched, and the
anti-Derrida secondary literature quite wide. I remember, for instance, attending a
meeting of the Husserl Circle, at Washington University, in St. Louis, in the early 1980s,
which was entirely devoted to Derrida's then controversial reading of Husserl. After
several papers showing this or that flaw in Derrida's reading, one participating scholar
presented a parody of the great parodist. This was not only the most amusing and
entertaining paper of the conference, but somehow it also seemed the most appropriate
too. Deconstruction is a technique, a bit like "spell check" on the computer (though
perhaps in reverse), not a philosophy. If we have learned anything from it, and if we are
not clowns, it is that we must not take deconstruction too seriously. Nonetheless, I would
be remiss if I did not mention at least one excellent book – balanced and thoughtful –
deeply critical of Derrida's reading of Husserl: J. Claude Evans, *Strategies of Deconstruction:
Derrida and the Myth of the Voice* (Minneapolis: University of Minnesota Press, 1991).

thought, but rather because signs signify across the essential absences exerted by differential contexts of signs, contexts such as language and history. The whole of Derrida's "deconstruction," the entire "play" of his many subsequent and varied writings, then, finds its original justification in the critique he launched, in *Speech and Phenomena*, against the "philosophy of presence" that he there attempts to show is the motivating and determining force of Husserlian intuition, and hence of the whole of phenomenology, and hence of the whole of science, and hence of the West as such.

But Levinas, like most careful Husserl scholars, recognizes that Husserl was already quite aware of the slippage of meaning that Derrida, for his part, is so keen to exploit and explode into a critique of the West. Since Levinas's work was published in 1930, perforce it makes no mention of Derrida or his "critique" of Husserl which only appear thirty-seven years later. Nonetheless, Levinas already answers Derrida *avant la lettre*, as it were. Levinas makes it perfectly clear that Husserl distinguishes two types of related intuition. On the one hand, there is transcendent or "external intuition," where consciousness is always only presented with one side of a material object (thus one sees, for example, one side, then another, and then another – successive sides – of the Statue of Liberty). On the other hand, and quite different, there is "internal intuition," where consciousness can be present to the whole of its object, since its object is nothing other than an object-of-consciousness (for instance an intuition into the idea of a "unit" or the idea of "point"). The temporal as well as spatial limitations of transcendent or "external intuition" are obvious. Bergson, years earlier, had already pointed out that even God must wait for sugar to melt in tea. Descartes, in his second *Meditation*, had described how "men who pass in the street" might well turn out, upon closer inspection, to be "automatic machines." For these reasons, the results of external intuition, however much based on fulfilled intuitions, remain both tentative and subject to revision.

Furthermore, thirty-seven years before Derrida's brainstorms regarding the sign as a "trace," Levinas has this to say about the "inadequation" inherent to and recognized by Husserl's account of the temporal limitations of inner or "*internal* intuition":

It is only internal intuition which can present the ideal of adequation. Only internal intuition has its object all at once before itself. Even if a certain inadequation is also proper to immanent perception, because of the temporal character of consciousness and the fact that the objects of reflection are constantly falling into the past, for Husserl this inadequation is of another type than that of transcendent perception. As we have shown, there is an abyss between the adequation of internal perception [with its specific type of inadequation] and the inadequation of external perception.[39]

Thus Husserl himself – without a touch of Derrida's derision – already recognized the inherent "inadequation" of even an adequate internal intuition, owing to its inherent temporal dispersion. Adequation in internal perception is never anything more, Levinas goes on to say, than an "ideal," hence something necessarily and infinitely *deferred*. These remarks are in no way intended to make Husserl a Derridaian, not at all. Husserl, unlike Derrida, grasps the manner in which deferral – not to mention finitude and responsibility – is essential to science itself. The inherent deferral of sense, recognized by Husserl, is also one reason, beyond those discussed in chapter 1, why Husserl speaks of science in terms of "infinite tasks." Derrida – who not only "criticizes" Husserl's phenomenology as a "philosophy of presence," but later uses this same criticism against Levinas's ethical metaphysics (and against everyone else, for that matter) – apparently did not read these lines from Levinas on the theory of intuition in Husserl's phenomenology.

Derrida's *mistake* is to have confused the inadequation essential to internal intuition, due to the temporal ecstasies of consciousness (Husserl's "protentions" and "retentions"), with the inadequacy essential to external intuition, due to the spatial perspectives of perception. By confusing and conflating these two different types of inadequation, inserting the spatiality of "writing," as Derrida calls the graphic dimension of signification,[40] into the temporality of consciousness, Derrida falls into – indeed welcomes! – a *sophisti-*

[39] *TIHP*, p. 136.
[40] See, especially, Jacques Derrida, *Of Grammatology* (Baltimore: Johns Hopkins University Press, 1974), whose two parts are called "Writing Before the Letter" (pp. 1–93) and "Nature, Culture, Writing" (pp. 95–316); and also Jacques Derrida, trans. G. C. Spivak, *Writing and Difference*, trans. Alan Bass (Chicago: University of Chicago Press, 1978).

*cal* abyss of his own invention. That is to say, he embraces the quick loss of meaning rather than the more arduous, indeed infinite, truth-seeking gathering of meaning inherent in the inadequation (Derrida will call it "deferral of sense") necessary to intuition. Furthermore, the bold claim to have dissolved the distinction between "internal" and "external" (or, on another plane, between "subjective" and "objective"), and hence to be writing from neither one position nor the other, but nonetheless (somehow) to still "be" (without privileging presence) prior to both, does not save the day, as it were, because any such dissolution or undercutting would follow from Derrida's original misreading, and therefore could not be used to defend it. To "argue" in this way would be – for those who do recognize argumentation – to succumb to what is called circular reasoning, assuming what must in fact be proven. It is a standard rhetorical device in the arsenal of sophists.[41] One Husserl scholar has suggested that perhaps Derrida simply *wanted* to go down into this abyss and merely "used" Husserl's first *Logical Investigation* as a foil.[42] Bad scholarship or deliberate manipulation, Derrida's reading of Husserl is a misreading. The irony is that Derrida's real master, Heidegger, built his philosophy of ecstatic temporality upon Husserl's time analyses, for which he was publicly grateful.[43]

Levinas, for his part, in contrast to Derrida, distinguishes and recognizes the several types of inadequation – internal and external, temporal and spatial – as essential dimensions within Husserl's theory of intuition. Furthermore, he will recognize that in the

[41] For what is perhaps the largest array of sophistical rhetorical devices ever assembled in one collection, see the *Adversus Mathematicos* (Loeb Classical Library) of Sextus Empiricus (late 2nd early 3rd cent. C.E.).

[42] Although generous to the extent that he admits one may take up Derrida's project independent of the validity or rigor of his reading of Husserl, i.e., that Derrida's reading of Husserl was simply an occasion to say what Derrida would have said in any event, Evans will also note that from a critical point of view: "Setting up straw men and blowing them down – even in the name of parody and fiction – simply will not do the job." Evans, *Strategies of Deconstruction*, p. 177; see also p. xviii.

[43] As we saw above (see footnote 3), Heidegger actually edited Husserl's 1905 lectures on inner-time consciousness. There is no doubt that *Being and Time* would not have been possible without Husserl's phenomenological studies of temporality. None of this suggests, however, that Heideggerian temporality simply reproduces Husserlian internal-time consciousness, for it does not – indeed Heidegger makes fundamental revisions; nor that our account of Derrida's misreading of Husserl means that Husserl's account of time is without problems, for it is not.

context of *ethical* exegesis – as opposed to phenomenology proper – the "inadequation" of consciousness need not be grasped on the epistemological plane at all. We will turn to these developments in the next chapter and thereafter. Levinas will discover a non-epistemological and "non-intentional" consciousness subtending what for Husserl is the irreducible intentional character of consciousness as such. For Levinas the "inadequation" of consciousness is not, as it is for Derrida, an occasion to celebrate the equivocalness or absence/presence of sense, but rather an opening to an even more positive dimension of sense, one exceeding both phenomenology and deconstruction: ethical signification.

### SOME HUSSERLIAN REPERCUSSIONS IN LEVINAS: REGIONS, CONCRETUDE, AND THE ORIGIN OF PHILOSOPHY

What effect did his early study of intuition have on Levinas's own work, on his ethical metaphysics? With regard to Heidegger's influence, for instance, it is clear – as we see confirmed by Levinas's own admissions both in the text of *The Theory of Intuition in Husserl's Phenomenology* and later when referring back to this work – that not only did Levinas appropriate certain of Heidegger's basic criticisms of Husserl ("[w]e shall not fear to take into account problems raised by other philosophers, by students of Husserl, and, in particular, by Martin Heidegger, whose influence on this book will often be felt."[44]), specifically the charge that the Husserlian phenomenology is biased in favor of theoretical consciousness, objectification, material things, but that when Levinas tried to obviate the impact of this criticism, he did so by insinuating into Husserl a quasi-Heideggerian ontology ("in the guise of epistemology Husserl pursues interests that are essentially ontological"[45]). Though influenced, Levinas himself was never a Heideggerian. Still, Levinas does follow Heidegger in a certain formal sense. He, too, emphasizes the existential character and concretude of the philosophical results deriving from the phenomenological approach. This is what Sartre and many others also celebrated in the phenomenological method. No later than 1935 (and one can

[44] *TIHP*, p. xxxiii.      [45] Ibid., p. 124.

debate how much earlier), Levinas will have found an alternative
basis – ethics – to escape even the ontological framing of his own
original phenomenological insights. In 1934, in an article entitled
"Some Reflections on the Philosophy of Hitlerism,"[46] Levinas will
be critical, albeit indirectly and without proper names, of the
importance Heidegger gives to the notion of "mood" (*Stimmung*).
One senses, too, that as early as *The Theory of Intuition in Husserl's
Phenomenology*, Levinas is already critical – in a muted way, a hint,
to be sure – of Heidegger (and perhaps also Husserl) for missing
the significance of intersubjectivity, and thus for missing its ethical
significance.[47] This will be, in any event, Levinas's later criticism of
Heidegger's account of intersubjectivity in terms of the *Mitsein*
("being-with") of *Dasein*, in *Being and Time*, because it treats sociality
as an immanent characteristic of *Dasein* rather than as a transcendence.[48]

It is also clear, second, that it is not despite his ethically based
criticisms but precisely because of them that Levinas will continue
to appreciate not only the existential character and concretude
made possible by phenomenology, but also its unsurpassed scientific positivism. Because Husserlian phenomenology represents the
limit case of scientific positivism (intuition seeking the absolute or
presuppositionless origin of meaning), Levinas's break with it, in
the name of the higher vocation of ethics, is not due to some
undetected fault or lack in his conception of science. In such a case,
as, for example, with several "non-scientific" breaks with Hegel's
allegedly "absolute" science, science is able to recuperate its hu-

---

[46] Emmanuel Levinas, "Quelques réflexions sur la philosophie de l'hitlérisme," in *Esprit*,
vol. 2, no. 26, November 1934, pp. 199–208, reprinted in Emmanuel Levinas, *Les imprévus
de l'histoire* (Montpellier: Fata Morgana, 1994), pp. 35–41.

[47] See *TIHP*, the final paragraph of chapter seven, p. 151.

[48] See, e.g., the first (pp. 40–41) and last (pp. 93–94) pages of Emmanuel Levinas, *Time and
the Other* [*and Additional Essays*], trans. Richard A. Cohen (Pittsburgh: Duquesne University Press, 1987); p. 40–41: "[T]he other in Heidegger appears in the essential situation of
*Miteinandersein*, reciprocally being with one another . . . The preposition *mit* (with) here
describes the relationship. It is thus an association of side by side, around something,
around a common term and, more precisely, for Heidegger, around the truth. It is not
the face-to-face relationship, where each contributes everything, except the private fact
of one's existence . . . it is not the preposition *mit* that should describe the original
relationship with the other." Compare Martin Heidegger, *Being and Time*, trans. John
Macquarrie and Edward Robinson (New York: Harper & Row, 1962), section 26, "The
Dasein-with of Others and Everyday Being-with," pp. 153–163; p. 156: "Dasein in itself is
essentially Being-with."

bris. Rather, Levinas's break represents the essential priority of ethics over science in its fullest, broadest, most universal sense. Husserl's phenomenological conception of science, in other words, because of its depth and breadth, its genuine comprehensiveness, frees Levinas's critique of science from any charge of "straw man." Furthermore, in sharp contrast to Heidegger, Levinas's ethical critique is not only able to recognize the genuinely scientific character of science (i.e., its contribution to pure knowledge), and, beyond that, it is not only able to appreciate the enormous contributions of science to the convenience and health of society, but even more profoundly, his critique, because it is ethical, positively values the universality, the impartiality, and the mathematical character of scientific knowledge as all necessary components for the constitution of a *just* society. Here is not the place to develop this line of thought. The point is that it is not science or technology as such, but rather the hubris of science, its pretended hegemony, that Levinas criticizes. Here, then, regarding the scientific character of phenomenology, like two sides of the same coin, as it were, Husserl serves Levinas both negatively (transcending a genuine rather than a deficient mode of science) and positively (seeing science as contributing to and serving justice).

While the first point above, Levinas's assimilation of Heidegger's ontology to palliate Husserl's epistemology, appears directly in *The Theory of Intuition in Husserl's Phenomenology*, the second, the superiority of science conceived on an intuitional rather than an experiential basis, follows no less from its theses, as has been shown in the first section above.

It has been suggested[49] that the birth of Levinas's own thought, his intersubjective ethics, first appears five years after *The Theory of Intuition in Husserl's Phenomenology*, in a 1935 article entitled *"De l'évasion* ["Of Evasion"]." Such a view would be supported not only by certain internal textual evidence, but also by the decisive impact that same year[50] of Rosenzweig's *Star of Redemption* on Levinas. Nonetheless, with a vision strengthened by hindsight, no

[49] See the introduction by Jacques Rolland to the French edition of Emmanuel Levinas, *De l'évasion* (Montpellier: Fata Morgana, 1982), pp. 9–64.

[50] See François Poirie, *Emmanuel Levinas: Qui êtes-vous?* (Lyon: La Manufacture, 1987), p. 121. Also cited and discussed in Cohen, *Elevations*, p. 237.

doubt, I think we can discover certain insights in Levinas's book of 1930 that are later developed in Levinas's own distinctive philosophy. While these elements may not be the central themes or emphases of Levinas's mature thought, focused as it is on an intersubjective ethics, they nevertheless play essential if supporting roles in it. Here I will focus on three elements of Husserl's phenomenology that will have a continued impact on Levinas's thought: (1) the pluralism of phenomenological analyses; (2) concretude; and (3) the problem of breaking with naïveté.

Though the idea is certainly not original to Husserl, it is from his phenomenology, I think, that Levinas learns to account for a variety of levels of meaning in a variety of ways, without reducing one to another. That is to say, it is from Husserl's manner of separating multiple fields of signification and multiple layers of meaning within any one field that Levinas comes to appreciate how to reject, and the significance of rejecting, the *reductions* inherent in *system* driven theories, whether straightforward or dialectical. In *The Theory of Intuition in Husserl's Phenomenology* Levinas writes:

The constitution is different in each region. We have shown that the intuition of sensible objects is different from categorial and eidetic intuition. But in the sphere of individual objects, intuition is not uniform either. The *Einfühlung* [empathy], which is an act that reveals the conscious life of others, is a type of intuition different from sensible perception. The experience that reveals animal reality to us is different from that which makes us know, for example, a social phenomenon. Each region of objects has a special 'regional ontology' as well as a special mode of being an object of consciousness, i.e., each has a special constitution.[51]

(Let us note, too, that Levinas's choice of examples focuses on the *difference* between inter-human and other experiences.)

The results of Levinas's early appreciation for the multilayered and multivalent regions opened up by Husserl's phenomenology are evident in the primarily phenomenological sections of Levinas's own writings. In his early work of 1947, *Time and the Other*, for instance, Levinas describes the several distinct but interrelated layers of intentional meaning which progressively constitute a fully

[51] *TIHP*, p. 127.

fledged subjectivity and world: pure existence, hyperstasis (self-sensing), solitude, enjoyment, everydayness, worldliness, labor, death, reason, time, sociality. In *Existence and Existents*, which appeared at the same time as *Time and the Other*, we find the same layering of distinct phenomenological regions, indeed for the most part the very same layering: pure existence, fatigue, worldliness, place, possession, knowing, sociality, time, eros. The same multi-layered account, the same phenomenological fleshing out of subjectivity and world, where each region of meaning is described in its uniqueness even while it is related to other "founding" and "founded" regions of meaning, appears in sections two, three, and four of Levinas's mature philosophical work of 1961, *Totality and Infinity*: enjoyment, dwelling, labor, possession, representation, sociality, commerce, eros. Unlike the two earlier works, which are for the most part (but not entirely) phenomenological studies, in *Totality and Infinity* the significance of ethics and justice, which Levinas conceives in a supra-phenomenological fashion, introduces an alterity which reorients the nominative character of any strictly Husserlian description. It thus introjects into the "originary" dimension of the constituting ego the higher imperative and prescriptive dimension of intersubjective obligations and responsibilities. The Husserlian return of meaning to its origin in the constituting ego – even if "absolute" – is insufficient, from a Levinasian point of view, owing to an even deeper, "ab-solute," or more elevated level of ethical consciousness. Levinas will characterize the ethical rupture of intentional consciousness in a variety of ways throughout his many writings, for example, as "insomnia," "trauma," "prophecy," "substitution," or "non-indifference." We will review the significance of these terms and others in chapter 6. Because he does attend to the priority of ethical signification, Levinas breaks with the Husserlian model of phenomenology – where, as he has shown in *The Theory of Intuition in Husserl's Phenomenology*, intuition, linked to representation, is the final evidential court of appeal for all meaning – even if he retains its appreciation for the differences that distinguish different regions of meaning.

Another issue raised in *The Theory of Intuition in Husserl's Phenomenology*, and of great subsequent importance for Levinas, has to do with the question of the very possibility of phenomenology, the possibility of a "reduction" to the phenomenological sphere of meaning. We must first recall why this topic is important and why it was so hotly debated in the early twentieth century. For Husserl, natural, ordinary, or pre-philosophical consciousness is essentially naïve. "The naïveté consists," Levinas writes, "in accepting objects as given and existing, without questioning the meaning of this existence and of the 'fact of its being given' (*Gegebenheit*)."[52] The naïveté or dogmatism of the natural attitude consists in being blind to the essential contribution of consciousness to the constitution of meaning. The exact sciences, too, for all their admirable precision, are as guilty as ordinary consciousness of this naïveté. Phenomenology, in contrast, as we have seen, attempts to describe the origin of meaning as a function of consciousness, as a product of its meaning-giving acts, deriving from its intentionality as a constitutive activity. Thus the inaugural moment of phenomenology, as it were, the breakthrough to the phenomenological sphere of meaning, with its multiple fields, requires a break with the naïveté of the natural attitude, from its naïve or dogmatic realism – its dogmatic slumber. To effect this break Husserl speaks of the methodological requirement of an "epoche," "bracketing," or "reduction," of the natural attitude's naïveté. What is at stake in the question of the possibility of such a "reduction," then, is the beginning of philosophy as such – Aristotle's *thauma*, "wonder," or perhaps even more deeply, his *aporia*, "argumentative impasse." What is at stake is the birth of philosophy. Not its end, but its beginning: What gives rise to philosophy? What motivates philosophizing?

Of Husserl's account of the neutralization of naïve belief, Levinas writes in *The Theory of Intuition in Husserl's Phenomenology* that: "For Husserl, philosophical intuition is a reflection on life considered in all its concrete fullness and wealth, a life which is considered but no longer lived. The reflection upon life is divorced from life itself."[53] And: "Hence the great merit of the theory of the phenomenological reduction (the method which leads us to the phenomenological consciousness) is to have shown, at least negatively, that the existence of consciousness and its relation to the

[52] TIHP, p. 122.    [53] Ibid., p. 142.

world must be conceived in a way totally different from the
existence of a part in a whole."[54] Consciousness is not within-the-
world, like "a part in a whole," but rather is the source, the origin,
the ground of the meaningful world as such. No consciousness, no
"world." Such is the vision opened up by the reduction. But
consciousness in the natural attitude seems in no way to even
suspect its own full responsibility for signification. It in no way
even suspects the ideality of meaning. How, then, does one get
from one attitude to the other, from naïve ignorance, however
much knowledge or information it "knows," to genuine philosophical responsibility, which sees consciousness as the source of
all meaning? Again, what triggers philosophy?

   Another lesson Levinas learns from Husserl must be introduced
at this juncture. Overcoming naïveté is important not because it
leads to a reconstruction of reality based on abstract philosophical
speculation, as the rationalists thought, but rather because it leads
to the concrete. Eliminating unacknowledged naïveté leads to the
concrete for the first time. Husserl's "idealism," far from losing
touch with "reality," signifies an even greater commitment to
existence – such is Levinas's reading. "The phenomenological
reduction," Levinas writes, "is precisely the method by which we
are going back to concrete man. Because of it, we discover the field
of pure consciousness where we can practice philosophical intuition."[55] This move to the concrete is, as we saw earlier, precisely
what in 1932 Sartre most appreciated about phenomenology, as
Levinas presented it in *The Theory of Intuition in Husserl's Phenomenology*. Levinas's appreciation for Husserl's appreciation for the concrete allows him to include Husserl, along with Heidegger, in his
1949 collection of secondary essays that he entitles *Discovering
Existence with Husserl and Heidegger*. Phenomenology, returning to
consciousness, discovers not ideas but existence. This is Levinas's
position, in any event, at a time when many interpreters of Husserl
felt that his phenomenology had veered into the typical abstractions of philosophical idealism. For Levinas, on the contrary,
"[t]he phenomenological epoche does not destroy the truths
proper to the natural attitude but wants only to clarify their

---

[54] Ibid., p. 146.     [55] Ibid.

sense."[56] Thus it is more concrete because more fully informed about the true signification of signification.

In fairness to the idealist reading of Husserl, however, we must not forget, as noted above, that Levinas recognizes and questions a certain "wavering," "indecision," or "obscurity"[57] in Husserl regarding the relation of immanence to transcendence. This will remain a troubling issue in Husserlian phenomenology throughout its career. What Levinas does not question, because like Sartre he is glad for it, is that Husserl had succeeded in opening the door to the concrete, to meaning as lived, including practical significations such as "goal," "end," "purpose," and "value." Purpose would no longer be a gloss that can be stripped off of reality in the name of science, but is rather of a piece with the constitution of the real as meaningful.

To return to our question: What motivates the naturally naïve person to take up a phenomenological outlook, to turn away from an attitude of realism, naïve or sophisticated, to the apparently so radically different attitude of phenomenological idealism? "The natural attitude is not purely contemplative; the world is not purely an object of scientific investigation," Levinas writes. "Yet it seems that man *suddenly* accomplishes the phenomenological reduction by a purely theoretical act of reflection on life. Husserl offers no explanation for this change of attitude and does not even consider it a problem. Husserl does not raise the metaphysical problem of the situation of the *Homo philosophus*."[58] But whether raised or not, the initiation of philosophy is a problem.

Eugen Fink made this issue famous within the phenomenological movement. Three years after the publication of Levinas's *The Theory of Intuition in Husserl's Phenomenology*, Fink published, in *Kant-Studien* (vol. 38, 1933), his now oft-cited article, "The Phenomenological Philosophy of Edmund Husserl and Contemporary Criticism."[59] In this article, as the title suggests, Fink compares Husserl and Kant (the neo-Kantianism of Rickert). What lends additional luster to this article, beyond its intrinsic clarity and

---

[56] Ibid., p. 147.    [57] Ibid., p. 150.    [58] Ibid., p. 142.

[59] Eugen Fink, "The Phenomenological Philosophy of Edmund Husserl and Contemporary Criticism," in R. O. Elveton, ed. and trans., *The Phenomenology of Husserl: Selected Critical Readings* (Chicago: Quadrangle Books, 1970), pp. 74–147.

penetration, is Husserl's prefatory endorsement. Husserl affirms
"that it [Fink's article] contains no sentence which I could not
completely accept as my own or openly acknowledge as my own
conviction."[60] In this article, in the course of his comparison and
contrast between phenomenology and critical philosophy, Fink
takes up the line that we have just seen Levinas articulate in *The
Theory of Intuition in Husserl's Phenomenology*: namely, that the phenomenological reduction is entirely *unmotivated*, that nothing in the
natural attitude leads to or induces a break with the realist naïveté
that is the essence of the natural attitude. "In the natural attitude,"
Fink writes, "we know nothing of the status of the world within the
universe of absolute life."[61] Also: "Every being in the world is
situated within horizons of familiarity . . . The reduction leads us
into the darkness of something unknown, something with which
we have not been previously familiar in terms of its formal style of
being."[62] Nothing in the world compares to the attitude of the
phenomenologist, hence nothing in the world can motivate it.
Attaining the phenomenological attitude, then, seems something
of a miracle, perhaps predestined for some (that strange breed:
"philosophers") and denied to others (the "masses," no doubt).
But then its findings, too, must appear no less mad than do the
ravings of the one who having escaped Plato's cave returns to
liberate those still enchained.[63]

Although the issue of the motivation for the phenomenological
reduction at first sight may appear to be a narrow technical
question only of interest within phenomenology, in fact a great
deal rides on it, and not for phenomenology alone. The issue is
really, as has been indicated, that of the beginning of philosophy,

---

[60] Edmund Husserl, "Preface" (to Fink's article, in ibid., p. 74.
[61] Fink, "The Phenomenological Philosophy of Edmund Husserl and Contemporary
Criticism," in ibid., p. 139.      [62] Ibid., p. 127.
[63] Of him, the true seer, Plato has Socrates say (*Republic*, Book Seven, trans. Allan Bloom),
517a: "[W]ouldn't he be the source of laughter, and wouldn't it be said of him that he
went up and came back with his eyes corrupted, and that it's not even worth trying to go
up? And if they were somehow able to get their hands on and kill the man who attempts
to release and lead up, wouldn't they kill him?" Although the Nazis did precisely this –
mockery, corruption charges, murder – to the Jews and the Jewish vision of morality,
they metaphorically did the same also to genuine science. It is precisely this degradation
of science, and the scientific destiny of the West, that Husserl so valiantly but ineffectively
warned against in his final writings.

of "*homo philosophus*," as Levinas calls the philosopher. In the natural attitude one is within-the-world, an entity amongst others; in the phenomenological attitude one attends to the constitution of "worldliness" as such. Instead of being-in-the-world, a part in a whole whose meaning is somehow already given, already "there" (*Da*), the philosopher attends to the very worldliness of the world, to the whole, to the original constitution of all meaning. Getting from one perspective to the other, then, is of great importance, insofar as it is important to avoid ignorance and the dangers that follow from ignorance.

In *The Theory of Intuition in Husserl's Phenomenology*, Levinas offers another line of approach. He shows that Husserl's reduction is not as radical as Fink – Fink's Husserl – would have it. Indeed, Husserl cushions the apparent radicality of the philosopher's freedom, muting the abruptness of the break between the natural and the philosophical attitudes. What Levinas shows is that because Husserl has already made theory primary in the natural attitude, one cannot be totally surprised by its alleged eruption and radical extension in the philosophical attitude. In the concluding chapter of *The Theory of Intuition in Husserl's Phenomenology*, Levinas writes:

[B]y virtue of the primacy of theory, Husserl does not wonder how this "neutralization" of our life, which nevertheless is still an act of our life, has its foundation in life. The freedom and the impulse which lead us to reduction and philosophical intuition present by themselves nothing new with respect to the freedom and stimulation of theory. The latter is taken as primary, so that Husserl gives himself the freedom of theory just as he gives himself theory.

Consequently, despite the revolutionary character of the phenomenological reduction, the revolution which it accomplishes is, in Husserl's philosophy, possible only to the extent that the natural attitude is theoretical.[64]

Hence, "the phenomenological reduction needs no explanation."[65] The reduction would simply be an extension or exacerbation of a theoretical attitude already in place, as it were, latently or weakly, in the natural attitude. Fink, however, with Husserl's endorsement, will later argue, quite cogently, that such a

[64] *TIHP*, p. 157.    [65] Ibid.

gradualist interpretation cannot make sense, since it would undermine the absolute radicality of the philosophical attitude, compromising it with the very pre-philosophical attitude whose essential
structure it aims to unravel from the absolute ground zero up.

Accepting Fink's point, but reversing its value, in the preface to
his *Phenomenology of Perception*,[66] Merleau-Ponty will turn the alleged
"contamination," the unavoidable "intertwining" or "chiasm" of
interrogating and interrogated, or of the pre-philosophical attitude
and the philosophical attitude, into the very virtue of the phenomenological reduction and the centerpiece of his own distinctive
philosophy. Rather than being a problem to be overcome, a thorn
in the side of absolute consciousness, it would reflect the very
essence of worldliness as such. Knowing and known would be
inextricably linked. As we have indicated in chapter 1, Merleau-
Ponty extends the Bergsonian heritage. Bergson, however, unlike
Husserl and Merleau-Ponty, spends very little time elaborating his
method. It is clear, of course, that the great difference between
pre-philosophical rationality and philosophical intuition is the
difference between a thought guided by utilitarian interests and a
thought guided by speculative interests alone. The difference,
however, may seem to be one of quantity, quantity of what
Bergson calls "effort," rather than a difference of kind. But this
effort and the change in outlook it effects, opening up the entire
field of "duration," is nonetheless considerable, certainly no less
considerable than Husserl's shift from the natural to the phenomenological attitude, to the extent that Bergson will speak of "the
essentially active, I might almost say violent, character of metaphysical intuition."[67]

Sartre, for his part, sides with Fink against Bergson and
Merleau-Ponty. Opting for radical discontinuity, he radically dis-
avows any contamination between the non-philosophical and the
philosophical. It is upon this rupture that Sartre builds his ontological dualism, with an entirely unmotivated freedom – the
for-itself – that is the origin of all meaning, on the one side, and an
entirely dense or opaque being – the in-itself – that by itself is
completely devoid of sense, on the other. It seems to me that this
radical dualism makes Sartre's philosophy more "modern" than

[66] Merleau-Ponty, *Phenomenology of Perception*, pp. vii–xxi.
[67] Bergson, *Introduction to Metaphysics*, trans. T. E. Hulme, p. 45.

"contemporary," more a rationalist construction than an ecological thought, in the sense that we have given to these terms in chapter 1. Seeing the consequences of answering the question of the motivation of philosophy one way or the other, as in Merleau-Ponty and Sartre, should impress us once again with the importance of this question. It is no less important to Heidegger and Levinas, who both take a different route.

Neither Levinas nor Heidegger is content to make the transcendental position of philosophy a function either of (1) the exacerbation of an already present theoretical attitude (Levinas's Husserl), a position which solves the problem of the motivation of philosophy but introduces the new problematic of philosophy's purity, *or* (2) the rather mysterious, and hence highly problematic, view that the "reduction" to the philosophical attitude is entirely unmotivated (Fink's Husserl). The new question, then, for Heidegger and Levinas, insofar as they reject both interpretations of Husserl's "explanation" for the emergence of philosophy, is to discover what does break the everyday self of its naïve realism, its vision of itself as within a given world.

In *Being and Time*, Heidegger answers this question by describing the everyday world in terms of ready-to-hand (*zuhanden*) instruments. It is when these instruments, which function smoothly within an unreflective practical world, break down, that they become transformed into what Heidegger calls "present-at-hand" (*vorhanden*) objects, that is to say, objects subject to theoretical scrutiny. Thus, in an apparent reversal of Bergson, theory depends on praxis. But the reversal is only apparent insofar as praxis itself depends on ontology and "thinking" (*Denken*). "Objects" refer back to "instruments," and the instrumentality, the "in-order-to" (*das Um-zu*) of the world of praxis, refers back to the human person (*Dasein*) who uses instruments or theorizes objects. Thus the question of the origin of philosophy does not depend on the break from praxis to theory, but rather on the break from praxis. Theory too, as Husserl had shown, can be naïve; but for Heidegger it is doubly naïve. What, then, "breaks" a person from the natural non-philosophical attitude in both its practical aspect, which for Heidegger is primary, and/or its theoretical aspect, which is derivative?

Heidegger's answer is now famous: *death, being-toward-death (Sein-*

*zum-Tode*). Rejecting the theoretical prejudice that Levinas shows is Husserl's, and not satisfied with an "unmotivated" shift from the naïve realism of praxis to philosophical thinking, Heidegger sees in the peculiar transcendence of death – being-toward-death, the "possibility of impossibility," the ultimate possibility of human finitude – the power sufficient to break human subjectivity from its self-alienation within-the-world ("inauthenticity") to achieve insightful and individualized retrieval of itself ("authenticity"). Opened up by a "conscience" (*Gewissen*) aware of Dasein's own "being-toward-death," authentic Dasein discovers itself to be the very question or "issue" of being, an openness to the revelation of meaning. Unlike Husserl, for whom, owing to his bias toward theory, meaning originates in absolute consciousness, for Heidegger meaning originates in Being (*Seindes*), or in the "house of Being," language. But returning to our interests: it is being-toward-death that is the Heideggerian "existentialized" version of the Husserlian reduction, the shift into philosophy, that through which someone is converted from ordinary naïve realism to a gripping appropriation of and by the question of "fundamental ontology." Transcendence in Heidegger is thus a function of an essentially ruptured immanence, of Dasein's retrieval of its own mortality – its "ownmost" (*eigenst*) possibility, "not to be outstripped" (*unuberholbare*) – and through that retrieval a becoming open to the thought of Being.

While appreciating the concretude of Heidegger's phenomenology, Levinas will decry, just as he decries in Husserl, its immanence:

In the finitude of time the "being-toward-death" of *Being and Time* stretches out – despite all the renewals of handed down philosophy that this brilliant book brings – the meaningful remains enclosed within the immanence of the *Jemeinigkeit* [Mineness] of the *Dasein* that *has to be* and that thus – in spite of the denunciation of being as presence – still belongs to a philosophy of presence.[68]

---

[68] Emmanuel Levinas, "Diachrony and Representation" (1982), in Levinas, *Time and the Other*, trans. Cohen, pp. 115–116. Levinas's critique of the immanence or "ownness" of Heidegger's account of Dasein was probably influenced by Martin Buber's earlier critique along the same lines. In his 1938 inaugural address at Hebrew University, published under the title "What is Man?" ["*Was is der Mensch?*"], Buber had said: "Apparently nothing more remains now to the solitary man but to seek an intimate

Levinas, too, like Heidegger, will reject both versions of the Husserlian explanation for philosophy, seeing the rise of philosophy neither in the exacerbation of an autochthonous theorizing nor in its unaccountable upsurge. But Levinas will also reject, as we have briefly noted, the Heideggerian account of being-toward-death as the absolute rupture of mundane subjectivity. Here is not the place to rehearse the details and nuances of Levinas's arguments against Heidegger, which can be found in *Time and the Other*, *Existence and Existents*, and *Totality and Infinity*. Suffice to say that Dasein's deathboundedness, and the ontological homecoming it opens up, are for Levinas not sufficiently other, not radically transcendent enough. Death, Levinas will argue, is not the "possibility of impossibility," which after all is *still a possibility*, but rather the "impossibility of possibility," heralding a more radical alterity. Being-toward-death does not open a person to the genuine origin of meaning, but rather derives its meaning, Levinas will claim, from social life. For Levinas one lives and dies for others. The alterity of the other person, an ethical alterity, is the most radical sense (or "non-sense") of transcendence, and the only sense that can properly "break" the subject of its sphere of immanence. What for Levinas effects the irretrievable break from naïve immersion within the world is not dying, then, but the encounter – ethically charged – with the alterity of the other person. Responsibility for the other, and not responsibility for being,[69] is the beginning of philosophy. Shame before the other, and not spontaneous reflection or exacerbation or being-toward-death, breaks the subject of its naïveté and, by opening up the dimension of goodness, opens up the requirement to be just, and hence the

communication with himself. This is the basic situation from which Heidegger's philosophy arises. And thereby the anthropological question, which the man who has become solitary discovers afresh, the question about the essence of man and about his relation to the being of what is, has been replaced by another question, the one which Heidegger calls the fundamental-ontological question, about human existence in its relation to its *own* being. There remains, however, one irrefragable fact, that one can stretch out one's hands to one's image or reflection in a mirror, but not to one's real self . . . Human life possesses absolute meaning through transcending in practice its own conditioned nature . . . Human life touches on absoluteness in virtue of its dialogical character . . . Heidegger's 'existence' is monological." Martin Buber, *Between Man and Man*, trans. Roger G. Smith (New York: Macmillan, 1965), p. 167.

[69] See Richard A. Cohen, "Dasein's Responsibility for Being," in *Philosophy Today*, vol. 77, no. 4, Winter 1983, pp. 317–325.

requirement for philosophy.[70] In this way, taking the "break" with naïveté to be neither a theoretical nor an ontological event but an ethical event, Levinas at once not only reorients the relation of ethics to epistemology and ontology, and not only provides an account of the beginning of philosophy, but, even more important-ly, *justifies* philosophy.

The point at hand, however, is more modest: to indicate that already in *The Theory of Intuition in Husserl's Phenomenology*, which is to say, already in 1930, Levinas raises fundamental questions within phenomenology that lead – taking a novel route – to the ethical metaphysics that is Levinas's distinctive twist and advance, as we have seen, beyond Bergson, Husserl, Heidegger, and Merleau-Ponty, his distinct and uplifting contribution to contemporary thought.

[70] For a closer look at the relations between morality and justice and justice and philosophy, see chapter eight, "G-d in Levinas: The Justification of Justice and Philosophy," in Cohen, *Elevations*, pp. 173–94.

# CHAPTER 3

# *The good work of Edmund Husserl*

In this chapter, by turning to an article that Levinas wrote on Husserl in 1940 – "The Work of Edmund Husserl"[1] – we will, at one stroke, continue and develop the themes of chapters 1 and 2. That is to say, by means of a close examination of one of Levinas's still early readings of Husserl, we will find that Levinas "discovers" at the heart of phenomenological consciousness the very Bergsonian intertwining of activity and passivity that defines contemporary thought. In later chapters, especially chapters 6 and 7, we will elaborate Levinas's ethical metaphysics in its own terms, without reference to Husserl. Here, however, we will follow Levinas's own route into his ethical metaphysics, a route that traverses and surpasses Husserlian phenomenology.

But Levinas's route – the route to ethics for an educated Westerner – is not accidental or fortuitous. And this means, too, that it is in some sense never done with. Let us recall, Husserl presents the science of phenomenology as the most advanced outpost of the Western quest for knowledge. Both supplementing and surpassing the natural and social sciences, it would be knowledge of the most radical, comprehensive, and rigorous kind. As such it would represent, as we have seen, the most advanced form of the scientific spirit of the West. Hence, given the universality of science and the value of knowledge, phenomenology would represent, for a devoted scientific thinker such as Husserl, following a long philosophical tradition, the very humanity of the human. At the heart of the human would be the philosopher, the knower. It is an old

---

[1] Levinas's "L'oeuvre d'Edmond Husserl" first appeared in 1940, in the January–February issue of the *Revue Philosophique de la France et de l'Étranger* (vol. 129, Nos. 1–2). See note 8 below.

theme in the West, already well developed in ancient Greece. In the middle ages it found expression with those theologians who considered the intellect the heart of the soul. It is the defining characteristic of the modern period: rationality as the core not only of the human but also, and even more fundamentally, of the universe. The destiny of the West as a scientific civilization, in any event, is the oft-repeated theme dear to Husserl's stirring meta-philosophical accounts of phenomenology enunciated in the dark days of the 1930s.[2] But for Levinas science alone is not enough. The heart of the human lies in morality and justice, not in knowledge, indispensable though knowledge be. To show this, however, Levinas must show, more specifically, that phenomenology – that is, genuine science – is not enough.

We have already seen, examining certain themes in his 1930 book *The Theory of Intuition in Husserl's Phenomenology*, that Levinas was well qualified for this task. Not only did he study under Husserl in 1928–29, he became one of the world's leading and most influential expositors of phenomenology. Indeed, by 1949 Levinas had published a sufficient number of articles on phenomenology to gather them into a collection: *Discovering Existence in Husserl and Heidegger*[3] (expanded 2nd edition, 1967). These two volumes were instrumental in introducing Husserlian phenomenology (and, to a lesser extent, the Heideggerian version) to France. Later, in 1973, André Orianne's English translation of *The Theory of Intuition in Husserl's Phenomenology*[4] helped introduce phenomenology to America. As recently as 1998, a collection of

[2] See, most especially, Husserl's lecture of 7 May 1935, at the University of Prague, "Philosophy and the Crisis of European Man," in Edmund Husserl, *Phenomenology and the Crisis of Philosophy*, ed. and trans. Quentin Lauer (New York: Harper & Row, 1965), pp. 149–192; and Edmund Husserl, *The Crisis of European Science and Transcendental Phenomenology*, published as vol. IV of *Husserliana* (The Hague: Martinus Nijhoff, 1954), parts one and two of which were published in 1936 in the Belgrade review *Philosophia*.

[3] Emmanuel Levinas, *En découvrant l'éxistence avec Husserl et Heidegger* (Paris: Vrin, 1949; 2nd expanded edn., 1967).

[4] Emmanuel Levinas, *The Theory of Intuition in Husserl's Phenomenology*, trans. André Orianne (Evanston: Northwestern University Press, 1973; with new preface by Richard A. Cohen, 1995). Earlier, in 1967, Joseph Kockelmans had translated and introduced chapter six, "The Intuition of Essences," of Levinas's book, for inclusion in *The Philosophy of Edmund Husserl and its Interpretations*, ed. J. Kockelmans (New York: Doubleday, 1967), pp. 87–117, intro. pp. 83–5.

Levinas's articles on Husserl appeared in English.[5] But Levinas is not simply one of the great expositors and practitioners of phenomenology.

He was also, in his own right, one of the great philosophers of the twentieth century (and, who knows, perhaps in the history of philosophy). In many volumes – most notably *Totality and Infinity* (1961) and *Otherwise than Being or Beyond Essence* (1974), which we will look at in chapter 5 – and many articles, and a career of teaching, he produced, as we know, a profound and far-reaching ethical metaphysics. Thus he was both faithful and unfaithful to Husserlian phenomenology, like Heidegger and Merleau-Ponty and Sartre, and all the great phenomenologists. Levinas, too, it seems to me, was the one philosopher in the twentieth century to offer an alternative path for thinking, engaged with, but deeper than – or higher than – and in essential opposition to, the *Denken* of Heidegger. We know Heidegger's reorientation of phenomenology toward the question of being, the ontological difference, the turn to language, and we will examine it again in the next chapter in relation to Levinas's alternative. In this chapter, however, let us ask how Levinas brought phenomenology from its scientific origins, its predilection for theory, to ethical imperatives.

The fateful conjunction of faithful Husserlian expositor and post-Husserlian independent philosopher already appears in the first words of the title Levinas selected for his collection, *Discovering Existence with Husserl and Heidegger*. We would be very wrong to separate these terms, to think of *discovering* as the dry scientific method opened up by Husserl, say, and *existence* as the rich ontological horizons opened up by Heidegger. Rather, the terms are wedded to one another (as indicated by the rest of the title: Husserl *and* Heidegger). Already in Husserl, so Levinas will show, one finds the inextricable and fruitful bond between knowing and existing. But the expression "discovering existence" goes further. It will suggest an essential ambiguity at the heart of the scientific quest, and hence at the heart of Western humanity. It is an ambiguity for which we have been prepared by Bergson, the ambiguity between *construction* and *reception*, activity and passivity, interest and dis-

5  Emmanuel Levinas, *Discovering Existence with Husserl*, ed. and trans. Richard A. Cohen and Michael B. Smith (Evanston: Northwestern University Press, 1998).

interest, choosing and chosen. It is an ambiguity Levinas will eventually elaborate in terms of self and other, height and responsibility – and thus in ethical terms.[6] This ambiguity, which in modern philosophy is treated as a dichotomy, divided empiricists and idealists. It is the same ambiguity that, as we saw in the previous chapter, is the centerpiece of the phenomenology developed by Merleau-Ponty. But for our purposes, it is an ambiguity which, when properly interpreted, that is to say, when appreciated in its ethical signification, is not only central to Levinas's ethical vision of philosophy, but effects a transcending of phenomenology at the very heart of phenomenology.

What is this ambiguity? Phenomenology, as we know, seeks the origin of meaning. Its seeks not just this or that origin – psychological, sociological or historical origins, say – but the absolute origin of meaning, the ground of meaning without any presupposition whatsoever. What Levinas discovers, however, is an essential ambiguity in the very "place" where phenomenology claims to have found the origin of meaning, that is to say, in the meaning-bestowing (*Sinngebung*) character of consciousness. What Levinas discovers is that the things discovered, "the things themselves," at once surrender to meaning and solicit the meaning to which they surrender, hence that they are both constituted and constituting. Philosophy, the quest for the true, is thus both a bold and a delicate enterprise. Husserl was sensitive to the epistemological dangers that lurk on all sides at this juncture, in grasping the very act of meaning-bestowal. There are risks of pride, of insufficient vigilance, of imposing meaning, and the seductions of complacency, insufficient self-awareness, being imposed upon. He was thus, as he called himself, a "perpetual beginner," steadfast in the tentativeness of truth, to the end open to the self-correcting progress of science. But if science is nonetheless more than diplomacy (sophism), it remains less than conviction (self-certainty), except for certain formal convictions such as perpetually beginning again.

[6] One Levinas scholar goes so far as to make the notion of "ambiguity" (usually associated with the thought of Merleau-Ponty, after the book by Alphonse de Waelhens, entitled *Une philosophie de l'ambiguité: L'éxistentialisme de M. Merleau-Ponty*, 1951) the centerpiece of Levinas's thought; see Jacques Rolland, "L'Ambiguité comme façon de l'autrement," in Jean Greisch and Jacques Rolland, eds., *Emmanuel Levinas: L'éthique comme philosophie première* (Paris: Les Editions du Cert, 1993), pp. 427–445.

We must ask, however, whether the tentativeness of knowledge, the provisional character of scientific truth (and of philosophy *qua* epistemology) is also true of wisdom. We must ask, with Levinas, "whether, beyond knowledge and its hold on being, a *more urgent* [my italics] form does not emerge, that of wisdom."[7] Does not another dimension altogether, an ethical dimension, so Levinas will suggest, open up in the conjunction of activity and passivity at the very origin of meaning? Does not the passivity at the root of signification signify not simply the openness to meaning, to signs, to evidence, but more urgently an openness to a unique signifier: the other person? Levinas will answer yes. It is this that he sees in the extraordinary signification of inter-subjectivity, toward which he was already pushing Husserl's phenomenology in 1930, on the final page of *The Theory of Intuition in Husserl's Phenomenology*. At the heart of phenomenology, then, would be a rupture with phenomenology. "One sees, in any event," Levinas wrote of his own ethical thought in 1947, "that it is not phenomenological to the end."[8]

In this chapter I am going to turn, as I have indicated, to an early article by Levinas, published in 1940, just as "world war" was breaking out in Europe: "The Work of Edmund Husserl." Levinas had this article reprinted in the 1949 first edition, and again in the 1967 second expanded edition, of his collection, *Discovering Existence with Husserl and Heidegger*.[9] I have selected this article not because it is the clearest or most developed articulation of the ambiguity I wish to bring to light. Many later articles are much clearer and more developed. Rather, I have selected it precisely because this article on Husserl's "work" is for the most part expository. Nonetheless, other than teaching Husserl's phenomenology, it also already contains, as I intend to show, a distinctively Levinasian dimension, an opening onto the ethical. Husserl had hoped to save Europe from its madness with the cry of "Return to science!" His

7 Levinas, "Ethics as First Philosophy," trans. Séan Hand and Michael Temple, in Emmanuel Levinas, *The Levinas Reader*, ed. Séan Hand (Oxford: Blackwell, 1989), p. 78.
8 Emmanuel Levinas, *Time and the Other* [*and Additional Essays*], trans. Richard A. Cohen (Pittsburgh: Duquesne University Press, 1987), p. 78.
9 This article appears as chapter four of the English language collection, *Discovering Existence with Husserl* (pp. 47–87, 184–188). Unless otherwise indicated, all references in the present chapter are to its English translation in that volume, hence page numbers will be omitted.

words went unheeded, and science – pseudo-science, to be sure – blithely contributed to the horror. Even before the war, however, we will see that Levinas already understood that the true battle cry for peace and against war was more drastic, more compelling than Husserl's. Science was unable to save Europe from the Nazis, let alone to save its own institutions (laboratories, universities, research centers) from pseudo-science. But the Nazis, their ideology, their wars, did not simply represent bad science. The problem was deeper. The Nazis and everything they represented was first and foremost *evil*. Thus Levinas understood that while Husserl was right, that genuine science and Nazi ideology were incompatible, he understood more profoundly that the Nazis would have to be opposed on the field of morality and justice. The battle cry would be: "Against evil, for the good!" It would thus be a spiritual battle cry, though one that would be able, in dark and drastic times, to muster real armies for real battles. The genuine problem was not epistemological but ethical. Twenty years after the war, after the Holocaust, Levinas would write: "The true problem for us Westerners is not so much to refuse violence as to question ourselves about a struggle against violence which, without blanching in non-resistance to evil, could still avoid the institution of violence out of this very struggle."[10]

"The Work of Edmund Husserl" appeared in 1940, in the January–February issue of the *Revue Philosophique de la France et de l'Etranger* (vol. 129, nos. 1–2). Thus it appeared just a few months prior to Levinas's four-year wartime internment, and prior to the post-war elaboration of his own distinctive philosophy, which began, at least in book form, in *Existence and Existents* (1947) and *Time and the Other* (1947). But it also appeared prior to both of Merleau-Ponty's inaugural works, *The Structure of Behavior*,[11] published in 1942, and *The Phenomenology of Perception*, published in 1947. I mention this because earlier I suggested that there is a similarity

---

[10] Emmanuel Levinas, *Otherwise than Being or Beyond Essence*, trans. Alphonso Lingis (The Hague: Martinus Nijhoff, 1981), p. 177.

[11] Maurice Merleau-Ponty, *The Structure of Behavior*, trans. Alden L. Fisher (Boston: Beacon Press, 1963). While this work, for the most part a scholarly study in social psychology, is more expository and certainly less original than Merleau-Ponty's *The Phenomenology of Perception*, it does contain, nonetheless, what Raymond Aron called "the root of his thought."

between Merleau-Ponty's phenomenology of ambiguity and the topic of this chapter, namely, the meeting of activity and passivity in Levinas's notion of "discovering existence." My point, then, is that "The Work of Edmund Husserl" appeared before there could be any possible influence of Merleau-Ponty upon Levinas. Unlike several of Levinas's later articles, on phenomenology or on themes dear to his own thought, one cannot claim to find in this article of 1940 the influence of a philosophy that Merleau-Ponty had not yet formulated. In fact, considering the chronological relation, along with their mutual devotion to Husserl's phenomenology, the reverse influence would be far more likely, though on this point I reserve any speculation.

Of course, more important than the question of influence is the matter of the different uses to which Levinas and Merleau-Ponty put their shared notion of the juncture of activity and passivity at the deepest levels of consciousness and sensibility. Merleau-Ponty's elaboration of this zero point of signification remains within the sphere of ontology, and in this way, though highly original, represents a development of what we could call the Heideggerian school of phenomenology. (I would even go one step further: it seems to me that Merleau-Ponty's development of phenomenology from *The Phenomenology of Perception* to *The Visible and the Invisible* is of far greater significance than Heidegger's own "poetic" development in his later thought.) Levinas, in contrast, breaking with both Husserl and Heidegger, shows the root of both epistemology and ontology in ethics. Thus, as we shall see, Levinas's interpretation of the intimate interaction of activity and passivity will be integrated into a fundamentally ethical perspective, even if this ethical reading is not at all as evident in 1940 (and then perhaps only retrospectively) as it will most definitely – indeed definitively – become after the war. So let us turn once again to Husserl.

Levinas's ethics, as we know, is not simply a philosophical ethics, self-grounded in reason. It is a "religious" ethics, a "Jewish humanism,"[12] as he called it, a "humanism of patience,"[13] rather

[12] Levinas, "For a Jewish Humanism," in Emmanuel Levinas, *Difficult Freedom*, trans. Séan Hand (Baltimore: Johns Hopkins University Press, 1990), pp. 273–276.
[13] Levinas, "Antihumanism and Education," in ibid., p. 287.

than a "pure humanism, a humanism without Torah."[14] I will later, in chapter 7, suggest that the expression "ethical exegesis" – the latter, exegesis, usually restricted to religious hermeneutics, but when joined to ethics exemplified, for Levinas, by the discussions of the Talmudic rabbis and sages (and by Levinas's own many Talmudic readings[15]) – best captures the specifically Levinasian manner of "doing" – or outdoing – phenomenology. But I think this thought bears mentioning even now, even if only as a promissory note. Husserl's eidetic and genetic analyses of meaning, showing levels of "founded" and "founding" essences or significations, are transcended, in Levinas's reading, by an account that is oriented as an ethical excess. Ethical transcendence, involving the excess of the other's alterity, as mortality and suffering, and the excess of the self's passivity, as responsibility and obligation, is found to irreducibly jolt human sensibility. It is a jolt such that the nominative and the prescriptive cannot be separated, making the integrity of their unity surpass the pure descriptions Husserl sought. One can, and Levinas will, call this transcendence by religious as well as by ethical names. In any event, at the very moment it is discovered at the heart of phenomenology, it surpasses phenomenology.

In "The Work of Edmund Husserl" neither religious themes nor religious language appear. This is just as one would expect from an exposition of the phenomenology Husserl proposed as rigorous science and philosophy of science. It is true, of course, that certain "religious" terms and references occasionally appear. In section six, for instance, Levinas writes: "The miracle of clarity is the very miracle of thought," but obviously the term "miracle" is here used in a metaphorical rather than a supernatural sense. In section seven, Levinas notes that because to perceive external things is necessarily to "synthesize diverse successive aspects of things," even God's perception of external things would unravel successively. But surely this invocation bears witness to nothing

---

[14] Levinas, "Model of the West," in Emmanuel Levinas, *Beyond the Verse*, trans. Gary D. Mole (Bloomington: Indiana University Press, 1994), p. 32.

[15] See Emmanuel Levinas, *Nine Talmudic Readings*, trans. Annette Aronowicz (Bloomington: Indiana University Press, 1990); Emmanuel Levinas, *New Talmudic Readings*, trans. Richard A. Cohen (Pittsburgh: Duquesne University Press, 1999); and Levinas, *Beyond the Verse*, for many of Levinas's Talmudic Readings.

more (and nothing less) than Levinas making a Husserlian variation on a familiar Bergsonian theme regarding the irreversible directionality of time. In section nine, while contrasting Husserl's notion of intentionality with the medieval notion of the same, Levinas parenthetically refers to "Saint Anselm's argument" regarding levels of being. But this reference is not developed and stands as an allusion. Finally, in section thirteen, Levinas again mentions God, but only to say that one "cannot take seriously the brief indications Husserl gives about God in the *Ideas.*" It is surely not to these remarks, little more than asides, that we must turn to see the essential links joining exposition, phenomenology, and the beginnings of an ethical account of consciousness and meaning.

Rather, to understand and appreciate Levinas's insights and innovations, we must take up the task named in the title of Levinas's article: we must enter into the *work* of Edmund Husserl (just as with Hegel one must enter into the "labor of thought"), attending not to passing remarks or allusions, but to an existence discovered and to the discovering of it. Levinas does not simply write "about" phenomenology, as if one could track its intuitions while remaining safely somewhere else, at a distance; he engages phenomenological thought, following Husserl's directions, pursuing his visions, and at the same time keeping the distance that science itself requires. We shall focus our attention on section six, entitled "Intentionality." Here, Levinas begins with *intentionality* and ends with *intuition*, two pillars of phenomenology, or so Levinas had presented them a decade earlier in *The Theory of Intuition in Husserl's Phenomenology*, as we saw earlier in chapter 2.

We are all familiar with the phenomenological account of consciousness as intentionality: to be conscious is always to be conscious-of . . . something. It is in all the introductions to phenomenology. But Levinas wants to make sure that we grasp the true sense of intentionality. It is *not* a celebration of the *relation* or *correlation* between "subject" and "object," since for Husserl intentionality "is nothing like the relations between real objects." Phenomenology – by means of its famous *epoche* – precisely overcomes the naïveté of all forms of realism. Rather, and Levinas underlines this point, intentionality "*is essentially the act of bestowing a meaning.*" Hence the exteriority of the "object" of intentional consciousness has a different sense than that of the object of the pre-phenom-enological attitude, the naïvely encountered so-called "real" object. Unlike the real object, the intentional object is the object *as meant*, the object as an object *of consciousness*. This is a big difference. The phenomenological epoch opens the scientific inquirer – the phenomenologist – to the character of consciousness as meaning bestowing (*Sinngebung*).

Levinas continues and deepens his analysis of the intentional essence of consciousness, consciousness as meaning bestowal. To bestow meaning is to *identify*. "For Husserl to think is to identify." Logicians characterize this activity as predication, the work of the copula, and symbolize its schematic form as "S is p" ("Subject" is "predicate"). But Husserl's conception is broader, for he finds identification in all meaning constitution, whether linguistic (and propositional), perceptual, emotive, memorial, or otherwise. Fur-thermore, so Levinas continues, to identify is to *synthesize*, to gather together the diverse, to find unity in multiplicity. And it turns out that the unity of these mental operations – meaning as identifying, identifying as synthesizing – is precisely what Husserl means by *representation*. In chapter two we spoke of Husserl's predilection for the theoretical. Now we can see even more clearly why Husserl, beyond his scientific bent, has this preference: it is precisely be-cause he sees at the heart of conscious activity the activity of meaning bestowal or representation. Because meanings depend on representation, a theoretical consciousness underlies all meaning.

Highlighting the fundamental movements of consciousness with simple yet striking formulations, Levinas allows us to see how for Husserl representation is "at once universal and primary." While there are many different kinds of intentionality, such as, perceiv-ing-perceived, desiring-desired, feeling-felt, judging-judged, and so on, each with its own regional integrity, all of them revolve around synthesizing acts. Identification, synthesis, that is, repre-sentation, is the *idée fixe* of Husserl's conception of consciousness, the Ariadne's thread running through all intentionality. Thus, Levinas writes, "representation, in the sense we have just specified, is found necessarily at the basis of intention, even non-theoretical intention." "Through this synthesis all mental life participates in representation."

Consciousness grasped as intentional activity, according to Husserl's account, thus lends itself to two foci. On the one hand there are the various non-theoretical intentions, such as perception, memory, imagination, feeling, in their *regional integrity* and inter-relationships. On the other hand, there is the trans-regional *representational core* of all intentional activity. As we know, without neglecting substantial studies of the former (e.g., "time," "life world"), Husserl, in his published works, not only tended to con- centrate on the latter (e.g., "logic," "signifying") but also often seemed to exaggerate its significance and become mired in the methodological difficulties to which its primacy led. This duality within phenomenology – between specific regions of meaning and a trans-regional representational core – accounts also for its great fecundity and for the wide divergences that would separate Husserl's greatest disciples. Emphasis on the intentional integrity of non-theoretical regions of signification played, according to Levinas, "a considerable role in the phenomenologies of Scheler and Heidegger," for example. In contrast, we can say, emphasis on a simplified or stripped down version of the representational core of consciousness served as the centerpiece of Sartre's existential phenomenology.[16]

By grasping will, feeling, desire, judgment, etc., not as real things (not, that is to say, in terms of "primary" "objective" qualities and "secondary" "subjective" qualities) but as *meanings* legitimate in their own right, whole new regions of signification could now be taken no less seriously by phenomenological science than the more limited set of quantifiable significations ("space," "force," "movement," etc.) which alone the natural sciences had hitherto taken seriously. Phenomenology, then, as Husserl insisted, would be genuine science, comprehensive knowledge. It would be science not by rejecting but by integrating the natural sciences into their proper and broader horizons of sense. Indeed, Levinas will claim that precisely the legitimization of multiple non-theoretical regions of signification, overturning the naïvely realist prejudices of the natural attitude and pre-

---

[16] Sartre's truncation of Husserl's conception already appeared in 1936 in *The Transcendence of the Ego*, trans. Forrest Williams and Robert Kirkpatrick (New York: The Noonday Press, 1957).

phenomenological science, "is perhaps the most fecund idea contributed by phenomenology" – despite Husserl's own predilection for the representational core of consciousness.

But Levinas's "exposition" does not stop here, where many others, in the name of one region of signification or another, or by way of recoiling from Husserl's predilection for theory, have chosen to deride or derail Husserl. As an expositor and a philosopher, Levinas probes further in an effort not to shadow but to shed light on the significance of the primacy Husserl saw in representation. Levinas is phenomenologist enough to know that phenomenology is a science, hence an ongoing, self-correcting, communal venture, anathema to all scholasticism, all merely logical avoidance of contradiction. Phenomenology demands *Leistung*, a production or performance by the inquirer; it requires the *work* of thought. All its results, all of its claims, remain tentative, more or less secure hypotheses to be verified, confirmed, disconfirmed, deepened, broadened, recontextualized, reconstructed, and otherwise reworked by seekers of truth who are themselves always part of a larger community of inquirers, and of humanity more widely. In a word, one must think through phenomenological results, to confirm or question them. Thus it is in the true spirit of Husserlian phenomenology that Levinas refuses to stand on some high horse (for or against theory), but rather asks of Husserl: "What is the significance of the presence of the act of identification at the basis of intentions that have nothing intellectual about them?" Answering this, Levinas will come to the final link joining identification and intuition.

If for Husserl representation lies at the bottom of all forms of consciousness, it is because identification culminates in *self-evidence*, in the self-evident. This point is so fundamental and so important – for any epistemological interest, that is to say, for any interest in truth – that it is difficult to grasp why so many philosophers seem to have lost sight of it. Whatever one might say or want from a "theoretical" or ideological point of view, *de facto*, consciousness always has a stop, is conscious of . . . *something*. If it is to have a stop for a *scientific* consciousness, that is to say, in the name of the *true*, that stop must be brought about through carefully controlled, repeatable intuitions into self-evident givens. Such is the zero point of phenomenological science. "The process of identification can be infinite," Levinas notes, "but it is concluded in self-evidence – in the presence of the object in person before consciousness."

Despite certain logical or formal temptations to deny the impact of self-evidence, despite the wilder ideological appeal of a Heraclitean vertigo, the seductive fanfare of "dissemination" or "deferral" of commitment, the alleged freedom of a purely "virtual" reality, Husserlian intentionality is not reducible to some interesting or provocative form of the "bad infinite." It is not reducible to a fancied regress of consciousness-of . . . consciousness-of . . . consciousness-of . . . ad infinitum (or, on the semiotic level: sense-of . . . sense-of . . . sense-of . . . ad infinitum). The primitive *fact* – like it or not – is that there is meaning. Meaning makes sense. The philosophical task is not to make nonsense of sense, which is easy enough, and happens all the time (and not just in academia), but to make sense of sense. Regardless of all superstructures of meaning (economic, psychoanalytic, sociological, ideological, historical, etc.), there is meaning, Husserl claims, because representation, which is the ultimate movement of consciousness, ends in self-evidence.

This means, in turn, that intentionality and intuition, representation and self-evidence, are linked. Their meeting is neither arbitrary, nor prudent, nor weak. It is not a function. It is not undercut by metaphysics. It is presupposed and not a presupposition. Levinas succinctly captures the connection: "Self-evidence realizes, as it were, the aspirations of identification." Thus we reach the answer to Levinas's probing question regarding the privileged status of representation for Husserl. "To say that at the basis of every intention – even affective or relative intentions – representation is found, is to conceive the whole of mental life on the model of light." (Here, too, by the way, is where Levinas makes the remark cited above: "The miracle of clarity is the very miracle of thought.") Intentionality *qua* representation, consciousness undergirded and guaranteed by intuition ending in self-evidence, "is the very penetration to the true." "The theory of intentionality in Husserl," Levinas writes, "identifies mind with intellection, and intellection with light." Phenomenology is science, knowledge, light – the light of all lights. Husserl is a scientist, come what may – to the end.

Having penetrated thus far, it is precisely at this point in his exposition, at the true depths of Husserl's thought, that Levinas – philosopher – will "discover" a novel interpretation. What Levinas discovers is that with Husserl's theory of intentional consciousness, linked as it is to intuition and hence to self-evidence, a new way is opened to mediate the difference between *constituting and constituted meaning.* Let us recall the itinerary of phenomenology. Husserl's approach is to discover in the givenness of meaning (found in the natural attitude) a constituted meaning (after the epoche), that is, meaning constituted by consciousness. Further, he discovers in the conscious constitution of meaning, consciousness as meaning bestowal, the self-constitution of consciousness (after the "transcendental reduction"), hence the absolute origin of all meaning constitution in "absolute consciousness." Thus while it is true that consciousness has a stop in self-evidence, it is no less true that consciousness – now "absolute consciousness" – reappropriates that self-evidence into itself as its absolute source. Here, then, lies the "idealist" tendency of Husserl's thought in his preference for representation. It is this tendency that his disciples reject.

Levinas, for his part, will see in the conjunction of constituted and constituting a completely novel approach to signification, and a completely novel signification of signification. Levinas writes:

If we wanted to distance ourselves from Husserl's terminology and characteristic mode of expression, we would say that self-evidence is a unique situation: in the case of self-evidence the mind, *while receiving something foreign, is also the origin of what it receives* [my italics]. It is always active. The fact that in self-evidence the world is a given, that there is always a given for the mind, is not only found to be in agreement with the idea of activity, but is presupposed by that activity. A given world is a world where we can be free without this freedom being purely negative. The self-evidence of a given world – more than the non-engagement of the mind in things – is the positive accomplishment of freedom. The primacy of theory in Husserl's philosophy is ultimately linked to the liberal inspiration that we are seeking to make clear through this essay. The light of self-evidence is the sole tie with being that posits us as an origin of being, that is, as freedom.

I am certainly not going to say that we can discover in this citation a full-blown version of Levinas's ethical metaphysics. That would be a retrospective fallacy. I do want to suggest, however, that in this conjunction of activity and passivity at the deepest depths of consciousness, in which "the mind, while receiving something foreign, is also the origin of what it receives," we have something very much like the *structure* of the ruptured consciousness – a "more" in a "less," "dia-chrony," a passivity outside the reach of conscious activity – that in his own thought becomes the ethical root of consciousness and the deeper core of subjectivity. What we witness, in "The Work of Edmund Husserl," is that interaction of active intentional consciousness and passive non-intentional con- sciousness, that "intimate incarnation,"[17] that in his own thought Levinas will distinguish not in terms of "reflective" and "pre- reflective consciousness," as does Husserl, as if passivity were always only an unclear or indistinct thought, but in terms of a deeper moral conflict between the equilibrium of "good con- science" and the disturbance of "bad conscience." Passivity – beneath identity, without status, vulnerable, exposed – does not simply raise the question of truth or of being, but rather, *more urgently*, for Levinas, it raises the issue of one's "right to be."[18] Of course, this ethical elaboration is just barely found, just hinted at, in 1940.

Already, in "The Work of Edmund Husserl," Levinas detects in the conjunction of constituting meaning and constituted meaning, activity and passivity, a new form of freedom and the "liberal inspiration" of Husserlian phenomenology. Freedom henceforth means neither an absorption in an intellectualized real – whether Spinoza's substance, Hegel's spirit or Heidegger's being or four- fold – nor a "non-engagement of the mind in things" – whether Kant's transcendental apperception, Brunschvicg's judgment, Husserl's transcendental ego, or Sartre's for-itself. Freedom is neither in-the-world nor out-of-the-world, but both at the same time, constituted by what it constitutes, "the origin of what it receives." Again, we detect a Bergsonian theme. What Levinas discovers, then, in existence – *in nuce*, in a 1940 Husserlian

---

[17] "Ethics as First Philosophy," in Levinas, *The Levinas Reader*, p. 79.
[18] Ibid., pp. 82, 86.

meditation – is a central motif of his own ethical metaphysics: "finite"[19] or "difficult"[20] freedom.

Levinas continues, in section eleven, entitled "The Ego, Time, and Freedom":

Thought is thus not simply a domain in which the ego manifests its freedom; the fact of having meaning – is the very manifestation of freedom. The opposition between activity and theory is eliminated by Husserl in his conception of self-evidence. This is the whole originality of his theory of intentionality and freedom. Intentionality is nothing but the very accomplishment of freedom.

Freedom and meaning are thus linked, arise together and are bound to one another. To reduce one to the other, for whatever purpose, whether for knowledge or for being, would only create abstractions of both, distorting the meaning of meaning into an arbitrary construct (abstract freedom) or an infallible oracle (abstract necessity).

Levinas sees the concrete intersection of freedom and meaning to be especially evident at the level of consciousness that Husserl (and Heidegger) take to be ultimate, namely, consciousness in its temporal self-constitution. "[N]ote," Levinas writes, "that the antinomy of spontaneity and passivity is eliminated in the mind grasped at the level of the *Urimpression*." Levinas brings this "Husserlian" insight to bear against what is surely Heidegger's conception of fundamental "historicity." He continues: "Here also Husserl remains faithful to his fundamental metaphysical intentions: mind is the inwardness of a meaning to thought, the freedom of intellection. Time accomplishes this freedom; it does not exist prior to the mind, does not engage it in a history in which it could be overwhelmed. Historical time is constituted. History is explained by thought." That history does not overwhelm consciousness, that historical time is both constituting and constituted, does this not mean that consciousness understood as real freedom, as the zero point and unity of activity and passivity, *is at once made by history and makes the history it is made by*? And does this not mean that, as becomes explicit in Levinas's later writings, going beyond

---

[19] See Emmanuel Levinas, *Totalité et infini* (The Hague: Martinus Nijhoff, 1961), p. 199; *Totality and Infinity*, trans. A. Lingis (Pittsburgh: Duquesne University Press, 1969), p. 223; and "Finite Freedom," in *Otherwise than Being or Beyond Essence*, pp. 121–129.

[20] *Difficult Freedom* is the title of a collection of Jewish writings by Levinas (see n. 12).

Husserl, a truly human freedom is one capable of *judging* history?[21] And thus that therefore ethics precedes ontology? Levinas will say yes: metaphysics (relation to the absolutely other) precedes ontology, and therefore one can judge the history within which one is engaged. We will return to Levinas's confrontation with Heidegger in the next chapter. Now I wish to continue our examination of the intersection of activity and passivity at the heart of consciousness by turning, with Levinas, to certain differences between Husserl and Kant.

In a later article of 1959, "Intentionality and Metaphysics" (included in the expanded second edition of *Discovering Existence with Husserl and Heidegger*), Levinas explicitly takes Husserl to task for interpreting the intersection of constituting and constituted as a "little perception."[22] Husserl's interpretation serves only to reproduce rather than to account for the excess – the "non-intentionality" – in consciousness that he had in fact discovered. Though Levinas acknowledges the "great contribution" of Husserl's account of intentionality, because it forever undermines a subject–object interpretation of consciousness and meaning, he joins Kant in characterizing the alterity of freedom in *moral* rather than in theoretical terms. Thus in the same paragraph of this 1959 article, Levinas will note: "Kant refuses to interpret transcendental activity as intuitive . . . Here Kant is bolder than Husserl."[23] The excess Husserl himself calls "transcendence within immanence" must, for Levinas, as for Kant, lie altogether outside an epistemological framework altogether, hence beyond the reach of intuition. What Husserl discovered – passivity – at the heart of consciousness (the activity of meaning bestowal) was "something" beyond evidence, hence beyond phenomenology proper.

For Levinas the paradoxical notion of the passivity of conscious-

---

[21] One could cite from many of Levinas's writings. From a "Jewish" writing: "But must we not accord to man the right to judge, in the name of moral conscience, the history to which on the one hand he belongs, rather than leave his right to judge to anonymous history?" "A Religion for Adults," in *Difficult Freedom*, p. 23. From a "philosophical" writing: "Though of myself I am not exterior to history, I do find in the Other a point that is absolute with regard to history – not by amalgamating with the Other, but in speaking with him. History is worked over by the ruptures of history, in which a judgment is borne upon it. When man truly approaches the Other he is uprooted from history." *Totality and Infinity*, p. 52.

[22] Levinas, "Intentionality and Metaphysics," in *Discovering Existence with Husserl*, p. 134.

[23] Ibid., p. 124.

ness indicates that consciousness, per impossibile, is imposed upon, "put" upon – but obviously not by a "given," not by "evidence." Rather, the only exteriority "adequate" to the passivity of consciousness is a passivity that must exceed the very adequacy or telos of consciousness itself, exceed its intentional character. An "outside" that remains outside, exterior to knowledge, beyond its reach, otherwise than a knowing, can only come to consciousness as moral imperative – what Levinas will call the "face" (*visage*) of the other person. The passivity of consciousness, in other words, indicates not an epistemological failure, but the inalterable "fact" that consciousness has been "put into question" – moral question – by the other person. Somehow consciousness is made conscious beyond its power of thematizing or representing. Thus consciousness is made to be more awake than intentional consciousness, and this "more awake" is precisely, so Levinas will argue, a moral sensibility, a responsiveness to the other's moral demands – that is, responsibility, moral election. Only a moral alterity would be other enough, as it were, to "strike" consciousness into passivity. We will return to these themes.

Beyond their formal agreement that consciousness cannot be contained by the activity of knowing, Levinas and Kant part company, however, regarding the character of the morality that exceeds representational consciousness. For Kant, who remains bound to the very epistemological perspective whose limits he saw with utmost clarity, the transcendence of morality transpires as respect for self-legislated law, the same law in the other as in oneself. For Levinas, in contrast, the rupture of transcendence – the impossible passivity of consciousness – occurs as the alterity of the other person impinging on self-consciousness, overloading it as moral obligation, in an inescapable yet non-contractual responsibility to and for the other. The passivity of consciousness means that it is humbled, as it were, by an excess not fully its own, outside its reach, beyond its grasp, yet nonetheless still meaningful, even if Husserl – understandably – re-inscribed this horizon and excess into the space of a scientific epistemology.

The path Levinas blazes in 1940, via Husserl, will of course be elaborated, developed and amplified in his subsequent writings. No doubt it is true, too, that we are able to detect the originality of

Levinas's early reading of Husserl because of its subsequent elaboration. Ethics is the very heart of Levinas's thought. His special contribution to philosophy has precisely been to show this centrality. Not only does he say that ethics is the heart of philosophy (as had already been argued by those who make Kant's second *Critique* [*of Practical Reason*] primary, or by the very life of Socrates), but he thinks and writes in such a way that thought and life truly begin in ethics. Levinas's ethical metaphysics serves as a powerful wedge for a radical critique of the dominant post-Husserlian phenomenologies of the early and mid twentieth century. That ethics precedes ontology will be reason to reject Heidegger, as we will see in the next chapter, and reason to revise Merleau-Ponty, to the extent that Merleau-Ponty continues within the ontological horizons opened up by Heidegger. That freedom involves passivity will be reason to reject the purity of Sartre's "existentialist" freedom.[24]

Levinas's 1940 reflections on Husserl – of course seen with hindsight – also provide us some foresight into the intimate relation Levinas will see between the science of phenomenology and the disciplined freedom characteristic of Talmudic commentary and hence of Jewish life, life imbued with Torah, exegetical existence, in its broadest sense. Eliciting and elicited eliciting one another, "letters" (text) calling for "spirit" (commentary), spirit finding itself through letters – is this not, in another register, the consciousness that Husserl describes,[25] even if he remained bound to an inadequate epistemology to interpret his own discovery (as did Kant more than a century earlier)? Levinas is the first to have seen the deeper consequences of Husserl's insights into the passivity of consciousness. He is the first to have seen that the surplus of consciousness is not an epistemological anomaly, but an ethical

[24] *La transcendence de l'ego* had been published four years earlier in 1936; *Being and Nothingness* would be published three years later in 1943, making no mention of Levinas's Husserl studies. Heidegger, for his part, never responded to or even mentioned Levinas's Husserl studies, his ethical metaphysics, or his radical critique of Heideggerian thought.

[25] In the light of all the above, it is fascinating to read, in Dorion Cairns' diary of his conversations with Husserl and Eugen Fink, the following entry for 12 November 1931: "Husserl said that in the Gottingen days [1901–1916] he used to describe '*originär*' *Gegebenheit* ('originary' givenness) as the object calling out, '*Ich bin da!*' ('Here I am!')." Dorion Cairns, *Conversations with Husserl and Fink*, ed. by the Husserl-Archives in Louvain (The Hague: Martinus Nijhoff, 1976), p. 40.

surplus. Consciousness would be – paradoxically – bound by that from which it is free, and freed by that to which it is bound. Consciousness would thus find itself deeper than its own *origin* and *arche*, "traumatized," as Levinas will later say, by the "an-archy" of an irretrievable *beginning – Bereshit* (בראשית) – lived concretely as the moral priority of the other.

Is this "discovery," hinted at in a Husserlian meditation of 1940, so far, then, from the "figure of inspiration" to which Levinas refers, commenting on a commentary, in 1985: "They say the Levites who carried the Holy Ark of the Tabernacle across the desert were also carried by that Ark: a parable that is probably the true figure of inspiration."?[26] Is it not also a recognizable if distant version of what Levinas means when he writes: "[T]here is an inseparable bond between God's descent and his eleva-tion"?[27] And would not Jacob's ladder – angels going up and down, transcendence linked to immanence – be yet another figure of such inspired reading, the very discovery of existence?

One final question: Was Husserl unaware of the ethical dimen-sions of his thought? Who can believe it? Husserl, whose voice rang like a clarion cry in the dark days of the 1930s, certainly grasped the centrality of ethics, even if for him it was still the ethics of science, hence an ethics instrumental for a scientific humanity. Husserl's vision of ethics, bound to his deeper commitment to science, will in no way be Levinas's. Yet, do we not sense the presence of Levinas in Husserl when, not despite his attachment to science but because of it, we discover Husserl – in a conversation with Eugen Fink, on 22 September 1931 – speak of the telos of science as being dependent on the *honesty* of scientists? Truth dependent on sincerity – this will be a central theme of *Totality and Infinity*. Why, finally, are we not at all surprised that Husserl continued this conversation about science by invoking Dostoyevsky? Nor are we entirely astonished that he quoted pre-cisely the one sentence from *The Brothers Karamazov* that Levinas, decades later, will cite repeatedly.[28] "I must be able to affirm the

---

[26] From "Judaism and Kenosis," in Emmanuel Levinas, *In the Time of the Nations*, trans. Michael B. Smith (Bloomington: Indiana University Press, 1994), p. 121.

[27] Ibid., p. 115.

[28] See, e.g., Levinas, "God and Philosophy," trans. Richard A. Cohen and Alphonso

acts of others as well as my own acts" – so Husserl is reported to have said. And then, the report continues: "Husserl quoted Dostoyevsky as saying each is guilty for the guilt of all."[29]

Lingis, in *The Levinas Reader*, p. 182: "Each of us is guilty before everyone, for everyone and for each one, and I more than others." Of course it is the last part of this citation that is most Levinasian.

[29] Cairns, *Conversations with Husserl and Fink*, p. 35. For Husserl, intellectual dishonesty is a betrayal of humankind. The scientist, discoverer of truth, member of the community of scientists, is responsible to and for all humanity. Levinas, of course, often cites this very same sentence from Dostoyevsky; see, e.g., *Time and the Other*, p. 108; *Ethics and Infinity*, trans. Richard A. Cohen (Pittsburgh: Duquesne University Press, 1985), p. 98; "God and Philosophy," in *The Levinas Reader*, p. 182; "Apropos of Buber: Some Notes," in *Outside the Subject*, trans. Michael B. Smith (Stanford: Stanford University Press, 1993), p. 44.

# CHAPTER 4

# *Better than a questionable Heidegger*

> The whole of biblical thought remains pure silence in
> Heideggerian hermeneutics.
>
> Levinas "Preface,"[1]

An unavoidable issue emerges when it becomes clear that one must go beyond the strictly scientific intent of phenomenology. That is to say, two very different paths surpass Husserl's rigorous and comprehensive science of phenomena: ontology and ethics, being and the good. Up to this point, when here and there we have encountered this issue, for example in Levinas's dissatisfaction with the immanence or "mineness" (*Jemeinigkeit*) of be-ing (despite Heidegger's completely contrary intent[2]), I have repeatedly posed Levinas's ethical metaphysics against Heidegger's fundamental ontology. Heidegger's ontology is not fundamental enough, or rather, because it is fundamental it has lost sight of that which

---

[1] Emmanuel Levinas, "Preface," to Marlène Zarader, *Heidegger et les paroles de l'origine* (Paris: Vrin, 1990). Three relevant rhetorical questions precede the sentence I have cited: "The thought of being – in the subjective and objective sense of this genitive – does it bear no trace whatsoever of that which had arisen before the morning of Greece or which, as Sacred History, had – perhaps inopportunely – inter-vened in the history of being? Do its stories and its prophecies, and its martyrs' miseries, lead only to the counter-senses in the reading of pre-Socratic fragments? Our European history, is it not a becoming whereby an inextinguishable Israel 'happens' [*se passe*] – *sich ereignet* – in the midst of a Christian Europe?"

[2] Levinas is quite aware of Heidegger's contrary intent. He writes: "In the finitude of time the 'being-toward-death' of *Being and Time* sketches out – despite all the renewals of handed down philosophy that this brilliant book brings – the meaningful remains enclosed within the immanence of the *Jemeinigkeit* of the *Dasein* that *has to be* and that thus – in spite of the denunciation of being as presence – still belongs to a philosophy of presence." Levinas, "Diachrony and Representation," in Emmanuel Levinas, *Time and the Other and Additional Essays*, trans. Richard A. Cohen (Pittsburgh: Duquesne University Press, 1987), pp. 115–116.

exceeds even the fundamental, that is, the meta-physical, the "good beyond being." In this chapter we will consider the opposition between ontology and ethics more closely. There can be no doubt that Heidegger's thought, and its prolongation by his epigones (Derrida perhaps first and foremost among them), has found a large following, to put the matter in merely sociological terms. But its allure is deeper than sociology, or rather, its sociological effect follows from its deeper allure. Or so it claims.

Of course, with the name Heidegger, one cannot be fully or even partially responsible if one ignores other questions, disturbing questions. But perhaps, except for certain sycophantic followers (and Heidegger has had them), these are not at all "other" questions. Let us see. In any event, here I will not explicitly examine the terrible but necessary question – rather the fact – of Heidegger's Nazi politics. It is nonetheless an unavoidable issue, and does indeed reappear, in more or less disguised form, even when it is not sought for, and perhaps especially then. In this chapter the matter at hand is not politics, however, or not politics directly. Rather it is the question of two radically different approaches to philosophy, or, more precisely, two radically opposed approaches to philosophy.[3] It is first a matter of appreciating – understanding, grasping – what and how Heidegger's thought thinks, what it accomplishes. But to appreciate is not necessarily to agree or to affirm. With Levinas's aid we will indeed glimpse limitations in Heideggerian thought, limitations that Heidegger himself, to be sure, but also so many Heideggerians, have had great difficulty acknowledging. This difficulty is itself a symptom, it seems to me, of a deeper difficulty. Or it is a compound of a limitation: immanence blinded by self-absorption, in a blindness that plagues Heideggerian thought, as if its very close-mindedness were the sign of its open-mindedness.[4] The issue in this chapter, then, has to do

---

[3] Adriaan Peperzak, *Beyond: The Philosophy of Emmanuel Levinas* (Evanston: Northwestern University Press, 1997), in a chapter entitled "On Levinas's Criticism of Heidegger," puts this same point as follows: "The greatest difficulty of a confrontation between Heidegger and Levinas is that they do not give two answers to one and the same question, but ask two different yet kindred questions, as is always the case when radical thinkers approach the origins of reality and thought" (p. 205).

[4] I am not thinking specifically of the authorial "blindness" that for Paul de Man, in *Blindness and Insight: Essays in the Rhetoric of Contemporary Criticism*, 2nd revised edition (Minneapolis: University of Minnesota Press, 1983), opens the door to critical "insight,"

with the very nature of philosophy or, if you will, with life, with the proper height of metaphysics, and the proper depth of ontology, according to Heidegger and Levinas.

The critique of metaphysics in our day has not been a simple revival of the Enlightenment attack on provincialism and superstition. Grown more wary, it is an attack on the surface as well as the soul of Western metaphysics. It is an attack on "presence" as such, on the "metaphysics of presence," the overt and covert drive toward presence, self-presence, evidence, self-evidence, certainty, self-certainty. "Metaphysics," Heidegger pronounces, "is the history of this truth. It tells us what what-is is by conceptualizing the 'is-ness' of what-is. In the is-ness of what-is metaphysics thinks the thought of Being, but without being able to reflect on the truth of Being with its particular mode of thought."[5] Heidegger has taught us to grasp and to *think* – rather than to conceptualize or "calculate" – through the subtle metaphysics that hides in language, in the self-presence of its formal, representational, foundational, willful and subjectivist tendencies. To learn to think, to think Being, or to think the thinking of Being, the philosopher must learn from poets,[6] from those who listen.

something on the model of the "Freudian slip." Rather, having raised the name of Paul de Man (d. 1983), I am thinking of a deeper and more dangerous moral blindness, e.g., the blindness that prevented (and still prevents) the Derridaian Heideggerians (including Derrida) from denouncing – or even acknowledging! – the grievous *moral* error of the young Paul de Man, who for two years, from 1940 to 1942, provided active journalistic support for the Nazi cause in his native Belgium. On this sorry chapter in twentieth-century intellectual history, see the excellent account – scholarly, balanced and with its moral compass intact – by David Lehman, *Signs of the Times: Deconstruction and the Fall of Paul de Man* (New York: Simon & Schuster, 1992). Because it came afterwards, the de Man chapter is in its own way even sorrier than the original Heidegger chapter, that is, the scandal of the Heideggerians who for decades minimized the fact and significance of Heidegger's pre-war and wartime Nazi party membership, and his (loud) post-war silence. On the latter, see Victor Farias, *Heidegger and Nazism*, ed. Joseph Margolis and Tom Rockmore, French trans. Paul Burrell, German trans. Gabriel R. Ricci (Philadelphia: Temple University Press, 1989).

5  Heidegger, "What is Metaphysics?" trans. R. F. C. Hull and Alan Crick, in Martin Heidegger, *Existence and Being*, ed. Werner Brock (Chicago: Henry Regnery Co., 1949), p. 351.

6  Heidegger very often comments on poems. In *What is Called Thinking?*, trans. Fred D. Wieck and J. Glenn Gray (New York: Harper & Row, 1968), originally published in 1954 (*Was Heisst Denken?*), he writes: "What is stated poetically, and what is stated in thought, are never identical; but there are times when they are the same – those times when the gulf separating poesy and thinking is a clean and decisive cleft. This can occur when poesy is lofty, and thinking profound" (p. 20). See also Martin Heidegger, *Poetry, Language, Thought*, trans. Albert Hofstadter (New York: Harper & Row, 1971).

Heidegger has taught that the history of Western thought and culture since its Greek beginnings has been an "onto-theology," an "ontic" theology in the guise of ontology.[7] What is truly present is not the hidden or manifest unfolding of what is, but *a being* with more being (real or eminent being) than the passing show of existence (appearance). This preeminent being – idea, energy, substance, position, concept, dialectic, will to power, will to will – would serve as the model or foundation for what being its poor relations – beings – might have. The world would be but the reflection, the re-presentation, of God, substance, transcendental ego, and so on. Beings in the world, then, are images of a being beyond the world, and philosophy would be the detection of that true being beyond its appearances. But none of this would be "thinking," the thinking of Being, Being's thinking, as Heidegger understands it. To think would be to hearken to the voice – to the language – of Be-ing.

Against the idealism of onto-theo-logy, Heidegger reintroduces the world to thought. Focused neither on beings in the world nor on a being beyond the world, he turns to being-in-the-world as such, the "worldhood" (*Weltlichkeit*) of the world. "This possibility of conceiving contingency and facticity not as facts presented to intellection but as the act of intellection," Levinas wrote in 1951, "constitutes the great novelty of contemporary ontology."[8] Because consciousness is intentional, as Husserl taught, and intentionality is not a subject–object relationship, as Husserl also taught, meaning arises out of an engagement, an involvement, an interaction between constituting and constituted. Rejecting Husserl's reduction to "absolute consciousness," Heidegger will characterize this interaction in the most concrete terms, first of all in terms of a mortal human existence and then, more deeply, in terms of the epochal historical situation in which human existence is embedded and from which it derives its meaning. Thus he thinks of the world, this world in its historical coming to be and passing away, the "worlding" of the world, as being pre-

[7] See Heidegger, "The Onto-Theo-Logical Constitution of Metaphysics," in Martin Heidegger, *Identity and Difference* [*Identität und Differenz*, 1957], trans. Joan Stambaugh (New York: Harper & Row, 1969), pp. 42–74.

[8] Levinas, "Is Ontology Fundamental?," in Emmanuel Levinas, *Entre Nous*, trans. Michael B. Smith and Barbara Harshav (New York: Columbia University Press, 1998), p. 2.

served and revealed – for the philosopher and poet – in language, "the house of being." Heidegger proposes the difficult task of thinking without recourse to the metaphysics of presence, teasing language from its accumulated epistemological biases, open to the very "openness" from out of which meaning arises. Just as Bergson saw in scientific thinking the interest not of pure philosophical speculation but rather of practical activity, and just as Husserl saw in the "natural attitude" an unexamined, and hence naïve, realism, Heidegger sees in ordinary knowing and theory a deadening epistemological prejudice toward self-presence and self-certainty. Opposing this tendency, Heidegger seeks the "essence of truth" elsewhere, in what he calls Being's donation of meaning, the verbality of be-ing, freed of the narrowing logic of non-contradiction, identity, and presence – freed, that is to say, of the forcing and manhandling constitutive of metaphysics. Heidegger has sought this language even if it meant, indeed precisely inasmuch as it requires, the "destruction" (what Derrida later called "deconstruction") of the entire history of Western thought. Nonetheless, extending a long tradition, like Descartes and Husserl, and like many other philosophers who sought solid foundations for truth, Heidegger would be a "beginner." His beginning, however, would be not with the human but with Be-ing. "This can occur," Heidegger declared, "when poesy is lofty, and thinking profound."[9] Heady thoughts.

But, before we are carried away in the heights of thinking, if we are indeed privileged with such a gift, let us pause to ask a question one must ask of all things, and hence also of "thinking." It is a question anyone should ask, philosophers included, but it is also a question that the horrors of the twentieth century – the Holocaust above all, or below all – have, we can hope, burned into our consciousness. For it is a burning question: What role is assigned to ethics in such a thought? Heidegger, as we know, rarely speaks of ethics, of the imperatives of morality and justice. His admirers might have us believe that his thought – genuine "thinking" – is too lofty, too precious, too rarified for such merely human concerns. But this is not the place to review the sorry history of denial

[9] See n. 3 and above.

within the Heideggerian camp. What is the role of ethics for *Denken*?

While Heidegger claims his own task is neither to support nor to oppose this or that worldly morality,[10] it becomes clear that with the end of traditional philosophy, the task of genuine thinking is itself an ethics. That is to say, if ethics has to do with moral imperatives, with what is, let us say (without yet specifying), "best" to do, then it is clear that nothing is more important for Heidegger (for Being!) than "thinking." What becomes most needful is a responsibility for the world, a caring for what is as it is, a shepherding, a letting be (*Gelassenheit*), an allowance for being's generosity, an attunement to the gift-giving of worlds. The life of the philosopher/poet is most needful, the greatest imperative, especially in these "most dangerous" times when Be-ing is being silenced by "technology." Heidegger will not hesitate to remind us that for the Greeks, before the corruption of thought – that is, before thought became merely a human construction – "the life of beholding, is, especially in its purest form as thinking, the highest doing."[11] Being, not the human, is to rule. Ontology becomes indebtedness to what is, a quiet listening, vigilant against its own interference, cautious of its own interventions, careful not to disturb. In a word, thinking becomes a loving-kindness. Or, as Heidegger expresses it, "thinking is thanking."

Is being – or be-ing – enough for the ethical? Is not ethics by its nature metaphysical, beyond being? Does it not depend on the essentially metaphysical distinction between "what is," verbal or not, and "what ought to be"? Does not ethics place more weight on the question of one's "right to be" than on the question (of the philosophers, and Hamlet) of being or non-being? Would this not mean, as Heidegger supposes, that ethics is essentially confined to ontics, and hence can rise no higher than to onto-theo-logy, to the

---

[10] In *Being and Time*, Heidegger simply locates the core structure of Dasein, i.e., "being-guilty" (*Schuldigsein*) or "care" (*Sorge*), at a "deeper" level than morality. Thus he can write: "The primordial 'Being-guilty' cannot be defined by morality, since morality already presupposes it for itself" (Section 58, p. 332). Moralities, then, would be "ontic," while Dasein, when it is authentically itself (*eigentlich*), is "ontological," the "issue (*darum*) of being."

[11] Martin Heidegger, *The Question Concerning Technology and Other Essays*, trans. William Lovitt (New York: Harper & Row, 1977), p. 164.

sanctions a being claims to hold over beings, unable to be "appropriated by" (*Ereignis*) the profounder significance of the "ontological difference"? These are ultimate, and hence difficult, questions.

For Nietzsche, like Heidegger, the era of metaphysics – the history of a long error[12] – the moralization of beings, the blindness of subjectivism, is over, exposed, unmasked in its deceptive presumptions. A new age and a new humanity are called for, an age of honesty, courage and innocence. Henceforth, existence will be affirmed joyously, gaily, in its coming to be and its passing away, in its expenditure without reservation, its bountifulness. Henceforth our obligations will be our own, to our own forces, resolute, authentic, in the self-conscious creation of value or, as Heidegger would have it, in the quiet hearkening to being. Ontology would be deeper than ethics as the will to power and being are deeper than self-deceptive human ideologies.

And yet Levinas insists on ethics, on a metaphysical responsibility, an exorbitant and infinite responsibility for other human beings, to care not for being, for the unraveling of its plot, nor to open the gates of a repressed will to power, but to care for what is beyond and against being, moved first by the alterity of the other person. The deepest question consists not in the question of being, but rather in the question of the self's *right* to be. And this question, raising issues beyond the reach of – and more important than – phenomenology and ontology, can only be answered "otherwise than being or beyond essence." The answer to this question, which presses harder – is more *urgent*, more emphatic – than the question of being, determines the answers to all other questions. Ethics would thus precede ontology.

In speaking this way, has Levinas perhaps misunderstood the critique of metaphysics? Is his yet another, even if subtler, return to slave morality, a fall into ontics, a forgetfulness of being, weighed down by the spirit of gravity? It is an irrepressible question, but let us also note that his writings provoke us to ask what *is* the status of ethics in a post-metaphysical age? Does the end of onto-theo-logy at the same time mean the end of metaphysics? Was metaphysics

---

[12] See Friedrich Nietzsche, *Twilight of the Idols*, "How the 'True World' Finally Became a Fable: The History of an Error," trans. Walter Kaufmann, in *The Portable Nietzsche*, ed. and trans. Walter Kaufmann (New York: Viking Press, 1954), pp. 485–486.

only onto-theo-logy, philosophy of presence? Levinas's unique place is to say no. His unique place is to insist that, quite to the contrary, ethics only comes into its own with the collapse of onto-theo-logy. This is not a matter of reversing a reversal. It is rather to appreciate the value of the critique ("destruction" [*Destruktion*],[13] "deconstruction") of onto-theo-logy without over-valuing and distorting that critique by totalizing it.

For Levinas, the critique of metaphysics, the critique of the philosophy of presence, indeed ends onto-theo-logical ethics, the ethics of transcendent sanction, of other-worldly principles and rules. Yet in the *correctness* of the critique of metaphysics he discerns another alternative than the joyous dance of existence, the poetic language of being, or – here we are thinking of Heidegger's disciple, Derrida, but there are many others besides him – the playful, detached games of language. Ethics is more serious, more pressing. He discerns that with the critique of the philosophy of presence we can now recognize that all along ontology, whether onto-theo-logical or not, has been the wrong standard for ethics, that it is an *inferior* standard. Ethics not only survives the so-called "end of metaphysics," it finally (and perhaps first) comes into its own with that end. How is this so?

Here again, precautions must be taken. Heidegger has taught us the care for language. It has been suggested – by Heidegger, and by Derrida more recently[14] – that philosophy lies in a certain questioning and not in answers. "For questioning," Heidegger writes, "is the piety of thought."[15] The real difficulty with question-ing, however, lies in the questions themselves, in the places they can take us unawares. Presupposed in the question of the status of ethics, so we are taught by the philosophy of questioning, is the

---

[13] See Martin Heidegger, *What is Philosophy?*, trans. Jean T. Wilde and William Kluback (New Haven: College & University Press, no date), pp. 71–73: "Destruction does not mean destroying but dismantling, liquidating, putting to one side the merely historical assertions about the history of philosophy. Destruction means – to open our ears, to make ourselves free for what speaks to us in tradition as the Being of beings."

[14] That philosophy lies in questioning and not in answers is a constant theme of both Heidegger and Derrida. See my *Elevations: The Height of the Good in Rosenzweig and Levinas* (Chicago: University of Chicago Press, 1994), chapter fourteen, "Derrida's (Mal)reading of Levinas" (pp. 305–321), especially pp. 307–308.

[15] Heidegger, *The Question Concerning Technology and Other Essays*, trans. Lovitt, p. 35. This citation is the concluding sentence of the article after which this book is named.

question of just what ethics is. What is ethics? Are moralities essentially onto-theo-logical, as Heidegger and Nietzsche insist, or do they manifest something else, something quite different, with different structures and demands, with a different relation to manifestation itself? Could it be that questioning – or a certain sort of questioning, precisely a questioning obsessed with a certain kind of difference, a difference playing between signs, certain signs – cannot see this "difference"? Taking up Heidegger's care for language, but against the tendency of his thinking, as we shall see, we must with no less care uncover the metaphysical intrigues of language – and a "certain" kind of philosophizing – precisely to escape and avoid misunderstanding the status of ethics in a post-onto-theo-logical age. The very questioning of ethics may disguise more than it reveals – a suggestion scandalous for the philosophy of questioning, but more excellent than scandal.

Heidegger's question, the question of essence – which is for him *the* question of philosophy – when applied to ethics, asking "What is ethics?," indeed seems to be the most philosophical of questions. "What is thinking?" "What is poetry?" "What is technology?" And now: "What is ethics?" But if in this question itself we can uncover a hidden onto-theo-logical bent, then we are on the way to grasping its inappropriateness with regard to ethics, if it is the case that ethics survives the end of metaphysics. Perhaps, too, by pursuing this line of inquiry, questioning questioning, the somber aura of mystery and strangeness that surrounds the later writings of Heidegger, his meandering path out of metaphysics by way of certain German poets and pre-Socratic fragments, can be grasped in an entirely new way. But do we not already sense the difference between asking about ethics and asking about thinking, poetry, technology, a thing, and the like? The latter are "reflective," questions about determinations of being. But the former, the ethical, is it a determination of being? Is it not rather a command-ment beyond being?

We know how Heidegger proceeds with his questions. To ask, "What is . . .?" is to ask for the "essence" of what one is asking about. And the "essence" is not within the domain of that about which one asks – poetry, technology, the thing, etc. – but rather opens up the domain of philosophy, or what Heidegger later prefers to call "thinking."[16] The essence of technology is not technological. Technology is a determination of being, but the essence of technology opens up a philosophical reflection on the determination of being. It "allows" or "lets be" Be-ing in its manner of giving beings. So, too, following this logic, the essence of ethics would not be ethical. Ethics, too, would be rooted in the generosity of being. But what if, and this is our *challenge*, the very question of essence, the "What is . . .?" question, is itself metaphysically compromised? What if, in other words, being were not the be-all and end-all?

The mind rebels. What could be more *essential* to any sort of intelligent inquiry, to any sort of thinking, than to ask what something *is*? If it is true that seeking to know what something is no longer means to seek a definition, whether by means of genus and differentia or efficient causality, then it must still mean to discover an essence, as Heidegger would have it, going beyond even the "four causes" of Aristotle: to know the manifestation of what is, and, more deeply, to uncover the gathering and separating of the "ontological difference" that gives out the manifest, the manifestation of the manifest. What is more unavoidable before getting caught up in the directives of ethics, then – or anything else for that matter, such as the "enframing" of technology – than to ask what it is, to ask *what ethics is*, and to discover if ethics is onto-theo-logical and hence metaphysical in the corrupting sense? It is already clear, then, that Heidegger's ontology is "fundamental" in at least two senses. Ontology would require asking of all and everything (ethics included): What is it? It would be an unavoidable and ultimate question. And then, second, philosophical to the end, in answering this question ontology would proceed to raise the question of the meaning of Be-ing as such.

Since Socrates, thought has been intimately tied to the cautions

---

[16] See, e.g., "The Essence of Truth," in Heidegger, *Existence and Being*, trans. Brock, pp. 292–324; Heidegger writes: "*The essence of truth is freedom* . . . Freedom is the *essence* of truth itself. 'Essence' is understood here as the basis of the inner possibility of whatever is accepted in the first place and generally admitted as 'known'." Or, in "The Question Concerning Technology," in Heidegger, *The Question Concerning Technology and Other Essays*, trans. Lovitt, we find, p. 35: "The essence of technology is nothing technological." Also indicative are the titles to many of Heidegger's writings: "What is Philosophy?", "What is Metaphysics?", *What is a Thing?*, *What is Called Thinking?*, etc.

that inhere in the question of essence. In the *Euthrypho* Plato has Socrates ask: "What is piety?" Piety, it turns out, is a kind of justice (though we never learn exactly what kind). So, in the *Republic* Plato has Socrates ask: "What is justice?" Socrates' life and, he would claim, the life of the city, not only depend on asking these questions, that life – at its best – *consists* in asking these questions. Unless we are to lose our true selves in the nonsense (foolishness, stupidity, childishness, ignorance) of enthusiasm or passion, we must always first ask and know what something is before committing ourselves to action or belief regarding it. Indeed, such caution has become the very action of the philosopher, the philosopher's reserve and wariness. It is in this sense that philosophy is *theoria*, "theory," vision, a seeing prior to doing. Philosophy – to never be duped – is anything but enthusiastic. Knowledge of the essence, essential knowledge, precedes the existential.[17] Essence in this sense is not some abstraction, however, but rather a way of life, the philosophical life, the true life. Socrates thought before he acted: he pauses before the symposium – he will be late – to contemplate, to deliberate, to reflect, to ask what's what, to feed his mind before his body. "To know the good," he taught, "is to do the good"; so bound were thinking and human being. Socrates defeated the "ignorance" of opponent after opponent with his questioning. His interlocutors learned that they must *first* know the good (or justice, or piety, etc.) in order to *then* do the good (or be just, or pious, etc.), that they must be philosophers, lovers of wisdom before all else. As the manner of his death makes literal, Socrates is the original "talking head," and his talk consists of a relentless questioning.

But Nietzsche and Heidegger have made Socrates suspect too. Their suspicions, the inversion and infiltration of metaphysics they point to, are not, however, what I wish to pursue for the moment. Rather, it is the essentialist form these suspicions still take that matters here. We must ask what the "What is . . .?" question is. In Socrates' hands it led to the inversion of consciousness and in-

[17] This in no way implies what is today called (vituperatively) "essentialism," by which is meant the pretense that what is in fact historical or changing is in truth eternal and unchanging, e.g., "human nature," "the feminine," "love." The charge (or bludgeon) of "essentialism" today, however, is all too often little more than a righteous piece of rhetoric or ideology.

stincts, the inversion of reflection and convention, the sacrifice of the latter to the former. But what of this question in Heidegger's hands? What is at issue, at stake, or, more importantly, what is not at issue, what is not at stake in the question of essence? Is there an "unsaid" deeper even than essence?

Are we not in need, then, of more precautions than Socrates, and than Heidegger? Must we not step back from *the* question of essence to raise another question – another sort of question, if it is a question at all – in order to recognize another circularity than that of simple repetition when asking, "*What is* the 'What is . . .?' question?" At first glance the question of essence seems to beg the question. Is our new suspicion, then, that Heidegger begs the question of metaphysics when he asks, "What is poetry?" or "What is thinking?"? Yet his thought is insistently anti-metaphysical. Why, then, does he retain the metaphysical question *par excellence*? Aware of just such an objection, he proposes, against the vicious circle of the *petitio principi*, an alternative: the productive circularity of hermeneutic questioning.[18] To ask, "What is . . .?" does not partake of onto-theo-logy if one acknowledges (1) that the answer can never be fixed absolutely, but calls essentially, endlessly, for additional "What is . . .?" questions. Dialectical refinement here replaces vicious circularity. Further, beyond the open-mindedness called for by dialectical refinement, hermeneutic questioning (2) insists on avoiding subjective impositions, on avoiding "reading into" rather than "hearkening to" things. One must hearken to the things themselves, ultimately to being, in a careful

---

[18] Heidegger pointedly relied upon the productive circularity of hermeneutic questioning, as he makes quite clear from the very start of *Being and Time* (paragraph two): "In working out our question [the question of the meaning of being], have we not 'presupposed' something which only the answer can bring? Formal objections such as the argument about 'circular reasoning' which can easily be cited at any time in the study of first principles, are always sterile when one is considering concrete ways of investigating" (Martin Heidegger, *Being and Time*, trans. John Macquarrie and Edward Robinson (New York: Harper & Row, 1962), p. 27). One proceeds to unravel the question of the meaning of being, Heidegger will say, because being itself contains surface "fore" [*Vor*]-structures of its own deeper self-interpretation. This issue is the same as the one we raised toward the end of chapter 2, above, concerning the origin of philosophy in terms of the motivation (or lack of motivation) for Husserl's "reduction." In a muted form, the ambiguity we saw there in Husserl's thought is again found in Heidegger's: the everyday self already has a "fore"-shadowing of its deeper ontological engagement, but at the same time it must *somehow* be jolted from its everydayness through an "anxious" recognition of its own mortality and by means of a silent "voice of conscience."

*Exceeding phenomenology*

attunement to what is. Heidegger has learned his lessons from Husserl.[19]

But does a hermeneutic questioning with all its refinement and care, one that succeeds, let us say, in avoiding onto-theo-logy, does it succeed also in avoiding all viciousness? Certainly it means to convert a simple fallacy into a productive inquiry, opening a path for thought.[20] But is it not the case, however, that despite bringing a sensitive receptivity to bear, to ask what something is leads to asking what something else is, and so on and so forth, *ad infinitum*? If being, as Heidegger suggests, is the revelation of beings (through language, the "house of being") in their being, then what reveals the revelation of being? Or, if there is no absolute (and what else is Heidegger suggesting with the terms "freedom" and *"Abgrund"*?), does not this line of thought once again end with Dasein? And thus does it not once again end precisely with the endlessness of subjectivity – call it either the "issue of being" or the "closure" of that same issue – that Heidegger himself wanted to avoid? Can it be no more than coincidence that the "voice" of being that was silent in

[19] But the contrast with Husserl must not be blurred. Husserl spent an enormous effort, not found in Heidegger, to keep his phenomenological method a "rigorous science." Though Levinas is certainly right that one must not make an obsession of method, perhaps Heidegger has erred in the opposite direction. I do not think it any accident, that is to say, that critical readers of Heidegger have never been able, with the best of will, to shake off the suspicion (to put this matter in its mildest form) that the "voice of being" is in fact a modulation, echo or outright ventriloquy of Heidegger's own voice.

[20] But relying on sensitivity to "fore"-structures, at the expense of critical reflection, opens the door to an egomaniacal, mythic, and sometimes nearly nonsensical logomania. That one finds this in many followers of deconstruction hardly needs emphasizing. This is perhaps its very authorization. It was certainly found in the late Heidegger. And it is found to this day among "orthodox" Heideggerians. For instance, at a conference held at Schloss Elmau in July of 1999 (on "Exodus from Being: Beyond Heidegger"), Peter Sloterdijk took it upon himself to defend Heidegger. But his presentation, which began by "interpreting" the history of Western philosophy and civilization as if it were the sweet exchange of letters between friends (to my mind a completely fantastic if imaginative romantic myth), was clearly unwilling – or unable? – to make the simple but basic distinction between private and public spheres of meaning. While such a "reading" is perhaps of literary interest, it can hardly be taken seriously from a philosophical or scientific point of view. But precisely because it thinks itself serious, i.e., the "future of thinking," it has dire consequences – or rather, it has had dire consequences, even if its present practitioners continue to refuse to acknowledge them. The rest of Sloterdijk's presentation was, to no surprise, a confused patchwork of conflated significations haphazardly – but ever so ponderously – taken from the regions of solitude, family, morality and justice. What this means, however, is that justice, the realm of the universal, of law, cannot be distinguished from personal preferences. And *this*, so I would argue, is far more dangerous than technology's alleged occultation of being.

conscience comes to speak a very human language, let us admit, even in the voice of the poets? What is disturbing in this is not simply the infinity of interpretive depth, which has the virtue of escaping onto-theo-logy and remaining true to the way of things, of beings and being, to the coming to be and passing away of being. Rather, the problem lies in the influence the endlessly open horizon of such thinking exerts on the unregulated way of such thought. That is, the problem lies in what seems to be the very virtue of hermeneutic thought, namely, the doggedness of the "What is . . .?" question, in its inability to escape itself, to escape being and essence. It is as if one were witnessing a dialectical *compensation*: for an endlessly formless freedom (the opening of the opening, etc.), the philosopher (Heidegger, Derrida, et al.) would hold desperately to the *form* of essential questioning. Levinas will call this free-floating adventure "the temptation of temptation," a "continual disengagement," which is perhaps nothing other than the "ego" or "philosophy, in contrast to a wisdom."[21]

But (and how can we avoid reverting again and again to this "but"?) what could be more inescapable than being and essence? Isn't such a "problem" mere silliness, or a return to onto-theo-logy, the craving for a beyond? In what way is the doggedness of essential questioning a constraint or viciousness? In what way is an attuned predisposition toward being and essence – what else could there be? – a flaw?

The only way such questioning can be recognized as problematic (but is "problematic" the right word?) is by introducing another sort of questioning, a questioning structured entirely otherwise, while at the same time structured in a way that is not itself onto-theo-logical. Perhaps it is not even a questioning, or at least it is not an essential questioning. Such a questioning would not be possible, inasmuch as "possibility" is limited to theory or to ontology. But such a question – if it is a question at all – is the ethical question. Rather than asking what ethics is, in the hope of finding out whether ethics is onto-theo-logical or not, one can ask if ethics is *better* than being. One can ask: "Is that good?" or "Is that evil?" These are not questions of being. This sort of question is not

---

[21] Levinas, "The Temptation of Temptation," in Emmanuel Levinas, *Nine Talmudic Readings*, trans. Annette Aronowicz (Bloomington: Indiana University Press, 1990), p. 34.

an essential question. It does not – no matter how respectfully – call for more vision, more knowledge. In fact, it is a wisdom that *already knows* – but without faith or "experience" – that good is good and evil is evil. It knows this without its questions becoming merely "rhetorical" questions. This is because their force lies elsewhere, outside the domain of the epistemological or ontological.

The ethical question does not merely contrast with the question of essence, as if ontological and ethical questions operated on the same horizon, under the same light. They are not on the same plane. Or, we could say, if the ontological or essential question opens up horizontally, to the manifestation of manifestation, then the moral question rises diagonally, to the goodness of the good.[22] Furthermore, the question of essence – "What is ethics?" – positively and precisely *excludes* the force of the ethical question. It defuses the ethical question in advance. Because it takes itself to be the ultimate and comprehensive question, the "fundamental" question, it collapses the "what ought to be" of ethics into the "what is" of ontology. It does not do this through some ill will, but in the very nature of its questioning. Thus, to take what is perhaps the most striking evidence for this blindness: the *Seinsfrage* by essence does not grasp the Holocaust. Or, to put this another way, the *Seinsfrage* as *Seinsfrage*, in all its depth, in all the severity and

[22] It is because he does not appreciate this radical difference in "angle," i.e., the irreducible moral character of Levinas's "saying," in contrast to the ontological character of Heidegger's "thinking," that Thomas Carl Wall, in *Radical Passivity: Levinas, Blanchot, and Agamben* (Albany: State University of New York Press, 1999), reduces the other's alterity once again to an affectation of the self, to its "finitude," to the self as "an image of nothing, of no one" (p. 4), and is thus able to characterize Levinas's work as "repeating Heidegger in terms of ethics" (p. 63), and to say that "Levinas *is* Heidegger in French . . ." (p. 63). Wall, in a word, thinks of ethics as a gloss on a pre-existent radical alterity, a pure alterity, as it were, when in fact alterity – the alterity of the other – is radical only as moral imperative. Surreptitiously, then, Wall treats alterity as an essence – precisely the seductive temptation of Heideggerian thought. Such a reading is guided, I believe, by a prior uncritical adoption of Derrida's reading of Levinas. In contrast, Simon Critchley, in *The Ethics of Deconstruction: Derrida and Levinas* (Oxford: Blackwell, 1992), recognizes that precisely the *ethical* determination of alterity, such as Levinas understands ethics, is required to "supplement" (p. 236) what would otherwise become the "empty formalism" (p. 237) of the deconstructive approach. What this supplement means, for Critchley, is that the questioning advocated by deconstruction, unless it is to be "publicly useless and politically pernicious" (ibid.), as it was in the case of Heidegger, must be relocated into a political context whose condition is recognized to be alterity grasped as moral responsibility, i.e., alterity as Levinas understands it.

grace of its thinking, still cannot raise the issue of the Holocaust as evil. Above, I almost said of the question of essence that "it *obscures*" the ethical question, but the point is that the very standards of obscurity and clarity are already standards of being and essence. In contrast, the approach of the ethical question, its force, its ethics, is and must be immediately one of moral height, of obligation and responsibility not for what is, but for what ought to be. Ethics is not merely different from thinking, in which case it would eventually be absorbed by thinking's play of differences, its differential field. Rather, ethics is radically and irreducibly "otherwise than being or beyond essence." To say it is impossible or that it does not exist is quite right, but only according to the limited standards of a resolute epistemology. But to go beyond epistemology does not make ethics thoughtless, a matter of faith, or idiosyncratic experience, or a particular history. Indeed, ethics is thoughtfulness itself. It is significance, an absolute deeper than significations.

Are we not now left with two questions rather than one? With the end of onto-theo-logical metaphysics: (1) is ethics still *better*? Does the term "better" still carry *moral* force, divorced from reality claims, from beings such as idea, substance, God, transcendental ego, etc., and from the being of being? Or, there remains what appears to be the most philosophical of questions: (2) what is ethics really, if it is anything at all, with the end of onto-theo-logical metaphysics? Is not ethics an entirely conditioned realm, part of an "epochal being" that itself emerges from the revelatory be-ing of being? Depending on which sort of question one asks first, or which sort of question is taken to be first, an ethical or an ontological result follows. It seems, then, that the viciousness of question begging has merely been doubled rather than vitiated. Ethical questions yield ethical answers (perhaps). Essential questions yield essential answers.

If the term "importance" is to have any sense at all, it is important to see that the ambivalence suggested above is not the case, or that if it is the case then such ambivalence arises, and the "fault" lies, with essential questioning. To be, according to Levinas, is not enough, even if such being takes responsibility for the unfolding of being, for the ongoing revelation of worlds. And perhaps especially then, when it seems most full of itself, does being lose its full significance. There is, we have suggested, a trap in essential questioning, an *ad infinitum* neglectful of its own conditions. Morality, in Levinas's view, imposes itself "prior" to essence and being, conditioning them. Not, however, because the good is installed in a Heaven above or in some identity behind identities. This would just take the ontological move one step back, would again succumb to onto-theo-logy, once more confusing ethics with ontology, as if what "ought to be" somehow "is." Nietzsche had already tracked down and exposed such illusions, "worlds" behind worlds.

*What* ethics is does not survive the end of metaphysics – but only because ethics never *was* or *is* anything. Ethics does not have an essence. Its "essence," so to speak, is precisely not to have an essence, but rather to unsettle essences. Its "identity" is precisely not to have an identity, but rather to undo identities.[23] Its "being" is not to be but to be *better than being*. Ethics is more vigilant, more sober, more alert than be-ing. It is a heightening of consciousness beyond the circuits of intentionality, that is to say, of synthesis, self-sameness, recurrence. Ethics is precisely ethics by disturbing the complacency of being (or of non-being, being's correlate). "To be or not to be," Levinas has said, "is it the final question?" The more basic – more pressing – question is the question of one's "right to be". Here the question is not a reflective one, in one's own being or in the being of beings, but rather a matter of being put-into-question by the other person. Is not my being, in its being, a usurpation of the other's being? Shame, not wonder, would be the origin of responsibility.

Ethics occurs not as the generosity of an *Abgrund*, but as an "an-archy," the disruption of being itself, a disruption arising from the irreducible agitation of a moral compassion. Not, however, as we shall see in chapter 9 with regard to Paul Ricoeur, in the self-absorbed passion of my own compassion, my sympathy, still *my* feeling, but rather in my compassion or "mercy" (French: *miséricorde*; Hebrew: *rachamim*, רחמימ[24]) – disruption, disturbance,

---

[23] Levinas will entitle an article of 1970 "No Identity"; in Emmanuel Levinas, *Collected Philosophical Papers*, ed. and trans. Alphonso Lingis (Dordrecht: Martinus Nijhoff, 1987), pp. 141–51.    [24] See ibid., p. 147, footnote no. 6.

distress – for the other's passion, for the other's suffering, the other's mortality.[25] This priority is affirmed without recourse to principles, without vision, in the irrecoverable shock of being-for-the-other-person before being-for-oneself, being-with-others or being-in-the-world, to name some of the contemporary philosophical formulae of post-metaphysical thought. Kant, as we have seen, had already understood the non-ontological and non-epistemological character of the ethical. But when he tried to articulate this "beyond" he succumbed to the language and outlook of epistemology, as if ethics were a peculiar kind of knowledge still. Levinas, in contrast, succeeds in speaking about ethics ethically. This is his special genius. His writings are not sermons, to be sure, but neither are they pure science or phenomenology in the strict Husserlian sense. Ethical priority occurs as the moral height of the other person, the angle of a "diagonal," an asymmetry cutting across the circuits of being, essence, identity, manifestation, principles – in brief, over all the circuits of self-sameness, the sphere of the ego or of being. To speak of the ethical ethically is to invoke an excellence other than the *arete* of the Greeks, beyond – because otherwise and better than – the shining or show (*Scheinen*) of fame or being. It is the excellence of an excess, an in-finity, that is not hubris but obligation and responsibility.

There is more to being than being. The surplus of the other's non-encompassable alterity – not the alterity of horizons – is the way morality intrudes, disturbs, and commands being – from height and destitution. It is the demand made by the very "face" of the other in a nakedness, a bursting of forms, an excess or vulgarity, that pierces the face that can be objectified, measured, photographed. "The face," Levinas says, "is what one cannot kill, or it is that whose *meaning* consists in saying 'thou shalt not kill.' Murder, it is true, is a banal fact; one can kill the Other; the ethical exigency is not an ontological necessity. The prohibition against killing does not render murder impossible."[26] It renders it evil. One can kill, but it is better – against all calculation, against machinations – not

[25] Levinas: "Perhaps justice is founded on the mastery of passion." Levinas, "As Old as the World," *Nine Talmudic Readings*, p. 76.
[26] Emmanuel Levinas, *Ethics and Infinity*, trans. Richard A. Cohen (Pittsburgh: Duquesne University Press, 1985), p. 87.

to kill, however much this "better" escapes thematization, representation, formalization, idealization, identification, and all the
cautions of essential thinking. Not only the instincts, natural
powers, inclinations, and animal being of the ethical agent are
transformed, made ashamed, but also consciousness is deepened,
alerted, insomniac, awakened from the dogmatic slumbers of
self-consciousness![27] One does the good before knowing it – ethics
lies in this "before," eternally scandalous to thought.

Neither my consciousness nor my instincts are sufficient to the
excessive demand the other places on me. The other is demanding
not by explicitly asking for this or that, but by the very force –
pacific – of an alterity that signifies the proximity of another,
proximity that from the first is already demanding. Consciousness
and instinct are cut to the quick. Yet shattered – as shattered, a
fission, "despite oneself,"[28] for "no one is good voluntarily"[29] – the
subject rises to the occasion, subjected to the other in a superlative
passivity, saying, "Here I am" (French: "*Me voici*"; Hebrew:
"הנני", *hineni*). Vulnerable and available at once, such is moral
subjectivity, subject to the other before itself. It is passive because
always already beholden to the other, before any activity, freedom,
or choice, hence before contract, charity, or even welcome. The
crux of morality lies in the non-encompassable yet non-indifferent
relation between the "better" and "being." The moral subject
does not thematize this relation but undergoes it. It is a relation
like no other, a "distance which is also proximity," Levinas wrote
in his 1979 preface to *Time and the Other*, " – which is not a
coincidence or a lost union, but signifies all the surplus or all the
*goodness* of an original sociality."[30] Responsibility in proximity with
the other, Levinas continues, is "*more precious* than the fact of being
given."[31] It is also more demanding.

---

[27] In an audacious formulation, referring to the "slumber" of cognitive consciousness, but
beyond Kant, referring, too, to the link between ethical transcendence and the divine,
Levinas writes: "It is not the proofs of God's existence that matter to us here, but the
breakup of consciousness, which is not a repression into the unconscious, but a sobering
up or an awakening, jolting the 'dogmatic slumber' which sleeps at the bottom of every
consciousness resting on its object." Levinas, "God and Philosophy," trans. Richard A.
Cohen, in Emmanuel Levinas, *The Levinas Reader*, ed. Séan Hand (Oxford, Blackwell,
1989), p. 173.    [28] Levinas, "No Identity," ibid., p. 146.
[29] Emmanuel Levinas, *Otherwise than Being or Beyond Essence*, trans. Alphonso Lingis (The
Hague: Martinus Nijhoff, 1981), p. 138.    [30] Levinas, *Time and the Other*, p. 32.
[31] Ibid.

As such, facing the other, subject to the other, the moral relation precedes thematization. To reduce it to a theme, a principle, a being, an *arche*, was the mistake of onto-theo-logy. To let being flow in the poetry of language, in its alleged gift-giving or in its play of equivocations, is also to turn from an ethical exigency to an ontological one, to *conatus essendi*, "will to power," "issue of being," or to the complacency, the self-satisfaction of aesthetics. Morality *occurs* – to return positively to Socrates – across the hiatus of a saying (*dire*), what Martin Buber called "dialogue," not in the contents of a discourse, in the continuities or discontinuities of what is said (*dit*), but in sincerity and the demand for response. "It is better," Socrates said, "to suffer evil than to do it." Socrates may not have realized that he could not *prove* this point, even though it was in effect while he spoke. Sincerity and the responsibility to respond to the other are, for Levinas, precisely the terms of an inordinate responsibility, the infinite responsibility of being-for-the-other *before* oneself – the ethical relation. What is said can always be unsaid, re-said or revised – it is the *saying* of it, the intrusion such saying effects, the interruption it inserts into continuities, as well as the passivity it calls forth, beneath identity, that accomplishes the *priority* and *anteriority* of ethics. Transcendence, the ab-solute, an-archy, not in the differential play *within* the said, in the "verbality of the verb," or in "difference," but in a human saying, the sincerity and authority of the "face" facing. The only alterity sufficiently other to provoke response, to subject the subject to the subjection of response – which for Levinas is subjectivity itself, and the meaning of meaning, the event of ethics – is the absolute alterity of the other person encountered in the excessive immediacy of the face-to-face.

Radical alterity figures in Levinas's thought not as a flaw, ignorance, obscurity, childishness, laziness, celebration, or deferral. Rather it is the non-thematizable charge through which ethics commands. "What ought to be" – one responding to the other – relates to "what is" – being, essence, manifestation, phenomenon, identity – not by some subtle or crude conversion into "what is," but by overcharging, disturbing, raising it to a moral height of which it is not by itself capable. The alterity of the other raises the subject in a severe responsibility that bears all the weight of the world's seriousness in a non-indifference – with no ontological basis – for the other. And it then comes to raise the world itself, transforming it into an environment of justice wherein morality receives its necessary and proper support. These are the exigencies – for morality, for justice – that guide Levinas's thought. Indeed, they are the exigencies that guide thought, thought which is otherwise lost in the fathomless reaches of space, time, and meaning.

Is not such an ethics too abstract? Not at all, indeed, it is all too concrete, painfully so. To be for-the-other before oneself is no small matter. It may be rare, but it is not abstract. When in the late 1930s the British colonial administrators asked Gandhi what he expected from his annoying non-violent agitation, the Mahatma (Great Soul!) replied that he expected the British would quit India. They would quit India *on their own* because they would come to see that they were *wrong* to occupy and rule it. Moral force is a scandal for ontological thinking, whether that thinking would like to be gently attuned to being or to forcefully impose its subjective will. The power of morality is effective in a different way than the power of identities, whether political or poetic, whether knowledge or administration, whether unified or diffused. Moral force escapes and judges the synthesizing, centralizing forces – the powers that be.

Morality is forceful not because it opposes power with more power, on the same plane, with a bigger army, more guns, a finer microscope or a grander space program, but rather because it opposes power with what appears to be weakness and vulnerability but is actually sincerity, responsibility, and justice. To the calculations of power, morality opposes *less* than power can conquer. With their lathi sticks the British occupational police struck their opponents and hurt them dreadfully. But at the same time each hit was an indication of their own injustice, their own inhumanity, and with each blow non-violently received they were taught a moral lesson. Not that they were *necessarily* taught a lesson: ethics is not ontology, it is not necessary. One can kill. Moral force, however, the proximity of the face-to-face, the height and destitution of the other, is the ever patient counterbalance to all the powers of the world, including nuclear power. Moral force *is* not stronger than the powers of being and essence, the totalizing, synthesizing powers, it is *better*, and this is its ultimate strength.

Can Levinas's ethical metaphysics be reduced, then, to the escapist lament of slavery, failure, cowardice, and inability? Is it a rationalization? Surely it can be approached this way. But such an approach is indeed a reduction, a moral blindness. There is a great difference between the "forgetting" involved in moral height, and the "blindness" involved in moral evil. "Does the subject escape the concept and essence . . . only in resignation and illusion, against which at the hour of truth or of the inevitable awakening, essence is stronger?" Levinas asks. He answers that to grasp the singularity of the subject morally commanded, one must "understand the subjectivity of the subject *beyond essence*, as on the basis of an *escape* from the concept, a forgetting of being and non-being. Not of an 'unregulated' forgetting . . . but a forgetting that would be an ignorance in the sense that nobility *ignores* what is not noble."[32] Noble ignorance, noble vision – moral attentiveness to the other, at one's own expense, for the other before oneself, such is one's true self, the self as vocation. Such an ignorance is not blind, however, for it knows too much, more than it can comprehend, more than what can be comprehended – an infinite responsibility and obligation before others.

Human violence cannot be seriously thought outside of ethics. Or, to say this otherwise and paradoxically, outside of ethics the violence of human violence is evil. Levinas will say:

> The true problem for us Westerners is not so much to refuse violence as to question ourselves about a struggle against violence which without blanching in non-resistance to evil, could avoid the institution of violence out of this very struggle. Does not the war against war perpetuate that which it is called to make disappear, and consecrate war and its virile virtues in good conscience? One has to reconsider the meaning of a certain human weakness, and no longer see in patience only the reverse side of the ontological finitude of the human. But for that one has to be patient oneself without asking patience of the others – and for that one has to admit a difference between oneself and the others.[33]

Only this difference, between oneself and the others, only the individuation of self – the self as a singularity, the election of the self – that occurs as non-indifference to the plight and height of the

[32] Levinas, *Otherwise than Being or Beyond Essence*, p. 177.    [33] Ibid.

others, as morality, related yet separate from others, is capable – through its very "weakness" – of holding the march of historical being in check. Only ethics can judge, rather than simply record, appreciate or celebrate the alleged "epochal unfolding of being," and thereby find the true meaning of history as part of humanity's "holy history" ("*histoire saint*"), its quest for morality and justice.

# 11

## *Good and evil*

# CHAPTER 5

# *Alterity and alteration: development of an opus*

Thus far I have presented Levinas's thought in relation to Husserl's phenomenology and Heidegger's ontology. I have sought to show early influences and departures. The real heart of Levinas's thought, however, appears later, in his two major philosophical works, *Totality and Infinity*, published in 1961, and *Otherwise than Being or Beyond Essence*, published in 1974.

The topic of this short chapter is twofold. First, it broadly characterizes the structure, themes, and aims of these two books, either of which would alone have established Levinas's reputation as a major philosopher. Second, and again broadly, it clarifies the relation of one to the other. My claim will be that though each book stands independently, together they form two natural parts of a united front, namely, Levinas's inter-subjective ethics. *Totality and Infinity* is primarily concerned to establish the radical and ethically compelling transcendence of the other person. *Otherwise than Being or Beyond Essence*, on the other hand, is primarily concerned to show the repercussion of this transcendence in the ethical constitution of moral subjectivity. We have already seen these two emphases, transcendence and the impact of transcendence on the self, in the ethical expression "for-the-other before oneself." The sequence of Levinas's two major works mimics the very priority of ethics itself, namely the moral height and precedence of the other before the self, and the radical alteration of selfhood in the face of the alterity of the other. At the same time, insofar as each book stands on its own, is a *magnum opus* in its own right, each covers most of the subject matter found in the other, though admittedly with different emphases.

*Otherwise than Being or Beyond Essence* is the last of Levinas's four original philosophical books, including not only *Totality and Infinity*, but the two earlier, shorter, and more schematic works: *Time and the Other* (1947) and *Existence and Existents* (1947). These four works, seen in sequence, elaborate an increasingly rich and refined philosophy of ethical metaphysics, built upon careful phenomenological investigations and Levinas's unique appreciation for the extraordinary weight, or height, of moral exigencies. These exigencies are the moral obligations and responsibilities and the call to justice that inform the whole of social life and constitute the very humanity of the human. They always command the center of Levinas's thought. The sheer originality and range, as well as the critical penetration, of Levinas's vision demand nothing less than a fundamental reorientation of the Western spirit – philosophy, logic, rhetoric, praxis, ontology, science, art, politics, religion – in the light of the demands of morality and justice. Here, in ethics, what is at work is not merely light, or a contemplative illumination of light, but at once light and moral command, a commanding light,[1] the peculiar conjunction and structure – "diachrony" – guiding Western thought and spirit.

A striking continuity links Levinas's writings. We have already seen just how early, already in 1930, he saw the importance of inter-subjectivity. At the heart of all his original work lies the irreducible ethical proximity of one human being to another – morality; and through that encounter, the relation of one to all – justice. Each successive text branches out, filigrees, presents successively richer, fuller, more nuanced analyses, testifying to the cornucopian genius of Levinas's central ethical vision. Almost organic, this process of amplification is an interesting and compelling "method." Built on, or starting with, phenomenology, it does not, as we have seen, ultimately remain there, but rises to the ethical. It combines description and prescription, the normative and the vocative, showing how one opens onto the other, the ethical – which is to never be done with "saying" (*dire*) and "re-saying" (*redire*) and "un-saying" (*dedire*) the "said" (*dit*) – having

---

[1] Commenting on an expression used in Exodus 20:15 ("And all the people *perceived the thundering* . . ."), Rashi (Rabbi Solomon ben Isaac, 1040–1105) writes: "They saw that which should be heard, which is impossible to see in another place [other than at the Revelation at Mount Sinai]."

the last word, as it were. All of Levinas's work is such a saying and re-saying. Spanning the last two thirds of the twentieth century, it offers a vision whose "argument" unfolds by a process of amplification, augmentation, expansion, extension, magnification, intensification, enlargement, as if Levinas's later writings were commentaries – exegesis – on the earlier ones. And they are. A sentence in an earlier text becomes a section in a later one, which in turn expands into an entire chapter later on. Latent implications are elaborated. Suggestions are amplified. Nuances are tightened, specified, sharpened. Levinas's works work, then, by a manner of philosophical donation that in its own way mimics the moral responsibility that is its subject matter, increasing to the measure that it is borne. *Otherwise than Being or Beyond Essence* and *Totality and Infinity*, especially, are intimately bound to one another in this way. They are companion works: like two tablets (or the two tablets that are also one tablet), or like Jacob's ladder with "the angels of God ascending and descending on it,"[2] each book amplifies, deepens, and explains the other. Of course, because *Otherwise than Being or Beyond Essence* is the later volume by thirteen years, there are some developments in it that do not appear, or do not appear in precisely the same form, in *Totality and Infinity*. These differences notwithstanding, the two volumes stand in a special harmony, a complementarity of mutual intensification: *Totality and Infinity* coming first like the other person, *Otherwise than Being or Beyond Essence* coming second like the moral self.

To be sure, both are works of ethical metaphysics. They are distinguished less by a difference in content than by a difference in emphasis. The four parts of *Totality and Infinity* deal successively with justice, sensibility, alterity, and eros. The key to the volume, however, driving all of it, is clearly part three, on the radical moral transcendence of the other person, the first "command" of the ethics of the face-to-face. The discussion of justice and other topics in part one is ultimately motivated by and built upon this ethics. The same can be said of the other parts too. The phenomenological analyses of part two, of enjoyment, affectivity, dwelling, labor, possession, and representation, at once build up to this

---

[2] Genesis 25:12.

transcendence and at the same time find their deeper sense in it. This, by the way, is also exactly how *Time and the Other* and *Existence and Existents* are structured: by a drive to transcendence that bursts the bounds of a Husserlian phenomenology. The account of eros in the concluding fourth part of *Totality and Infinity*, where the meaning of transcendence is understood in terms of sensuous contact (caress, voluptuousness, fecundity) and family relations (paternity,[3] filiality, fraternity), reveals yet another way in which inter-subjectivity is conditioned, and hence another dimension of ethical transcendence, linking humanity across the time of human generations. Following from and augmenting the ethical meta-physics developed in *Totality and Infinity*, the two central themes of *Otherwise than Being or Beyond Essence* are the moral sensibility of the moral subject (vulnerability, patience, substitution), and the ethical foundation of language and signification (saying, witness, proph-ecy). To be sure, the latter themes are announced in *Totality and Infinity*, but they are pronounced in *Otherwise than Being or Beyond Essence*. Again, like the ethical relation itself and its priorities, *Totality and Infinity* focuses on the commanding *otherness* of ethical alterity, *Otherwise than Being or Beyond Essence* on the commanded *passivity* of ethical subjectivity.

The primary labor and accomplishment of *Totality and Infinity*, then, is the articulation and elaboration of the otherness of the other person as moral "height and destitution." The task is in-herently difficult. But it is also difficult because philosophy has traditionally been oriented not by the transcendence of ethics but by the integrative or synthetic concerns of ontology and epistemol-ogy. It is not simply that "being and thinking are one," they have been the only one. The wisdom philosophy loves has been defined as and by knowledge. But for Levinas, contra Parmenides, contra Hegel, contra Heidegger, there is a deeper stratum of significance underlying and ultimately justifying knowledge. This significance – ethical – derives from the dynamics of inter-subjective encounter. Genuine transcendence, transcendence that is not a homecoming

---

[3] I have left out the notion of "maternity," which will be taken up in chapter 6 below. For a detailed account of Levinas's analyses of eros in part four of *Totality and Infinity*, see chapter nine, "The Metaphysics of Gender," of my *Elevations: The Height of the Good in Rosenzweig and Levinas* (Chicago: University of Chicago Press, 1994), pp. 195–219.

(Abraham, not Odysseus), is found in what Levinas call the "face" (*visage*) of the other, the trace of an imperative height. The appearance of the alterity of the other is not an appearance at all, but the enigma of a command that bursts through all appearance: "Thou shalt not murder." The other "is" unique, not a function of a context, just as the moral self, responsible for this other, "is" also unique. One must put the copula (in this case "is") in quotes, because the other, as moral other, and the self, as moral self, burst the bounds of being. "Thou shalt not murder" – this is how Levinas articulates the pacific force of morality, unsettling the more or less sophisticated economies of interest (self-interest) that the self can find for itself in sensibility, labor, knowledge, and reason. The "face" is at once the visage of the other, his or her face, and a metonomy standing for the whole body of the other,[4] and even more broadly for otherness as moral command, whether the other person is literally present or not. For the self facing the face only an excessive desire – a metaphysical desire, a desire without term, without finality – the desire for goodness, always insufficient to meet its obligations and responsibilities and the call to justice, can do justice to the radical otherness of the other person who faces.

*Otherwise than Being or Beyond Essence* elaborates this ethics of radical alterity by turning back to the moral sensibility of the subject awakened by the other. It turns to the moral subject's unique temporal and moral "de-phasing," whereby it is "de-nucleated" of its substantiality, "an-archic," "fissured" in its very identity, a "traumatized" psyche, held "hostage" by the other to the point of "obsession." We will look more closely at this moral subjectivity in the next chapter, "Maternal body/maternal psyche." A few indications will do here. The moral subject arises in subjection, "despite itself," introjected by an alterity deeper than its own synthetic activities, undergoing an "immemorial past" never contracted in the present, the trace of a "dia-chrony." It is self as "substitution" for the other, like a "skin turned inside out," hostage to and for the other's needs, for the other's life, all the way

---

4 See Emmanuel Levinas, *Totality and Infinity*, trans. Alphonso Lingis (Pittsburgh: Duquesne University Press, 1969), p. 75: "The nakedness of his face extends into the nakedness of the body." Levinas somewhere extends the notion of the "face" to include even an arm sculpted by Rodin.

to being responsible for the other's responsibility, including the other's evil, expiating even the other's persecution. I am I as my brother's keeper, all the way to the point that one could die for the other. The moral self bears the other like a pregnancy, the other within the same. Or like prophecy, speaking the other's words. Such is the moral self – an inspired and elected subjection. Here the alterity of the other is no less radical than it was in *Totality and Infinity*. The "asymmetry" of the I–you relation – the priority of the other, the other before the self – is in no way diminished. Indeed, precisely because the other is morally *prior* to the self, and the moral self is for the other *before* itself, it is fitting that *Totality and Infinity*, with its emphasis on radical alterity, comes before *Otherwise than Being or Beyond Essence*, with its emphasis on moral selfhood. In *Otherwise than Being or Beyond Essence* Levinas's focus is precisely on the asymmetrical repercussion of the moral height of the other on the moral sensibility of the self. In the face of a natural inclination toward selfishness, toward the complacency of immanence, the interests of self-interest, what does it mean, he is asking, to be morally beholden to the other? What does it mean to be responsible? What precisely, beyond the circuits of self-sameness (whether practice or knowledge) are the structures of a responsible self? Here his aim is to account for the shock, the implosion, of a radically ethical alterity – the moral force of the other – on a subjectivity whose very subjectivity is constituted as moral subjection to and for the other.

In *Otherwise than Being or Beyond Essence* there is also a new emphasis on language, on what Levinas calls "the saying" [*dire*] of the said [*dit*]." No doubt, in *Totality and Infinity* Levinas had already named "the relation with the Other, discourse."[5] There he had already understood that "language presupposes interlocutors, a plurality,"[6] and that "the formal structure of language thereby announces the ethical inviolability of the Other."[7] There he had already analyzed the ethical significance of language as "expression": the signifying or surplus of the other's "saying," calling the

---

[5] See, Levinas, *Totality and Infinity*, p. 39: "We shall try to show that the *relation* between the same and the other . . . is language"; or, p. 97: "A relation between terms that resist totalization, that absolve themselves from the relation or that specify it, is possible only as language."    [6] Ibid., p. 73.    [7] Ibid., p. 195.

economies of logic, reason, representation, thematization, signification, and disclosure into question. The excessive significance of
signifying was explicated in terms of teaching, speech, command,
judgment, prophecy, apology, saying and "unsaying the said."
"Language," Levinas had written, "is perhaps to be defined as the
very power to break the continuity of being or of history."[8]
*Otherwise than Being or Beyond Essence* amplifies and nuances these
analyses, turning from the infinity of the other's expression to the
inexhaustible responsiveness of the self's response as a saying.

In both books, Levinas's primary protagonist is Heidegger. In
earlier chapters we have already seen how close and how far
Levinas is from Husserl's phenomenology and Heidegger's ontology. The title and the content of *Otherwise than Being or Beyond
Essence* alert us to the priority Levinas gives to his ongoing and
fundamental contestation of Heideggerian thinking. *Otherwise* than
Heideggerian being; *beyond* Heideggerian essence. In the after-
math of the failure of modern science to ground itself, to form a
seamless totality, a new and future *gigantamachia* has arisen in the
twentieth century and will remain for the new millennium. It is the
struggle for philosophy's future – for the destiny of the West –
between ethics and aesthetics, the struggle of David and Goliath,
Bible and Homer, revelation and oracles: Levinas versus
Heidegger. Given the enormous stature of Heideggerian thought
in twentieth-century philosophy, despite the obvious moral failure
of both Heidegger personally and the *Seinsfrage* objectively,[9]
Levinas is perhaps the only philosopher who at the most fundamental levels of insight has seen all the way through and beyond
*Denken*. One can see their dispute, as we have remarked in earlier
chapters, as one over the heritage of Husserlian phenomenology.
Whereas Heidegger, in *Being and Time*, was led to surpass phenomenology in the direction of *ontology*, through a renewal of "the
question of being," Levinas, in *Totality and Infinity*, also surpasses
phenomenology, but in the direction of *ethics*, through the even
more sober exigencies of moral responsibility and the call to
justice.

[8] Ibid.
[9] I am thinking, of course, of Heidegger's membership in the Nazi party, and of the marked
failure of the *Seinsfrage*, as *Seinsfrage*, to respond to – let alone to grasp – the Holocaust.

As we have already discussed earlier,[10] Edmund Husserl – teacher of both Heidegger and Levinas – had pushed science to new and genuine limits. He had convincingly shown that modern mathematical science would have to expand to return to its original telos: to be a fully justified, verifiable, self-correcting account of the whole. Science, to remain science, would no longer be able to reduce away "secondary qualities" on the basis of an unjustified but presupposed realist bias ultimately satisfied only with mathematical certitude. Rather, it would have to expose all evidences, including the evidences of consciousness *taken on their own terms*. Vast domains of signification hitherto dismissed as unscientific or pre-scientific, *mere* perception, *mere* imagination, *mere* worldliness, *mere* duration, etc., not to mention the domains of value, purpose, telos, etc., all reduced to one form or another of an allegedly illusory subjectivism, would be restored to scientific status by phenomenology. Phenomenology would rigorously investigate and uncover the invariant structures ("essences") constitutive of their meaning. Phenomenology, which would include the natural sciences as but one part, would be the true name of science. It would be a vast collaborative effort, ultimately uniting humankind in the name of science. And it has had stunning results. Maurice Merleau-Ponty's *Phenomenology of Perception*, to name but one, presented brilliant and novel analyses of perception, not by explaining away perception in terms of causality or a transcendental logic, but by uncovering and describing its inherent sense, its inner coherence. Levinas's own thinking – both before and after Merleau-Ponty, as we have seen, following lines of thought similar to those elaborated in the *Phenomenology of Perception* (as well as earlier phenomenological lines of thought inaugurated by Bergson and Husserl, also followed by Merleau-Ponty) – integrated and transformed phenomenological insights into a fundamentally ethical vision of philosophy.

Heidegger did the same for time in *Being and Time*. Developing the earlier insights of Bergson, who first uncovered the interpenetrating dimensions of time that he called "duration," and of Husserl, who further unpacked this thick interpenetrating duration in terms

[10] See chapter 2 above.

of the synthesizing temporality of futural "protentions" and past "retentions," Heidegger also uncovered beneath an artificial, spatialized "clock time" the deeper structures of an "ecstatic" temporality. In this way, in *Being and Time*, he linked time to human praxis, theoretical knowledge, mortality, worldliness, history, and ultimately to the very revelation of being. But precisely here, where *Being and Time* is most original, on Heidegger's own turf, as it were, on the subject of time, Levinas would propose an even deeper vision. Undercutting all the forms of ecstatic temporality and the practical and ontological structures they supported, whether in Bergson, Husserl, or Heidegger, Levinas discovered an even sharper sense of time in "proximity," in the very de-phasing of moral subjectivity, the one-for-the-other. Time itself (as Levinas had already declared as early as 1947[11]) would be constituted inter-subjectively, hence ethically. Not "being and time," but "the other and time" or, what amounts to the same thing, "ethics and time." The transcending dimensions constitutive of time – the pastness of the past, the futurity of the future – would derive not from the subject alone, or from its historical context, but from the ethical transcendence of the inter-subjective relation. The disruption of identity that "is" identity, that which Levinas understood as the moral subjectivity of the for-the-other, would at the same time function to "de-nucleate" self-presence, shattering the presence of the present with an "immemorial past never present" and "a future always future," both encountered in proximity to the other. Moral selfhood, proximity, would hence also be "diachrony," the ultimate sense of time. Thus both Heidegger and Levinas launch their radically differing philosophies by means of careful analyses of time and sensibility: anxious mortal being in Heidegger, obligated moral responsibility in Levinas.

In addition to contesting Heidegger's theory of ecstatic time by proposing his own theory of intersubjective and ethical time,

---

[11] See the concluding pages of *Time and the Other* and *Existence and Existents*. In the latter volume, Levinas writes: "If time is not the illusion of a movement, pawing the ground, then the absolute alterity of another instant cannot be found in the subject, who is definitively *himself*. This alterity comes to me only from the other. Is not sociality something more than the source of our representation of time: is it not time itself?" Emmanuel Levinas, *Existence and Existents*, trans. Alphonso Lingis (The Hague: Martinus Nijhoff, 1978), p. 93.

Levinas also challenges Heidegger's account of sensibility. Here, too, Levinas is challenging one of the fundamentals of Heideggerian thought, the priority of praxis over theory. And here, too, Levinas challenges Heidegger not through a simple reversal, a defense of theory over praxis, in this instance, but by means of closer, more sensitive analyses of sensibility itself. A layer of meaning Levinas calls "enjoyment" (*jouissance*) would be the deepest sense of sensibility. One of the most profound discoveries of *Totality and Infinity* and Levinas's earlier works, a discovery amplified in *Otherwise than Being or Beyond Essence*, this sense of sensibility lies deeper than the embodiment and worldliness Heidegger described in *Being and Time*. There embodiment had been described, beneath theory, in terms of instrumental praxis, mortal anxiety, and historical engagement in being. No one who has read *Being and Time* has not been impressed by its stunning phenomenological analyses of the instrumentality of the "ready-to-hand" (*Zuhanden*) as the ground of the "present-at-hand" (*Vorhanden*), giving rise to theory. The phenomenological analyses of part two of *Totality and Infinity*, however, uncover a more originary layer of meaning. Sensibility, Levinas discovers, does not first emerge as praxis caught up in a larger network of the "in-order-to" (*das Um-zu*) – the "referential totality (*Verweisungsganzheit*) – which ultimately implicates Dasein. Rather, sensibility is first the sheer enjoyment of sensations, a "carefree" contentment with sensing itself. Embodiment, sensibility, flesh, is first a self-satisfaction and an enjoyment of elemental sensations, the sun on one's arms, the breeze in the air, indifferent to the higher-level significations of instrumentality and theory.

This discovery of the status of enjoyment, so seemingly innocuous, has important consequences. It means that the very independence of subjectivity, its original separation and individuation, would lie more deeply embedded in sensibility than the synthesizing temporal ecstasies of praxis, worldliness, or anxiety, as Heidegger thought. The circuits of subjectivity would already have begun in the very sensing of sensations. But this will mean that the transcendence of the other (or time), the ethical impact of the other on the self, the self as moral subjection, is felt more deeply, in the deepest recesses of the flesh. Levinas already saw these two related radicalizations, of the self-sameness or immanence of the self and of the transcendence necessary to disrupt it, as early as *Time and the Other*, whose aim, stated on its first page, is "on the one hand, to deepen the notion of solitude and, on the other, to consider the opportunities that time ['the very relationship of the subject with the Other'] offers to solitude."[12] Morality thus strikes the subject at once from further and more closely than Husserl or Heidegger conceived. It emerges as compassion, as a suffering for the other, a *suffering for the suffering of the other*. It is thus not one's own mortality, one's being-toward-death, that is definitive of human individuation, but the other's. The other is mortal, therefore I am obligated. Perhaps, in a generous reading, we might think that Heidegger's famous dismissal of morality, in *Being and Time*, as derivative and "ontic"[13] (and worse, his real-life dismissal of morality) derives from this oversight regarding the real depth to which *human and moral* being is implicated in sensibility. Humanity is sensible from the bottom, as it were, in enjoyment, to the top, in ethical responsibility and justice. One does not only suffer for the suffering of the other, one redresses that suffering, concretely. "The *material* needs of the other," Levinas is fond of quoting the nineteenth-century Eastern European rabbi Israel Lipkin (Salanter), "are my spiritual needs."[14] The interpenetrating structure of sensibility and ethics (and time) undercuts the foundational status of the meaning-bestowing acts of Husserlian intentionality as well as the freedom Heidegger discovered in the essence of truth.

The peculiar de-formalized excesses, asymmetries and priorities

---

[12] Emmanuel Levinas, *Time and the Other and Additional Essays*, trans. Richard A. Cohen (Pittsburgh: Duquesne University Press, 1987), p. 39.

[13] See, e.g., paragraph 58: "Essential Being-guilty is, equiprimordially, the existential condition for the possibility of the 'morally' good and for that of the 'morally' evil – that is, for morality in general and for the possible forms which this may take factically. The primordial 'Being-guilty' cannot be defined by morality, since morality already presupposes it for itself." Martin Heidegger, *Being and Time*, trans. John Macquarrie and Edward Robinson (New York: Harper & Row, 1962), p. 332.

[14] For more on Rabbi Israel Salanter, founder of the "*Musar*" (ethical self-development) movement within traditional Judaism, see Louis Ginzberg, "Rabbi Israel Salanter," in Judah Goldin, ed., *The Jewish Expression* (New York: Bantam Books, 1970), pp. 419–451 (originally delivered as a lecture at the Jewish Theological Seminary, 25 February 1904); Menahem G. Glenn, *Israel Salanter: Religious-Ethical Thinker: The Story of a Religious-Ethical Current in Nineteenth Century Judaism* (New York: Bloch Publishing Company, 1953). Salanter's teacher and "spiritual founder of the Musar movement" was Joseph Zundel of Salant (1786–1866).

of ethics – commanding height of the other, subjection of self, other-before-the-self, diachrony deeper than synthesis, otherwise than being and beyond essence – in conjunction with a commitment to the method of phenomenology, account not only for the relation between *Totality and Infinity* and *Otherwise than Being or Beyond Essence*, but also for the peculiar structure of each of these two texts. In *Totality and Infinity* ethics appears both before (part one) and after (part three) a phenomenological account of sensibility as "separated" being (part two). Morality and justice appear *before* a phenomenology because *ethical priorities* have priority over the a priori syntheses – the intentionality – constitutive of such regions of signification as sensibility, praxis, knowledge, and history, phenomenologically grasped. Morality and justice appear *after* a phenomenology, on the other hand, because the selfishness of the self is its "naïve" or "natural" position. So, too, mimicking and reproducing this order, knowledge (whether theory or praxis) presents itself as a search for origins, as "first philosophy," as re-presentation of presence. Thus knowledge finds itself inverted by ethics, "traumatized"[15] by a *beginning* that, per impossibile, precedes its *origin*, piercing the ironclad self-presence of first philosophy with moral responsibilities and obligations. Levinas will name this peculiar structure the "anterior posteriorly."[16] Phenomenology and ontology are thus too early and too late for ethics. They are too late, because the priorities of ethics precisely take priority over knowledge and being, are more important, more demanding, exert a greater exigency. They are too early because in tracing meanings to their origin in consciousness, in intentional-

---

[15] Levinas uses this psychological terminology not, as we have seen, because he believes that consciousness can be explained through psychology, but rather because what philosophy has hitherto taken to be an *origin* or *arche* in fact succumbs, as we are here indicating, to a prior and more pressing *beginning* in the other person. As we shall see in the next chapter, for Levinas knowledge does indeed succumb to the relativism and deferral of a bottomless psychoanalysis when and only when it does not recognize its absolute beginning in morality. Morality, with its non-intentional structure, is thus the ultimate "trauma" for a representational consciousness caught up in its own self-presence and for this very reason reduced to a psychology. This is an interesting line of thought: precisely when consciousness aims most to avoid psychologism, by resolutely maintaining itself within the sphere of cognition, it is precisely then that it is reduced to psychologism. Morality would thus be the "cure" for consciousness sick with itself – sick of itself! Thus Nietzsche, always so perceptive, is consistent when he conceives of consciousness as essentially sick, *but only because* he rejects morality as morality, i.e., as an absolute.

[16] Levinas, *Totality and Infinity*, p. 170; see also p. 54.

ity, or in the "clearing" or the "opening," the self-presence of phenomenology and the circuits of being cannot catch sight of the deeper ethical vigilance – Levinas calls it "insomnia" – of which even absolute transcendental consciousness and the be-ing of being is but a mode. Thus phenomenology and ontology, at their best, are obliged to obliquely catch sight of the "trace" of an ethical alterity to which they are nonetheless, in a deeper moral adherence, fully beholden.

The *tracing* of diachrony – ethical excess – also structures *Otherwise than Being or Beyond Essence*. Chapter one, entitled "The Argument," like part one of *Totality and Infinity*, is a *beginning* prior to *origins*. The demands of goodness do not wait for the completion of knowledge (though the demand for justice required by the demand for goodness provides the very motivation for the thematization and quantification proper to knowledge). Socrates was exactly wrong: to know the good before doing the good is neither to know the good nor to do the good. The Israelites at the foot of Mount Sinai understood the order of ethics better: "We will do and we will hearken."[17] Chapters two through five of *Otherwise than Being or Beyond Essence*, entitled "The Exposition," renew Levinas's earlier ethico-phenomenological account of sensibility. They build upon and extend the results of *Totality and Infinity*, elucidating an ethics fully aware of its sensible dimension, the inordinate passivity – passion and compassion – of a subjectivity driven to the point of trauma and obsession by the in-finite moral demands of the other. The final section of this book, having two titles, "In Other Words" and "Outside,"[18] like the last section of *Totality and Infinity*, "Conclusions," is neither final nor conclusive. They are re-formulations and renewals, re-saying (*redire*) the saying of the said – in an unending process, as exegesis, as ethics. I have compared this unending exegetical process to the ever renewed and ever novel annual reading of the Hebrew Bible (Five Books of Moses) in the Jewish Sabbath liturgy.

*Otherwise than Being or Beyond Essence* advances Levinas's ethical

---

[17] *Exodus* 24:7: "נעשה ונשמע"

[18] "Outside" in French is "*Au dehors.*" But, as is so often the case with key terms of Levinas's French, one thinks of a Hebrew equivalent, in this case *ha'chutzah* (החוצה). Even more particularly, one thinks of this word as used in Genesis 15:5: "And He took him [Abraham] outside . . ." The Midrash interprets God's taking Abraham "outside" to mean taking him outside the realm of reason and nature.

challenge into the deepest recesses of Heidegger's later "turn" (*Kehre*) to the "end of metaphysics." In this last phase of his thought Heidegger turned to – was attuned by – the poetry/"piety of thought," "letting be" (*Gellasenheit*), a "hearkening" to the epochal revelatory gift of "appropriation" (*Ereignis*), of "the fourfold" (*die Vierung*) of "earth, sky, gods and mortals," of language as "the house of being." In *Totality and Infinity* Levinas had already sharply objected to this phase of Heidegger's itinerary: "Speaking," he wrote, "rather than 'letting be,' solicits the Other."[19] In *Otherwise than Being or Beyond Essence* he refines and amplifies this challenge. Before language is a poetic hearkening, it is radical ethical sincerity: saying as "my exposure without reserve to the other,"[20] inspiration, witness, prophecy, risk, glory – "proximity and not truth about proximity."[21] Levinas will challenge the distant and delicate fluttering of the verbality of the verb "to be", and the poetic "epochal" language that in the later Heidegger comes to substitute itself for the earlier more straightforward ontology of being. The saying of the said comes not as the anonymous voice of "language languaging," as Heidegger would have it. Rather, saying – and un-saying, and re-saying – is the moral cry of the other, an appeal that finds voice in the moral self who through its own lips speaks to and for the other – responsible to and for the other.

An edifying case regarding Levinas vis-à-vis Heideggerian thought concerns Jacques Derrida – Heidegger's most celebrated and faithful disciple in France. Despite his fundamental adherence to the Heideggerian conception of philosophy as questioning, or, more precisely, of philosophy as language questioning itself, the "originality" of Derrida's own thought came from reducing Levinas's notion of the "trace" to the internal movement, at once semiotic and semantic, of signs, the immanent generator of meaning Heidegger called "language languaging." For Levinas, as we know, the trace is an ethical structure, not equivalent to the internal movement of signs, indeed exceeding all structures of immanence, as what gives significance to signification precisely by remaining "exterior" or "an-archic" or "outside." Language

---

[19] Levinas, *Totality and Infinity*, p. 195.
[20] Emmanuel Levinas, *Otherwise than Being or Beyond Essence*, trans. Alphonso Lingis (The Hague: Martinus Nijhoff, 1981), p. 168.    [21] Ibid., p. 120.

would be meaningful not because its signs interact, in a historically limited variety of combinations, with one another, but because interlocutors rise to responsibilities and obligations for one another. Levinas's trace, in a word, is the sincerity of the face. In Derrida's hands, however, the trace would become a founding concept of deconstruction. Diachrony, for Derrida, would become the central semiotic/semantic structure of language, what he calls "*differance*" or "undecidability." The price, however, for this displacement and loss of transcendence, this attempt to locate the trace within language, is the neutralization of its moral force. I have written at length on this point – the amorality, hence the immorality, of deconstruction – in the final chapter of *Elevations*, entitled "Derrida's (Mal)reading of Levinas."[22] But it is not merely, indeed not at all, an academic matter. The price of this price, already all too high in Heidegger's membership in the Nazi party and his silence about the Nazis and the Holocaust after the war, is again paid by Derrida – thankfully on a smaller scale – both in his inability and unwillingness to condemn the Nazi writings of Paul de Man and, perhaps worse, in his vicious attack on those who had the moral sense to condemn them.[23] It is no doubt true that Levinas's trace demands the "violation" of the formal structures of logic, inasmuch as the demands of ethics precede and transcend the requirements of epistemology and ontology. Such "violence", nonetheless, is precisely against moral complacency. It pales in comparison to the moral cowardness and violence, with very real consequences, perpetrated by those who – like Heidegger and Derrida – would neutralize the moral force of saying, mystifying and burying the humanity of the human under an avalanche of

---

[22] Cohen, *Elevations*, pp. 305–321.

[23] On Derrida, deconstruction, and the Paul de Man affair, see the balanced and morally sensible account by David Lehman, *Signs of the Times: Deconstruction and the Fall of Paul de Man* (New York: Poseidon Press, 1991, 1992). On Heidegger's moral corruption, among other volumes (e.g., Victor Farias, *Heidegger and Nazism*, trans. Paul Burrell [Philadelphia: Temple University Press, 1989], and Gunther Neske and Emil Kettering, eds., *Martin Heidegger and National Socialism* [New York: Paragon House, 1990]), see Berel Lang, *Heidegger's Silence* (Ithaca: Cornell University Press, 1996). On Derrida's adherence to Heideggerian *Denken*, it is evident throughout his writings, but see especially Jacques Derrida, *Of Spirit: Heidegger and the Question*, trans. Geoffrey Bennington and Rachel Bowlby (Chicago: University of Chicago Press, 1989).

ambiguities, indifferent to the mortal suffering of the other person, and in this way hiding behind the masks and ruses of language, language reduced to rhetoric, escaping responsibilities and obligations by saying "adieu" to Levinas.

On the final pages of *Otherwise than Being or Beyond Essence*, Levinas writes:

And I still interrupt the ultimate discourse in which all the discourses are stated, in saying it to one that listens to it, and who is situated outside the said that the discourse says, outside all it includes. That is true of the discussion I am elaborating at this very moment. This reference to an interlocutor permanently breaks through the text that the discourse claims to weave in thematizing and enveloping all things.[24]

[24] Levinas, *Otherwise than Being or Beyond Essence*, p. 170.

CHAPTER 6

# *Maternal body / maternal psyche: contra psychoanalytic philosophy*

For rabbinic Jews, the human being was defined as a body – animated, to be sure, by a soul – while for Hellenistic Jews (such as Philo) and (at least many Greek-speaking) Christians (such as Paul), the essence of a human being is a soul housed in a body.

Daniel Boyarin, *Carnal Israel*[1]

The psyche is the other in the same without alienating the same.

Emmanuel Levinas, *Otherwise than Being or Beyond Essence*[2]

In truth, both religion and ethics have the same intent. They both strive to elevate one from the limiting filth of self-love and to bring one to the pinnacle of loving others.

Rabbi Yehuda Ashlag, *Kabbalah: A Gift of the Bible.*[3]

The first part of this book, "Exceeding Phenomenology," comprising chapters one through four, aimed to show certain defining points of convergence and divergence between Levinas's ethical

[1] Daniel Boyarin, *Carnal Israel: Reading Sex in Talmudic Culture* (Berkeley: University of California Press, 1993), p. 5.
[2] Emmanuel Levinas, *Otherwise than Being or Beyond Essence* (hereafter: *OBBE*), trans. Alphonso Lingis (The Hague: Martinus Nijhoff, 1981), p. 112.
[3] Rabbi Yehuda Ashlag, *Kabbalah: A Gift of the Bible*, trans. Samuel R. Anteby (Jerusalem: Research Center of Kabbalah Books Edition, 1984), p. 72. This book by Rabbi Ashlag (1885–1955), a twentieth-century Talmudic commentator and Kabbalist, speaks in the religious language and to the sensibilities of an "orthodox" community of believers. In this it differs from the primarily philosophical vocabulary of Levinas's writings. Nonetheless, Ashlag's thought shows certain remarkable conceptual similarities with Levinas's exegetical ethical metaphysics. For one aspect of the comparison between their two worlds, see David Hansel, "L'origine chez Rabbi Yehouda Halevy Ashlag: Tsimtsoum de Dieu ou tsimsoum du Monde?" ["Origin in Rabbi Yehuda Halevy Ashlag: Tsimtsum of God or tsimtsum of the World?]", unpublished manuscript, available at < http:// ghansel.free.fr >.

161

metaphysics and the epistemological and ontological philosophies of Bergson, Husserl, and Heidegger primarily (but also Merleau-Ponty, Sartre, Derrida, to name some others). Its second part, "Good and Evil," which comprises the rest of the book, is less comparative and critical than expository and positive. The previous chapter, chapter 5, began this process. It briefly reviewed the most general "themes" of Levinas's philosophy and did so by at the same time revealing the complementary relationship binding Levinas's two major works, *Totality and Infinity* and *Otherwise than Being or Beyond Essence*. The work of the present chapter is also positive. It aims to illuminate Levinas's radically ethical conception of human being by tracing the notion of the "psyche" (*"psychisme"*), primarily through its appearance on the pages of *Otherwise than Being or Beyond Essence*. As we saw in chapter 5, this work, along with *Totality and Infinity*, elaborates Levinas's most developed and mature philosophical thought. More specifically, as we saw, while *Totality and Infinity* was primarily concerned to establish the ethical transcendence of the other person, *Otherwise than Being or Beyond Essence* is primarily concerned to articulate the impact of that transcendence in the moral self. It is this moral self, for-the-other before itself, that Levinas will call the "psyche." Much of the secondary literature on Levinas has focused on alterity, transcendence, the trace of the other. This is certainly proper, insofar as ethical transcendence is the first and deepest (or highest) force of all of Levinas's thought. Here, however, I am primarily concerned with that – or rather him or her – upon whom that transcendence "impacts," i.e., the moral *subject*. What does it mean not just to have this or that morality, but to be[4] a moral self? What is the structure of moral subjectivity? These two questions guide this chapter.

Before turning to the psyche, however, I want first to take a brief look at two introductory considerations regarding psychology and a psychologist. It is in the discipline of psychology, after all, rather

---

[4] Perhaps with this juxtaposition of the verbs "to have" and "to be," it is time to mention the name Gabriel Marcel, who authored a volume entitled *Being and Having* in 1935, and was an important personal and philosophical influence on Levinas. I freely admit that my book would be improved by adding Marcel's thought to those with whom I have compared and contrasted Levinas's. (The same might also be said, *mutatis mutandi*, of Martin Buber and Abraham Joshua Heschel.) I have tried, however, to focus more narrowly on the phenomenological school.

than philosophy or ethics, that today one ordinarily thinks of the "psyche." In order to provide a certain context, the first section presents a brief review of Levinas's general comments regarding psychology, psychoanalysis and Freud. Strictly speaking these comments are restricted in scope, dealing with one discipline among many. But because the real work of this chapter is to trace the notion of the "psyche," a notion of central importance to Levinas, it is best to start with these narrower considerations, in order to avoid being erroneously limited by them later. There is one important result of this quick examination of Levinas's comments on psychology. This is the stunning idea (which we touched upon in the previous chapter[5]), that independent of ethics the whole of consciousness, even and perhaps especially when – philosophical, scientific, phenomenological – it seeks the origins of things, is in a certain sense *merely* psychological. The next section examines the likely influence of Charles Blondel (1876–1939), professor of psychology and Levinas's mentor at the University of Strasbourg, where Levinas pursued his university studies, starting in 1923 at the age of seventeen. Both of these introductory sections are relatively short, however, because the weight of Levinas's positive and original contribution to philosophy (and thus also to a potential re-conceptualization of psychology) lies not with occasional or even comprehensive remarks about psychology and psychoanalysis, nor, obviously, with his relation to Blondel. Rather it lies with his conception of the psyche – the "maternal psyche," which is the primary subject matter of this chapter, as found in the third and fourth sections below.

### COMMENTS ON PSYCHOLOGY, PHENOMENOLOGY, PSYCHOANALYSIS, FREUD

Scattered throughout Levinas's many writings one finds brief comments on psychology, and on psychoanalysis and Freud more particularly.[6]

---

[5] See chapter 5, n. 15, p. 156.

[6] Steven Gans has written an article entitled "Levinas and Freud: Talmudic Inflections in Ethics and Psychoanalysis" (in Séan Hand, ed., *Facing the Other: The Ethics of Emmanuel Levinas* [Richmond, VA: Curzon Press, 1996], pp. 45–61), in which he argues "that the Levinasian Talmudic hermeneutic opens the possibility of making audible the muted Talmudic basis of Freud's psychoanalytic practice and shows the way toward the

One of the most sustained discussions of psychology is found on the final pages of chapter seven of *The Theory of Intuition in Husserl's Phenomenology*. Levinas's concern there, however, occurs within what seem to be the narrow confines of a technical question regarding the significance and depth of the phenomenological method and phenomenological science. It is a matter of the difference between psychology and phenomenology. This question may seem technical and narrow, but it is of course also the very important issue of distinguishing philosophy from non-philosophy, that is to say, a matter of distinguishing truth from opinion, the absolute (phenomenology) from the relative ("psychologism"). Early in his career, Husserl had named his new method "descriptive psychology" or "phenomenological psychology." He will soon shed these names, however, no doubt to avoid any appearance of "psychologism," and name his new philosophy "phenomenology" and "phenomenological philosophy." Levinas discusses psychology in *The Theory of Intuition in Husserl's Phenomenology*, then, in order to elucidate Husserl's mature conception of the radical difference between psychology and phenomenology.

Though radically different, psychology is for Husserl nonetheless strictly parallel, overlapping, or coincident (*Deckung*) with phe-

---

development of an ethical psychoanalysis" (p. 45). While the latter project, an "ethical psychoanalysis," appears eminently sensible, and has already been initiated in George Kunz's *The Paradox of Power and Weakness: Levinas and an Alternative Paradigm for Psychology* (Albany: State University of New York Press, 1998), the former notion, that there is a "muted Talmudic basis of Freud's psychoanalytic practice," and that this is what Levinas's "Talmudic hermeneutics" makes audible, strikes me as pure fantasy. Talmud and Talmudic hermeneutics are not something a Jew has in his or her blood, or that one picks up by osmosis. One must rather study Talmud, something I am unaware that Freud did. If Freud had been born in India, this sort of thinking leads us to believe, one would no doubt "discover" a muted Hindu hermeneutics at the basis of psychoanalytic practice. If one must discover such bases, I think it far more likely that Freud's psychoanalytic practice has a muted Catholic confessional basis than a Jewish Talmudic one. Along these same lines – racist I think – one "discovers" a rabbinic hermeneutics in the writings of Derrida, because, so I can only suppose, he was *born* Jewish. Among others, Susan Handelman tends toward this line of caricature in speaking of "Reb Derrida," as she calls him, in *The Slayers of Moses: The Emergence of Rabbinic Interpretation in Modern Literary Theory* (Albany: State University of New York Press, 1982). In contrast to Gans, however, Handelman spells out with some precision what she means by the rabbinic interpretation that she will discover in Freud, Lacan, Derrida, and Harold Bloom. She also, though several years later, in *Fragments of Redemption: Jewish Thought and Literary Theory in Benjamin, Scholem, and Levinas* (Bloomington: Indiana University Press, 1991), comes to appreciate the genuinely Talmudic hermeneutics at work in Levinas's thought.

nomenology in every particular. This is one more reason, no doubt, for the seductive attraction of "psychologism." The findings of one discipline are precisely mimicked by the other. But, and this is the all-important difference, the ultimate *sense* – the ultimate *meaning* or *significance* – of their findings differs radically. Psychology and "psychological consciousness" remain for Husserl "natural" or worldly like all non-phenomenological sciences. Phenomenology, in contrast, by utilizing the strict method of "epoche" or "reduction" – that is to say, by means of a deliberate *bracketing or suspension of the realist belief that defines and limits the natural attitude, along with a concomitant and positive reflective awareness of consciousness as "intentionality," that is, as meaning-giving*, ultimately grounded in transcendental consciousness – attains the absolute, the final constitutive origin of all meaning.[7] Phenomenology, we might say, is depth psychology purified of ontological presuppositions (which is doubtless why at first Husserl had been willing to call phenomenology "descriptive psychology"). Or, to put this difference in yet another way: psychology is one natural science among many, pursuing the logic of its particular and distinctive subject matter, the psyche, while phenomenology is philosophy as "rigorous science," at once transcending and accounting for the whole. Thus the difference between psychology and phenomenology is the radical difference between one natural science, in this case psychology, and the absolute science of philosophy. Of course this does not preclude a phenomenological reworking of the field of psychology, and such, precisely, is transcendental phenomenology.

Though Levinas's discussion of psychology and phenomenology in chapter seven of *The Theory of Intuition in Husserl's Phenomenology* sheds little light on Levinas's own conception of the psyche, it does reveal what will always be his dissatisfaction with any purely psychological accounts of reality. This, his argument against "psy-

---

[7] It is interesting to note that Bergson, whose philosophy of intuition in many ways anticipated Husserl's phenomenology, often used what he called "psychology" – without "psychologism" – as the method for his own fundamental researches. For example, in *The Two Sources of Morality and Religion*, his last book, published in 1932, we find the following typical sentence: "If we confine ourselves to psychology, as we have done, if we reconstitute, by an effort of introspection, the . . ., we find that . . ." Henri Bergson, *The Two Sources of Morality and Religion*, trans. R. Ashley Audra and Cloudesley Brereton (New York: Doubleday, 1935), p. 163.

chologism," which he shares with Husserl, and which he shares with all philosophers, is, though negative, very important, especially in our day when psychology has attained such enormous prestige in the popular mind. For Levinas, as for Husserl, psychology does not get to the root of things, does not reach ultimate significations or ultimate significance.[8] The methodological limitation of psychology follows from the distinction, summarized above, between a relative and an absolute science. The issue that is important, positively, for Levinas, is to say precisely what is the absolute that resists psychologism. And here Levinas parts company from Husserl: not phenomenology, that is, a more rigorous science, but rather ethics, the ethical metaphysics of the face-to-face, provides the *absolute* – transcendence – capable of putting a stop to the psychologizing of consciousness.

Husserl's powerful, indeed definitive, critique of "psychologism" appeared in the "Prolegomena" to his *Logical Investigations* of 1901–02. There, bringing to bear brilliant and unrelenting argumentation, Husserl attacked any purely psychological account of signification as a relativism, and hence as a skepticism, hence lacking in truth, and hence contradicting its own claims to scientific validity. In Levinas's discussion of psychology and phenomenology in chapter seven of *The Theory of Intuition in Husserl's Phenomenology*, it is quite interesting – in terms of discerning the point of departure for Levinas's own thinking – to note that in addition to pointing to the limitation of psychology revealed in the contrast Husserl makes between psychology and phenomenology, in the final two paragraphs of this same chapter, as we have seen, Levinas argues that phenomenology must pursue its own studies of inter-subjectivity. What this leads to, as we know, in the development of his own distinctive thought, is the recognition that it is

---

[8] This is also Buber's criticism of Jung. Namely, that by taking religion to be nothing but a "psychic event," i.e., an immanent event within the psyche, whether conscious or unconscious, Jung has deliberately reduced religion to psychology and lost sight of its most essential dimension – transcendence. Buber's criticism is that while Jung is certainly free as a psychologist to treat religion as a psychological phenomenon, he nonetheless has overstepped his authority as a psychologist when he *reduces* religion to a psychological phenomenon. See Martin Buber, "Religion and Modern Thinking," trans. Maurice S. Friedman, in Buber, *Eclipse of God* (New York: Harper & Row, 1957), pp. 63–92, endnotes, 141–144 (on Jung especially pp. 78–92; as well as "Supplement: Reply to C. G. Jung," pp. 133–137).

ethics (because for Levinas the deepest signification of inter-subjectivity is precisely ethical) rather than philosophy that puts a stop to the psychologizing of consciousness.

All this – the signification of consciousness as psychology, philosophy, and ethics – is made perfectly explicit, in a subsection entitled "Discourse and Ethics," in an article of Levinas's entitled "The *I* and Totality," published in 1954.[9] In this article Levinas elaborates the stunning thesis that considered independent of the ab-solute of ethics (i.e. ethical transcendence), consciousness strives to but cannot establish an origin for itself. Thus, precisely when it is most "philosophical," that is, seeking absolute origins, it is the most psychological. Psychoanalysis, then, would be the very structure of a consciousness seeking epistemological or ontological conditions, that is, a consciousness detached from its "true" (ethical) absolute. "If self-knowledge rests on conditions," Levinas writes, "no knowledge, even reflective, even psychoanalytic, has a beginning."[10] Earlier I distinguished "origin" from "beginning," the latter referring to consciousness in relation to the absolute transcendence of the other person. Without a beginning, then, absorbed in the search for origins, consciousness would be essentially the project of a psycho-analysis. But because, or if, it is deprived of its genuine ethical beginning, it will become ensnared in its own *mythology* rather than discover the origin it inevitably seeks. Thus, in a powerful passage, Levinas writes:

Psychoanalysis is, in its philosophical essence, the end result of rationalism: it places the same demands on reflection that reflection placed on naively thinking thought. The non-philosophical end result of psychoanalysis consists in a predilection for some fundamental, but elementary, fables – the libido, sadism, or masochism, the Oedipus complex, repression of the origin, aggressiveness [let me add Heidegger's "fourfold" of "earth, sky, gods and mortal"] – which, incomprehensibly, would alone be unequivocal, alone in not translating (or masking or symbolizing) a reality more profound than themselves: the end terms of psychological intelligibility. The fact of their having been collected from among the debris of the most diverse civilizations and called myths adds nothing to their worth as clarifying ideas, and at most evinces a return to

9 In Emmanuel Levinas, *Entre Nous: On Thinking-of-the-Other*, trans. Michael B. Smith and Barbara Harshav (New York: Columbia University Press, 1998), pp. 13–38.
10 Ibid., p. 31.

the mythologies, which is even more amazing since forty centuries of monotheism have had no other goal than to liberate humanity from their obsessive grip. Still, the petrifying effect of myths must be distinguished from the comfort they are thought to offer the intelligence.[11]

I could not refrain from interpolating Heidegger's "fourfold" among the arbitrary and mythic "origins" of consciousness, but one can certainly add Nietzsche's "will to power" (Levinas's "aggressiveness"), Schopenhauer's "world will," or Spinoza's "*conatus essendi*." In the end, they are all more or less sophisticated variations on the ancient formula of Thales: "All is water." Consciousness, as Kant showed definitively in the "Paralogisms" (not to mention the "Antinomies") of the "Dialectic" of his *Critique of Pure Reason*, is not self-contained. When philosophy, from within the resources of *ratio* alone, pretends to enunciate the "set of all sets," it simply mythologizes. Or, as Levinas put it: "psychoanalysis is, in its philosophical essence, the end result of rationalism."

And the way out? How does one (or is there an) escape either from an endless psycho-analysis, if one has the integrity to continue to seek conditions, or, even worse, from the arbitrariness of the mythology that emerges from an always premature end to the psycho-analytic process? The answer is in Levinas's great discovery: ethics, the ab-solute of the ethical transcendence of the other. I again cite Levinas at length:

But we cannot find our way out of that whole phantasmagoria – we do not begin the work of criticism itself – except in terms of a fixed point. That fixed point can be no incontestable truth, no "certain" statement, which would always be subject to psychoanalysis; but the absolute of an interlocutor, of a being, and not that of a truth about beings. He is not affirmed as a truth, but is believed. Faith or trust – which does not mean here a second source of knowledge, but which is assumed by every theoretical statement. Faith is not the knowledge of a truth about which one might be doubtful or certain. Beyond these modalities, it is the face to face encounter . . . Language cannot encompass the other: the other, the concept of whom we are using at this very moment, is not invoked as a concept, but as a person. In speech, we do not just think of the interlocutor, we speak to him.[12]

Without ethics, in other words, consciousness would be endless

---

[11] Ibid.     [12] Ibid., p. 32.

self-analysis or psycho-analysis (endlessly seeking conditions), or it would be arbitrarily, and hence dumbly, embedded in myth. Either unmasking or masked, it would be an endless costume party. But, as we shall see shortly when discussing Levinas's notion of the "maternal body" or "maternal psyche," *ethics* is not only the "truth," the higher or ab-solute truth, it is also the *cure* for the psychoanalysis of consciousness. "It is not through psychoanalysis, leading back to myths, that I can dominate the totality of which I am a part – but by encountering a being who is not in the system, a transcendent being."[13] These are truly remarkable pages, published in 1954.

Before moving on from this discussion, it is interesting to note that Levinas assimilates the endless "deferral" of sense found in Derrida's philosophy of deconstruction to the very same endlessness found in philosophy *qua* psychoanalysis. Levinas makes this equation in an article entitled "The Thinking of Being and the Question of the Other," first published in 1986, in a collection of his articles entitled *Of God Who Comes to Mind.*[14] In the previous chapter we began by noting that the "critique of metaphysics," or the "end of metaphysics," means criticizing both depths and surfaces, that is, criticizing not only worlds *behind* worlds, but the very coherence or stability of the *world* as such. The latter task, Levinas will say in this article of 1986, is Derrida's questioning of the "privilege of presence." But he will also note that Derrida's critique of the illusion of immediacy "cuts across traditional philosophy with a demarcation line similar to that of Kantianism."[15] Just as Kantian Reason (*Vernunft*) cannot give a definitive or final "depth" (or transcendental) account, that is, a coherent and comprehensive account of the totality, so, too, Kantian Understanding (*Verstand*) cannot give a definitive or final "surface" (or empirical) account, that is, a coherent and complete account of all conditions. Like the latter, but on the plane of reference rather than causality, what Derrida's deconstruction discovers – and exacerbates – is that "the signified, which is always to come in the signifier, never manages to take shape."[16] "This," Levinas writes, "is a view that

---

[13] Ibid., p. 34.
[14] See Emmanuel Levinas, *Of God Who Comes to Mind*, trans. Bettina Bergo (Stanford: Stanford University Press, 1998), pp. 111–21.    [15] Ibid., p. 116.    [16] Ibid., p. 117.

corresponds with what is perhaps the profoundest discovery of psychoanalysis: the dissimulative essence of the symbol. Lived experience would be repressed by the linguistic signs creating the texture of its apparent presence: an interminable play of signifiers postponing forever – repressing – the signified."[17] But this means that Levinas's critique of philosophy *qua* psychoanalysis applies also to deconstruction. His critique, let us remember, is that when philosophy attempts to ground itself in itself, that is, in epistemology or ontology, it sinks into a bottomless abyss, or, worse, it invents a mythological "bottom." Thus, Levinas writes of deconstruction:

Yet this is a critique that nevertheless remains faithful in some fashion to the gnoseological signification of meaning, precisely to the degree to which the deconstruction of intuition and the perpetual deferral of presence, which deconstruction shows, is thought exclusively from presence itself, which is treated as a norm.[18]

Thus, like philosophy *qua* psychoanalysis, deconstruction in attacking or deconstructing presence is at the same time, and no less resolutely, defending presence. This is precisely what Levinas said about deconstruction one year earlier, in an interview of 1985: "I have often wondered, with respect to Derrida, whether the *differance* of the present which leads him to the deconstruction of notions does not attest to the prestige that eternity retains in his eyes, the 'great present,' *being*, which corresponds to the priority of the *theoretical* and the truth of the theoretical, in relation to which temporality would be failure. I wonder," Levinas continues, contrasting his own thought to that of Derrida, "if time – in its very dia-chrony – is not *better* than eternity."[19] What both rationalism and deconstruction do not realize, and why they both devolve into psychoanalysis, is that genuine transcendence is ethical: the face of the other.

Before concluding this section, I want to note that in both *Time and the Other* (1947) and *Totality and Infinity* (1961), Levinas will criticize Freud by name for having begun his theory of psychoanalysis with libidinal desire and pleasure without having

[17] Ibid.      [18] Ibid.
[19] Levinas, "Violence of the Face," in Emmanuel Levinas, *Alterity and Transcendence*, trans. Michael B. Smith (New York: Columbia University Press, 1999), p. 173.

delved into them deeper.[20] Psychology is not deep enough. In an interview of 1982, entitled "Philosophy, Justice, and Love,"[21] Levinas will declare (in a remark that reminds us of another more personal statement, about Blondel, that he made in an interview of the same year[22]): "Before Eros there was the Face . . . I have never been a Freudian."[23] Levinas will consider his notion of the "maternal psyche" not only a challenge to Husserl, and to philosophical rationalism, but to Freudian accounts of the psyche as well.[24]

Through what at first sight seems like an odd reversal or twist, in *Difficult Freedom* and *Otherwise than Being or Beyond Essence*, Levinas accuses psychology and psychoanalysis, along with sociology (and on some occasions also Marxism, political economy, structuralism, linguistics, and political economy as well), of being too suspicious, for reductively detecting "symptoms or superstructures"[25] where straightforward meanings are intended by interlocutors.[26] In fact there is no reversal at all. This new accusation – really the charge of "ideology" – is a variation of the criticism we saw above, that psychology is not deep enough. Its lack of depth, we must remember, can lead either to an interminable analysis or to a hasty, indeed mythological, stop. Here psychology is accused of a hasty

---

[20] See Emmanuel Levinas, *Le temps et l'autre* (Paris: Presses Universitaires de France, 1994), p. 83; *Totalité et infini* (The Hague: Martinus Nijhoff, 1970), p. 253.

[21] Levinas, *Entre Nous*, pp. 104–121.

[22] 'Dialogue with Emmanuel Levinas," ed. and trans. Richard Kearney, in Richard A. Cohen, ed., *Face to Face with Levinas* (Albany: State University of New York Press, 1986), p. 13: "Blondel, one of his [Bergson's] disciples, developed a specifically Bergsonian psychology quite hostile to Freud – a hostility that made a deep and lasting impression on me."

[23] Levinas, *Entre Nous*, p. 113. A comment by Leo Strauss seems appropriate here: "It is safer to try to understand the low in the light of the high than the high in the light of the low. In doing the latter one necessarily distorts the high, whereas in doing the former one does not deprive the low of the freedom to reveal itself fully as what it is." Leo Strauss, 1962 Preface to English edition of *Spinoza's Critique of Religion*, in Judah Goldin, ed., *The Jewish Expression* (London: Yale University Press, 1976), p. 345.

[24] For Levinas's most sustained discussion of eros, and its relation to ethics, see the brilliant analyses of section four, "Beyond the Face," in *Totality and Infinity* (pp. 254–285). Let me also recommend chapter nine, "The Metaphysics of Gender," of my own book, *Elevations: The Height of the Good in Rosenzweig and Levinas* (Chicago: University of Chicago Press, 1994), pp. 195–219.

[25] Emmanuel Levinas, *Difficile liberté*, 4th edn. (Paris: Albin Michel, 1976), p. 266.

[26] See ibid., pp. 157, 234, 266, 267, 376; Emmanuel Levinas, *Autrement qu'être ou au-delà de l'essence* (The Hague: Martinus Nijhoff, 1974), p. 75.

stop, of trying to appear deeper than it is by reading meanings into significations at the expense of a more immediate, more direct, and more compelling ethical significance. For Levinas, as we shall see, it is the other – the one who faces – who speaks to me and to whom I speak. The radical alterity of the other does not lie in that person's "complexes," or bank account, or nationality, though these and other similar "superstructures" certainly have a role to play. Their role, however, is auxiliary and not primary. In attending first to symptoms and superstructures – approaching the other as would a detective – psychology is diverted from the more originary and peremptory meaning of the ethical event of proximity. Freudianism, in the name of analysis, effects a sort of epistemological epoche or reserve, but by trying to register more, by treating the other's psyche as a symptom (like one's own psyche, since everything is reduced to a symptomology), it ends by being in contact with less. Thus "depth" psychology precisely misses the ethico-metaphysical impact of alterity and the sensibility that we, following Levinas, are calling maternal body/maternal psyche.

## THE INFLUENCE OF CHARLES BLONDEL

Charles Blondel was a distinguished professor of psychology at the University of Strasbourg and in his day – the first third of the twentieth century – was a well-known theorist of psychology. He authored a number of books in psychology and philosophy – *The Morbid Consciousness* (1914), *Psychoanalysis* (1924), *Primitive Mentality* (1926), *Introduction to Collective Psychology* (1928), *The Psychology of Marcel Proust* (1932), and *Suicide* (1933), none of which are translated into English – that were well received and commented upon. Blondel was also Levinas's teacher at Strasbourg in the 1920s. It is difficult to ascertain his precise influence on Levinas because Levinas makes only one brief explicit reference to Blondel's work, that is to say, to its content. In an interview conducted by Richard Kearney in the early 1980s, Levinas remarks that Blondel had "developed a specifically Bergsonian psychology quite hostile to Freud – a hostility that made a deep and lasting impression on me."[27] We have seen this, Levinas's hostility to Freud, above.

---

[27] See n. 21 above, p. 171.

Beyond this particular lesson learned, we know that Levinas had felt close to Blondel as a person and maintained a lifelong respect for him. In another interview, fifty years after having been his student, Levinas remembers of his earlier relationship to Blondel that "he became very quickly a man to whom I could say everything."[28] Today we would call such a teacher a "mentor." In yet another interview, also conducted in the 1980s, Levinas testifies that Blondel was one of the "four professors to whom, in my spirit, I attach an incomparable prestige"[29] – note the present tense, more than half a century later. Throughout his entire life, then, Levinas held both the man and the educator in the highest regard. In this section I would like to suggest some more specific ways that Blondel may have influenced Levinas.

Blondel opposed Freud. How or on what basis did he oppose Freud? What Blondel contested was the central Freudian notion of the "unconscious," and its alleged influence on, or interaction with, conscious life. In its stead, he defended a very different model for grasping what he preferred to call the difference not between the conscious and the unconscious but rather between the "voluntary" and the "involuntary." To understand this difference, let us first note that Blondel gained professional recognition due to his insistence on the social or "collective" dimension of individual psychology – without, for all that, reducing the individual to a pure node of sociality. Of course, we see this same emphasis on the social, again without reducing the individual to its social being, in Levinas. At all stages of personal development, according to Blondel, the individual and society must be understood together. "Will and reason," for instance, the former so often interpreted as a function or faculty of the individual, are for Blondel "the two splendid presents that society deposits in our cradle."[30] So, too, "affective states" are penetrated by social significations.

[28] Interview with François Poirie, 1986, in François Poirie, ed., *Emmanuel Levinas: Qui êtes-vous?* (Lyon: La Manufacture, 1987), p. 70.

[29] Emmanuel Levinas, *Ethics and Infinity*, trans. Richard A. Cohen (Pittsburgh: Duquesne University Press, 1985), p. 25; also see footnote one on p. 25 for a selected bibliography of Charles Blondel. The other three professors were: Maurice Halbwachs (1877–1945; martyred), Maurice Pradines (1891–1958), and Henri Carteron (1891–1929).

[30] Cited in Armand Cuvillier, *Cours de philosophie*, vol. I (Paris: Armand Colin, 1954), p. 41. I have not been able to track this citation down, but in all likelihood it is taken from Charles Blondel, *Introduction à la psychologie collective* (Paris: Armand Colin, 1928).

Social significations, Blondel also fully recognizes, depend on civilization and hence on history. Now, insofar as social significations penetrate all the way to the deepest constitutive layers of affective states, will, and reason, Blondel understands that the voluntary and the involuntary, far from being radically distinct, are on a continuum.

The difference between the voluntary and the involuntary, then, is neither a difference in kind, say that between a civilized construct and animal instincts, nor, for that matter, a difference between "conscious" and "unconscious" in the Freudian sense of these terms.[31] For Blondel, the "voluntary" represents gestures or significations deemed "opportune" or socially viable. The "involuntary," in contrast, represents not an essentially uncivilized reservoir of drives, as Freud proposed (or a depth grammar or semiotics, according to Lacan), but rather gestures and significations determined *by society* to be *anti-social* or "inopportune": gestures and significations deemed contrary to public mores, manners, and morals. Thus sociality, a social continuum of the acceptable and the unacceptable, and not an animal residue or a theoretical postulate, determines the difference and the fluid boundary between the voluntary and the involuntary. It is clear, in any case, that according to Blondel's model the difference between the voluntary and the involuntary is accounted for without resorting to the hypothesis of a primitive unconscious (mechanical or linguistic) substructure.

The difference between voluntary and involuntary gestures and significations, then, would stem from a combination of two related factors: (1) socially constructed meanings in relation to (2) the individual's attentiveness or attention. The latter recalls Bergson's notion that all consciousness is a "tension," a tension that when relaxed tends toward matter (indeed, in Bergson's later work "matter" is precisely a relaxed consciousness) and that when tensed tends toward spirit. For Blondel, the normal or adjusted subject, belonging to and more or less molded by a particular community of subjects, that is, belonging to a specific and particu-

---

[31] Even recognizing that in Freud there are several possible "models," e.g. a mechanical pressure system, or a linguistic model (Lacan), for the relationship between the conscious and the unconscious.

lar culture or civilization, is a subject attentive to rehearsing only socially accepted gestures and significations (including a certain socially determined margin of creative originality). These are precisely the gestures and significations that are considered voluntary. The same subject, again as an active/passive member of a particular community, culture or civilization, is such a member precisely because he or she recognizes certain other gestures and significations to be anti-social and hence socially unacceptable. When these gestures and significations perchance occur, they, in contrast to the first set of gestures and significations, will seem to be more or less accidents, errors or mistakes. They are considered to be more or less the products of inattention, and hence more or less involuntary. Thus, rather than being a function of a natural or primitive division between the conscious and a repressed unconscious, the difference between the voluntary and involuntary, for Blondel, is bound to the always more or less conscious (= attentive) dissemination and assimilation of cultural significations.

There is another noteworthy consequence of the weight Blondel places on the sociality of the human individual. Different communities, cultures, and civilizations, are different precisely because they divide the realm of what counts as significant or objective ("real/unreal," "opportune/inopportune") differently. Thus they also divide what counts as voluntary and involuntary differently. What is considered involuntary in one culture (e.g. a burp or body odor) could well be considered voluntary in another, and vice versa. Further, what is considered voluntary at one point in time in one community, culture or civilization, could well have been considered involuntary at another time. Behaviors and significations that today in America are taken to be sexist or racist, for example, and hence taken to be subject to moral evaluation, and hence considered to be products of freedom or conscious control, could also be considered – at an earlier time, or in a sub-culture, or in another place at the same time – "involuntary" and hence non-moral behaviors. At a different time or in a different place, the immoral behaviors of one culture might be considered "part of the nature of things," "unremarkable," "a matter of course," in another. Thinking of the voluntary and involuntary in this way, then, opens values to a much more radical cultural critique than does a naturalization of this division, such as Freud's. Blondel's psychology, in any event, is based on giving greater credence to the impact of societal mores and morals on the conscious attention, will, and affective states of the individual.

Aside from the particular details or the explanatory force of Blondel's account (characterized somewhat schematically above), it is clear that at least three dimensions of his model resonate closely with Levinas's subsequent thought. First, there is the strong bond between reason and will and social significations. Reason and will, and hence affectivity itself, are constituted in relation to others and to the cultural and historical significations that organize societies. Having said this, we must also note that, like Blondel, Levinas will be careful to resist any totalizing or complete historicization of the subject. One of the most important moments of his thought, a moment essential to its ethical dimension, especially in terms of the passivity/activity of the moral subject, is the original *independence* of the subject. In all four of his philosophical books, Levinas will insist on the subject's origin in a sensible "hypostasis," its "separation" *qua* self-sensing – what Levinas terms the self as "enjoyment" (*jouissance*) – both from a "lower level" of undifferentiated anonymous existence ("there is," *il y a*), and from all the "higher levels" of signification determined by the inner needs of such a separated being (e.g., its fragility) and its various relations to more or less exterior social dimensions ("dwelling," "family," "ethics," "justice"). Levinas's thought – like Blondel's – is neither purely social nor purely individualistic.

Second, and related, there is the strong link both Blondel and Levinas maintain between will and conscious attention. This yields an account in Levinas attuned to the social inflection, as it were, of attention and will. The will is not simply an animal given, a natural force, power, or instinct,[32] but rather is a transfiguration resulting from the encounter with transcendence. The moral will, as we shall see below, begins in shame, shameful of its brute power, in the recognition that one can murder. The moral will "originates"

---

[32] According to Gilles Deleuze's reading, in *Nietzsche and Philosophy*, trans. Hugh Tomlinson (New York: Columbia University Press, 1983), so naturally given does Nietzsche consider the will that he felt its level of force could be quantified to determine differences between one person and another. We can add that his famous "*amor fati*," while in some sense grounded in a metaphysical doctrine of "Eternal Return," at the same time also expresses the inexorable givenness of the particular will.

outside itself (what we earlier called its "beginning" prior to its "origin"), in response to the face of the other as moral command, as, more particularly, the "Thou shalt not murder" directed to the physical powers of the "natural" subject. What this means, in line with Blondel, is that moral will is more or less a discipline, is more or less a manner of conscious attentiveness or responsiveness to the other. Levinas will call this moral layer, this conscientiousness of consciousness, "non-intentional," precisely because it comes from the outside, hence exceeds the immanent circuits of meaning-bestowal that characterize intentional consciousness according to Husserl's analyses. Following Bergson, for Levinas the deepest attention, instead of being the most self-conscious consciousness in the sense favored by philosophers, namely, the most active consciousness (from Aristotle's "thought thinking itself," to the medieval "active intellect," to Hegel's "concept"), involves an extreme passivity precisely because it is a responsiveness to the other. This is the "maternal psyche" to which we will turn shortly.

Third, and again related to the first point above, and perhaps most important of all three points, there is the fact that for Blondel as for Levinas one cannot separate sociality, which penetrates the individual from birth, from *morality*. Of course Levinas makes this – ethics – the centerpiece of his thought, but it is also present in Blondel. This third dimension (indeed all three components and their links) is highlighted in the following citation taken from Blondel. This citation has the additional value of having the French psychologist Henri Pieron (1881–1964), with whom Blondel both agrees and disagrees, here play a role analogous to that of Husserl for Levinas.[33] Blondel writes:

Pieron is right to want psychology not to bother with the moral value of the principles that dictate the conduct it studies. According to him, voluntary activity is purely and simply intentional activity, and all intentional conduct, whatever the value of ends and means, is voluntary

---

[33] Despite its relevance in this citation, the analogy does not hold for long, however, because unlike Husserl, who defended "inner consciousness," the "transcendental ego" as the source of all meaning, Pieron held the opposite position, arguing against introspection altogether (contra Bergson), and as such was a precursor of behaviorism, psychophysiology and neuro-science. Pieron taught at the prestigious Collège de France from 1923 to 1950. He was author, among other writings, of: *L'évolution de la mémoire* (1910); *Le Cerveau et la pensée* (1921); *La sensation guide de la vie* (1945), *Vocabulaire de la psychologie* (1957); and *De l'actinie à l'homme* (1958).

activity. But no psychology of behavior, unless it is to remain incomplete, can make an abstraction of the conduct called moral, whatever be, for the moralist, the value of the ethics to which this conduct submits. All intentional conduct, if it is not pure impulsion, implies, good or bad, a system of values, and reveals itself the more intentional the more it is coherent, that is to say, not only the means for it to better conform to an end, but even more when the end is harmonized with an ensemble of designs antecedently following interest. Now in every epoch of the evolution of humanity the model of a system of values has been the system of values called moral.[34]

For Blondel, the will, the voluntary, that for which one is respon-sible, is linked to a psychological attention sensitive to what society permits and does not permit. For Blondel, also, what society permits and does not permit is inextricably bound to questions of morality and justice. These links, between consciousness, sociality, attention, and morality, will all later be reflected in Levinas's thought.

More specifically, given all the above, perhaps we can now also see Blondel's influence behind Levinas's concluding remarks in *The Theory of Intuition in Husserl's Phenomenology* regarding the import-ance of inter-subjectivity for phenomenology.[35] Looking back to-day, given the work of Levinas, and perhaps even more so that of Alfred Schutz, whose important volume *The Phenomenology of the Social World*[36] was published in 1932, the theme of inter-subjectivity seems so naturally central to phenomenology.[37] But this was not always so, and was certainly not at all obvious within the phenom-enological movement in 1930. In 1930, this theme, the importance of inter-subjectivity, the importance of the collective, would have

---

[34] Charles Blondel, "Les Volitions," in G. Dumas, *Nouveau Traité de psychologie*, vol. IV (1930), p. 362, note; cited in Maurice Pradines, *Traité de psychologie generale*, vol. II (Paris: Presses Universitaires de France, 1946), p. 383.

[35] We discussed these remarks in chapters 2 and 3 above.

[36] Alfred Schutz, *The Phenomenology of the Social World*, trans. George Walsh and Frederick Lehnert (Evanston: Northwestern University Press, 1967); German original: *Der sinnhaft Aufbau der sozialen Welt* (Vienna: Julius Springer, 1932).

[37] No doubt the "dialogical thinking" of Martin Buber, whose influential book *I and Thou* was first published in 1923, also influenced Levinas (not to mention the possible influence of Eugen Rosenstock-Huessy and Franz Rosenzweig) on this score. But within phenom-enology, in contrast to "religious thought," Levinas and Schutz were pioneers cham-pioning the centrality of the social. Schutz's orientation, however, unlike Levinas's, remained epistemological rather than ethical.

been associated with the work of Charles Blondel. Let us recall what Levinas wrote at the end of his Husserl book:

> Concrete being is not what exists for only one consciousness. In the very idea of concrete being is contained the idea of an intersubjective world. If we limit ourselves to describing the constitution of objects in an individual consciousness, in an *ego*, the *egological reduction* can be only a first step toward phenomenology. We must also discover "others" and the intersubjective world.[38]

If, as some have claimed, Levinas's appreciation for phenomenology's discovery of the "concrete" is evidence of Heidegger's influence (though, to be fair to the founder of phenomenology, this discovery of the concrete is no less evidence of Husserl's influence), then surely it is no less likely that Levinas's revolutionary recognition of the fundamental importance of intersubjectivity for phenomenology (and ethics), is evidence of Blondel's influence.

Of course, in his book on Husserl it is no surprise that Levinas credits Husserl himself for being seriously interested in intersubjectivity: "this intersubjective reduction and all the problems that arise from it have much preoccupied Husserl."[39] Levinas's teacher at Strasbourg is not mentioned, and never will be mentioned (with one minor exception) in Levinas's published writings.[40] In his Husserl book, Levinas will list specific relevant topics dealt with by Husserl: "the perception of our body and its analogy with the body of others"; "the life which manifests in this other body a type of existence analogous to mine"; "the characteristic of the constitution proper to intersubjectivity"; "the existence of man as a person and the history and origin of consciousness"; "a problem such as that of destiny"; "the constitution of immanent time and of cosmic time"; and he concludes this list by pointing to Husserl's "unpublished works" on intersubjectivity, stating that, though they "have been very influential" (a reference to Heidegger no doubt), "we are not authorized to use them prior to their publication."[41] I

[38] Emmanuel Levinas, *The Theory of Intuition in Husserl's Phenomenology*, 2nd edn., trans. André Orianne (Evanston: Northwestern University Press, 1995), p. 150.    [39] Ibid., p. 151.

[40] With the one exception of the listing of Blondel's name along with Levinas's three other primary teachers at Strasbourg (Halbwachs, Pradines, Carteron), in the short biographical article, appropriatedly entitled "Signature," published at the end of Emmanuel Levinas, *Difficult Freedom*, trans. Séan Hand (Baltimore: Johns Hopkins University Press, 1990), p. 291.

[41] Levinas, *The Theory of Intuition in Husserl's Phenomenology*, p. 151.

have no doubt that these remarks crediting Husserl are both true and sincerely meant. What I am suggesting, however, is more modest than a displacement of or transference upon Husserl. It is simply the likelihood that Levinas's own attention and interest were drawn to "transcendental intersubjectivity," to the social dimension of self and signification, and also, subsequently, to the irreducible role of morality and justice in the constitution of meaning, at least in part owing to the influence of his mentor, Charles Blondel.

Interesting as is Levinas's relationship to Blondel, and as important as are Levinas's insights into the fundamentally psycho-analytical character of rationalist consciousness and its inevitable deconstruction when self-absorbed, it is time now to turn to Levinas's positive and original account of the psyche *qua* moral subjectivity.

## MATERNAL BODY/MATERNAL PSYCHE

In a chapter entitled "Psyche or the Separation of the Knower from the Known," from his book *Preface to Plato*,[42] Eric A. Havelock, then Emeritus Sterling Professor of Classics at Yale University, presents a well-reasoned and studious account of the nature and origin of the pysche in ancient Greek culture. The psyche emerged, so he argues, through a paradigm shift whereby "the Homeric state of mind gave way to the Platonic."[43] What does this mean? In contrast to the Homeric mentality, in which one became a person by "a mechanism of self-surrender to the poetic performance, and of self-identification with the situations and the stories related in the performance," the Platonic mentality demanded "self-consciousness emancipated from the condition of an oral culture." "The *psyche*," Havelock continues, "which slowly asserts itself in independence of the poetic performance and the poetized [*sic*] tradition had to be the reflective, thoughtful, critical psyche, or it could be nothing."[44] For Havelock, then, the "Platonic" psyche, in contrast to and liberated from the participa-

[42] Eric A. Havelock, *Preface to Plato* (Cambridge, MA: Harvard University Press, 1963), pp. 197–214.    [43] Ibid., p. 198.
[44] Ibid., p. 200.

tory or mimetic ethos of the oral-poetic "Homeric state of mind," is the independent, self-reflective, self-conscious, the critical, thinking ego. This same division, between a participatory-poetic consciousness and an independent-reflective consciousness, structures Nietzsche's work, too, from his first books, especially *The Birth of Tragedy*, with its distinction between Dionysian frenzy and Apollonian contemplation, to his last, *The Genealogy of Morals*, *The Wagner Case* and the *Twilight of the Idols*, with their distinction between reflective religious/scientific consciousness and productive artistic consciousness.

What Havelock and Nietzsche do not consider, however, is a third option. Introducing this – in all its radicality – is precisely Levinas's contribution. The break with poetic-participatory consciousness, or "mythic" consciousness, occurs not with reflective consciousness, which reproduces the immanent circuits of participatory consciousness at a reflective or intentional level, but rather with moral consciousness, which is structured entirely otherwise – as both response and responsibility – than both mythic and reflective consciousness.

Thus, while the individualized psyche does indeed mark a departure from the participatory selfhood of the mimetic aesthetic tradition, it may nonetheless be the case that selfhood must be interpreted according to a still deeper interpretation than that arising from and reflecting the reflective, critical, or contemplative self-consciousness Havelock and Nietzsche both attribute – the one to praise, the other to criticize – to Plato. It seems to me that Havelock has been overly influenced by Heidegger, who has taken up Nietzsche's line of thought (purified, so we are meant to believe, of Nietzsche's metaphysics of the will[45]) by seeing beneath the theory and practice of human beings a deeper poetic-participatory engagement in being. But behind Heidegger, despite but at the same time in line with his "turn," stands Nietzsche and the entire romantic tradition. Or, to put this matter in the sociological terms

---

[45] See Martin Heidegger, *Nietzsche*, vols. I–IV, trans. David Farrell Krell (vols. I and II) and Frank A. Capuzzi (vols. III and IV) (New York: Harper & Row, I, 1979; II, 1984; III, 1987; IV, 1982); and Heidegger, "The Word of Nietzsche: 'God is Dead'," in Martin Heidegger, *The Question Concerning Technology and Other Essays*, trans. William Lovitt (New York: Harper & Row, 1977), pp. 53–112.

of Ferdinand Tönnies's influential work of 1887, *Community and Society*,[46] Heidegger has opted for "community" (*Gemeinschaft*) in contrast to "society" (*Gesellschaft*), that is to say, for the participatory community of being in contrast to the atomistic individual (*subjectum*) of society. But this entire framework and the central opposition upon which it is based, its opposition between reflective objectifying consciousness (*Gegenstand*) and participatory openness to being (*Aletheia*), proves, in the face of Levinas's ethical metaphysics, to be unduly limited. It will have to be interpreted anew from the ethical perspective it suppresses, wittingly or not.

But these are introductory remarks, providing a brief historical and neat conceptual context. It is clear that Levinas does not define the self cognitively. Indeed, he does not "define" the self at all, does not consider the self to be a specification of a genus, an instance of a generality, or a part of a whole. Despite the theories of Jacques Lacan,[47] who thinks of the self by itself, or in relation to the world, the self constituted as a mirroring of itself, the self for Levinas is not first a spectacle, an object seen from the outside. The self is the first person singular. However, singularity must not be confused with individuality. Every spatial-temporal entity is individual, unique because no other entity occupies the same space at the same time. But this uniqueness does not constitute selfhood. Odd as it may seem, Kant already saw something like singularity in his account of the "parallogisms" of reason in the "Dialectic" of the *Critique of Pure Reason*. The self could not know itself, not because all the data was not in, but because the knowing self essentially exceeded the self known. For Kant, however, the impossibility of objectifying the self was understood in epistemological terms, as a rupture or breakdown in knowing.[48] For Levinas, in contrast, the human psyche – ego, self, subjectivity, soul, I – is from

[46] Ferdinand Tönnies, *Community and Society*, trans. Charles P. Loomis (New York: Harper & Row, 1963).

[47] See, especially, Jacques Lacan, *Écrits: A Selection*, trans. Alan Sheridan (New York: W. W. Norton Co., 1977); also Richard Boothby, *Death and Desire: Psychoanalytic Theory in Lacan's Return to Freud* (New York: Routledge, Chapman and Hall, 1991).

[48] Even if one grants the priority of the second critique over the first, Kant still thinks of practical reason in terms of theoretical reason, i.e., in terms of self-legislation and obedience to law. The greatness of Levinas's philosophy is to have truly thought reason based in ethics. In the history of philosophy, perhaps only the Platonic dialogue has done the same.

the first not a scientific object, not even a failed or deferred scientific object, but a moral event, an event of sensibility deeper than rationality.

Singularity is a function of moral responsibility, the irreplaceability of the moral agent. We shall shortly see how moral selfhood is at once both singular and social: singular as social, social as singular, precisely because both these terms, the singular and the social, must be understood originally in moral rather than epistemological terms. For the moment, however, let us first appreciate the shift in grounds Levinas's account requires. What does it mean positively and concretely for the human self not to be, or not to be originally, an object or spectacle seen from the outside? An examination of Levinas's reading of Husserl, influenced partly by his teacher, Charles Blondel, reveals Levinas's account to be both concrete and rooted in the intersubjective. Nonetheless, it does not mean, as one might think, that selfhood will be presented exclusively as the intersection or node of interactions or transactions within a social network or differential (e.g., as seen in Freud and Jung), or that it is the motivational zero point of certain social values (e.g., as seen in Köhler, Maslow, Adler, and Erikson). Rather, more deeply and specifically, it means that selfhood emerges *as* the bearer of obligations and responsibilities for the other. The human self, in other words, is constituted by – constituted in, constituted as – the inescapable exigencies of moral obligations and responsibilities. The self, one might say, is pressed into service, service to others. It does not volunteer – it is enlisted. Beneath or rather better than the for-itself of reason, beneath or rather better than the for-itself of willfulness, or the alleged dissipation or annihilation of the will in frenzy or poetic hearkening, for Levinas it is in the passivity of its very sensibility that the self is itself as for-the-other.

The self is therefore not an entity with moral qualities, a substance with moral attributes. To say "the self is for-the-other" does not mean that first there is a self and then this self becomes "for-the-other," but rather that insofar as the self is for-the-other it is itself. Its original way of being is moral. Or, to say this differently, to be originally is to be morally. "To be or not to be," Levinas has

written, "is not the question."[49] The question is to be good. Not to
be, but the right to be. The self is thus not only its "brother's
keeper," but it is *as* its brother's keeper, and only insofar as it is its
brother's keeper. The self lived in the first person singular, me,
myself, I, is a singularity deriving its singularity, its irreplaceability,
its non-substitutability – what Levinas, borrowing religious language, calls its "election" – from its moral responsibility to and for
the other. Moral sensibility, in other words, cuts deeper than the
instincts of animal sensibility, the willfulness of human desire, the
reflection of human reason, or the vertigo of poetic attunement.
One is stunned or, to use one of Levinas's terms, "traumatized,"
by the other. But the impact of the other is not a brute force, it is a
moral force: there is a responsibility to respond, obligation to and
for the other.

Responsibility for the other thus cuts deeper than egoism's
for-itself. One is chosen before choosing. Here, it seems to me, lies
Levinas's great insight and achievement: the absolute primacy of
morality and, built on morality, of justice. Here, too, lie fertile
grounds for an ethical reconfiguration of psychology. To have seen
that the core of what it is to be human, the distinctively human, the
very psyche, is from the first and at bottom to be conceived – and
not merely conceived but lived – within the imperative vectors of
morality and justice, rather than in terms of the motivations,
drives, and interactions of instincts or knowledge, creativity or
productivity, technology or ontology, or aesthetics – this is the
challenge of Levinas's thought. No doubt the circuits of the for-
itself are potential forces. When realized for the self at the expense
of the other and of others, they are forces of evil. But they are now,
in Levinas's account, seen to be refusals of a deeper moral force,
the pacific force of goodness, the prior moral authority commanding the self from the heights of the other. This sort of thinking
provokes an upheaval in thought. It requires a reversal of thinking
that Kant wanted but could not accomplish: thought grounded in
morality.

When Levinas characterizes the psyche as a moral psyche he
means that its "for-the-other" is from the first a moral event. It is

49 Levinas, *Ethics and Infinity*, p. 10.

moral more essentially, as it were, than essence itself.[50] That is to say, selfhood is for-the-other more deeply than its essence, substance, will, reason, transcendental ego, substance-as-subject, freedom, will-to-power, resoluteness, *Gelassenheit*, and all the formulae of self-sameness – whether individual or participatory – philosophy has proposed for selfhood hitherto. For Levinas, in contrast, the self stands in relation to a far greater transcendence, indeed an *absolute* transcendence, than the alterity recognized and integrated into these formulae. And this transcendence, as we know, is the transcendence of the other person – absolute yet in relation. Such a relation, with what is both out of relation and in relation, hence a relation that exceeds all the relations (inherence, causality, reciprocity) and modalities of relation (possibility, existence, necessity) *known* by philosophy,[51] can only "be" as the moral relation. Here selfhood is selfhood not through syntheses of self-identification, whether mine or the world's (spirit, substance, etc.), but rather as a "non-identity," a being "put into question" or a "de-nucleation" by the other. The self is thus a dis-equilibrium, not such that it loses itself, is annihilated, is non-being, but precisely such that it finds itself wholly given over to the other in moral responsibility for the other – all the way, under extreme circumstances, unto death.

The veritable self is thus "for-the-other" before it is for-itself – chosen before choosing. Its very existence is as "the-other-in-the-same," the "other in me." These abstract formulae, repeated by Levinas again and again in *Otherwise than Being or Beyond Essence* and elsewhere, are in no way meant as "glosses" on an already constituted self, or as metaphors for something else, but rather as the most general or all-encompassing articulations of an exceedingly concrete, imperative disordering of selfhood understood in all its other expressions (having, knowing, being, etc.). These formulae – for-the-other, put-into-question, other-in-the-same, and so on – are the most basic expressions of Levinas's ethical wisdom, of his conception of the psyche. What do they mean?

---

[50] Regarding the issue of "essence," see chapter 4 above.

[51] I have, for convenience, provided Kant's "categories" of relation and modality, but the ethical relation exceeds all relations of *having, knowing,* or *being.* The very specificity of the ethical relation is its excess – or infinity – as moral obligation.

SENSIBILITY AND SIGNIFICATION

To flesh out the meaning of these seemingly abstract expressions, in this section we are going to turn to Levinas's most sustained discussion of the psyche. This occurs in the third chapter, "Sensibility and Proximity," of *Otherwise than Being or Beyond Essence*. When Levinas speaks of the psyche elsewhere in his writings (for example, in *Totality and Infinity*), he does so in the direction of the trajectory articulated in that chapter.

The first time Levinas refers positively to the psyche in *Otherwise than Being or Beyond Essence* he begins by linking it to a sensibility exceeding Husserl's notion of intentionality. For Levinas the psyche is a breach and not a bastion of self-consciousness. Levinas's deepest account of this breach has to do with its time: "dia-chrony," the self pierced by time's transcendent dimensions, the irrecuperable past and the unforeseeable future, which for Levinas come to the self as a function of the time of the other.[52] Since Kant, and in some sense even earlier in Augustine, philosophers have understood that time is "the form of subjectivity." Until the contemporary period of thought, however, such time was more or less dismissed in the name of "eternity." Now, since Bergson, as we have seen, the issue has been to show precisely the nature of inner time and its relation to other forms of time such as "clock time" or historical time. Bergson showed that clock time, or the time of a "time line," is not really time at all but the measure of motion, hence a spatialized "time." Inner time, which is genuine time, in contrast, he named "duration," and characterized it in terms of a creatively developing inter-penetration of past, present, and future. Levinas's notion of dia-chrony, in contrast to Bergson's duration, while referring still to "the form of subjectivity," refers to the self not in continuity with past and future, but rather ruptured by an "immemorial past" and an "unforeseeable future." For Levinas what is key to time is the alterity of its dimensions, not their continuity. Thus Levinas breaks with the more harmonious images of identity one obtains when thinking of time in terms of projections and continuities as in Bergson, but also with the

---

[52] For Levinas's account of time, see my *Elevations*, chapter six, "On Temporality and Time," pp. 133–161.

syntheses of "retentions" and "protentions" in Husserl's "inner time consciousness," or Heidegger's existential version of Husserlian time, the "ecstatic" syntheses of Dasein as "temporality," time as futural projection and historical retrieval. For Levinas in contrast to all these visions of inner time as extensivity, the psyche is diachrony, and diachrony is ruptured time, self pierced by a past and a future not its own but the other's.

The key to the intrusions of past, the pastness of the past, and future, the futurity of the future, that constitute the psyche as diachrony is that they are not produced by the subject. If they were they would reduce to one form or another of projection or synthesis, which is exactly what Levinas rejects. How, then, can the other affect the self without either being reduced to self or inaugurating a war of absorption, other-into-self or self-into-other,[53] that is to say, how can the other affect the self, or the self be affected by the other, such that otherness retains its transcendence? Levinas's answer is, of course, by means of moral transcendence, the transcendence that demands more than can satisfy it, putting a "more" into a "less." Here Levinas speaks of this alteration of the self in terms of time (i.e., diachrony). The psyche, ruptured by diachronous time, is affected by the moral alterity of the other. Such alterity retains its alterity insofar as it is received by a self inordinately responsible for the other. It is quite striking, then, that diachrony – which is to say, time – the psyche and morality all arise together. Furthermore, the moral other can have this effect on the self precisely because it affects the self beneath or beyond or across the identifying power of the self's reason and will, reaching the self in its very sensibility, that is to say, in its sensibility as a passivity. This "inspiration" of the self in its passivity, due to its sensible vulnerability to the other, leads Levinas to name the

---

[53] Treating "negation" existentially, both Hegel and Sartre conceive inter-subjectivity as a war. In *Being and Nothingness* (1943), Sartre conceives the self as pure negation or the pure activity of the for-itself. Such a self cannot, by definition, brook alterity. For Sartre, unlike Hegel, negation does not lead to sublimation (*aufheben*). Thus, per impossibile, there are multiple selves, each the absolute negation of the other. Hegel, however, who treats substance (in-itself) as subject (for-itself), ends by this maneuver with a reality that is both in-itself and for-itself, absorbing the transcendence of all finite individuals into its one absolute spirit (*Geist*). Thus, on the existential plane, Sartre is to Hegel as, on the purely logical or rational plane, Leibniz is to Spinoza. Neither "substance" nor "negation" are concepts adequate to account for genuine transcendence.

morally affected body, the psyche as responsible in its depths for the other, "the maternal body."

From this overview, it is time to turn to specific texts. I cite at some length Levinas's first positive, and very rich reference to the psyche in *Otherwise than Being or Beyond Essence*:

Indeed in the transcendence of intentionality diachrony is reflected, that is, the psyche itself, in which the inspiration of the same by the other is articulated as a responsibility for another, in proximity. Sensibility is in this way situated back in the human exception. But one has to go back from this reflection to the diachrony itself, which is the-one-for-the-other in proximity. It is then not a particular signification. The one-for-another has the form of sensibility or vulnerability, pure passivity or susceptibility, passive to the point of becoming an inspiration, that is, alterity in the same, the trope of the body animated by the soul, psyche in the form of a hand that gives even the bread taken from its own mouth. Here the psyche is the maternal body.[54]

While the penultimate image – "a hand that gives even the bread taken from its own mouth" – is without doubt excessive and moving, the final image – "the maternal body" – is even more extreme: the other literally within oneself. One can hardly imagine the "one-for-the-other" in any greater sense than that portrayed by the image of the woman "with child," the woman who shares her very body with the body of the other, protecting and nurturing the other. The other morally encountered is "in-me" as if the other were literally in my body, the other's pain my pain, the other's suffering my suffering. The psyche is born in this introjection. But it is introjection of a very special sort: moral introjection. To go beneath or farther than reflection, beneath or farther than "thematizing consciousness," beneath or farther than Husserlian intentionality altogether, to find the genuine concreteness of the psyche is to see the psyche as *responsiveness* to moral exigency, to moral imperative. More aware, more alert, more vigilant, more conscious, if one can say this, than self-consciousness, is the moral acuity of the psyche. Consciousness is under-girded by conscientiousness. Self-consciousness must be awakened by the other.[55]

---

54 Levinas, *OBBE*, p. 67.
55 It is interesting that Nietzsche, too, though he adamantly opposes conscientiousness and concern for others, also recognizes in the very origin of consciousness a disturbing, even painful, relation to the other. See, Nietzsche, *Genealogy of Morals*, essay two, section

It is interesting that in emphasizing the above point, Levinas is returning to the very parallelism in Husserl that he had treated more than forty-four years earlier in *The Theory of Intuition in Husserl's Phenomenology*, the alleged "strict parallelism" between phenomenology and psychology that we have examined in earlier chapters. Here he writes:

Between the signification proper to the sensible and that of thematization and the thematized as thematized, the abyss is much greater than the parallelism constantly affirmed by Husserl between all the "qualities" or "theses" of intentionality would allow one to suppose. This parallelism would imply the equivalence of the psyche and the intentional. In renouncing intentionality as a guiding thread toward the eidos of the psyche, which would command the eidos of sensibility, our analyses will follow sensibility in its prenatural signification to the maternal, where, in proximity, signification signifies before it gets bent into *perseverance in being* in the midst of a Nature.[56]

What is remarkable about this claim is that Levinas exactly reverses the priorities that Husserl, like all philosophers, had insisted upon in the name of phenomenological philosophy. For Levinas it is not thematizing intentionality that augments and completes psycho-logy, as Husserl wanted, but rather the reverse. It is the psyche – as diachrony, proximity, maternal body – that exceeds and supplements thematization and ontology – in a word, that exceeds philosophy as hitherto conceived. Of course, while pointing out this radical reversal, we must not neglect to say that for Levinas, as for Husserl regarding phenomenology, this new status of the psyche in no way suggests an endorsement of the relativism of "psychologism," a point that Levinas emphasizes in the above citation by using the term *eidos*. It is consciousness that takes itself to be independent of the ethical force of the maternal psyche that sinks into the bottomless abyss of psycho-analysis (or, to use the current "semiotic" equivalent to the abyss of psycho-analysis, into deconstruction). Though Levinas will see the psyche as a deeper structure than self-consciousness, his writings (his

---

sixteen. Of course, for Nietzsche this makes consciousness humanity's "weakest and most fallible organ." For more on the failure of Nietzsche's rejection of "love of the neighbor" in contrast to Levinas's maternal psyche, see my *Elevations*, chapter three, "Rosenzweig versus Nietzsche," pp. 67–89.     [56] Levinas, *OBBE*, p. 68.

"thematizations," as it were) nevertheless are efforts to articulate this structure, to present to readers "the eidos of the psyche," however daunting a task the presentation of such a structure in writing may be. We will return to this point, a point Derrida has used as a wedge – the question of Levinas's discourse – later.

## SENSIBILITY AND PSYCHE

The remarks above present Levinas's notion of the "psyche" as it appears at the end of subsection two, "Sensibility and Signification," of *Otherwise than Being or Beyond Essence*. We now turn to subsection three, "Sensibility and Psyche." Below, I will present a series of citations, for the most part following the order of their appearance in "Sensibility and Psyche," followed by my comments.

The psyche is the form of a peculiar dephasing, a loosening up or unclamping of identity: the same prevented from coinciding with itself, at odds, torn up from its rest, between sleep and insomnia, panting, shivering. It is not an abdication of the same, now alienated and slave to the other, but an abnegation of oneself fully responsible for the other.[57]

We have seen that this "peculiar dephasing" is diachrony, the self ruptured by "times" not its own but the other's. The other has already passed before being constituted in the memory of the self, hence passes in an "immemorial past" from the viewpoint of the self. The other is also yet to come, coming from "unforeseeable future," beyond the farthest projects of the self. Both this past recalcitrant to memory and this future recalcitrant to forecast, disturb the self-presence of the self. Levinas speaks of the psyche in terms of attention, "between sleep and insomnia," as an alertness, a wakefulness, a vigilance. In the face of the other's radical alterity the self, though disturbed, indeed overwhelmed, is nonetheless neither annihilated nor alienated. Rather, it finds itself, "torn up from its rest," disabused of its complacency, because taken up in greater exigencies. It is as the obligation of an unceasing responsibility for the other.

[57] Ibid., pp. 68–69.

In the form of responsibility, the psyche in the soul is the other in me, a malady of identity, both accused and *self*, the same for the other, the same by the other. Qui pro quo, it is a substitution, extraordinary.[58]

For Levinas the non-identity of the self has higher priority, is more important, is better, than the complacency of identity. The self is in the accusative, *for* the other, *to* the other – responsible to and for the other. The psyche is like a "malady" because it is already shattered prior to its identity. This shattered non-identity is shattered not from a purely epistemological, ontological or psychological point of view (as Kant, Heidegger or Lacan, respectively, would argue), but rather insofar as it rises to a higher cause than identity: being for the other before oneself.

But there are psychological consequences. In a footnote to the above citation Levinas writes: "The soul is the other in me. The psyche, the-one-for-the-other, can be a possession and a psychosis; the soul is already a seed of folly."[59] Because the psyche is the self in the most extreme proximity of the other and in its greatest vulnerability to the other, it is also liable to a non-moral collapse, liable, that is to say, to genuine psychosis. "The soul is a seed of folly" because the healthy soul, the healthy psyche – to say "moral psyche" is a redundancy – is not an armed self-enclosed fortress but an openness to the other, and hence also the possibility of malady, dishabilitating vulnerability, illness, mental breakdown, psychosis. One can be mentally ill because one can be morally responsible! The road from mental illness to mental health is not to create from a shattered ego a fortress ego, as much pop psychology seems to suggest, but rather to regain one's obligations, one's responsibilities to and for the other. The other is neither enemy nor demon, but rather "the poor, the widow, the orphan, the stranger," one for whom my concern makes sense. The road of morality is a rocky one, and not just in and of itself: one is tempted on the one hand by refusal of the other, by "hardness of heart," immorality, evil, and on the other, there is the danger of collapse, of excess, of psychosis and folly. Moral maturity – the psyche – is not a given. To find one's balance – the balance of dis-equilibrium, disturbance, "bad conscience," obsession – under the extreme

[58] Ibid., p. 69.    [59] Ibid., p. 191.

pressure of the other, is precisely to respond morally to the other.

The animation, the very pneuma of the psyche, alterity in identity, is the identity of a body exposed to the other, becoming "for the other," the possibility of giving.[60]

Levinas does not separate pneuma and psyche in his analysis of the "soul." Precisely the vulnerability of the body is at the same time its exposure as psyche, its capacity to "suffer for the suffering of others," a formula Levinas uses elsewhere to speak of the morality of the one-for-the-other. In speaking of Heidegger's account, in *Being and Time*, of the difference between the "present-to-hand" (*Vorhandenheit*, objectivity, and the object, *Gegenstand*), and the deeper structure Heidegger sees in praxis, in the "ready-to-hand," (*Zuhandenheit*, instrumental relations, the "in-order-to," *das Um-zu*) which leads ultimately to *Dasein*, the "being-there" of human being, Levinas once remarked that Heidegger had altogether neglected not only the hand that begs but also the hand that gives.[61] This means that all meaning – the significant – does not refer back to my being, as Heidegger and a long philosophical tradition have thought, even though it *can* always be referred back to my being or to the being of which I am a part ("world," "*Geist*," "earth-sky-gods-mortals," "Be-ing," "Concept," "Will," "will to power," "substance," "essence," "idea," etc.). Rather, what is meaningful originates in my being responsible to and for the other, originates in the disordering of my being by the other. To make this distinction between the beginning of meaning in the for-the-other and the recuperation of meaning in the for-itself, Levinas distinguishes, as we have seen, "saying" (*dire*) and "the said" (*le dit*). Here, this distinction appears as that between the "psyche" and "system." Thus his account of the psyche turns from diachrony and incarnation to the "signifyingness" (*signifiant*) and signification diachrony and incarnation imply.

---

[60] Ibid., p. 69.

[61] Private conversation, August 1986. In "From Ethics to Exegesis," in *In the Time of the Nations*, Levinas writes: "The face of the other, in its defenseless nakedness – is it not already (despite the countenance this bareness may put on) an asking? A beggar's asking, miserable mortal. But at the same time it is an authority summoning me to 'appear,' summoning me to respond." Emmanuel Levinas, *In the Time of the Nations*, trans. Michael B. Smith (Bloomington: Indiana University Press, 1994), p. 110.

The signifyingness they ["the affective, the axiological, the active, the sensible, hunger, thirst, desire, admiration"] bear in a system, in the said, in the simultaneity of a particular language, is borrowed from this prior psyche, which is signifyingness *par excellence*. In a system signification is due to the definition of terms by one another in the synchrony of a totality, where the whole is the finality of the elements.[62]

Levinas distinguishes that which derives its meaning from its place within a differential network of signs, whether a system or a deferral of signs, "the synchrony of a totality, where the whole is the finality of the elements," from the more profound meaningfulness of "the sensible, hunger, thirst, desire," etc., which derive their significance not within a differential network of signs, but precisely by piercing through such networks, breaking up synchronies, upsetting totalities, coming from the "outside," "exterior," "other," with demands more demanding than signs referring to signs, demanding more attention, demanding my attention, demanding me as attention, me as *moral* attention. Such demands are more excellent, better, morally superior, than the demands of organized and organizing signs. They are more meaningful. And the meaning of systems, synchronies, totalities, "the said" – their justice and justification – derives ultimately from this more excellent, more compelling moral significance. This deeper meaning, however, can be and too often is suppressed, ignored, neglected, shut out and otherwise refused – precisely in the name of the system or differential network it in fact charges with significance in the first place. To understand the psyche in its moral character must not be confused with miraculously making the world moral, on the one hand, but neither can it be confused with having an "objective" account of the psyche in its relation to the other.

It is indeed clear that the psyche can thus have a sense like any other term of the language stated, showing itself in the said, in tales or writing. A psychic fact can have sense as referred to another psychic fact, like any element of the world of the experience called exterior.[63]

Just as the other person can be refused, the depth structure of the psyche itself can be – and usually has been – refused/refuted by theory. Indeed, it is likely to be refused by theory precisely

---

[62] Levinas, *OBBE*, p. 69.    [63] Ibid., p. 69.

because theory seeks to know, to explain, to order. There is nothing wrong with theory or science, to be sure, indeed they are necessary; but they nonetheless and naturally tend not only toward the orderly, the synchronic, but toward the ordering of the orderly as if it were the whole. Theory has a tendency to be blinded by its own light. Levinas is not opposed to science, he is opposed to the confusion of explanation and explained, or rather he is opposed to their totalization. He is opposed to the confusion of the disorder at the source of order for yet another order. "Chaos theory," then, would precisely be what he rejects: to read into every "chaos" an "order" of another order. According to "chaos theory" what appears chaotic or disordered is in fact, from another level, higher or lower, orderly. But for Levinas the breakthrough of the other into the self is so fundamentally and so essentially out of order that it is "otherwise than being or beyond essence." The other is always more than the self bargains for, more than the self wants, more than what the self can handle. Yet the self is precisely response in the face of this excess. The true self is precisely an insufficiency, a "trauma" that is not psychotic but the psyche *qua* responsibility for the other. Here what Levinas is noting is that not only can and do people refuse one another, ignore one another, behave indifferently to the suffering of others, but theory and theorizing, too, can and do betray the genuine meaning of the psyche as for-the-other. Not only does theory, in the name of objectivity, whether for or against (i.e., theory against theory), shy away from morality, but the "object" of morality exceeds its grasp – and thus, paradoxically, even and especially in the name of objectivity it would lose its truth. Objectivity is not surpassed by subjectivity, as Kierkegaard thought, or by aesthetic construction, as Nietzsche thought, but by morality.

The meaning of perception, hunger, sensation, etc., as notions signifies through the correlation of terms in the simultaneity of a linguistic system. It has to be distinguished from the signifyingness of the-one-for-the-other, the psyche that animates perception, hunger and sensation.[64]

Such phenomena as hunger, sensation, desire, etc. (are they really "phenomena" at all?) can thus be distinguished according to

[64] Ibid., p. 70.

two levels of meaning: "objective," signification as the manner in which they make sense within a system, actual or deferred; "subjective," signifying in the sense of making demands upon the self. It is precisely this exigency, this im-position – this "saying" – that escapes every position and positioning, "the said," and yet is the very animation of the psyche. By an exasperation or abuse of language – an "exasperation" or "abuse" only from the point of view of the said, but a moral exigency for saying – Levinas forces his readers to attend to the difference between the said and the saying that animates it. Levinas's language – the hyperbolic style of his discourse, the overloading of sense he demands, the impositional "rhetoric" of exigency – peculiar though it may be, is anything but the "violence" for which Derrida accused it.[65] It is an ethical exacerbation parallel to, indeed reflecting, morality itself, an effort to awaken a "saying," or a glimpse at the "saying" that underlies and conditions the significations "said." It is an effort of rhetoric – sweet rhetoric[66] – that must be continually renewed and

---

[65] Derrida, like Hegel, is a philosopher of immanence, even if he is so by celebrating the unresolved and *unresolvable* tension of a linguistic and differential dialectic. "I have often wondered," Levinas writes, "with respect to Derrida, whether the *différance* of the present which leads him to the deconstruction of notions does not attest to the prestige that eternity retains in his eyes, the 'great present,' *being*, which corresponds to the priority of the *theoretical* and the truth of the theoretical, in relation to which temporality would be failure. I wonder if time – in its very dia-chrony – is not *better* than eternity and the order of the Good itself." "Violence of the Face," an interview with Angelo Bianchi (1985), in Emmanuel Levinas, *Alterity and Transcendence*, ed. Pierre Hayat, trans. Michael B. Smith (New York: Columbia University Press, 1999), p. 173.

[66] "The education of the soul," Richard M. Weaver writes in *The Ethics of Rhetoric* (South Bend: Regnery/Gateway, 1953), apropos Plato's *Phaedrus*, "is not a process of bringing it into correspondence with a physical structure like the eternal world [see preceding note above], but rather a process of rightly affecting its motion. By this conception, a soul which is rightly affected calls that good which is good; but a soul which is wrongly turned calls that good which is evil. What Plato has prepared us to see is that the virtuous rhetorician, who is a lover of truth, has a soul of such movement that its dialectical perceptions are consonant with those of a divine mind. Or, in the language of more technical philosophy, this soul is aware of axiological systems which have ontic status." Regarding this last sentence, Levinas would of course say that ethics precedes ontology. Thus his rhetoric – for it is not deductive logic that guides Levinas's thought – is "sweet" rather than manipulative.

Of Levinas's rhetoric, Steven G. Smith has perceptively written: "For Levinas, the non-coercive reason pertaining to the ethical or the human – '*Raison, comme l'un pour l'autre!* [Reason as the one for the other!]' – is not a deficient reason. The non-coerciveness of moral reason is the very rationality of genuine reason distinct from mechanical necessity. The rhetorical appeal of a discourse is again distinguished from logical structure, but as a donation instead of a privation, i.e., as 'sweet' reason – the

*Good and evil*

continually re-said. By means of what I am calling philosophical exegesis, a reawakening of meaning producing a meaningfulness more awake than the meaning signs accrue in relation to one another, Levinas points to the sparks or traces of the signifyingness that lies at the root of all signification, the one-for-the-other. Thus his discourse is "reflective" in a specifically ethical sense.

The said shows, but betrays (shows by betraying) the dieresis, the disorder of the psyche that animates the *consciousness of*, and which, in the philosophical order of the said, is called transcendence. But it is not in the said that the psyche signifies, even though it is manifested there. Signification is the-one-for-the-other which characterizes an identity that does not coincide with itself.[67]

The said, the thematized, the represented, cannot "capture" the dis-order of the living psyche. By itself, as if masks masked only other masks, it is but a simulacrum, a bottomless pit or an endless psycho-analysis, however frightening or fascinating. But the face operates with a different difference. It pierces all masks and is the source of their significance, in the sense that one can distinguish (and today, as always, there are those who refuse this distinction) life from theatre. At first glance it is astonishing, in terms of Levinas's intellectual itinerary, that we see him here, in the above citation, going so far as to question the strength of the term "transcendence," which in *Totality and Infinity* carried much of his effort to exceed the said. But the said must be continually re-said, each word much be continually revivified. In philosophy – ethical philosophy – there are no "magic words," no sacraments of the holy.

With his finely honed "rhetoric," what Levinas is pointing to in his writings is the psyche as the very animation of the body, the very "lived," as it were, of the "lived body." "Here," Levinas writes, "animation is not a metaphor."[68] The distinction and

---

sweetness of which reflects obedience to the Good rather than the deceptive sugar-coating of ill rhetoric. Unlike the monolithic Reason formed by logic, or by the one Being or Spirit or History, the sweet reason proposed by Levinas is the positive production of *plurality*, on the assumption that plurality is better than the One . . . On this view 'rhetoric' is rehabilitated and even enthroned in the intersubjective drama of philosophy." Steven G. Smith, *The Argument to the Other: Reason Beyond Reason in the Thought of Karl Barth and Emmanuel Levinas* (Chico, CA: Scholars Press, 1983), pp. 190–191.

[67] Levinas, *OBBE*, p. 70.  [68] Ibid.

difference Merleau-Ponty's phenomenological studies uncovered between the "*corps-propre*" (lived body) and the "*corps*" (body as object) depend not, as he thought, on ontology, however much revised, as in the brilliant formulations of *The Visible and the Invisible* (1968), but rather on the psyche, that is to say, as a function of moral intersubjectivity, the imperative of saying as distinct from the totalizing of the said. Levinas's claim – radical as it may seem – is that moral intersubjectivity, the one-for-the-other, is nothing less than the animation of the body, that is to say, of the human body and not merely of an animal vitality such as could be kept going with "life support" systems. If one has ever witnessed a body "living" – maintained, "kept alive" – solely by means of a mechanical life support system, and hence knows graphically the difference between such a body and the person one knew, then one understands what Levinas means by saying that animation itself depends on social interaction. One's very "life," then, the life not simply of animal vitality but of *humanity*, is breathed into the self, as it were, by the other.[69] In this sense the psyche – the one-for-the-other – lies at the ground of humanity, and in relation to it, as we have said already, evil and inhumanity would be second-order phenomena, the *refusal* of a prior humanity – respiration without inspiration.

Having touched on the subject of the "abuse" of language and the betrayal of saying in the said, let us reiterate the point above regarding sweet rhetoric. Statements such as these quoted above, and the care with which Levinas writes, show clearly that Levinas is quite aware that he is stretching and must stretch language, pushing to its limits to show a signifyingness beyond the bounds of the grammar, the semiotics, and even the semantics of a linguistic system. Of the vulnerability of the animated body, the "maternal body," for example, he will speak of a "passivity more passive than all passivity." Thus one must think passivity and a passivity beyond the passivity one can think. Of the impact of the other, proximity, he will write of "the *immediacy* of the other, more

---

[69] Compare Genesis, 2:7: "And the Lord God formed the man of dust from the ground, and He blew into his nostrils the soul of life; and man became a living being." Or, so I am suggesting, one could equally conclude this verse: "and a living being became man." I will return to this point in the next chapter.

immediate still than immediate identity in its quietude as a nature."[70] Thus, likewise, one must think immediacy and an immediacy beyond the immediacy one can think. One must think the
"more in the less," to retrieve a formula (whose "philosophical
dignity" is derived from Descartes's Third Meditation) from *Totality and Infinity*. Levinas must betray the betrayal inherent in what is
said – its tendency to congeal, to mirror itself, to mistake the
proximity of its signs for the proximity of the other – to allow
a glimpse at the saying underlying, animating, giving life to
language. There are, as I have said, no magic words. Levinas's
work – the work of Levinas's work – as we are now attempting to
appreciate by examining his extraordinary use of the term
"psyche," deepening its sense further than its "usual" or "habit-
ual" psychological meaning, requires a constant renewal of sense
through an exegetical over-determination of meaning, through
commentary upon commentary upon commentary, in an unending enhancement and augmentation of meanings that ever slip
away into the false objectivity of thematization, as if a meaning
could finally be grasped once and for all and kept like museum
pieces. Dia-chrony, ethical proximity, the dis-order of the one-for-
the-other, "is" always better than order, even the "order" – the
complacency of "good conscience" – of a presumed ethical axiol-
ogy. Thus Levinas's language works by a kind of exacerbation of
meaning, an exaggeration or interruption of the betrayal of meaning in themes. The reader does not simply grasp what Levinas has
to say, rather one grasps and at the same time – or in the difference
of time that is dia-chrony – is overloaded by it. Colin Davis, then,
despite his suggestive insights into the complexity of Levinas's
thought, is mistaken to criticize Levinas's "central notions" for
being "inadequately defined."[71] Levinas's central notions intrinsi-

---

[70] Levinas, *OBBE*, p. 84.

[71] Colin Davis, *Levinas: An Introduction* (Notre Dame: University of Notre Dame Press, 1996),
p. 143. Only because he separates the alterity of the other from moral force, a separation
that undermines all of Levinas's thought, can Davis think of Levinas as a "chameleon"
(p. 144), "lacking rigor" (p. 143), "elusive" (p. 141), and speak of this alleged semantic
indeterminacy as the "Levinas effect" (p. 140). Levinas's destabilizations – the non-
identity, dia-chrony or de-nucleation at the heart of his writings – are very specific. They
are ethical, that is to say, they are based in and upon the imperative force of the face that
is irreducibly moral: "Thou shalt not murder." Davis is simply mistaken – for the above
reason – when he writes that: "Levinas offers an ethics without rules, imperatives,

cally and necessarily cannot be "defined," precisely because, as moral force, i.e., as infinition, they defy definition and must defy definition. The entire labor of Levinas's thought is not to define the psyche, but to compellingly express its moral excess.

To betray the betrayal of language, Levinas will often also resort to "religious" language to express the rupture of the psyche that is its ab-original signifyingness. In fact, shaking up the I, disrupting the complacency of the ego, meaning comes toward the self, imposes itself, rather than meaning deriving from the self's grasp, its comprehension. To capture this movement toward the self, Levinas uses the peculiar formula: "God who comes to mind" (*Dieu qui vient à l'idée*), even naming one of his books with this expression. This "coming to" "constitutes" the self not as some mythological figure outside the self (i.e., as "persona"), but precisely as the insufficiency of the self's response to the other, which is to say, positively, as a responsibility always required to be more responsible to the other in and as one's own self. In this way the self is "more immediate still than immediate identity." Psyche, *penetralia mentis*, "is" the other, the other in me as me, self as response to the other. Levinas, quite evidently, also uses "psychological" terminology, speaking of "trauma," "psychosis," "obsession." The psyche "is" traumatization by the other. The psyche "is" obsession, obsessed with the other, obsessed by the other, obsessed for the other.

The psyche or animation is the way a relationship between uneven terms, without any common time, arrives at relationship. Non-objectifiable, non-contemporaneous, it can only signify non-indifference. An animate body or an incarnate identity is the signifyingness of this non-indifference.[72]

Again, animation, incarnation, are inseparable from the psyche, from "non-indifference" to the other, which is why one must speak of "maternal body" and "maternal psyche" as equivalent and

maxims or clear objectives other than a passionate moral conviction that the Other should be heard" (p. 144). The other must not only be heard, but must be cared for, and this requires not only the giving of food and shelter, but also all the institutions and laws, the "rules, imperatives, maxims," of a just society. The "clear objective" of Levinas's ethics is the recognition that the infinite demands of morality also include the demands of justice.    [72] Levinas, *OBBE*, p. 70.

inseparable expressions. Although moral selfhood is not a matter of being or ontology, and is even antithetical to the self understood as *conatus essendi*, "perseverence in being," there is nonetheless nothing "ethereal" about the psyche. The sensibility of the self is exposure, vulnerability and response – moral response, a response that is at once a responsibility, a giving and caring for the other's needs. We have already seen Levinas use a striking formula, one that he will repeat again in *Otherwise than Being or Beyond Essence*: "bread taken from one's own mouth" to be given to the other. This image – and it is surely not only an "image" – concretizes or specifies the significance of the responsive-giving sensibility that is the psyche. "Signification signifies . . . in nourishing, clothing, lodging, in maternal relations."[73] Again, there is nothing dreamy or "spiritual" about Levinas's account of the psyche. "The other's material needs are my spiritual needs," Levinas has said repeatedly, quoting the formula of an important nineteenth-century Lithuanian ethicist and Talmudist, Rabbi Israel Lipkin ("Salanter") (1810–83).[74] Nothing could be more immediate, more concrete, more pressing than the other's suffering. The psyche is non-indifference to the needs – both spiritual and material – of the other. Incarnation, the psyche, is thus an inter-humanity, "fraternity." For this reason, beyond morality, Levinas will also see "the latent birth of justice in signification"[75] in the psyche. This is to say that not only morality, my obligation to the other, but justice, my obligation to all others, derives from and inheres in the maternal psyche. Here is not the place to develop this striking notion, that justice, too, derives from the carnal sensitivity of the psyche.[76]

The following is the final reference to the psyche in the "Sensibility and Psyche" subsection of chapter three of *Otherwise than Being or Beyond Essence*:

We have shown that the one-for-the-other characteristic of the psyche, signification, is not an ordinary formal relation, but the whole gravity of the body extirpated from its *conatus*. It is a passivity more passive still than

---

73 Ibid., p. 77.        74 On Rabbi Israel Salanter, see n. 14 of chapter 5 above, p. 155.
75 Levinas, *OBBE*, p. 71.
76 For more on the relation between morality and justice in Levinas, especially in contrast to Spinoza, see my article, "Justice and the State in the Thought of Levinas and Spinoza," in *Epoche: A Journal for the History of Philosophy*, vol. 4, no. 1, 1996, pp. 55–70; and chapter eight of *Elevations*, pp. 173–194.

any passivity that is antithetical to an act, a nudity more naked than all "academic" nudity, exposed to the point of outpouring, effusion and prayer . . . It is the passivity of being-for-another, which is possible only in the form of giving the very bread I eat. But for this one has to first enjoy one's bread, not in order to have the merit of giving it, but in order to give it with one's heart, to give oneself in giving it.[77]

In contrast to *conatus essendi*, "perseverance in being," a term Levinas borrows from Spinoza but broadens to characterize the essence of the self *qua* for-itself-regardless-of-the-other, the psyche is "outpouring, effusion and prayer." Invoking this religious terminology, Levinas here follows a long Jewish tradition for which prayer is sacrifice, self-sacrifice.[78] But again following a long Jewish tradition, such a self must not be mistaken for an ascetic self. Responsibility for the other, even infinite responsibility, though a "suffering," must not be confused with self-denial. There is no self-denial here for the sake of self-denial, that is to say, for the sake of the self, as if it were the improvement of the self that was at stake in its suffering. It is the other who comes first. As we shall see later, in chapter 9, when discussing Paul Ricoeur's alternative conception of moral selfhood in relation to the alterity of the other person, there is a great temptation to think of moral selfhood in terms of self-esteem. Just as one can always facilely say, because of the inevitable reflexivity of human consciousness, that whatever anyone does – however "altruistic" it appears, it is nevertheless done for oneself, to make oneself happy, there is an equivalent temptation to say that being for-the-other is ultimately, or even more deeply, for the sake of oneself. This is wrongheaded, but, as I have said, we will return to confront this line of thinking later.

---

[77] Levinas, *OBBE*, p. 72.

[78] It is interesting to note that after the destruction of the second Temple in ancient Jerusalem, the Jewish sages declared that henceforth prayers would substitute for the grain, bird, and animal sacrifices hitherto performed at the Temple altars. Prayer, too, then, instead of simply being a request from God for oneself, would be a request from God for others. "Far from being a demand addressed to God, prayer consists in the 'elevation, surrender and *adherence* of the soul to the heights.' . . . For the self (*moi*), prayer means that, instead of seeking one's own salvation, one secures that of others." Levinas, "Prayer Without Demand," trans. Sarah Richmond, in Emmanuel Levinas, *The Levinas Reader*, ed. Séan Hand (Oxford: Blackwell, 1989), pp. 232–233 (Levinas's citation is taken from the *Nefesh ha'Hayyim* (*The Soul of Life*) of Rabbi Hayyim of Volozhyn (1759–1821), founder of the famous Volozhyn yeshiva and chief disciple of Rabbi Elijah the Gaon of Vilna (1720–1797)).

Here, it is important to note that for Levinas the moral self is indeed a sacrifice. This is why Levinas speaks of "prayer," and "giving the very bread I eat." Rather than self-denial, or what one receives, Levinas is first concerned with giving, with the giving of clothing, shelter, food, warmth. But, and this point must be underlined, it is a giving that is also a giving of the self.[79] Thus it is the positivity of the for-the-other – a for-the-other whose acuity is felt to the extent that the self, in its sensibility, is sensible to the value of pleasure, indeed tends by itself toward enjoyment, toward satisfaction and contentment – that makes giving at once a giving to the other and a giving of oneself over to the other. In giving, and not merely in feeling, one suffers for the other's suffering. In this way the psyche is sacrifice and hence prayer.

This brief review concludes our examination of the discussion of the psyche in the subsection of *Otherwise than Being or Beyond Essence* entitled "Sensibility and Psyche," begun in the prior subsection, "Sensibility and Signification." Some, but not all, that we have seen is that Levinas's "notion" of the psyche (1) requires conceiving selfhood more deeply than the synthesizing circuits of self-consciousness or willfulness; (2) comes to the self insofar as the self is for-the-other before being for-itself; (3) is the internalization of the basic moral imperative imposed by and in responsiveness to the very alterity of the other; (4) manifests itself as the "me" or "I" of "my" responsibility to and for the other, the self as the singularity of obligation to the other, (5) which responsibilities and obligations

---

[79] An interesting "story" – *aggadah* – from the Babylonian Talmud, *Moed Katan* 28a, illustrates this point regarding the relation between giving and giving of the self: "[The angel of death] could not gain access to Rabbi Chiya. One day the [angel] adopted the guise of a pauper, knocked on his door and asked, 'Give me bread.' He gave him. [The angel] said, 'If you take pity upon a pauper, why do you not take pity on the [angel] of death?' He proved [who he was] by showing him a rod of fire. [Rabbi Chiya] then yielded his life to him." The commentary of Rabbi Chaim Schmulevitz (1902–78, (disciple of Rabbi Salanter and head of the Mir Yeshivah [Mir, Shanghai and Jerusalem]) explains: "This story is incomprehensible. What parallel did the angel of death find between the giving of a morsel of bread to a pauper and the giving up of one's life? The answer is that the angel of death was well aware of Rabbi Chiya's profundity of heart. He knew that when Rabbi Chiya gave even a crust of bread to the beggar, he did not only give it with heart; rather it was his very heart that he gave. Therefore, the angel of death was able to ask him 'to have pity on him' and surrender his life on the basis of the kindness expressed in the act of charity." In *Sichos Mussar: Reb Chaim's Discourses*, 2nd edn., trans. Eliyahu Meir Klugman and A. Scheinman, ed. Samson R. Weiss (Brooklyn: Mesorah Publications, 1998), pp. 132–133.

are more significant, more meaningful than any other significations even though and precisely because they do not originate in
the self but from the other, and hence are "an-archic" in origin
and give meaning to all significations; (6) is the very animation of
the body, its incarnation, its life, (7) and connects one person to
another across a global inter-humanity of such sensibility, linking
one to the other through the imperative to care; (8) is the ever
disturbing moral task of providing for the real needs of the other
(and others: justice); (9) is experienced by the self as sacrifice
because of sensibility's countervailing but natural tendency toward
its own self-satisfaction, contentment, and complacency. This conception of the psyche is built upon and serves as an elaboration of
Levinas's original conception of time as dia-chrony: the psyche as
the time of ethical inter-subjectivity.

In the following section, on the basis of selected citations, I am
going to examine various additional insights regarding the psyche
found on the subsequent pages of *Otherwise than Being or Beyond
Essence* where the insights we have already seen are developed.

### INSOMNIA, INSPIRATION, ELEVATION, EXPIATION, SUBSTITUTION PROPHECY, REVELATION, HUMANITY

The psyche is disturbed in its responsibility to and for the other to
the point of "insomnia":

> It is set up as it were in the accusative form, from the first responsible and
> not being able to slip away. This impossibility to slip off even into death is
> the point where, beyond the insomnia which can still be dissimulated, the
> subject is a saying, an uncovering oneself to the other – a psyche.[80]

Related to this use of the term "insomnia" we might think of our
earlier use of the term "obsession": the other obsesses the self,
the self is obsession with the other.[81] When Levinas resorts to

---

[80] Levinas, *OBBE*, p. 85; see also endnote 16, p. 192.

[81] It is interesting to note that "insomnia" is one of the very few terms in Levinas's corpus to
undergo a radical change in sense, or rather in context. In 1947, in section one of *Time and
the Other*, Levinas had used it to describe the "vigilance without end" of the "there is [il y
a]" (p. 48), anonymous existence without existents. The "there is" – like an insomnia,
night, the absence of all existents, "an atmospheric density, a plenitude of the void, or the
murmur of silence" (ibid., p. 46) – continues to play an important role throughout
Levinas's philosophy. But in his later writings, as we see here in *Otherwise than Being or*

psychological language it is not to characterize the psyche as unhealthy as did Nietzsche. Rather, it is to give rhetorical force to the impact, the immediacy, the directness, the implosion of the other in the self, and to the self as an alert moral responsiveness to this imposition. Levinas borrows from psychological terminology, using the "excess" that is sickness – trauma, obsession, insomnia – to understand or point to what exceeds understanding: ethical proximity. Proximity occurs otherwise than under the judgment of health and sickness, or rather it is the condition for discriminating and preferring health to sickness. But its excess, which is ethical and not pathological, is *like* the excesses of a pathology. The image of the psyche as insomnia is in keeping with Levinas's characterizations, in *Otherwise than Being or Beyond Essence*, and increasingly in his later writings, of moral consciousness as a "wakefulness," a "vigilance," an "extreme attention." Proximity, the self's moral singularity, irreplaceable before the other, hence its individuation as a self through an extreme sense of obligation and responsibility, is for the self *like* an "insomnia," the self kept awake not by itself but by the other. But actually, because for Levinas ethics precedes ontology, it is the psychological notion of "insomnia," and "obsession" and "trauma," that are like the ethical notions of the same. "This insomnia," the insomnia of moral proximity, Levinas writes, "is the psyche."[82] The (pathological) insomniac wants to sleep but cannot. A person would rather not be troubled by another, but there, before the other, the self – me, no one else, psyche – is troubled by the other, is a moral self, and as such rises to the occasion to aid the other. One would rather not bother. One would rather be left alone. But the other's troubles take priority over my own comforts. This moral insomnia reminds us of another of Levinas's formulae for the psyche, the biblical expression, "here I am" [Hebrew: הנני, *hineni*], referring to an availability, a vulnerability, a responsiveness to the call of the other. God calls Abraham, and Abraham responds: "Here I am." Abraham calls Isaac, and Isaac responds: "Here I am." "Here I am" – already a sacrifice. Insomniac, the self is wakened by the other and for the other, by its obligations to and for the other.

---

*Beyond Essence*, Levinas will use the term "insomnia" to describe the moral consciousness more wakeful than self-consciousness, i.e., the psyche.        [82] Levinas, *OBBE*, p. 87.

But lest this troubling of the self, the psyche, "insomnia," seem like a terrible affliction, we must not forget that it is actually an "inspiration." Let us remember the citation at the head of this chapter, the very "definition" of the psyche: "The psyche is the other in the same without alienating the same."[83] It is the non-alienation of the self in its obsession with the other that leads Levinas to the religious language of inspiration, meaning both "breath" (respiration, inspiration, expiration) and the "spiritual" (in Hebrew: רוח, *ruach* = "breath" = "spirit").

I am summoned as someone irreplaceable. I exist through the other and for the other, but without this being alienation: I am inspired. This inspiration is the psyche. The psyche can signify this alterity in the same without alienation in the form of incarnation, as being-in-one's-skin, having-the-other-in-one's-skin.[84]

The self as for-the-other is as such irreplaceable. Hence only in this way is the self *singular*, truly in the first person singular, i.e., "I," "me," "myself." Paradoxical as it may sound to logic, the self is itself when and only when it is for-the-other. And it is itself to the extent that it is for-the-other. The psyche is thus a deepening process: the more one responds, the more one gives, the more one "is." One does not give in order to receive, but by giving one becomes oneself. This "dialectic" of a giving that is a receiving is the "inspiration" of the psyche – its "election," as Levinas else-where calls this inspiration. In invoking the term "election" Levinas is recalling the Jewish sense of a "chosen people," mean-ing a people chosen not for physical or animal domination (the war of all against all) but an ethical domination (the peace of one for all), for the humility and greatness of a global moral responsibility. Both of these terms, "inspiration" and "election," do not refer to dreams or beautiful ideals. They are not "spiritual" notions, angelic, above and beyond matter. Rather they refer concretely to incarnate beings, self and other, others who are needy, a self that can help others materially. Thus the other does not affect the self in some ghostlike or imaginary "kingdom," or in another world, but viscerally, in one's skin, like a turning of the self inside out, as if the self were naked, exposed to the other's needs as if they were

[83] Ibid., p. 112.  [84] Ibid., p. 114–115.

one's own. Earlier I called this the self as its "brother's keeper." "I
am my brother's keeper" is for Levinas literally true: the I is I as,
and insofar as, it is its brother's keeper. Individuation is not an
affair of my death but of the other's death, the other's mortality,
the other's suffering. To be concerned in this way for the other is
election, what Levinas here calls the inspiration of the psyche.
One's very breathing is for-the-other: "what we are here calling
oneself, or the other in the same, where inspiration arouses respiration, the very pneuma of the psyche."[85] Inspired by the other, not
only does one respire for the other but, let us add, one can expire
for the other too – responsibility goes all the way to death, being-
for-the-other unto death. Such is the transcendence of the other
that at the same time – or in dia-chrony – it is the depth of the self.

The psyche as "inspiration" is one of Levinas's ways of express-
ing the "ambiguity" or "ambivalence" of a self whose *ownmost*
selfhood is "*put*" into it by the other. Selfhood – first person
singularity, psyche – is not alienated by introjection, but rather
raised up, lifted to its proper moral stature, again, elected to moral
responsibility. This "raising," "lifting," and "election," are not
physical but moral heights. Levinas calls

the subjectivity of the subject, its very psyche, a possibility of inspiration.
It is the possibility of being the author of what has been breathed in
unbeknownst to me, of having received, one knows not from where, that
of which I am the author. In the responsibility for the other we are at the
heart of the ambiguity of inspiration.[86]

Another term for this inspiration, one that, like the term "inspiration," captures the sense of being penetrated by another but at the
same time not alienated by this intrusion, but uplifted, is "elevation."

Inspiration, heteronomy, is the very pneuma of the psyche. Freedom is
borne by the responsibility it could not shoulder, an elevation and
inspiration without complacency. The for-the-other characteristic of the
subject can be interpreted neither as a guilt complex (which presupposes
an *initial* freedom), nor as a natural benevolence or divine "instinct," nor
as some love or some tendency to sacrifice.[87]

The moral self is not what it would be by itself, independent or
or indifferent to the other. This morality of "non-in-difference," as

[85] Ibid., p. 116.      [86] Ibid., p. 148–149.      [87] Ibid., p. 124.

Levinas also calls it, does not derive from some inner sanctum, some innate moral "tendency," "love," "divine 'instinct'" or "natural benevolence." The heart must be circumcised, to take up a biblical expression, because, like the circumcision of the body, this is not its original condition. Levinas thus rejects the hypotheses of those who, like the eighteenth-century British moralists Shaftesbury and Hutcheson, posit an innate moral sense. These positions are based on a false optimism, a wishful thinking about human "nature." They also promote a monadicism appropriate to cognition but foreign to a genuine moral sensibility. "By nature" humans are as capable of evil as of good. This point hardly has to be emphasized after a century that has seen gas, gulag and Auschwitz. Neither, then, more obviously, does Levinas abide by what he considers to be a mystification such as the hypothesis of a divinely implanted moral sensibility – a moral "soul" or God's "love" given somehow miraculously at birth or conception. To conceive the "soul" as something put into the body at some point in time, even if its residence there is temporary in the longer run, is but a Sunday School fable. This same childish thinking would have Commandments given once and for all at Mount Sinai. Rather, the soul, like commandments, is constantly put in us, and neither is a "something" at all. Neither, for those who outgrow or reject the fable of an "eternal soul" lodged in the body, does morality depend on a detached and self-contained freedom, for example the radical freedom of Fichte's self-positing ego or the equally radical freedom of Sartre's for-itself. Such a freedom, absolute in itself, is not only incapable of suffering the other's suffering, but must reduce all that is non-ego to what is ego. Levinas characterizes the psyche as "elevation" because the moral psyche, the maternal psyche, is *more* and not less than it is by itself. It is not its own ground, neither an island nor a fortress: hence it is, to invoke another Levinasian term, "an-archic."

An anarchic liberation, it emerges, without being assumed, without turning into a beginning, in inequality with oneself . . . in the undergoing by sensibility beyond its capacity to undergo. This describes the suffering and vulnerability of the sensible as *the other in me*. The other is in me and in the midst of my very identification.[88]

[88] Ibid., p. 124–125.

The moral self is elevated above itself, is oriented by the above, the "better," through its being for-the-other-before-itself. It is this, and this is the task it is. Selfhood is in this way not a finitude but an infinition: desire as desire, "satisfied" while insatiable, as obligation to and for the other. This way of being cannot therefore be reduced to a form of self-esteem because it is in no way a self-satisfaction. Rather, to the contrary, it is an insufficiency, a "fissure" or "de-nucleation" at the heart of identity – "like a cellular irritability; it is the impossibility of being silent, the scandal of sincerity."[89]

Chapter Four of *Otherwise than Being or Beyond Essence* is entitled "Substitution." Levinas explains that this chapter is the "germ"[90] of the entire book, which is "built around"[91] it. The notion of substitution, which we have already touched upon, is yet another way to understand the psyche. The self substitutes the concerns of the other for its own concerns. Rather, the other's concerns become its own. Levinas will speak of this movement as "expiation." As "skin turned inside out," the other-in-the-same, the self is transformed in responding to the other, elevated by rising to the other's needs; the self is an "expiation" for the other, and it is so precisely by putting itself in the other's shoes.

It is the null-place in which inspiration by the other is also expiation for the other, the psyche by which consciousness itself would come to signify. The psyche is not grafted on to a substance, but alters the substantiality of this substance which supports all things . . . Substitution is not the psychological event of compassion or intropathy in general, but makes possible the paradoxical psychological possibilities of putting oneself in the place of another.[92]

Once again, challenging the notion of subjectivity as source or ground of all significance, here, as with the overloading of the Husserlian notion of "intentionality" that we saw earlier, for Levinas the psyche as a substitution of the self for the other "alters the substantiality of this substance which supports all things."[93]

[89] Ibid., p. 143.    [90] Ibid., p. 193, n. 1.    [91] Ibid., p. xli.    [92] Ibid., p. 146.

[93] In *Totality and Infinity*, speaking of the erotic and the parental relations, the relation of lover and beloved, and that of parent and child, Levinas will use the term "transubstantiation" (p. 271), obviously borrowed from religion, to express the internalization of another's sensibility within one's own, the erotic embrace of two lovers whose desire for transcendence is "resolved," as Levinas puts it, in the birth of the child and the

Expiation is not a compassion, sympathy or empathy, because the self does not rest in-itself-for-itself and *add* these emotions to its own feelings, to its own identity. Rather, as expiation, the psyche is an uprooting of the self-sameness such that the other, as Levinas says, "orders me by my own voice."[94] The psyche is for-the-other, we have said, as a suffering of and for the suffering of the other. Regarding the psyche as expiation Levinas cites Dostoyevsky's words from *The Brothers Karamozov*: "Each of us is guilty of all and for all humans before all, and I more than the others."[95] Referring to this disordering of the self by the other for the other, in an article entitled "God and Philosophy," with the words of the prophet Micah (1:3–4) in mind, Levinas says of the impact of the other that inspires expiation: it "devastates its site like a devouring fire, catastrophying its site."[96] Of course, in our concern to grasp the intimate sensibility of the psyche, let us not forget, too, that the I expiating for the other does so not by basking in its own exquisite feelings, but far more concretely, by feeding the hungry, sheltering the exposed, comforting the hurt, healing the sick, defending the oppressed.

To stretch the reader's consciousness beyond the inevitable routines and habits of thought (the "said"), Levinas is not afraid to use religious terminology. In contrast to his use of psychological terminology, whose terms (psyche, trauma, obsession) Levinas overloads with the significance of an ethical transcendence, in the case of religious language, whose virtue is that transcendence is already a "given,"[97] Levinas's work is to charge this transcendence with its proper ethical significance.[98] In *Otherwise than Being or Beyond Essence*, which is a philosophical work, to be sure, he speaks of the psyche in terms of "prayer" and "inspiration," as we have seen, but also in terms of "prophecy" and "revelation." Religious terminology, whose excess philosophy has always suspected when it did not simply rule it out of hand for purely logical reasons, is

parent–child relation. This trans-substantial sensibility, in its moral dimension – suffering for the suffering of another – is what Levinas is referring to with the term "maternal body," and what I mean by "maternal psyche." [94] Levinas, *OBBE*, p. 147.

[95] Ibid., p. 146; see also Levinas, *Ethics and Infinity*, p. 98.

[96] Levinas, "God and Philosophy," in *The Levinas Reader*, p. 176.

[97] Transcendence is, of course, never "given."

[98] Negatively, this same work is to divest religious language of its mythological significance.

now understood in terms of the extra-ordinary transformation of a
being-for-itself into a being-for-the-other, that is, in terms of the
excess of moral responsibility and obligation. The infinition of
moral responsibility, increasing to the measure – and beyond the
measure – that it is embraced, exceeding all economy, is not only
"like" the infinity of the divine, it is precisely the way the divine
"passes" on earth. Even to say that ethics is God's detour, suggesting that God's passage through human relations is second best to
some other undisclosed short cut, is to pay obedience to a mythological picture of divine transcendence. No other route can be
articulated in human speech or for humanity. God's passage
through human relations, that is, through morality and justice, is
precisely God's passage on earth.[99] In his public discourse Levinas
does not speak of a person's alleged direct contact with God, of
religious experience or faith. When brought into public discourse
these "experiences" may well be inspiring testimonies or provide
personal witness, but they lack the compelling rhetorical force
required by philosophical discourse. When confused for the universal discourse of philosophy they inevitably turn into an over-
bearing imposition, sanctioned only by totalizing and violence.
Philosophy must dismiss this force. But the language of ethics does
not suffer from such a limitation. Its discourse is universal and
particular at the same time, or rather, dia-chronically. Its force is
that of moral singularity. Its impositions – responsibilities and
obligations – are constitutive of our deeper and better self, our
psyche. Indeed, morality is precisely the "reversal" of the desires of
the self, such that in place of narcissistic desires, desires for self-
satisfaction or self-aggrandizement, indifferent to others or imperial, the moral self desires what is least desirable: the other's
welfare, the other's well being. And this desire – inspired, elevated
– is precisely the psyche. It is also the height of "prophecy" and
"revelation" – an ethical elevation.

  The psyche is prophecy because its words, while its own, have

<hr />

[99] This recalls certain formulations – "Indications of divine justice are to be found only
    where just men reign" (chapter nineteen, trans. S. Shirley) – made by Spinoza in the
    concluding "political" chapter of his *Theological-Political Treatise*. For the difference
    between Spinoza's idea of the divine instituted through justice, and Levinas's very
    different conception, see my article, "Justice and the State in the Thought of Levinas and
    Spinoza," pp. 55–70.

been "received" – as moral order, as moral command – from the other. The face is revelation in this sense. Levinas is certainly not referring to any sort of spiritual ventriloquy – "talking in tongues" or "spirit possession" – for the self he means is a self morally inspired and not replaced or taken over. Levinas consistently opposes the model of a "participatory" self, a self absorbed into and factotum for nature, world, master, state, God. The psyche is a responsibility for the other, and not some slavish submission to the greater power of an exterior force, however dressed up in the language of glory. One may indeed be violated, forced by superior powers – such is the human condition, of frailty and finitude – but submission in this way does not characterize the moral self in its moral being. The subject is subject subject to the other – morally. Levinas rejects mythological consciousness and cults of participation where one becomes – willfully or not – part of a larger whole, losing the self in vertigo, under whatever name that whole is advertised. Religion, contra Kierkegaard, cannot require the sacrifice of morality and justice, since it is precisely the demand for morality and justice. Of the near sacrifice of Isaac, Levinas writes: "Perhaps Abraham's ear for hearing the voice that brought him back to the ethical order was the highest moment in this drama."[100] The righteousness of Abraham was greater than that of Noah because when God threatened to destroy human life it was Abraham, but not Noah, who challenged God, who demanded that God Himself conform to God's own standards of justice.[101] And this is why, too, Abraham and not Noah is called "our father." Thus we can understand Levinas's use of the term "prophecy." Prophecy is anything but the loss of self. It is sacrifice,

---

[100] Levinas, "Kierkegaard: Existence and Ethics," in Emmanuel Levinas, *Proper Names*, trans. Michael B. Smith (Stanford: Stanford University Press, 1996), p. 74.

[101] Compare Genesis 6:22, "Noah did according to everything God commanded him, so he did," to Genesis 18:23, "Abraham came forward and said, 'Will You also stamp out the righteous along with the wicked?'" Perhaps this is another way to understand the Talmud's praise for Abraham: "Abraham performed the commandments of the Torah before they were given" (Yoma 28b). To perform a commandment before it becomes a "given," a "said," is to first respond morally to the other. One does not perform a "good deed" (or "commandment," Hebrew: מצוה *mitzvah*) as one follows a recipe in cooking, reading what to do in a cookbook. The dialectic is deeper, that of dia-chrony, the self as a responding awakened by the command of the other, by saying, my saying of the other's needs, a saying put into me – prophecy.

true, but sacrifice as the self shattered by awesome obligations, the self *qua* irreplaceable, singular, morally responsible – ordered. Like the biblical prophets, one obeys a higher and better command prior to one's own desires or one's contractual consent. These demands not only do not override moral demands, they precisely are moral demands. In "God and Philosophy," Levinas writes of the situation:

. . . where I make myself the author of what I understand, inspiration. It constitutes, prior to the unity of apperception, the very psyche in the soul. In this inspiration, or "prophesying," I am the go-between for what I set forth . . . Prophesying is pure testimony, pure because prior to all disclosure; it is the subjection to an order before understanding the order . . . It is in prophesying that the Infinite passes – and awakens. As a transcendence, refusing objectification and dialogue, it signifies in an ethical way. It *signifies* in the sense in which one says *to mean an order*; it *orders*.[102]

Here Levinas is clearly making reference to and "universaliz-ing" the significance of the celebrated sequence of the response of the Jews who, at the foot of Mount Sinai, in response to God's offer to give them the Torah, respond by saying: "We will do and we will obey" (Exodus 24:7). Contrary to Socrates, for Levinas one does not first know the good in order to be able to do the good. Nothing precedes the good, not even God, and certainly not knowledge. To do the good one must first be responsive to the order of the good. This responsiveness is the passage of God on earth. Cain's question, "Am I my brother's keeper?," is for Levinas already too late, already evil. In *Otherwise than Being or Beyond Essence*, Levinas writes:

We call prophecy this reverting in which the perception of an order coincides with the signification of this order given to him that obeys it. Prophecy would thus be the very psyche in the soul: the other in the same, and all of man's spirituality would be prophetic.[103]

All of human spirituality would be prophetic because the very selfhood of the self, its psyche, would be moral response before all else. Levinas does not believe that the root formulae of religion are dogmatic declarations of faith such as: "I believe in God," or "I

---

[102] "God and Philosophy," in Levinas, *The Levinas Reader*, p. 184.
[103] Levinas, *OBBE*, p. 149.

affirm that God exists" or "is good," or "My Lord and Savior is . . ." These are words, "the said," and words by themselves can lie. "To bear witness to God is precisely not to state this extraordinary word, as though glory would be lodged in a theme and be posited as a thesis, or become being's essence."[104] Rather, bearing witness to God is precisely the psyche as inspired, elevated, prophecy – loving the neighbor before oneself. "It is sincerity, effusion of oneself, 'extraditing' of the self to the neighbor. Witness is humility and admission; it is made before all theology."[105] The psyche, Levinas will say, is the "Here I am" [*Me voici*], an availability to the other, a readiness to serve. And thus, finally, Levinas can speak of the psyche as "revelation." "Here there is an inversion of order: the revelation is made by him that receives it, by the inspired subject whose inspiration, alterity in the same, is the subjectivity or psyche of the subject."[106]

Levinas's exposition in *Otherwise than Being or Beyond Essence* goes on to show that the maternal psyche, the "inspired subject," requires and demands justice, too, a concern for others beyond the other whom one faces immediately and before whom the I is fully responsible. And with the requirement for justice comes the need for measurement, hence for science, philosophy, courts, and all the institutions required for good government. To discuss this topic properly, however, goes beyond the confines of our present discussion of the psyche. But justice must be mentioned, nonetheless, to avoid the mistake of thinking that the psyche is an affair of morality alone, or that morality can remain moral without justice – that is to say, without measure and law, without public institutional protections and equal treatment before the law. These are necessary – in our unredeemed world – to preserve the more fundamental inequality that "defines" the psyche, namely, the height of the other and the humility of the self. It is in the name of this central inequality, the psyche itself, the-other-before-itself, maternal, that the more distant, objective, yet fair equalities established by justice are required. They are required to protect all others, all of humanity, oneself included.

---

[104] Ibid.    [105] Ibid.    [106] Ibid., p. 156.

*Humanity*, then, is the final, broadest, most all-inclusive sense of the psyche in Levinas. In the concluding chapter of *Otherwise than Being or Beyond Essence*, he will write of "the psyche, humanity,"[107] as if these two terms – the one the most singular, the other the most universal – were interchangeable, as ultimately they are.

### CONCLUSION

For Levinas, as we have seen, the psyche is the inordinate responsibility of being-for-the-other-before-being-for-oneself. No one can doubt that one can be evil, that one can be less than one's better self, that one can refuse the other, ignore the appeal, reject the call, turn aside "the poor, the widow, the orphan, the stranger," take one's own "place in the sun" at the expense of others. To some extent we are always doing that, always insufficiently ourselves, never finished with morality, not yet at our full height. Let us not forget, distracted perhaps by a concern for morality and justice, the power of immorality and injustice, and the hold that they have on humanity. But this entire vision, of good and evil, of justice and injustice, depends not on evil and injustice, but on good and justice. From the point of view of epistemology and ontology this region of signification – this significance – the moral, is higher not lower, a surplus not a lack. Deeper or higher than egoism, and giving its usurpation its meaning in the first place, is the inspired self, the maternal psyche, concerned for others in its very being.

This expository journey into the psyche as elaborated in *Otherwise than Being or Beyond Essence* has shown a self successively characterized as: for-the-other, proximity, diachrony, responsibility, substitution, animation, incarnation, signifyingness, non-indifference, fraternity, passivity, nakedness, exposure, prayer, insomnia, irreplaceability, inspiration, election, elevation, disorder, an-archy, suffering, vulnerability, expiation, catastrophying, prophecy, fissure, de-nucleation, expiation, prophecy, revelation, and finally humanity. The structure of the self takes on all these meanings because it is not an object or thing or essence or substance, not a state of being, but a life lived with others. Its

[107] Ibid., p. 178.

fundamental non-identity – dia-chrony, proximity, saying – is greater than identity because it is better. Higher than the self-sameness of identity is responsibility for the other, and ultimately for all others. The self by itself is not meaningful enough, indeed not meaningful at all, even when fevered with the will to power. At bottom, one cannot remain faithful to the deep structure of the self and at the same time separate oneself from society, from the other – mortal and hence suffering – who comes first. And thus philosophy cannot divorce the prescriptive from the denotative.

My first person singularity, I, me, myself, the psyche, is constituted as a moral Atlas. Each and everyone upholds the whole world. So speaks ethics. But for morality, it is I – I alone, I as myself, I as the singular *par excellence* – that is such an Atlas. Such is righteousness, no worse for being unspoken, though the philosopher who writes an ethics must bring it to voice, and its voice must indeed be heard. The burden of the world is surely too heavy, and surely can be dropped – who in our time can doubt the existence of evil, in oneself, in others? – but goodness, kindness, consideration, solicitude, justice, do not thereby go away, do not thereby stop their inordinate appeals. Quite the reverse, the worse it gets the more is required, and the more that is given, the more there is that still must be given. To repeat the words of Dostoyevsky that Levinas is fond of citing: "Each of us is guilty of all and for all humans before all, and I more than the others." Or in the words of Rabbi Yehuda Ashlag: "All of Israel are responsible for one another, for the Torah was not given to them until each and every one of them was asked if he agreed to accept upon himself the commandment of loving another at the level specified by the words 'Love thy neighbor as thyself'."[108]

[108] Ashlag, *Kabbalah*, p. 46.

# CHAPTER 7

# Humanism and the rights of exegesis

This is an ascent within words, be they the most recent ones, to I know not what antiquity that is already to be translated, already to be deciphered. A dead language to be resuscitated, in order that its innumerable intentions may be reawakened! The latent birth of Scripture, of the book, of literature, and an appeal to interpretation, to exegesis, an appeal to the sages who solicit texts. A solicitation of solicitation – Revelation.

Levinas, "From Ethics to Exegesis"[1]

Revelation needs commentary in order to be rightly understood and applied – this is the far from self-evident religious doctrine out of which grew both the phenomenon of biblical exegesis and the Jewish tradition which it created.

Gershom Scholem, "Revelation and Tradition as<br>Religious Categories"[2]

The present chapter is central to this book. It is guided by two related aims. At its core it aims to explicate the nature and value of the ethico-exegetical approach that operates in Emmanuel Levinas's work. This approach is especially evident in his Talmudic Readings, but it is also operative throughout his philosophi-

---

[1] Levinas, "From Ethics to Exegesis," in Emmanuel Levinas, *In the Time of the Nations*, trans. Michael B. Smith (Bloomington: Indiana University Press, 1994), p. 110.

[2] Scholem, "Revelation and Tradition as Religious Categories" (1962), in Gershom Scholem, *The Messianic Idea in Judaism* (New York: Schocken Books, 1971), p. 287. This entire article (pp. 282–303) is relevant to the present chapter. In it, Scholem presents both non-kabbalistic and kabbalistic ways of understanding the inextricable relation between revelation and exegetical tradition. For an excellent and extended study of this same topic, the relation of revelation to exegesis, with particular attention paid to the modern period and its historical criticism, see also Jay M. Harris, *How Do We Know This? Midrash and the Fragmentation of Modern Judaism* (Albany: State University of New York Press, 1995).

cal writings proper. Exegesis, in Levinas's hands, signifies far more than what one might ordinarily expect from a method or technique of text analysis, and certainly far more than text analysis "limited" to so-called religious writings. The second aim, then, is to elucidate and appreciate the larger issues at stake by locating Levinas's exegetical approach, both critically and positively, within the broader ethical-metaphysical project of "biblical humanism" that drives his thought as a whole, and represents Levinas's distinctive contribution to contemporary thought. Though Levinas is certainly mindful that many, though certainly not all, of the texts he comments upon are chosen from the heart and soul of Jewish tradition, from the Talmud[3] and (through the Talmud) the Bible, his readings are an affair neither for Jews or Judaism alone, nor for spiritually inclined individuals and religious communities alone – large and important as these intended audiences are. The significance of Levinas's readings is universal, for all the world. Against a narrow conception of *ratio*, which nonetheless – and because of its very narrowness – will claim for itself totality, Levinas will defend the wider humanism of *wisdom* – of reason, that is to say, of a wisdom inseparable from virtue. That this is so, and how this is so, is what this chapter sets out to show.

## BIBLICAL HUMANISM

Levinas – and not only Levinas – has been accused of humanism. As if this were an accusation! Who are the accusers? What is the fault? Martin Heidegger, fresh from the horrors of the Nazi experience, fresh from *his own* twelve-year Nazi party membership, unapologetic, chose to denounce humanism two years after the war's end in his famous 1947 "Letter on Humanism." Not in the excesses of fascism, or mechanized impersonal war, or mass death,

---

[3] Georges Hansel, in chapter nineteen, "Le *Midrach* n'est pas une exégèse" ["The *Midrash* is not an Exegesis"], of his excellent book, *Explorations Talmudiques* (Paris: Editions Odile Jacob, 1998), convincingly shows that not all Talmudic reading is exegetical. Readings oriented to *halakhah*, Jewish "law," are very often not exegetical at all. Levinas, in his own Talmudic Reading, however, is quite clear – as Hansel, a fine Levinas scholar, clearly knows – that his approach deals only with *aggadah*, narratives, stories, incidents, and not at all with the derivation of *halakhah*. These two approaches, *halakhah* and *aggadah*, both worthy in their own right, have traditionally been kept separate in the Jewish tradition, while at the same time nurturing one another.

or the leveling of Rotterdam, Dresden, Hiroshima, or the Rape of Nanjing, or slave labor camps, or the crematoria at Auschwitz, but in humanism, of all things, would Heidegger discover the scourge of human willfulness, self-assertion, loss of being. Humanism would be held accountable not for an appreciation, however poorly actualized, of the humanity of the human – the "universal rights of man," as it promised – but rather for the terminal closure of ontological horizons brought about by a technological world-view triumphant beyond anyone's dreams, the nightmare. So much for the celebrated subtleties of *Denken*. In America, concerned with an altogether different transcendence, religious fundamentalists would rant against the evils of "secular humanism," condemned as prideful and godless, adulating the human while heedless of the divine. Scientific discoveries, biblical criticism, religious ecumenism, and social idealism would all be lumped together and scorned as Satanic. One reels from these peculiar accusations, from their perversity, their latent gnosticism. What strange bedfellows anti-humanism makes: the German philosopher Heidegger (and his loyal disciples) and American religious fundamentalists.

In the face of a global, perennial, and well-documented history of inhumanities – slavery, serfdom, economic and political disenfranchisement, repression, war, suppression of women and minorities, colonialism, mass starvation, torture, imperialism, genocide, tyranny, and more – can it really be humanism that is at fault? Can any stretch of reasoning or imagination, however adroit, convince us that humanism is to be lamented and denounced for being the root cause and culmination of barbarism, rather than its enemy? It seems far too clever, another case of the intellect's penchant for novel and simple explanations, for an oblivious but superior self-absorption, for arcane conspiracy theories, for semantic pyrotechnics – in a word, for losing perspective. Is it not possible, even likely, actually the very case, that precisely the reverse is true? Humanism – by which I mean, at the very least, a pragmatic and fundamental respect for the irreducible dignity and worth of each and every human being *qua* human being – is it not rather a great human good, and hence indirectly also a great *religious* good? Even more, is not humanism directly a religious good, perhaps even the highest, the greatest of religious goods, the very vocation of the individual as *homo re-ligiosus*, of humanity consecrated to the task of returning to God? Such is the case Levinas will make everywhere in his work. Humanity is not duped, but elevated, by morality. Morality is the very vocation of the human. And the human is a vocation for morality.

For Levinas, humanism, respect for the human *qua* human, does not derive from or remain limited to some Greek or Renaissance or Enlightenment "definition" of the human being: "rational animal," "worker," "artist," "*homo sapiens*," "*homo politicus*," "language user." Rather, more deeply, it recalls and animates a central biblical teaching, the idea – and not *merely* an idea – that each and every human being, regardless of differences in wealth, power, talent, position or status, is "created" in "the image and likeness of God." Humanity would be constituted not by the embrace of a unitary idea or hidden substructure, but across encounter – face-to-face. Though it may be incomprehensible, the trace of transcendence passes here through the very heart of humanity. All humans, and a humanity so dedicated, across the diversity of individuals, families, and nations – despite but not wholly indifferent to these distinctions as well as to historical differences in military, political, economic, and cultural achievements – is, in a profoundly meaningful sense, one humanity. This one global human community opens in but stretches beyond families, friends, neighbors, and fellow citizens, welcoming complete strangers, even enemies, binding together near and far, rich and poor, strong and weak, healthy and sick, ally and enemy, fortunate and wretched, good and evil. Here lie thick and complex concatenations of meanings and imperatives – significance and not merely signification – worthy not only of thought but also of life.

The Bible expresses this unity – universal fellowship, universal humanity, the humanity of the human, fraternity – not in the rational and exclusionary discursiveness of philosophical exposition, nor merely in the quasi-scientific terms of the biological and hence racist parentage of an Adam and Eve, or Noah and Naama, or finally of Abraham and Sarah. Rather, the Bible reveals the outstanding ethico-spiritual attributes of truth, righteousness, hospitality, and compassion that these biblical figures do not merely represent or comprehend or declaim, but which they live and breath and walk in the concrete and inspirational narratives of the Bible. "Paradigmatic" narratives, Levinas will call them, without excluding the inspiration driving all literature.[4] Here one finds loftiness with its feet on the ground, a human sensitivity attentive at once to heights and failings, to failings measured by heights. Is not the Bible as much a record of human failings as of human achievements, and as such a unique document in the spiritual order of the world? Neither a human comedy nor a human tragedy – for who stands outside looking in? – but a "holy" document whose holiness consists in recording the inspirations/ aspirations of a human community united under the just and merciful "eyes" of an invisible but inescapable God.

Just as Heidegger's penetrating critique of "onto-theology" unmasks the forced and illusory *mythologizing* inherent in religious primitivism (including its secular forms), such as is all too often found in American fundamentalism with its dogmatic spiritual diremptions and its contagious veneration of a being within being as the Supreme Being, so too Hans Jonas has with no less penetration shown the latent *paganism* of Heidegger's suggested alternative, his "turn" (*Kehre*), his entranced and entrancing pontifications calling for a heightened attunement to the no less exclusionary oracular (verbal) be-ing of beings. Paganism, Jonas warns, lies not merely in some dark and distant origin, antiquated, overcome once and for all, but rather in the winking complacency of a being all too certain of its own being-in-and-of-the-world.[5] Paganism is the assurance – naïve or sophisticated – of having one's place under the sun, one's destiny, one's fate – one's right to be. That this seductive appeal of the earth, as it were, continues to haunt and challenge civilization was already shown by Franz Rosenzweig in his great religious work *The Star of Redemption* (1921). Levinas first warned of it in 1934 in a short article modestly entitled

---

4  In "From Ethics to Exegesis," in *In the Time of the Nations*, as elsewhere, Levinas writes, inclusively: "Is not the prophetic gift latent in all inspiration, and is not inspiration the sublime ambiguity of human language?" (p. 112).
5  For references to Hans Jonas's writings and further discussion of the question of paganism in Heidegger, see my *Elevations: The Height of the Good in Rosenzweig and Levinas* (Chicago: University of Chicago Press, 1994), pp. 300–304.

"Some Reflections on the Philosophy of Hitlerism."[6] But the critique of the immanentist and totalizing mythologies of both "onto-theology," the divinization of a being, and "fundamental ontology," the divinization of *be-ing* itself, began neither with Heidegger nor with Jonas, nor with Bultmann, Buber, Rosenzweig or Nietzsche, nor with the rationally definitive and devastating aporia articulated in the Dialectic of Kant's *Critique of Pure Reason*, nor with Hume's urbane but hyperbolic skepticism, nor even with the "negative theology," the "God without being," of a Thomas Aquinas, as read, say, by Jean-Luc Marion. Nor did a genuine humanism have to wait centuries for Paul's declaration that "there is neither Jew nor Greek, there is neither slave nor free, there is neither male nor female," in Colossians 3:19. Rather, far earlier, out of an "immemorial past" at the very dawn of history and humanity – and always, at every moment, here, now, "in the beginning" of a continual dawning of history and humanity, out of an immemorial past whose immemoriality traces an insecurity in the heart of being upon which history and humanity dawn – humanism begins with a tradition as ancient, in the West, as the Hebraic. This tradition reveals a God who is uniquely one, at once immanent and transcendent, and for the same reason uniquely invisible, beyond being and essence, *more* imposing than the very presence of the present. The idea of such a beginning, ancient yet contemporary, a more in a less, whose peculiar time structure Levinas will call "diachrony," is immediately disturbing, excessive, provocative, unsettling – to all the powers that be.

The imperialism of ancient Rome – and all that is still represented by such a "Rome," that is to say, by imperialism, by statism, by both the overt and subtle powers of the powers that be – was outraged to find that within the innermost precinct of the great Jewish Temple in Jerusalem – a Temple at once spiritual and material, an ancient architectural "wonder of the world" and a spiritual wonder of all worlds, a building, with many courtyards and sanctuaries, with many elevations, surrounded and supported by the massive stone bulwarks which stand to this day – in its very

---

[6] Emmanuel Levinas, "Quelques réflexions sur la philosophie de l'hitlérisme," *Esprit*, vol. 2, no. 26, November 1934, pp. 199–208 reprinted in Emmanuel Levinas, *Les imprévus de l'histoire* (Montpellier: Fata Morgana, 1994), pp. 35–41.

heart and soul, in a chamber known as the "Holy of Holies," a *place* (מקום, *makom*, a term which is one of God's "names"!), there stood no icon, no statue, no oracle, no god, no image, nothing. There was only a box containing the hewn tablets of the Ten Commandments (known in Hebrew as the "Ten Words") given to Moses, to the Jewish people, and to all the nations of the world, at Mount Sinai.

A temple without an idol – an outrage to pagan sensibilities. Furthermore, the tablets in the Holy of Holies were *not* the tablets of the Ten Commandments given by God to Moses on Mount Sinai. The Bible, in its obsessive honesty, does not flinch from informing its readers of the first tablets that they were destroyed by Moses at the foot of Mount Sinai in response to the idol worship of God's own people (and here Israel is certainly a paradigm for all humanity). Many paintings attempt to depict this striking and awesome moment, the breaking of the first tablets. Carved and given by God, inscribed by God, the first tablets were smashed. Thus when God's commandments *were* presented to Israel, later, they were already haunted by a pre-original from the start. Absolute origins elude the human condition, or perhaps, if we are not hasty in our judgments, the very temporality of a beginning prior to the origin is what constitutes the humanity of the human condition. Just as the Bible begins with the second letter of the aleph-bet, and the Talmud has no first page, the tablets sheltered in the Temple were, from the very first, second.

The shattered first tablets were *too first*, as it were, too exalted, cut too far above the measure of humanity. The Midrash tells that their letters flew back to Heaven, leaving behind tablets too heavy for Moses to bear, and this would be why they fell to the ground. In the short time of the first tablets, given on high on the shrouded mountaintop above, in the plains far below the Jews persuaded themselves to imitate the idol worship of pagans, forming and worshipping a "golden calf." Too pure divinity yields only a debased humanity. It is a great lesson. The high and the low would have to be brought into conjunction, into unequal reciprocity; *religion (re-ligio)* would henceforth be necessary for the very human-ity of the human and the divinity of the divine. Distances – one of the topics Levinas discusses apropos a conversation "recorded" in the Talmud between Alexander the Great and the "Rabbis of the Negev"[7] – must be bridged. Paradoxically, too, from the other side, the transcendent God must transcend divine transcendence. Religion and humanism, then, would arise together in the warmth of *rachamim* (רחמים), a Hebrew term meaning "compassion," "mercy," "pity," a word whose root (ר-ח-מ) forms the letters of the word for "womb," and is yet another of God's names (see Exodus 34:6, "Compassionate" or "Merciful," רחום). In Isaiah, we hear God say of Himself (57:15): "I abide in exaltedness and holiness – but am with the contrite and lowly of spirit, to revive the spirit of the lowly and to revive the heart of the contrite."[8] Religion – the link between the human and the divine, the place of the divine (no Hermes) – would require of humans neither a blind obedience nor an alienated freedom, but rather the "difficult freedom" of biblical humanism, neither too high nor too low, neither ashes nor ice.

Kept in the Temple's Holy of Holies, in the Ark of the Covenant, were the second tablets of the Ten Commandments, commandments in which – as the Jews realized – one could rejoice, commandments one could both "remember" and "keep," both "follow" and "obey," despite failures, lapses, backsliding, defeat, and the concomitant constant need for repentance. Humans – neither demons nor angels, hence capable of both good and evil – would be "given" a Torah, would enter into relationship with a forgiving, merciful, and just God. In his Talmudic Reading of 1974, entitled "The Will of God and the Power of Humanity,"[9] Levinas shows how divine commandments realized through carefully regulated and humane judicial proceedings are no less than divine *rewards* and not simply divine retribution. The restitution accomplished through human punishment would also be a divine mercy. The commandments of the second tablets were the same commandments as the first, to be sure, but the stones of the second

---

[7] "Beyond the State in the State," in Levinas, *New Talmudic Readings*, trans. Richard A. Cohen (Pittsburgh: Duquesne University Press, 1999), pp. 79–107.

[8] For an interpretation of Isaiah and other Hebrew prophets, one cannot recommend too highly Abraham Joshua Heschel, *The Prophets*, vol. I and vol. II (New York: Harper & Row, 1962). On page 95 of vol. II , just to invoke one brief citation, Heschel writes: "Compassion is the root of God's relationship to man." Note, it is *God's* relationship to man that is compassionate.

[9] Levinas, *New Talmudic Readings*, pp. 47–77.

were carved and contributed by Moses, not by God (though still according to God's command). The significance of this difference has too often been overlooked. Coming second, taking second place, the humility of the other-before-the-self, the other-put-into-the-same, converts a certain firstness – the for-oneself, *of both God and man* – into an actual *relationship*, the most concrete and pressing of relationships, the exigencies of morality and justice breaking the bounds of both terms. In the same way, all that is "first" – first fruits, first crops, first sons – would have to be consecrated to God. The Infinite is not indifferent to the finite, nor is the finite indifferent to the Infinite. Abraham – first of the Jews, by God's command – is he who challenges even God according to God's own justice. We have already remarked on the superior righteousness of Abraham in relation to Noah's. What would be demanded would not be abjection but election, not slavery but service. To be in relationship with the divine would be a high calling.

Relationship with God – covenant – henceforth would involve the intersection of two heterogeneous times: pre-original or "immemorial" time and a disrupted present, a present troubled, put upon, overburdened, obligated – the "more in the less." Such is the time Levinas calls "diachrony," link and rupture at once. Diachrony would be the temporality of a "present" always already too late "in the beginning," burst by a past too past and, demanded by that very immemorial past, oriented toward a future too future. It is that that at the conclusion of *Totality and Infinity* Levinas calls "messianic time, where the perpetual is converted into the eternal."[10] Diachrony is no less the conjunction of two heterogeneous parties or partners, each with an irreducible part: God and humankind. God is brought down to the earth upon which humans live and breathe and walk, and humans are raised to their proper stature, raised to the heavenly heights serving God through His commands. Just as the divine disappears in human arrogance (the warranted complaint of fundamentalists, Heidegger, and all the religious traditions), so too humanity – the humanity and dignity of the human – disappears in an excessive

[10] Emmanuel Levinas, *Totality and Infinity*, trans. Alphonso Lingis (Pittsburgh: Duquesne University Press, 1969), p. 285.

absoluteness attributed to the mastery of God. Already this complex dialectic – two times, two partners, two registers of significance, the intertwining of being and morality, heterogeneous yet
making contact – is contained, for exegesis, in the allegedly simple
"Bible story" of the two sets of tablets of the Ten Commandments.

A modern reader of the Bible – and surely of the Talmud – may
be far too self-satisfied and utterly blinded by conceit (however
scholarly), and therefore dismiss as archaic or anachronistic, as
"poorly edited," or as childish, the significance of all the many
very obvious instances of twos (creations, Adams, Eves, brothers,
wives, animals, tablets, etc.) so carefully preserved in the oneness of
the Bible. As if these were simple errors. As if there were not
lessons here, too. Not merely in the remarkable subtlety, astute-
ness, and fruitfulness of their exegeses, but in the fundamental and
challenging moral truths they promulgate, Levinas's Talmudic
Readings awaken us from the slumber and pretense of tiresome
"academic" readings. Slimly based, lacking the commitment of a
deliberate choice, forever taking refuge in hypotheses, conjectures,
possibilities, the alleged open-mindedness of such approaches is in
truth but a more sophisticated form of close-mindedness. Open to
everything, nothing would count more than anything else. Open
to all possibilities, such approaches would be closed to self-implica-
tion, to responsibility. A safe openness, untouched, "free." But just
as humanity is elevated above animal instinct, even more
profoundly has it always already been elected to an even greater
sobriety, bound by greater obligations, than those which often
seem to suffice a critical intelligence seeking the impregnable
citadels and sophisticated groves of "academic" retreat. That
scholarship is admirable and worthy, Levinas would have been the
last to deny, and neither do I. But at the same time scholarship
alone is insufficient, inadequate for a fully human life, not only the
life of the mind but also life among people. Levinas – whose
philosophical rigor was pristine – would be the first to affirm this.
Indeed, to make such an affirmation requires nothing less and
reflects nothing more than precisely his philosophical rigor. "I am
inclined to believe," Levinas once said in an interview, "that in all
meaningful thought, transcendence is manifested or has been

reduced."[11] Exegesis is the effort not to reduce transcendence – either through philosophical abstraction, including theology, or mythical constructions, even in the name of piety.

   This is the lesson of the two tablets: divinity as absolute mastery reduces humanity to slavery, hence to subhumanity, hence to anti-humanism. Tablets divine – all too divine – would have too much authority, and hence none. Thus they would fall to the ground unheeded, would not command *humans*, would belittle humanity, take away dignity, freedom, produce humans less than human, helpless children, groveling suppliants. Such was the slavery in Egypt, naturally aligned with an escapist death cult and a sorcerer's religion.[12] From such slavery the Jews fled, a negative moment whose positivity lay in God's command, under the leadership of Moses and Aaron, where a people fled from evil with their feet and not only with mouths that prayed, on an exodus which continually moves away from slavery, but also toward and up the harder road of freedom, a permanent exodus but also a continual redemption, the very movement of a humanist vision of history. Tablets human – all too human – on the other hand would lack authority, would not *command* humans, would be commanded by humans, by instinct and will to power. Such is the "bad" humanism of the Tower of Babel, of Korach's rebellion, of the Golden Calf, built on the subjectivist or projective rhetoric decried by Heidegger, fundamentalism, and the religious traditions. Such humanism, however, to the extent that it claims for itself "truth" or "higher values," nevertheless must derive its force, albeit surreptitiously, from the very transcendence it is so often intent on deriding.

   Biblical humanism, in contrast, recognizes and requires the meeting of divine and human through moral command manifest in moral action, hence in human courts. It recognizes divine command in human response, human response as divinely com-

---

[11] "On Jewish Philosophy," interview with Françoise Armengaud, in Levinas, *In the Time of the Nations*, p. 175.
[12] It seems to me that Jan Assmann, in *Moses the Egyptian: The Memory of Egypt in Western Monotheism* (Cambridge: Harvard University Press, 1997), only confirms this point. We will return to this work later.

manded. It is ordered by a structure combining both absence and presence, being and beyond being, a moral structure. No doubt paradoxes abound in such a configuration. No doubt both rationalism, for reasons of logical consistency, and irrationalism, seeking an unbounded freedom, chaff under its greater vigilance. Such, however, is the difficult path of a fully human life, the life of the creature alert in moral exigencies, in the solicitous sobriety of civilized life, attentive to others, charged with obligations and responsibilities, not at all confined to the mind alone, to intellect "intellecting," and, it goes without saying, far more demanding than the impulsive vitality of nature. Rationalism and irrationalism alike would rather be left alone, would rather stay less sober, absorbed in their own affairs, mad or maddening, clever or dumb. The exegetical path, in contrast, requires a more extreme vigilance, an unremitting attention to the ethical alterity of the other.

PHILOSOPHY, RELIGION, AND MYTH (CONTRA SPINOZA)

Levinas's writings and readings are thus dedicated to a sober vigilance, to an attentiveness to and for the other, to a moral conscience and conscientiousness. They demonstrate the intimate link binding exegesis, humanism, and religion. To see this, it is important to see that exegesis, and the stories and layers of meaning it elaborates, must not be confused with myth. This, too, is a temptation of reason, an escape. What is beyond reason is not for that reason irrational. In fact, for Levinas "Jewish humanism" is precisely "a system of principles and disciplines that free human life from the prestige of myths, the discord they introduce into ideas and the cruelty they perpetuate in social customs."[13] The enemy of Judaism, the enemy of all ethical monotheism, and the enemy of genuine reason, then, would be myth, mythological thinking, mythologized life.

Such an opposition would recall Kant's opposition to "speculative" metaphysics, whose reifications and personifications confuse a regulative ideality with truth claims regarding reality. For Levinas a truly adult religion offers an alternative perspective attentive, as

---

[13] Levinas, "For a Jewish Humanism," in Emmanuel Levinas, *Difficult Freedom*, trans. Séan Hand (Baltimore: Johns Hopkins University Press, 1990), p. 273.

we have seen, to the transcendent through its manifestation in morality and justice. Concomitant with the moral consciousness of this attentiveness is the effort to rid the world of the violence that follows naturally from the irresponsibility confirmed and sustained by adherence to mythic constructions. Though Derrida, in his essay "Violence and Metaphysics," has accused Levinas's critique of philosophy of "violence," the true violence comes not from alerting philosophy to an ethical vigilance, whose transcendence Levinas rightly characterizes as "pacific," but rather from "the prestige of myths, the discord they introduce into ideas and the cruelty they perpetuate in social customs." Derrida's attack on Levinas would thus represent yet another chapter in rationality's longstanding fear of the "beyond," even if in the case of Derrida's deconstructive enterprise this fear would come, paradoxical though it sounds, from rationality's shadow, the irrational. Levinas is perfectly explicit about the double imperative – positive and negative – which gives sense to the various activities and beliefs that constitute the universal particularism[14] of Jewish life: "They hold a man freed from myths and identify spirit with justice."[15] In a single but double-edged exigency, religion would be a movement toward freedom – a difficult freedom, an engaged freedom, to be sure – at the same time that it is, and precisely because it is, a movement away from the violence perpetrated in the name of mythic constructions.

It is instructive, given the modern propensity of philosophy to oppose religion, to compare Levinas's opposition to myth to Spinoza's. Though Spinoza also opposed the mythic constructions of what he called "superstitious religion," Levinas insists that his own thought nonetheless stands "at the antipodes of Spinozism."[16] Spinoza's solution to the problem of superstition, and the fear upon which it is based, as well as the violence it promotes, is to reject religion altogether in the name of a physico-mathematical rationality, a *mathesis universalis*. Because, following a long philo-

[14] See my article, "Levinas and Benamozegh: Universalist Particularism or Israel and Humanity," given as a paper at the World Congress of Jewish Studies, Jerusalem, 30 July 1997, and at the American Academy of Religion, San Francisco, 23 November 1997; published in the *Proceedings of the Twelfth World Congress of Jewish Studies* (forthcoming).
[15] Levinas, *Difficult Freedom*, p. 276.　[16] Levinas, *Totality and Infinity*, p. 105.

sophical tradition, he believes that true freedom can only be found in scientific knowledge, that is, knowledge of the true, Spinoza identifies all religious discourse, indeed all discourse alternative to science, with bondage. It is precisely this conflation that modern thought promotes and against which, in consequence, we must be vigilant. Like Spinoza, in opposing myth Levinas also opposes superstition. But his opposition, in contrast to Spinoza's, does not require the repudiation of religious transcendence. "Judaism," Levinas has written, "appeals to a humanity devoid of myths – not because the marvelous is repugnant to its narrow soul but because myth, albeit sublime, introduces into the soul that troubled element, that impure element of magic and sorcery and that drunkenness of the Sacred and war, that prolong the animal within the civilized."[17] Both Spinoza and Levinas oppose prolonging "the animal within the civilized," but Spinoza's solution, science all the way down (and all the way up, so that up and down become meaningless), would throw out the baby with the bath water.[18] Judaism, for Levinas, is also a force to rid the world of the macabre hybrid demi-gods of Egypt, which are to give way to the one God – the One God of Israel, of all humanity. But this requires no intellectual compromise, no sacrifice of intellect, no believing because it is absurd – quite the reverse. His solution requires awakening myth, and not simply from ignorance in the name of knowledge, as if myth were only ignorance, only a stammering science, which it is not, and which is why science alone cannot eradicate myth. But rather and more powerfully it requires the

[17] Levinas, "Being a Westerner," in *Difficult Freedom*, p. 49.
[18] It is not because he rejects the term "holy," but because he is using it exclusively to refer to (and to reject) Heidegger's pagan notion of the sacred, i.e., the holy as abode, that we can agree with Adriaan Peperzak in the following: "Freed from all holy abodes, we can discover the authentic meaning of the human way of being-in-the-world: we are here in order to provide food and shelter for the Others. Dis-enchanting nature and demystifying the world are the reverse side of existing for the Infinite that exceeds all horizions." Peperzak, *Beyond: The Philosophy of Emmanuel Levinas* (Evanston: Northwestern University Press, 1997), p. 217. Let me also mention, in this regard, Dietrich Bonhoeffer's notion of "religionless Christianity," by which he meant, if I am not mistaken, something very much like the biblical humanism of which Levinas speaks: an engaged moral religiosity, transcending institutions not by eliminating them but by judging them. In any event, of it he writes, in a letter of 30 April 1944, while in prison: "The transcendence of epistemological theory has nothing to do with the transcendence of God. God is beyond in the midst of our life." Dietrich Bonhoeffer, *Letters and Papers from Prison* (The Enlarged Edition), ed. Eberhard Bethge (New York: Macmillan, 1972), p. 282.

awakening of myth from its indolence, its stupor, its dream, in the name of the more sober and shattering religious responsibilities of a moral and just humanity.

But, one might retort, are not the Bible itself, its stories of Noah's ark, tablets, golden calf, earth swallowing rebels, and the like, as well as the Midrash, and especially the Aggadah upon which Levinas often comments, which are so vital to Judaism, are they not vast compilations of myth? Are they not stories wherein the divine and human are depicted as interacting often in miraculous ways? And if this is so, and so it seems, how can one hope to eradicate myth by means of myth? Would this not simply perpetuate superstition? But these questions reveal an unexamined and prejudicial leveling of perspectives. Levinas does not fight myth with myth, superstition with superstition. Rather, in what seems like myth, in what could be misunderstood as myth, he understands the human by means of exegesis. It is a great difference.[19]

Levinas, in contrast to the entire thrust of modernity from Spinoza to Strauss and beyond, is not satisfied with a radical separation between philosophy and religion. "There is," he writes, "communication between faith and philosophy and not the notorious conflict. Communication in both directions."[20] The refusal to begin with an irreparable dualism – the refusal to separate reason and revelation, Athens and Jerusalem, philosophy and religion, is one of the great strengths of Levinas's thought. It extends and amplifies, let us note too, a long tradition of Jewish thought and action. The issue is obviously of great importance. In contrast to many philosophers and religious thinkers before him, Levinas overcomes the alleged opposition between science and religion by siding with neither pole. Nor does he glorify the tension of their allegedly indissoluble opposition. Rather, he shifts grounds and undercuts the intellectual temptations of this opposition by writing from a perspective whose unitary vantage point reveals the abstract and derivative character of either side taken independent-

---

[19] This same difference, centuries earlier, explains why Spinoza, who treated the Bible as myth (or for the ignorant as a very simpleminded moral primer), was so frustrated and infuriated by Maimonides who, despite an intellectual bent no less scientific than Spinoza's, read the Bible in the light of exegesis.

[20] "On Jewish Philosophy," in Levinas, *In the Time of the Nations*, p. 170.

ly of the other. If one insists on calling Levinas a "postmodern" – a label both fashionable and deplorable for its slackness and lack of purchase – it is not through any semiotic or semantic pyrotechnics, or through some clever technique, maneuver or intellectual fast step whose utility or significance is blown out of proportion. Rather, precisely and profoundly, it is because his thought challenges the separation of science and religion. And at the same time, he radically challenges, from an ethical perspective, the plethora of alternative challengers to the philosophical tradition, all the counter-philosophers who opt for various fine-tuned aesthetic perspectives, those upon whom I am perfectly content to bestow, as they are to accept, the questionable title "postmodern."

One of the intellectual moves central to modernity, perhaps even constitutive of modernity, has been the hegemonization of physico-mathematical science. We have heard it since Descartes: nothing is acceptable as having truth value – and nothing is acceptable except what has truth value – other than "clear and distinct ideas," that is to say, ideas as clear and distinct as mathematical ideas. Only what is as clear and distinct as mathematical ideas, and hence acceptable to cognition, the mind, would count as an account of the real. The real would be the clear and distinct, the clear and distinct would be the real. Or, as Hegel expresses this same notion: "The real is rational and the rational is real." The rest would be subjective, not only opinion and poetry (*poesis*), but ethics and politics too (this is surely the position of Spinoza, de Sade, Nietzsche – another set of odd bedfellows).

Of course, in recent years Heidegger and then Derrida have denounced this notion of rationality as a truncation of wisdom. Limiting the real to conformity with "clear and distinct" ideas would be an unwarranted privileging of presence. Against its domination they have opted for the entertaining but essentially labyrinthean path of an aesthetic-poetic alternative, as we saw in chapter 4 above. Heidegger turned from such rationality to a refined though somewhat arbitrary appreciation for vague pre-Socratic fragments and German poets, while Derrida, his most faithful disciple, picking up where the late Heidegger left off, turned to microscopic but essentially parasitic analyses of semantic equivocations in texts. There is no doubt that equivocations can always be found, just as the pre-Socratics and the poets – as Socrates already showed – can be made to speak many things. But the temporary solace of these clever meanderings, this technique of deconstructing texts, when taken with the utmost seriousness (Heidegger) or with the utmost irony (Derrida), comes at the high price of neglecting the prior and more important demands of ethics. Heidegger intones that "thinking is thanking," to which Levinas retorts: "Who is thankful for Auschwitz?" Derrida speaks, finally, in his most recent writings, of friendship,[21] of responsibilities,[22] and even of religion,[23] but in his delicate hands these dimensions lose their ethical exigency to become little more than texts to be warily deconstructed. These characterizations and the criticism underlying them may strike the reader as harsh, but the political consequences of an unchecked aesthetic worldview have, in fact, been far harsher.[24] Levinas challenges the hegemony of

[21] Jacques Derrida, *The Politics of Friendship*, trans. George Collins (New York: W. W. Norton, 1997).

[22] See, e.g., Jacques Derrida, *The Gift of Death*, trans. David Wills (Chicago: University of Chicago Press, 1995); and *Adieu: To Emmanuel Levinas*, trans. Pascale-Anne Brault and Michael Naas (Stanford: Stanford University Press, 1999).

[23] See Jacques Derrida, "Faith and Knowledge: the Two sources of 'Religion' at the Limits of Reason Alone," trans. Samuel Weber, in Jacques Derrida and Gianni Vattimo, eds., *Religion* (Stanford: Stanford University Press, 1998), pp. 1–78. It is more than merely interesting that Derrida's title mimics that of Hegel's essay of 1802–3, also called "Faith and Knowledge [*Glauben und Wissen*]." For a discussion of this conjunction (*avant la lettre*), see my *Elevations*, pp. 315–318.

[24] I remind readers, too, of our earlier reference (chapter 4, n. 4; p. 121) to David Lehman's disturbing account (*Signs of the Times: Deconstruction and the Fall of Paul de Man*) of Derrida's perverse defense of Paul de Man's mature subterfuge regarding his youthful pro-Nazi writings. I am obviously not convinced by Richard Kearney's alternative reading of Derrida's relation to Heidegger and Levinas in "Derrida's Ethical Re-Turn," in Gary B. Madison, ed., *Working Through Derrida* (Evanston: Northwestern University Press, 1993), pp. 28–50. Kearney's article is commendable for its directness and lucidity, qualities too often lacking in deconstructive circles. Nonetheless, while it makes a good case that Derrida has always been concerned with otherness – an incontestable point, it seems to me – nevertheless I do not see that he has shown that Derrida's concern for otherness is bound to ethics ethically, in the manner I have pointed to in chapter 4 and thoughout this volume. It is precisely the indetermination that haunts his conception of otherness that has always disturbed me about Derrida's thought. It is not simply that when he "deconstructs" a text there is no positive result, it is also that when he takes up such topics as friendship, responsibility, politics, and religion, Derrida does not appreciate the extra-ontological ethical *force* – or ethical *significance* – of the saying that precedes the said. For Levinas, in contrast, the face of the other, *qua* the command "Thou shalt not kill," is the source of all signification. Otherness is thus not some abstract or "pure" alterity, as Kearney suggests, as if this were the problem Derrida corrects with his loyalty to the Heideggerian "ontological difference," but rather and precisely otherness for Levinas is

epistemology (and its shadow anti-epistemology) and its concomitant truncation of reason, by means of an ethical metaphysics –
that is to say, by means of an ethical account of transcendence that
exceeds but at the same time requires knowledge. For reason to be
reasonable, so to speak, it must neither be rational alone, nor
absorbed by its irreducible poetic-rhetorical dimension; it must
rather be responsible.[25]

In the face of modern non-teleological science, the temptation
to simply separate religion and philosophy is great. A thinker of
modernity as clearheaded, self-conscious and insightful as Leo
Strauss develops many reasons to defend an irreconcilable conflict
between religion and philosophy, Athens and Jerusalem, reason
and revelation. But, so it seems to me, he has nonetheless, for all
his clarity, succumbed to a pervasive but unacknowledged
Spinozist presupposition underlying such a separation. It was
Spinoza, after all, who in the *Theologico-Political Treatise* explicitly,
trenchantly, and systematically separated reason from revelation,
differentiating them in terms of rational truth and irrational belief,
knowledge and ignorance, freedom and bondage. Spinoza, like

the mortality of the other and, in relation to that mortality, the potential immorality of
myself. I am also evidently not convinced by Christopher Norris's efforts, in the final
chapter of his book *Derrida* (Cambridge, MA: Harvard University Press, 1987), to argue
that Derrida's deconstructive enterprise is linked to Jewish ethical sources. Relying on
the work of Susan Handelman, Norris once again trots out what to my mind is a rather
loose and facile parallelism between Derrida's interpretative agility and the rigors of
rabbinic hermenetics (pp. 229–230), and then uncritically supports Derrida's misreading
of Levinas as another philosopher of an impossible beyond (p. 234). Of course, I would
certainly have been happy had Norris and Kearney, along with Critchley, been right
about the essential ethical dimension of deconstruction, but I see no convincing reasons
to hold this view. Rather, one must criticize Derrida precisely on this point, for his lack of
an irrreducibly ethical perspective: that is, rather than succumb to good intentions by
fabricating a wishful revisionist picture of Derrida, one must rather criticize his always
"double" thought from a Levinasian point of view. Or perhaps we must think, regarding
Derrida's army of literary-critical fellow travellers, and of Derrida himself in the De Man
affair, that these legions of deconstructionists have all been obtuse and have all completely misunderstood the genuine moral restraints built into deconstruction? This seems
highly unlikely, even insulting.

25 One thinks of Kierkegaard's distinction: "Aesthetic pathos keeps itself at a distance from
existence, or is in existence in a state of illusion; while existential pathos dedicates itself
more and more profoundly to the task of existing, and with the consciousness of what
existence is, penetrates all illusions, becoming more and more concrete through recon-
structing existence in action." Søoren Kierkegaard, *Concluding Unscientific Postscript*, trans.
David F. Swenson and Walter Lowrie (Princeton: Princeton University Press: 1941),
p. 387.

Strauss, Levinas and a long philosophical tradition, rightfully wanted to oppose and eradicate a superstitious, mythological type of religion. Against the fearful and potentially fearsome prejudices and the loss of human dignity that follows from submission to superstition, all three thinkers argue instead for a spiritually purified or "adult" conception of religion. Spinoza's position, however, is determined throughout by an unconditional acceptance of the modern physico-mathematical model of rationality and science. This was, in fact, the basis of Spinoza's critique of Descartes: Descartes was not modern enough, did not fully carry out his own commitment to mathematical truth, to clear and distinct ideas.

Spinoza argues that not only mythology but imagination *per se* is altogether incompetent to conceive the clear and distinct ideas which are to be the exclusive domain of genuine science. Spinoza's *Ethics* intends to be nothing other, and nothing less, than the self-understanding of science conceived as the only and complete system of truth. It aims to eradicate "knowledge of the first kind"[26] – that is, imagination, opinion, false ideas (everything Spinoza finds in the Bible) – for the sake of the fully coherent and progressively more determinate system of necessary and universal propositions (of material causality and deductive logic) which make up "knowledge of the second kind" – that is, scientific or fully rational knowledge. The *Ethics* is intended to be "the way of truth," to borrow a phrase from Parmenides' theodicy, in contrast to imagination and opinion, the "knowledge of the first kind" which Spinoza derides as capable only of falsity. Science is possible and the mind is free only when they are liberated from the pernicious influence of the imagination. By means of a mathematical standard, Spinoza completes – or aims to complete – the attack on myth and *poesis* begun by Parmenides, banishing them, as Plato had not been able, from the precincts of truth. Only the pure and complete self-transparency obtainable through the filter of mathematical clarity and distinctness, yielding universal and necessary

---

[26] Baruch Spinoza, *Ethics*, trans. Samuel Shirley (Indianapolis: Hackett Publishing Co., 1992), Part II, Scholium 2 to Proposition 40, and Proposition 41 (pp. 90–91). Spinoza explicitly equates "knowledge of the first kind" with " 'opinion' or 'imagination' " (Part II, Scholium 2 to Proposition 40; p. 90), and declares in Proposition 41: "Knowledge of the first kind is the only cause of falsity" (p. 91).

truth, as opposed to the impenetrable opacity and heteronomy of mythic tales and all products of the imagination (which leave humanity vulnerable and obedient to the external forces Levinas calls "magic and sorcery and that drunkenness of the Sacred and war"), would be adequate to a fully free and hence a fully human spirituality. Such is Spinoza's rigorous program of science *qua* ethics. Its price is the belittlement and its aim is the ultimate elimination of religion (as well as art, history, and morality).

For Spinoza, religion and theology, based in heteronomy, would be based in ignorance and untruth, would always already be a power politics. Everything other than rationality in relation to itself would be slavery. Hence the hyphenated title of Spinoza's treatise on religion, *Theologico-Political Treatise*, a book that does not simply treat religion and politics successively, as its table of contents might suggest, but treats them together because it reduces religion to a politics, to force relations, to a manipulation of meanings divorced from the discovery of truth. In chapter seven of the *Theologico-Political Treatise*, entitled "On the Interpretation of Scriptures," Spinoza declares that "the point at issue is *merely* [my italics] the meaning of the texts, not their truth."[27] His point, and the self-declared central aim of the entire *Theologico-Political Treatise*, is to sharply distinguish truth from meaning, rationality from theology. For all the talk of his rhetorical sensitivity to "persecution and the art of writing,"[28] Spinoza in no way hides his scorn for the ruses of religion and theology and their imaginary productions, despite their usefulness – given the ignorance of the "masses," the "multitude" – for a prudential political calculation. Thus Spinoza extends on the deepest philosophical plane, in the name of science, the divorce between fact and value that Machiavelli had earlier encouraged on the plane of political calculation. Thus the world is divided: science, philosophy, freedom, and calculation for the few; the Bible, religion, obedience, and ignorance for the many. Nietzsche will later admire this segregation of the few from the many, while shifting his criteria from knowledge and ignor-

---

[27] Baruch Spinoza, *Tractatus Theologico-Politicus*, trans. Samuel Shirley (Leiden: E. J. Brill, 1991), p. 143.
[28] This is, of course, the thesis and title of Leo Strauss's work, *Persecution and the Art of Writing* (Chicago: University of Chicago Press, 1988; originally published in 1952).

ance to strength and weakness, basing his thought, following Schopenhauer, unabashedly on the will rather than the intellect.

It is true that a thinker such as Strauss, unlike Spinoza, will recognize the independence and perhaps even the superiority of monotheism over mythology.[29] Unlike Spinoza, too, Strauss will argue that the rights of monotheistic religion are impregnable against philosophical criticism, that philosophy is as helpless to refute religion, since religion is not based on the intelligibility of argument, as religion is to refute philosophy, which is based on intelligible principles. Nonetheless, despite Strauss's differences from Spinoza, his position remains – wittingly or unwittingly – based on Spinozist premises, on a sharp and irreconcilable separation of the truths of philosophy from the claims, however unitary, of religion. Strauss remains committed to an irreconcilable opposition between autonomy and heteronomy. Levinas, in contrast, rejects this dichotomy, rejects its Spinozist philosophical presuppositions.[30] The plurality of myths poses the problem of contradiction and conflict, to be sure. But this problem is fatal only on the assumption that systematic or scientific philosophy has the last word. The genuine resolution of this problem, and of the alleged conflict of reason and revelation, lies neither in philosophy nor in religion taken separately. Reason and imagination – or, more broadly, reason and sensibility – while not reducible to one another, to be sure, are at the same time indispensable to one another. As we saw on the ontological plane in the very first chapter regarding Bergson, and in the previous chapter regarding the ethical character of the maternal psyche, consciousness is itself incarnate, incarnate as ethical consciousness. Or, to restate Spinoza's and Strauss's alleged opposition in terms of reason and will, the solution lies neither in reason without will – that is, will reduced to reason – nor in will without reason – that is, blind and stupid faith. Levinas's philosophical writings and his Talmudic

---

[29] Where exactly Strauss himself stands in the Athens/Jerusalem conflict he defends, where one must necessarily take one side or the other, continues to be subject to controversy in the secondary literature.

[30] In the name of the Jewish alternative, Emil Fackenheim has also attacked the Kantian dichotomy of autonomy and heteronomy. See chapter 14, "The Revealed Morality of Judaism and Modern Thought: A Confrontation with Kant," in Fackenheim, *Quest for Past and Future: Essays in Jewish Theology* (Boston: Beacon Press, 1968), pp. 204–228.

Readings demonstrate and rise to another way, a more exacting intersection of reason and religion across *exegesis*, across the ethical height of exegesis.

## CRITICISM AND THE LIFE OF EXEGESIS

The solution to the problem of myths contradicting myths lies neither in the abstract transparency of an allegedly pure reason, which eliminates imagination and free will along with myth, nor in the complementary but no less abstract opacity of blind faith, which denies free will and intellect. These alleged solutions in fact represent two sides of the same coin, a coin whose purchase is to separate reason from revelation. Nor does the solution lie in embracing myth as if on a higher plane. To rely on the polysemy of great poets or obscure fragments rescued from antiquity, seducing the resources of a frustrated philosophical reason with the alluring refinements of self-referring groundlessness, remains enchantment and complacency. In the poems of a Mallarmé, say, the enchantment of this self-contained world is just that, enchanting. But for philosophy, which has always claimed a higher responsibility, it would indeed be yet another version of blind faith, and as such would be – and has been – defenseless against moral and political manipulation. Such flights of "thinking" would be what Martin Buber has called "monologue" in contrast to "dialogue," about which, in reference to Heidegger specifically, he has rightly noted:

Monologue may certainly disguise itself ingeniously for a while as dialogue, one unknown layer after the other of the human self may certainly answer the inner address, so that man makes ever fresh discoveries and can suppose that he is really experiencing a "calling" and a "hearing"; but the hour of stark, final solitude comes when the dumbness of being becomes insuperable and the ontological categories no longer want to be applied to reality.[31]

Being talking to itself (revealing itself to itself) remains indistinguishable, in the final account, and with all the attendant problems of subjectivism, from the self talking to itself. Rather, the solution

[31] Buber, "What is Man?" (1938), in Martin Buber, *Between Man and Man*, trans. Ronald G. Smith (New York: Macmillan, 1972), p. 168.

lies in recognizing the deeper link between reason and faith in exegesis. Exegesis, Levinas writes, effects "a demythologizing of the text"[32] for the sake of a "wisdom of love"; it is indeed the very performance, manifestation or production of a wisdom that serves the ends of morality and justice: "*a difficult wisdom concerned with truths that correlate to virtues.*"[33]

In religion as in all the humanities, understanding is to the highest degree self-understanding. Hence it is dependent on hermeneutics or interpretation, because the object of human understanding here, in contrast to the object of explanation in the natural sciences, is the very same humanity that is the subject of human understanding. Religion is, in a word, self-understanding. And again, just as in the humanities, the fact that it is not "objective" in the manner of the natural sciences does not at all mean that understanding in religion is "subjective" in the sense of unregulated subjectivism. In contrast to the self-understanding obtained through literature or historical studies, religion is humanity's self-understanding in view of the absolute transcendence of God. To grasp the import of Levinas's philosophical contribution, his "solution" to the alleged opposition between science and religion, and the problem of myths conflicting with myths, we must, however, make a distinction between two modes of interpretation. These two modes of interpretation can be taken narrowly as two types of text interpretation or more broadly as two different existential stances toward truth and meaning. One is *criticism* and the other *exegesis*, of which Talmudic exegesis is for Levinas the exemplary case.

What criticism does is to interpret a text by explaining it in terms of more or less remote objective contexts. One understands the biblical flood story, for example, by comparing it, say, to a contemporaneous Mesopotamian flood story, or to our current scientific knowledge regarding floods. Or one understands Abraham's childhood, his opposition to idolatry, and his early departure from his hometown, by grasping the economic, social, and political contexts inferred from archeological digs in the ancient city of Ur as found in present-day Iraq. The key to

[32] "On Jewish Philosophy," in Levinas, *In the Time of the Nations*, p. 168.
[33] "For a Jewish Humanism," in Levinas, *Difficult Freedom*, p. 275, my italics.

criticism, then, is explanation by comparison and contrast derived from a text's insertion within local, regional, and ultimately global contexts – for example, meteorological, geological, geographical, historical, cultural, economic, political, religious, sociological, and linguistic contexts. One locates a text within a universal and objective differential field of texts and contexts. Criticism, in a word, though fundamentally self-understanding, owing to the nature of its regions of meaning, nonetheless relies primarily on explanation.

Exegesis, on the other hand, is text interpretation not through *explanation* derived from *objective* context alone, but through *understanding* derived from the text's as well as the subject's own *subjective* context. Though it does not exclude objective truth, for this too is also part of subjective context, it searches for subjective or internal truth as well. Exegesis, then, never loses sight of the self-understanding fundamental to the constitution of its regions of meaning. The term "subjective," borrowed from modern epistemology, may be misleading. Rather than restricting the explanation of a text's meaning to significations derived by comparing and contrasting its forms or structural characteristics with those of alternative cultures, exegesis would grasp the significance of a text by comparing and contrasting its content and intent with those from that text's own cultural tradition or from cultural traditions internally relevant to the text, *and* with cultural traditions which ultimately refer to the cultural context of the interpreter. One might call exegesis "relevant hermeneutics," regardless of how objectively remote the texts may be from the inquirer's own cultural-spiritual tradition. And the import of "relevance" – text as teaching – is irreducible because the inquirer and the text are bound, more or less remotely, within the all-embracing but infinite context of one humanity – humanism again. Here "all things human concern *me*."

Exegesis, then, is tributary of and contributes to the internal and ongoing self-revelatory dimension of a living textual tradition, while criticism adds to the external and objective knowledge of a universal science for which any particular text is but one text among others. Of course there are academic researchers who would claim to be content with criticism. The students of Max

Weber described his intellectual approach to society as that of "someone from an alien planet." "But the lucid labors of that science," Levinas notes of the critical approach, "have never been able, to this day, to take the place of that other reading, which is neither the private domain of the so-called 'orthodox' circles, nor the stylized daily practice of the underdeveloped classes."[34] "This exegesis," Levinas writes, "made the text speak; while critical philology speaks *of* the text. The one takes the text to be a source of teaching, the other treats it as a thing."[35] Franz Rosenzweig, in 1924, makes this point even more sharply, regarding, in this instance, understanding the significance of Jewish law: "[I]t is not at all that historical and sociological explanations are false," but rather that "in the light of the doing, of the right doing in which we experience the reality of the law, the explanations are of superficial and subsidiary importance."[36] Of course exegesis has no good reason to ignore the claims of criticism, but neither can it be limited or bound to them.

Before proceeding, an important point must be highlighted. To

[34] Levinas, "The Strings and the Wood," in Emmanuel Levinas, *Outside the Subject*, trans. Michael B. Smith (Stanford: Stanford University Press, 1994), p. 128.

[35] Levinas, "The State of Israel and the Religion of Israel," trans. Séan Hand, in Emmanuel Levinas, *The Levinas Reader*, ed. Séan Hand (Oxford: Blackwell, 1989), p. 263. Jay Harris, in *How Do We Know This?*, makes a similar point regarding the effects of historical criticism within the Jewish tradition: "In the end, then, we must say that the traditional historical school was quite successful in its efforts to rehabilitate the reputation of the rabbis as readers and jurists; they were much less successful in promoting continued attachment to a historicized rabbinic tradition in the modern world" (p. 210). Not only was Jewish historical criticism able to rehabilitate the reputation of the rabbis as readers and jurists against earlier and harsher critics such as Spinoza, it was also able to counter the all too often partisan and triumphalist historical criticism of Christian Bible scholars in their unequal approaches to Judaism and Christianity. On this second "passion" of what might otherwise seem to be a rather dry criticism, see, e.g., the excellent study by Susannah Heschel, *Abraham Geiger and the Jewish Jesus* (Chicago: University of Chicago Press, 1998). Perhaps here is also the place to recommend Richard A. Muller's erudite study of contemporary Christian theology, *The Study of Theology: From Biblical Interpretation to Contemporary Formulation* (Grand Rapids: Zondervan Publishing House, 1991), because it is especially attentive to the role of hermeneutics and ethics as essential dimensions of scriptural understanding.

[36] From a letter to several members of the *Lehrhaus* faculty, cited in Nahum N. Glatzer, ed., *Franz Rosenzweig: His Life and Thought* (New York: Schocken Books, 1967), p. 245. For an extended account of Rosenzweig's departure from the objectivity of academia for the personal involvement of Jewish community life and exegesis (of Yehuda Halevi), see my Introduction, "Rosenzweig's Rebbe Halevi: From the Academy to the Yeshiva," in *Ninety-Two Poems and Hymns of Yehuda Halevi*, ed. Richard A. Cohen, trans. Thomas Kovach, Eva Jospe, and Gily Gerda Schmidt (Albany: State University of New York Press, 2000), pp. x–xxvii.

distinguish exegesis and criticism in the above manner does not imply that the significance of exegesis is parochial or particular while that of criticism is universal. Both are universal. This must be highlighted because there is considerable prejudice against the claim to universality for exegesis. This comes from the side of those scholarly practitioners who, for one reason or another, limit themselves (or appear to limit themselves) exclusively to criticism. It sometimes even seems as if certain scholars derive their own worth – the value of their research – not so much from the universality of their own discourse, but rather from insisting on the narrow parochialism of an alternative exegetical discourse. Certainly, there is no doubt that one of the virtues of criticism is objectivity and the universality that objectivity implies. And, even further, to suggest that criticism serves or is itself a version of exegesis is in no way intended to undermine its objectivity. One of the prime virtues of exegesis, in contrast to myth, is also universality, even if it is not limited to the same principles of objectivity that the external perspective of criticism provides. Above and beyond, as it were, the objective scientific explanations gained through criticism, and above and beyond an exegesis which might want, according to its own self-interpretation, to contribute only to the internal growth of self-understanding within a particular living tradition (what might be called narrowly parochial in what Levinas has called "the so-called 'orthodox' circles"), exegesis is no less capable – and in its own way is more capable – of contributing to the self-understanding of humankind at large. It is precisely this point that Levinas – along with his contemporaries Martin Buber, Abraham Joshua Heschel and André Neher, to name only three fellow exegetes within the Jewish exegetical tradition – will insist upon and demonstrate. Moreover, he will further show that this is the case with rabbinical or Talmudic exegesis, where biblical narratives and stories of the sages and others are taken neither as authoritative myths nor as simpleminded children's tales, but, as we shall see, as exemplary *paradigms*. In sum, exegesis can be, and Talmudic exegesis is, an enlightened discourse, a wisdom for each and every individual, whether Jewish, Christian, Muslim, Confucian, Hindu, Buddhist, or atheist, to speak only of religious denominations. For precisely this reason, coupled with his recognition that Judaism is permeated through and through with rabbinic exegesis, Levinas calls the heart of Judaism a "Jewish humanism" or a "biblical humanism."[37] Exegesis, in this sense, like Judaism itself, is for humanity. "It may even be," Levinas muses rhetorically, knowing both the prestige and pride of criticism in today's intellectual circles and the inner greatness of religious traditions such as Judaism, "that a less naïve conception of the inspired Word than the one expiring beneath critical pens allows the true message to come through . . ."[38]

Another further, almost paradoxical, dimension of the distinction between criticism and exegesis, one that provides a basis for a critique of criticism from the point of view of exegesis, has to do with the naïvité of criticism! This will appear paradoxical at first sight since it is well known that criticism prides itself on its intellectual rigor and sophistication in comparison with what it believes to be the close-minded parochialism and ignorance of exegesis. Thus it enjoys castigating "orthodox" readings precisely for *their* naïveté. But as is often the case – so Shakespeare had already seen – in defensive protests, exactly the reverse of what is declared may be at work. The claim offered here, then, is that precisely because criticism decries and lacks the essential insight of exegesis, namely, a deep appreciation for transcendence, it suffers from superficiality. This was certainly Rosenzweig's point.[39] For this reason, too, Levinas accuses criticism of a naïveté on a par with that of the fundamentalist or literalist Bible readings that criticism and Levinas both reject. Levinas finds in criticism a hesitation, an insufficiency, a spiritual narrowness, that parallels – without being reducible to, or a simple reversal of – the disdain with which criticism looks down upon fundamentalist readings. "[F]or these

---

37 Levinas uses these expressions in several places. For "biblical humanism," see, e.g., *New Talmudic Readings*, p. 117.
38 "The Strings and the Wood," in Levinas, *Outside the Subject*, p. 126. Another author within the Jewish tradition no less appreciative of the universality and humanism of the most Jewish dimensions of Judaism was Rabbi Elijah Benamozegh (1823–1900), mentioned earlier (p. 228 n.14), whose remarkable work, *Israel and Humanity*, trans. Maxwell Luria (New York: Paulist Press, 1995), was – by happy coincidence? – republished in France by the same press, Albin Michel (Paris), in the same series, *Présences du Judaisme*, as Levinas's "Jewish" book, *Difficult Freedom*. (In fact, Benamozegh's work is advertised on the back cover of Levinas's!)
39 See my introduction, "Rosenzweig's Rebbe Halevi," to Rosenzweig, *Ninety-Two Poems and Hymns of Yehuda Halevi*, pp. xi–xxxii.

critical readers equally," Levinas writes, "transcendence continues to signify an exchange of data with God or an experience of the supernatural. Having descended to the underground of verbal signs, criticism has lost, under an artificial but apparently sufficient illumination, the philosophical certainties, right up to the desire to leave the Cave."[40] Thus Levinas will accuse criticism, in its haste to denounce fundamentalism, of conflating – and thereby over-looking – the humanity and subtlety of the exegetical approach with the narrow and simple mindedness of an exclusionary parochialism they both oppose.[41]

With the above distinction in mind, we are in a position to clarify the central role of exegesis in Levinas's conception of religion. His claim is, first of all, that Jewish spirituality is exegetical through and through. Just as Judaism cannot be separated from Torah, Torah cannot be separated from exegesis. One does not simply read the Bible through the Talmud, say, as if the Talmud were a gloss that could be stripped off. Rather, there is no pure Bible, but only a Bible interpreted, and there is a specifically "Jewish" Bible precisely owing to the Talmud. Or, more broadly, the truths of religion – of humanity in personal relation to transcendence – are truths exegetically revealed. Second, the exegesis that cannot be separated from Torah is a wisdom that combines understanding and virtue. This is what Spinoza failed to appreci-

---

[40] Levinas, *New Talmudic Readings*, p. 75.

[41] Here is the place to mention, but not the place to enter into, the extensive debates regarding the relative status of and the interrelationships between "explanation" and "understanding," and the role of prejudice and reason, articulated by Hans-Georg Gadamer, Jürgen Habermas, Carl Hempel, Paul Ricoeur, et al., building on the work of Wilhelm Dilthey (1833–1911). Except to note that Levinas's notion of exegesis has much in common with (though is not equivalent to) Gadamer's notion of *wirkungegeschichtliches Bewusstsein*, "consciousness of historical efficacy," or the "efficacy of history within understanding itself" (Hans-Georg Gadamer, *Truth and Method* [no translator named]; New York: Crossroad, 1982; p. 267; see especially, in Part Two, the subsection entitled "The principle of effective-history," pp. 267–274). One sees, for instance, the latent humanism – the integral unity of humanity – contained in Gadamer's contention that: "When our historical consciousness places itself within historical horizons, this does not entail passing into alien worlds unconnected in any way with our own, but together they constitute the one great horizon that moves from within and, beyond the frontiers of the present, embraces the historical depths of our self-consciousness. It is, in fact, a single horizon that embraces everything contained in historical consciousness" (ibid., p. 272). Is this not another way of saying that everything human affects me? And that therefore explanation is itself part of understanding?

ate. Morality is not some ignorance or failing of knowledge but its very source. Third, precisely because it eliminates the mythological, and because it aims at virtue, exegesis is a contribution to universal self-understanding. Levinas thus rejects the adequacy of both the rhetoric of an ostensive literalism as found in fundamentalist readings, which he will call "the negation of the spiritual and the source of all idolatry,"[42] and the rhetoric of a ostensive detachment derived from a strictly scientific or critical reading. The rhetoric of both these approaches, one in the name of single-minded conviction, the other in the name of open-minded disengagement, would be narrow forms of reading alien to the integral combination of multiple readers and multiple levels of meaning, and the prescriptive heights uncovered and unraveled through exegesis.

Levinas writes often of the peculiar genius of Talmudic exegesis, at once particular and universal, faithful to the concrete situations of the human yet resonating with trans-temporal significance. The significance of such a reading is universal not because it abstractly applies to everyone in general, as, for example, does the periodic table of chemistry, but rather because it concretely speaks to each and every individual in particular in his or her particularity. For Levinas, as I have indicated, Judaism is permeated throughout by exegesis. Owing to this immersion in reading and rereading – "interpretation and reinterpretation" (see below) – it avoids the moribund idolatries of literalism and scientism. In an article entitled "Contempt for the Torah as Idolatry," Levinas writes of the compulsory and mutual character of the exegetical interaction between reading and read as follows:

I wish to speak of the Torah as desirous of being a force warding off idolatry by its essence as Book, that is, by its very writing, signifying precisely prescription, and by the permanent reading it calls for – permanent reading or interpretation and reinterpretation or study; a book thus destined from the start for its Talmudic life. A book that is also by that very fact foreign to any blind commitment . . . The reading or study of a text that protects itself from the eventual idolatry of this very text, by renewing, through continual exegesis – and exegesis of that exegesis – the immutable letters and hearing the breath of the living God in them . . .

[42] Levinas, "Contempt for the Torah as Idolatry," in *In the Time of the Nations*, p. 67.

Reading and study taking on a liturgical meaning in Jewish culture: that of an entering . . . into society, into a covenant with the transcendent will . . . A liturgy of study as lofty as obedience to the precepts, but of a never-ending study, for one is never done with the other. Incompleteness that is the law of love: it is the future itself, the coming of a world that never ceases coming, but also the excellence of that coming compared to presence as persistence in being and in what has always been.[43]

A very rich citation indeed, for it profoundly recognizes both the necessity and the lofty status of exegesis. Levinas rejects the narrow literalism of blind faith, without, however, thereby rejecting the personalism, the existential rebound, the fervor of its commitment. In the same way, he rejects the free-floating abstractness, the alleged "superiority" of criticism (what Rosenzweig, years earlier, had decried as mere free-floating "possibility," the possible divorced from the actual, leading not to life but to a "phantom"[44] life), without thereby rejecting universality. Study, as "interpretation and reinterpretation," as "continual exegesis – and exegesis of that exegesis," and life would be inseparable.

In contrast to blind faith or detached criticism, exegesis produces and requires the engaged or existential self-transformation of the inquirer, through a back-and-forth movement, the very life of inquiry as dialogue between text and reader,[45] between reader and reader, between texts, readers, and reality across time, from an immemorial past to an ever distant future. "[T]he life of a Talmudist is nothing but the permanent renewal of the letter through the intelligence."[46] As we saw above, this renewal of the past would at the same time be the opening of the future – diachrony. For Levinas this manner of exegetical reading, this study, this life, results in "saving the text from being turned into a mere book, that is to say just a thing, and in once more allowing it to resonate with the great and living voice of teaching."[47]

---

[43] Ibid., pp. 58–59.
[44] Glatzer, ed., *Franz Rosenzweig*, pp. 97, 129.
[45] Basing himself on Buber rather than Levinas, Steven Kepnes will propose precisely such a model of reading in Part I of his book, *The Text as Thou: Martin Buber's Dialogical Hermeneutics and Narrative Theology* (Bloomington: Indiana University Press, 1992), pp. 3–78.
[46] Levinas, "As Old as the World," in Emmanuel Levinas, *Nine Talmudic Readings*, trans. Annette Aronowicz (Bloomington: Indiana University Press, 1990), p. 79.
[47] "The State of Israel and the Religion of Israel," in Levinas, *The Levinas Reader*, p. 263.

## FOUR CHARACTERISTICS OF EXEGESIS (CONTRA NIETZSCHE)

To be more precise, we must distinguish in exegesis four inter-related characteristics or dimensions: (1) concrete and productive integrity of spirit and letter; (2) pluralism of persons and readings; (3) virtue, or existential, self-transformative wisdom; and (4) authority, or the renewal of a living ethico-religious tradition.[48] It is interesting to note, given the academic popularity of Nietzsche and his epigones, that exegesis closely resembles, in its first three characteristics, Nietzsche's conception of interpretation. Regarding the fourth point, however, Levinas and Nietzsche radically part company. Nietzsche attacks, both from the pre-historical fantasy of the "blond beast" and from the post-humanist phantom of the *Übermensch*, the very ethico-religious tradition that Levinas defends and renews. The wide chasm that separates the outcomes of their respective perspectives measures the importance of the fourth dimension of exegesis – continuity with a living ethico-religious tradition – and serves to explain, as shall become fully clear later, why Levinas and Nietzsche only *seem* to agree regarding the first three characteristics. We turn now to a closer look at these four characteristics of exegesis.

(1) *Concrete and productive integrity of spirit and letter.* Following and developing the phenomenological insights of Henri Bergson and Merleau-Ponty, Levinas begins with the integral or dialectical unity of spirit and matter.[49] At the level of text interpretation, this translates into the integral unity of spirit and letter, meaning and text. Letters give rise to spirit, call for commentary,[50] and spirit is

---

[48] It should be noted from the start that Levinas's "interpretation" of rabbinic exegesis is in nowise idiosyncratic, wishful thinking, or invented. For a very fine account along the same lines of the living and authoritative dialectic operative in rabbinic exegesis – called "Intrinsic Inspiration" (p. lxv) – in contrast to both strict literalism and loose liberalism, see Howard Loewe's 1938 "Introduction" to C. G. Montefiore and H. Loewe, eds., *A Rabbinic Anthology* (New York: Schocken Books, 1974), especially pp. lv–lxxxi.

[49] Daniel Boyarin, *Carnal Israel: Reading Sex in Talmudic Culture* (Berkeley: University of California Press, 1993), will speak, as the title of his book indicates, of "carnal Israel." For Boyarin, as for Levinas, the notion of the integral unity of body and soul, matter and spirit, is both a content thought and lived and a root principle of hermeneutics.

[50] In *Sotah* 47b, the Torah is said to "beg from house to house to house" in order to get students. Cited in Montefiore and Loewe, eds., *A Rabbinic Anthology*, p. 668.

rooted in letters, in a textual richness that is one of the marks of sacred literature, or of literature taken in a sacred sense. It is because it begins with this integrity that exegesis succumbs neither to an impossible literalism of the letter, which Levinas derides as the "negation of all spirituality and the source of all idolatry,"[51] nor to a no less impossible detachment, an abstract or free-floating interpretation, which Levinas derides as "pious rhetoric . . . in which ambiguity, amidst unverifiable 'mysteries,' always finds a convenient shelter."[52] Literalism and spiritualism are both subjective in the worst sense: willful, unregulated, self-projections, rather than inspirations. Spirit detached from the letter – one might think of certain instances of Protestant Bible reading in America, or of Derrida and deconstruction – can give rise to an excessive and hence a falsely optimistic moralistic generosity,[53] to an "angelic" dreaminess inattentive and unattached to the historical situations and concrete motives of the human condition. By contrast, in exegesis, "through the apparent attachment to the letter, there is the extreme attention paid to the spirit of the biblical text and a hermeneutic which puts a passage . . . back into the context – and in the deepening – of the totality of the Bible."[54] To fly with a text, to be inspired by it and discover its inspiration, requires not that one have wings, that one hover above it. Rather, it requires that one's feet be firmly planted on the earth, in touch with the concrete, never losing sight of a properly human dignity: then one is able to find the wings of words that cry out to rise to their proper height and raise the reader to his or her proper height as well. Because the words demand to be interpreted, because they cannot be extricated from interpretation, exegesis is far from what

[51] In the Talmud we find the following remarkable declaration: "Jerusalem was destroyed only because they gave judgment therein literally in accordance with biblical law" (Baba Metzia, 30b).

[52] "Contempt for the Torah as Idolatry," in Levinas, *In the Time of the Nations*, p. 63.

[53] "The Pact," Emmanuel Levinas, in *Beyond the Verse*, trans. Gary Mole (Bloomington: Indiana University Press, 1994), p. 78–79: "A principle of generosity, but nothing but a principle . . . Every generous thought is threatened by its Stalinism. The great strength of the Talmud's casuistry is to be the special discipline which seeks in the particular the precise moment at which the general principle runs the danger of becoming its own contrary, and watches over the general in the light of the particular."

[54] "On Religious Language and the Fear of God," in ibid., p. 91. See also chapter 1 on Bergson in this volume for a fuller treatment of the integral unity of spirit and matter, letter and commentary.

Spinozist rationalism can only deride as "excessive and rash" "licence."[55] (It is not surprising, then, because it separates spirit and letter, that we can call Spinoza's rationalist reading of the Bible excessive and rash licence.)

(2) *Pluralism of persons and readings.* Exegesis not only yields but also requires multiple readings, multiple interpretations. This multiplicity, however, is not a flaw, as has all too often been asserted – happily or unhappily – based on the standard of an epistemological rigidity satisfied only in mathematics (and not even there). Rather, exegetical pluralism is a product of and tribute to the pluralism constitutive of human society. Thus it is a reflection of lived ethics, the pluralism of the face-to-face, on the one hand, as it is also a product of and tribute to that lived ethics, reflected in the essential pluralism (not "mere" or "unfortunate" ambiguity or equivocation) of textual meaning, on the other hand. What constitutes the fundamental truth of meaning, then, is not a common denominator, which would be reductive, but a unique service, the singularity of each one in the face of the other. "Each one of us Jews," Levinas once declared before presenting a public interpretation of Judaism, and without any false modesty, "retains his freedom of expression."[56] This qualification could well serve as a preface to all of Levinas's Talmudic Readings, as indeed to all reading and communication.

What this means, too, is that regardless of the depth and sincerity of one's own religious commitment, no single reader can appropriate the definitive mantle or chant of priest or pontiff (and even less of oracle). The revelatory or sacred character of texts and religions, unfolding within living exegetical traditions, cannot sanction closure within official dogma or catechism. Without opening itself to any and all interpretations, the Midrash insists that millions of interpretations of the Torah, more even for non-Jews than for Jews, were already given and hence legitimated at Sinai.[57] In Levinas's

---

[55] Spinoza, *Tractatus Theologico-Politicus*, trans. Shirley, chapter seven, p. 158. In this instance Spinoza is referring to Maimonides' exegesis.

[56] Levinas, "Judaism and Christianity," in *In the Time of the Nations*, p. 161.

[57] According to Midrash the Torah at Sinai was given to 600,000 souls, for each of whom it was received differently; and it was given with at least four ways of interpretation ("PaRDeS": literal; "Remes": allegorical; "D'rash": homiletic; "Sod": mystical), yielding 2,400,000 readings; and it was given even then to the seventy nations, yielding 170,400,000 readings; all of which is to say that there are innumerable legitimate readings, each necessary for a complete understanding of Torah; which is to say that the

vocabulary this also means that each human being retains his or her right of expression because that expression is not extraneous to truth, is not a merely subjective interference, or the source of merely secondary qualities. Rather, expression, commentary, dialogue, partnership in learning, are the necessary "manner" or "way" of truth itself, since truth cannot be true without reflecting rather than suppressing its actual conditions. Exegesis neither reduces singularity to universality, discarding it as "particularity," nor succumbs to a "war of all against all" where the strongest will, the most sincere witness, or the loudest voice prevails.

"Prophecy," Levinas will say, using this term in a broad sense, "is an essential dimension of truth."[58] This does not reduce truth to subjectivity, or diminish truth in the name of friendship, say – or it need not, because truth itself, for its full expression as a living, ongoing revelation, requires multiple expressions. Speaking of revelation and the multiplicity of legitimate readings, Levinas writes:

> The Revelation has a particular way of producing meaning, which lies in its calling upon the unique within me. It is as if a multiplicity of persons . . . as if each person, by virtue of his own uniqueness, were able to guarantee the revelation of one unique aspect of the truth, so that some of its facets would never have been revealed if certain people had been absent from mankind . . . I am suggesting that the totality of truth is made out of the contributions of a multiplicity of people: the uniqueness of each act of listening carries the secret of the text; the voice of Revelation, in precisely the inflection lent by each person's ear, is necessary for the truth of the Whole . . . The multiplicity of people, each one of them indispensable, is necessary to produce all the dimensions of meaning; the multiplicity of meanings is due to the multiplicity of people.[59]

Like Schleiermacher in this regard,[60] but based in an ethical singularity rather than the specification of individuality, Levinas will argue that there are, in principle, at least as many readings as

Torah is inexhaustible.

[58] Compare with Numbers 21:29: "Moses said to him [Joshua son of Nun], 'Are you being zealous for my sake? Would that the entire people of God could be prophets.'"

[59] Levinas, "Revelation in the Jewish Tradition," in *The Levinas Reader*, p. 195.

[60] "We all exist as 'someone.' Therefore each person has a greater receptivity for some religious perceptions and feelings than for others. In this manner every person's experience is different." F. D. E. Schleiermacher, "Speeches on Religion," in Edward Oakes, ed., *German Essays on Religion* (New York: Continuum, 1994), p. 56. Levinas, of course, does not reduce unique religious experience to "perceptions and feelings."

readers, since each reader brings (or can bring) his or her own unique concerns, insights, perspectives, heritage, to bear in understanding what a text can say, and what a text can say depends on this multiplicity of readers and readings. The singularization of the singular – the psyche – occurs as moral response to the other. This is the true beginning of meaning, and so too in "reading." "Each soul is called to exegesis," Levinas writes, "which is both regulated by the rigorous reading of the text and by the unicity – unique in all eternity – of its own contribution, which is also its discovery, the soul's share."[61] Each reader, then, is irreplaceable, just as each one is irreplaceable before the other.

Thus, too, in the revelation proper to religion "there is included a semantics that is absolute, inexhaustible, ever renewable through exegesis."[62] This inexhaustible pluralism and the diversity to which it gives rise are not a *flaw* or *problem* but rather a reflection of the irreducible alterity and personal challenge encountered in social relations. Debate, disputation, argumentation, disagreement, and dissension, like agreement, resolution, unanimity, and consensus, do not represent the provisional externals or contingencies of an absolute truth unable or not yet able or finally able to cohere with itself, but rather reflect the pluralism of humanity and the infinity of truth. "The innumerable sides of the absolute Truth live in the bosom of rabbinical debates or disputes, avoiding dogmatism, avoiding heresies."[63] Of the "innumerable" exegetical interpretations, Levinas writes: "Their diversity, their very contradictions, far from compromising the truths commented upon, are felt to be faithful to the Real, refractory to the System."[64] What is refractory to the system, then, is not the irrational but the dialogical, the exegetical. Revelation extends through the pluralism of persons[65] and readings throughout history right up to the present, as Levinas notes, recalling the celebrated insight of an

---

[61] Levinas, *New Talmudic Readings*, p. 76.

[62] "From Ethics to Exegesis," in Levinas, *In the Time of the Nations*, p. 112.

[63] Levinas, *New Talmudic Readings*, p. 87.

[64] "The Strings and the Wood," in Levinas, *Outside the Subject*, p. 130.

[65] In *Ta'an*, 7a: "A Rabbi said that as fire does not burn when isolated, so will the words of the Torah not be preserved when studied by oneself alone. Another said that the learned who are occupied in the study of the Law, each one by himself, deserve punishment, and they shall become fools." Cited in Montefiore and Loewe, eds., *A Rabbinic Anthology*, p. 107.

eighteenth-century rabbi for whom "the slightest question put to the schoolmaster by a novice constitutes an ineluctable articulation of the Revelation which was heard at Sinai."[66] Exegesis is precisely this "ineluctable articulation of the Revelation which was heard at Sinai." Pluralism and diversity, then, are not equivalent to loss and fragmentation. We shall return shortly to consider the discipline that brings even apparently contradictory truths together across a long history.

(3) *Virtue, or existential, self-transformative wisdom.* The third characteristic of exegesis is closely related to the second. This is because the dialectical or dialogical dimension of exegesis prevents it from being mere spectacle, something seen at a distance, in the third person, with clean hands.[67] Rather, it engages and hence transforms – and is meant to transform – its interlocutors in the first person. "I" and "you" (including the "you" which speaks through the text[68]) are thus not the same as "one" and "it," or the same as "self" and "other person." Precisely this difference makes all the difference because the third person impersonal is necessarily grounded in the first person singular. When "I" say "he," I say it *to* someone. That someone, who is a "you," and that "I," who is me, precede that about which one speaks: saying precedes the said. Likewise, exegesis lives because it engages the lives of those who engage in it.

This fundamental engagement accounts for why what is called "Talmud Torah," the study of sacred literature, which includes a vast range of literature, is in the Jewish tradition called "learning" (Yiddish: *lernen*). To study is to learn. This is also why the Yiddish term for synagogue, "*shul*," literally means "school." Not because

---

[66] "Revelation in the Jewish Tradition," in Levinas, *The Levinas Reader*, p. 195.

[67] In this regard we recall the fascinating teaching of the Talmud whereby the handling of sacred texts makes pure hands impure! This is indeed taken as a criterion of the holiness of a text, for instance, to confirm the sacred status of the Song of Songs and of Ecclesiastes.

[68] It is interesting in this regard that in orthodox yeshivah exegetical circles sometimes a revered sage-author becomes known and (re)named by the title of his primary book (e.g., Rabbi Yisroel Meir HaCohen Kagan [1838–1933] is known after his book as "Ha-*Chofetz Chaim*, [The "Will to Life"], Rabbi Meir Simcha HaCohen [1843–1923] is known as "Ha-*Or Someyach* [The "Joyful Light"]); and very often important religious books (*Midrash, Talmud*, commentaries, codes) are spoken of as if they were live personages, e.g., "The *Midrash* says . . .", or "The *Mishnah Torah* says . . ." rather than "Maimonides says . . ."

praying is learning, though it is,[69] but because learning is a kind of prayer, a holy service, a link to transcendence. A text is sacred not because it is inviolable, but precisely because it transfigures, engages, and in this way is "alive." The significance of a text – inseparable from exegesis – is neither a subjective projection, as if the self remained untouched and imposed itself on the text, nor an impossible literalism, as if the self again remained immaculately removed while discovering something outside itself, unmoved and unmovable in the text. Rather, significance is itself an existential enterprise, fraught with difficulties and dangers, but also rewards. It is an existential enterprise, an intertwining of inwardness and exteriority that emerges in and affects the interaction which is exegetical reading. Written Torah cannot be separated from Oral Torah without becoming "dry bones," just as Oral Torah cannot be separated from Written Torah without producing "beautiful souls," both of which are abstractions alien to the readers and writings they claim to elucidate.

The issue of the text's impact is not a matter of receiving new contents, new information, new data. The learning involved in study is not a matter of possessing a new or revised set of theses, to carry away in one's mental pocket, as it were. Rather, one is changed by the experience of learning. To expand one's erudition, to gain new objective knowledge, is not a negligible result, but it is not the primary purpose of study. Or, rather, gaining knowledge is not simply putting data into a pristine container, the mind: the container, the self, and the contained mutually affect each other. Thus the Talmud enjoins Talmudic study even for those poor students who retain nothing afterwards, that is, who retain no new data that they can repeat back later. While retaining such data is recommended, is indeed best, not retaining it, however, does not entirely negate the effect of study. Thus learning in Judaism is itself a quasi-liturgical activity. In contrast to criticism, which may alter an objective body of knowledge, in exegetical reading – even of the most obscure and seemingly impractical texts, texts, say, that refer

---

[69] A contemporary American lay commentator writes: "You're supposed to leave Jewish prayer services more inclined to do good and less inclined to do bad than when you came in, and this is achieved gradually, not in one step." Arnold Rosenberg, *Jewish Liturgy as a Spiritual System* (New York: Jason Aronson, 1997).

to rituals and practices that have not been performed for thousands of years – the reader is in principle still changed, transformed, uplifted, inspired by the reading. Thus, too, in learning, one's aim is never simply to put a learned idea into practice: the learning itself is also a practice. Indicative of this approach, it is often the case that after hours of intense Talmudic study, requiring great intelligence and diligence, as well as keen logical and analytical skills, to decipher, clarify and understand often obscure texts, students, after concluding their learning, may still ask: "And what do we [as observant Jews] actually do?" – and then look up the answer elsewhere in a contemporary code book! The Talmud is called an "ocean," indicating its vastness. But this image also suggests that, as in entering an ocean, the student gets wet, develops muscles, must swim for dear life – Talmudic study is a complete spiritual-intellectual immersion. In the same way one speaks of entering into the "world" of Plato, or Shakespeare. And because the words of the Torah are also called "fire," exegesis can also be called baptism by fire.

Exegesis cannot be action at a distance or pure intellection, and must be an existential project, because it contains an ineradicable *prescriptive* dimension. One does not learn about Temple ceremonies, say, in order to perform them; no one is oblivious to the fact that the Temple no longer stands. Rather, in learning about Temple rituals one also learns about one's relation to God, to others, the meaning of priesthood, sacrifice, holiness, purity, and so on. Nothing here is alien to today. Perhaps, too – and this level of meaning is never lost – one day the obsolete ceremonies *will* be performed. Who knows? Nothing can be discounted in the wealth of sacred meaning. There are levels and levels of significance. Also, it should not be forgotten, very often learning does have to do with practices and beliefs that are still current, and thus enriches them with new layers of significance. It was "study," Levinas writes, "that was considered valid as *association*, as covenant, as sociality with God – with his will, which, though not incarnate, is inscribed in the Torah."[70] If Torah is the recipe, and exegesis the cooking, then it is we who are the food – the holy sacrifice. Exegesis

---

[70] Levinas, "Judaism and Kenosis," in *Difficult Freedom*, p. 120.

tolerates neither detached knowledge nor blind faith, but promotes wisdom, a way of life, and a way toward a way of life, a combination of truth inextricably bound to behavior and behavior inextricably bound to truth. It is "a difficult wisdom," as Levinas has said, "concerned with truths that correlate to virtues." Its impetus is vertical as well as horizontal, finding the vertical in the horizontal – and hence it is diagonal as it is dialogical.[71]

Exegetical wisdom is difficult precisely because it operates neither above nor below the human condition, but speaks a *human* language. "The Torah speaks in the language of humans"[72] is a well-known adage of Jewish Torah study. Exegetical language is charged with prescriptive inspiration, with moral commands, duties, obligations, and responsibilities. It speaks to readers in their whole being as individuals, as family members, as members of communities, polities, and a global humanity, and not merely to intellects or to scholarly interests. Approached in this way, the sacred stories resist devolving into myths. "In opposition to the transfiguration into myth," Levinas writes, "(whether by degradation or sublimation) that threatens this 'profound past,' there stands the astonishing reality of today's Jews . . . As a defense against 'mythologizing,' . . . these traits also characterize the liturgy . . . At once commemoration of Holy History and a continuation of the events commemorated, the practices are, through *interpretation*, reinserted into the texture of those events."[73]

A final citation from Levinas will serve as a bridge from the third trait of exegesis, self-transformation, to the fourth, the authority of tradition, both set in contrast to what we above called "critical" hermeneutics:

The transmission, the *lelamed* [teaching], is an obligation distinct from the pure receptivity of study. For humankind entails the risk of a fossilization of acquired knowledge, depositing itself in our consciousness like some inert matter and being handed down in this ossified form from one generation to another. This congealment of the spiritual is not the same as its true transmission, whose essence lies elsewhere: in vitality, inven-

---

[71] Diagonal like the *mezuzah* marking the doorways of a Jewish home (see Deuteronomy 6:9). According to the Talmud the *mezuzah* must be either completely vertical or completely horizontal, and yet in practice it is diagonal – "reality" once again surpassing logic. [72] *Babylonian Talmud: Yevomoth 71a; Nedarim 22a; Avodah Zarah 27a;* and *Arachin 3a.*
[73] "The Strings and the Wood," in Levinas, *Outside the Subject,* p. 128.

tiveness and renewal which occur precisely through being taken up by way of tradition, or of a lesson taught to the other and assumed by the other.[74]

(4) *Authority, or the renewal of a living ethico-religious tradition.* The third characteristic of exegesis, self-transformation, is intimately linked to the fourth and perhaps most important characteristic of exegesis. This is its regulative principle: connection with a historical and more or less organized ethical tradition.[75] While interpre-

---

[74] "The Pact," in Levinas, *Beyond the Verse*, p. 79.

[75] In the preface to their recent book, *Thinking Biblically: Exegetical and Hermeneutic Studies*, trans. David Pellauer (Chicago: University of Chicago Press, 1998), authors André LaCocque and Paul Ricoeur also say that "the factor . . . the exegete most takes into account has to do with the connection between the text and a living community" (p. xii). They label this factor "textual dynamism" (p. xiii). Regarding the difference between a Jewish reading and a Christian reading of the Old Testament, one must wonder, however, what the authors were thinking when they wrote: "The First Testament is not abolished by the Second, but reinterpreted and, in this sense 'fulfilled' " (p. xiv). Presumably this left-handed disclaimer is written to acknowledge the legitimacy of a Jewish reading of the Bible. Unfortunately the allegedly "Jewish reading" LaCocque and Ricoeur have in mind remains almost entirely within the Christian picture of a Jewish reading, that is to say, it is a reading for the most part confined to the Old Testament, and completely unaware that a genuinely Jewish reading of the Old Testament necessarily puts into play the Jewish "New Testament," i.e., the Talmud. In the light of this exclusion one must wonder what the authors can mean when they claim that the Christian New Testament is on the "same trajectory" as the Old Testament, but "considerably ramified." This coming from two educated and sensitive Christian readers shows just how far traditional religious exegesis remains from the ethical exegesis that Levinas calls for and has produced in many writings. More positively, however, LaCocque and Ricoeur advise that "the Christian reading is not taken as a substitute but, rather, as an alternative to the traditional Jewish reading" (p. xiv). With this genuinely fine hermeneutical principle, which I have spoken of in terms of "multiple readings," one wishes that these authors had a better idea – as they should have – of what the "traditional Jewish reading" really is.

I think, however, that David Boyarin is far closer to Levinas's sensibilities regarding the third and fourth characteristics of exegesis, reflexivity and engagement in tradition. Boyarin writes of this aspect, which he names "generous critique," of his own method, which he names "cultural critique" (and more broadly, following Stephen Greenblatt, "Cultural Poetics" – a name I find less felicitous for reasons by now obvious): "It will have to be an account that is not judgmental but critical. Rather than apologetic, I shall call this mode of cultural critique . . . *generous critique*, a practice that seeks to criticize practice of the Other from the perspective of the desires and needs of here and now, without reifying that Other or placing myself in judgment over him or her in his or her there and then. I will suggest that such a practice is appropriate for any presentation of a past culture, but most imperative when the past is my own" (Boyarin, *Carnal Israel*, p. 21). What Boyarin in this citation names "criticism," Levinas would call "judgment" – "judging history" – but their sense, as the citation shows, is the same. It is, it seems to me, an essential dimension of exegesis, of which Jan Assmann's method of "mnemohistory" is precisely incapable (see n. 89 below).

tations are innumerable and inexhaustible, they are nonetheless rooted in past interpretations, in past texts, in texts that have a past, in a past aiming at a future, in a tradition which in the case of Judaism is, in Levinas's words, "as old as the world," that is to say, as old as the "humanity of the human." Certainly this is one of the central (exegetical) truths taught by the dating of the Jewish lunar calendar, nearly 6,000 years old. It tells the story not of the geology of the earth, or of the evolutionary origins of homo sapiens, but rather of the humanity of the human, the origins of *our* universe of meaning.[76] Adam would not be the first homo sapiens (for who, after all, did Cain go off and marry? a question asked by all third grade Sunday School students), but rather, as his very name ("Adam" = "human") suggests, the first human being – ideality and reality combined. As such, Adam serves as a paradigm: of intimate relations with God, with commandments, with a spouse, with nature, and so on. With Adam begins the history of "man," the human. What regulates exegesis, and at the same time frees it from both the excessive rigidity of objectivism and the excessive elasticity of subjectivism, is its living link to tradition.

This fourth characteristic of exegesis, then, is a specification or determination of the third characteristic, the dialectical interaction between texts, readers, history, and transcendence. It refers to specific historical commitments, and to the extensions of these commitments, these living interactions, under the guidance and weight of tradition. Levinas is thus able to remind his readers of the all-important conjunction of liberty and authority, originality and continuity, in exegesis:

There is, moreover, a means of discriminating between personal originality brought to bear upon the reading of the Book and the play of the phantasms of amateurs (or even charlatans): this is provided by the necessity of referring subjective findings to the continuity of readings through history, the tradition of commentaries which no excuse of direct inspiration from the text allows one to ignore. No "renewal" worthy of the name can dispense with these references.[77]

[76] On this point I recommend Leo Strauss's penetrating exegesis of the biblical genesis story in "On the Interpretation of Genesis," Leo Strauss, *Jewish Philosophy and the Crisis of Modernity*, ed. Kenneth Hart Green (Albany: State University of New York Press, 1997), pp. 359–376.

[77] "Revelation in Jewish Tradition," in Levinas, *The Levinas Reader*, p. 196.

Liberty, creativity, and revelation are bound by tradition, just as tradition lives through revelation, creativity, and liberty. Bergson's insight, that the present, building on the past, is essentially novel, has not been forgotten.

It is tradition, however, that provides a regulating context for the accumulating historical dialectic of a past renewed in the present and opening upon (and opening up) a novel future. Wakened by exegesis, both text and reader are made to link up with and reawaken a long history of prior exegesis. Along these same lines, Franz Rosenzweig once wrote "To read Hebrew implies a readiness to assume the total heritage of the language . . . Its [Hebrew's] growth is not that of an organism but of a treasure."[78] Just as every word of the sacred Hebrew literature resonates with and is linked to every other word of that literature, exactly so does every exegesis resonate with and link up with every other, in principle if not in fact. "To belong to a book," Levinas writes, "as one belongs to one's history!"[79] By an odd twist, then, what is today often referred to as Jewish "orthodox fundamentalism" is precisely the opposite of Christian Protestant "fundamentalism": the learned Jew opens the Bible to read it through the long historical lens of innumerable commentaries, while the latter opens the Bible and reads afresh as if for the first time. Both dimensions are necessary. Indeed, reading the Bible through commentaries includes reading it afresh for the first time. To read, even for the first time, is to reread, and to reread is to read for the first time. Exegesis is at once old and new, derivative and original – again, "diachrony." "There is nothing new under the sun," wrote Solomon in Ecclesiastes, not because everything has been said and done and therefore need not be said or done again, but because everything new renews, and every renewal is a new beginning, a new passing or passage of the past. Thus in the same text Solomon also writes: "The words of the wise are like goads." Levinas will recall a Talmudic metaphor, that the words of holy literature are like *embers*, embers that must be breathed upon to awaken flames, to give light.

Exegesis operates as and awakens a peculiar time structure: a past more past than origins, hence "immemorial," and a future

[78] Glatzer, ed., *Franz Rosenzweig*, pp. 268, 267.
[79] "The Strings and the Wood," in Levinas, *Outside the Subject*, p. 129.

more future than projections, hence "messianic." Through exegesis, wisdom reaches to the roots and heights of an always
ruptured and renewed human continuity. "It is the eternal anteriority of wisdom," Levinas writes, "with respect to science and
history."[80] The letters of Jewish tradition solicit interpretation
because the reader of sacred texts comes to them from neither
dead history nor mystifying mythology, but formed by the very
meanings whose meaning must be awakened anew. Reading produces rereading. Exegesis produces its own renewal. Thus for
Levinas, the tales, stories, narratives of Bible, Midrash, and Aggadah offer eternal "paradigms." The vivid concretude of the
Bible, Midrash, Halakhah, and Aggadah need not turn into fossils,
embedded in a long-gone stratum, true then but false now, as
modern, overly hasty, reformers and critics have suggested.
Rather, the stories and legal discussions remain rich treasure
houses of meaning, precisely to the extent that they remain alive
through exegesis, that is to say, to the extent that one finds them
applicable today. Not, of course, because when the ancient texts
speak of donkeys and wooden carts they already had automobiles
and trucks in mind, but rather because the human imperatives that
speak through these texts lend themselves to and require the
continual renewal of exegesis, right from the very start.[81] There is
no original word, but no obsolete word either – such is the unity of
humankind. "This essential unity of all languages," Rosenzweig
wrote, "and based on it the commandment for all human beings to
understand one another, is what creates the possibility and also the
task of translating – the possibility, the permissibility, and even the
obligation to translate."[82]

Exegesis is thus not some nefarious manipulation and distortion
of revelation, as Spinoza thought, because he wanted to bury
history and its revelations once and for all in the name of the latest
science. Rather, it is a continual animation, a permanent awakening, and the very revelation of revelation. It is mistaken to conceive

[80] Levinas, "Judaism and the Present," in *The Levinas Reader*, p. 257.
[81] The midrashic story of Moses, uncomprehending, sitting in the class of Rabbi Akiva,
who nonetheless expounds the Torah "in the name of Moses," is but one of many
indications that the sacred literature is itself aware of its own prolongation through
exegesis.     [82] Rosenzweig, *Ninety-Two Poems and Hymns of Yehuda Halevi*, p. xlvi.

revelation as once and done with, locked into the "once upon a time" of fable. Exegesis and revelation are inseparable, not once and forever done, but once and once again, again and again. The voice heard at Mount Sinai, deafening from the start, must be constantly modulated to the human ear. Prophecy – the revelation of revelation, exegesis – is never finished or sealed.

The time structure of exegesis is thus the very temporality of ethics, of the encounter of one with another, "I," and "you." It involves a notion Levinas early in his career called "trace," and later calls "diachrony." Just as the ethical imperative embedded in the disturbing alterity of the other opens up an unanticipated future more future than the projections of the self, so too it bores more deeply into the self than the self's syntheses, however passive; it fissures the self with responsibilities deeper than its recuperative powers of synthesis, its for-itself. Such is the ethics of the maternal psyche: for-the-other before itself. The constant deepening or continual elevation of the self effected by ethics, the "theme" of Levinas's philosophy and his Talmudic Readings – the for-the-other-before-oneself – is at work in exegesis. Only in this way, contrary to Derrida's eccentric misreading, can "I" and "you" meet not across violence but pacifically. Violence occurs when an irreducible alterity is reduced to sameness. Language is precisely the pacific medium of an encounter with that which exceeds the terms in encounter with one another. In this way a text can be a "you." The infinity of exegesis, linked to the pluralism of an ethically constituted humanity, and hence to religious-moral tradition, is thus yet another manifestation of the infinity proper to ethics, to the unending and ever greater obligations and responsibilities of persons to and for one another. "The Bible," Levinas writes, "*signifies* for all authentically human thought, for civilization *tout court*, whose authenticity can be recognized in peace, in *shalom*, and in the responsibility of one man for another."[83] Peace does not mean universal sameness, but ethical response to otherness. A living ethical tradition can therefore rest neither on the cold antiquarianism of museum maintenance nor on the fiery but free-floating exuberance of an unbridled avant-garde's permanent

[83] "On Jewish Philosophy," in Levinas, *In the Time of the Nations*, p. 172.

revolution or deconstruction. Rather, it requires continual renewal through continual inspiration. "We must isolate the ancient
examples," Levinas has written, "and extend them to the new
situations, principles and categories which they contain."[84]

We find Levinas both defending and demonstrating his commitment to interpretative paradigmatics, and his commitment to the
regulative authority of a living religious-ethical tradition, in his
1965 commentary on the Talmudic commentary *Sotah* 34b–35a.
This commentary concerns the biblical incident of the twelve
scouts who report on the status of the land of Israel to Moses in
Numbers 13:25–14:37.[85] All but Joshua and Caleb are executed
for calumny not only against the land of Israel but also, so
Levinas's commentary on this commentary will claim, against the
very existence of God. In effect, the Talmud suggests, by denying
that the Jews can attain the land of Israel, the scouts – except
Joshua and Caleb – are denying God's ability to fulfill His ancient
promises, His ability to reward the just and punish the unjust, His
very presence in holy history. In effect, then, the scouts represent,
as Levinas expresses it, "the denial of God's power, of holy history,
of divine promises and divine justice."[86] Levinas thus characterizes the issue at stake in this incident as a "crisis of atheism, a crisis
much more serious than the crisis of the Golden Calf. The Golden
Calf, that was still religious: one switched gods. Here, nothing is
left, one contests the very attributes of divinity."[87] What saved
Joshua and Caleb from the temptation of atheism to which the
other ten scouts succumbed? In Levinas's answer we find his
support for adherence to a living ethical tradition:

Here are indicated two ways of escaping temptation . . . Caleb's way of
resisting the seduction of the explorers (who, perhaps, sin only through an
excess of justice) consists in staying within the ancestral tradition, in
integrating himself within the rigorously national history of Israel, within
its transmitted customs, in entrusting himself to this land in which his
ancestors are buried, out of which good came into the world and from
which no evil can emerge: Caleb prostrates himself on the grave of
Abraham, Isaac, and Jacob at Hebron. Joshua's way is different.
Through the first two letters of his name, the idea of God was inserted

---

[84] "The State of Israel and the Religion of Israel," in Levinas, *The Levinas Reader*, pp.
262–263.
[85] Levinas, "Promised Land or Permitted Land," in *Nine Talmudic Readings*, pp. 51–69.
[86] Ibid., p. 58.    [87] Ibid., p. 57.

into his nature. Did he not accede to this honor through the teaching he received by serving Moses? No doubt this teaching received directly from the master was needed to preserve him from the temptation of the explorers.[88]

Caleb and Joshua thus represent two ways to escape the temptation of free-floating exploration, of unbounded interpretation: adherence to an ethico-religious tradition, and adherence to a teacher of ethico-religious tradition.[89] Freedom and command[90]

---

[88] Ibid., p. 59.

[89] In his lecture, Levinas thanks Dr. Henri Nerson and Theo Dreyfus for this part of his reading of *Sotah* 34b–35a (p. 59); I would like to thank Shmuel Wygoda for pointing out this reading to me as one appropriate to show the ethical limitations Levinas places on interpretative freedom.

Jan Assmann in *Moses the Egyptian: The Memory of Egypt in Western Monotheism* (Cambridge, MA: Harvard University Press, 1998), takes an alternative view which I would sum up as: to the victor goes the interpretation. He too wants to reject a purely "critical" hermeneutics, but he goes overboard in doing so, rejecting all moral standards as well. He writes: "The task of historical positivism consists in separating the historical from the mythical elements in memory and distinguishing the elements which retain the past from those which shape the present. In contrast, the task of mnemohistory [Assmann's approach] consists in analyzing the mythical elements in tradition and discovering their hidden agenda" (p. 10). And further on: "In other words, the past cannot be stored but always has to be 'processed' and mediated. This mediation depends on the semantic frames and needs of a given individual or society within a given present" (p. 14). But, I would argue, "semantic frames and needs" are hardly sufficient to maintain and distinguish between truth and falsehood, let alone right and wrong. By means of "mnemohistory" Assmann does not want to, and does not, distinguish myth from history. There is a much older name for this approach: sophism. It is the view that truth is really a matter of power politics, that might makes right, and to think otherwise is to be a dupe. In our time this is also the outlook of Nietzsche and his followers. The whole thrust of Levinas's work, however, is to say that morality is not a matter of being duped, quite the contrary, that reality is itself based upon morality. Thus exegesis, as I am presenting it in this work, is neither a science nor a game, but the effort to understand the real without discounting the priority of moral responsibilities and obligations.

In sharp contrast to Assmann, for Michael Fishbane, in *The Exegetical Imagination: On Jewish Thought and Theology*, published in the same year and by the same press (Cambridge, MA: Harvard University Press, 1998) as *Moses the Egyptian*, two of the three limits to "midrashic" interpretation that he singles out are ethical. "The first of these two is what the sages call *haggadot shel dofi*, midrashic interpretations which are designed to malign or mock the teachings or teachers of Scripture (*Sanhedrin* 99b)" (p. 21). This limitation aims "to thwart mean-spirited and potentially anarchic readings of Scriptures" (p. 21). The other is even more directly ethical. It has to do with "the limits which sin places on faithful interpretation. Indeed, this factor subverts the very possibility of Midrash" (p. 21).

[90] See Levinas, "Freedom and Command," in Emmanuel Levinas, *Collected Philosophical Papers*, ed. and trans. Alphonso Lingis (Dordrecht: Martinus Nijhoff, 1987), pp. 15–23. Here Levinas writes: "Freedom consists in instituting outside of oneself an order of reason, in entrusting the rational to a written text, in resorting to institutions . . . The supreme work of freedom consists in guaranteeing freedom. It can only be guaranteed by setting up a world where it would be spared the ordeals of tyranny" (p. 17).

are not incompatible but inextricable – one needs a tradition, and one needs a teacher.

The all-important difference between Levinasian exegesis and Nietzschean interpretation, then, can be stated boldly. Whereas Levinas locates exegesis within an ethico-religious tradition which demands selflessness, the humanist priority of being for the sake of the other before being for oneself, Nietzsche breaks from precisely this tradition – and from all ethico-religious tradition, indeed from all tradition as such – to proclaim the primacy of individual will, and hence the priority of being for the sake of oneself as a willful being over the alleged selflessness of being for the sake of the other (which Nietzsche, quite consistently, interprets as a weak, sick, slavish, and sublimated form of selfishness). One can hardly imagine a more radical opposition, recognized by both thinkers. Both retaining their freedom, the one submits to God, the other replaces God. For Nietzsche, as for Derrida, the weight of tradition, as orientation and direction in thinking and life, can only appear as an unwanted and heteronomous violence. Already in 1934, in one of his first philosophical writings, with great prevision Levinas links the willful anti-humanist spirit of Nietzschean thought – and of Heideggerian thought, which in typical German idealist fashion reifies individual human will into world will (again, the famous "turn," *Kehre*), before whose "voice" humans must humble themselves – to the oncoming horror of Nazism.[91] It is a strong charge, to be sure, but the Holocaust, no less than be-ing, must also be thought deeply, ethically.

Because Levinas renews tradition and Nietzsche rejects it altogether, Nietzschean interpretation radically reverses the value ("revaluation of all values") of all four characteristics of exegesis. While it too recognizes the integrity of spirit and matter, it aims at matter to the detriment of spirit. In France, Gilles Deleuze will pursue this Nietzschean atomization. Second, while Nietzschean interpretation also recognizes a multiplicity of readings and readers, it aims at their mutual alienation and dispersion, their dissolution, not at the community of *shalom*. It is Nietzsche's "ships passing in the night," his "Be happy, and then do what you

---

[91] Levinas, "Quelques réflexions sur la philosophie de l'hitlérisme," reprinted in Emmanuel Levinas, *Les imprévus de l'histoire* (Montpellier: Fata Morgana, 1994), pp. 35–41.

please."[92] While it too recognizes the imperative existential force of interpretation, its imperative is from and for itself alone, not for the other, or for the greater good which is also the individual good. For Levinasian exegesis, in contrast to Nietzschean interpretation, "the great miracle of the Bible," and by extension all of sacred literature, "lies not at all in the common literary origin, but, inversely, in the confluence of different literatures toward the same essential content . . . the ethical."[93] "We can now appreciate," he writes, "in its full weight the reference made by the Revelation to exegesis, to the freedom attaching to this exegesis and to the participation of the person listening to the Word, which makes itself heard now, but can also pass down the ages to announce the *same truth* [my italics] in different times."[94] These are not, or need not be, idle or simply beautiful words. But neither are they ontological necessities, allegedly ironclad "laws" of history. Genuine freedom is more difficult, more and less precarious. Texts, like life itself, call for interpretations, and only interpretations awaken texts – but not, as Nietzsche thought, to enforce one's own will, to exacerbate one's own isolation, to heighten alienation, but rather to enter into a living ethico-religious tradition dedicated to all of humankind, dedicated to the unending difficulties of morality and justice, which is nothing less and nothing more than the very process of sanctification, "biblical humanism."[95]

---

[92] See Henri Birault, "Beatitude in Nietzsche," in David B. Allison, ed., *The New Nietzsche* (Cambridge: MIT Press, 1985), pp. 219–31.

[93] Emmanuel Levinas, *Ethics and Infinity*, trans. Richard A. Cohen (Pittsburgh: Duquesne University Press, 1985), p. 115. Strauss makes a similiar point regarding the lack of significance religious consciousness finds "in contradictions and in repetitions which are not intended" in the Bible, but he makes this point not so much in the name of the unifying exigency of the ethico-religious tradition than in the name of the epistemological breakdown that necessarily results when a finite mind attempts to understand the doings of the one absolute and hence mysterious God. See Strauss, "On the Interpretation of Genesis," in *Jewish Philosophy and the Crisis of Modernity*, pp. 374–375.

[94] "Revelation in the Jewish Tradition," in Levinas, *The Levinas Reader*, p. 195.

[95] Of course Buber also understands the basic Jewish project to be one of "sanctification." Of ethics and sanctification in Levinas, Robert Gibbs has written: "Levinas calls this task ethics, but this is a translation of the Hebrew term *sanctification*." Robert Gibbs, *Correlations in Rosenzweig and Levinas* (Princeton: Princeton University Press, 1992), p. 187, cited by Alfred I. Tauber (p. 458), in "Outside the Subject: Levinas's Jewish Perspective on Time," in the excellent special Levinas issue subtitled "Levinas's Contribution to Contemporary Philosophy," *Graduate Faculty Philosophy Journal*, vol. 20, no. 2–vol. 21, no. 1, pp. 439–459.

### RENEWED THINKING AND SANCTIFIED LIFE

Such a conception of humanism, humanism fully conscious of itself in moral humility, aware of its inexorable link to the divine through exegetical life, would be able finally to reject abstract philosophical notions of freedom – with their dialectical partners: abstract philosophical notions of necessity. Thus it would also be able to reject certain self-declared "secular humanisms" which, in the name of abstract freedom and abstract necessity, have built self-distorting ideologies and launched havoc, usurping the name of the highest values. Feuerbach would have been more right than even he knew: genuine humanism would indeed be the expression of humankind's highest aspirations, its highest ideals, but this would in no way sever such idealism from the genuine and demanding transcendence – the transcendence of God – proper to religion. For along with a *humanism* more fully conscious of itself and of its intrinsic religious dimension, would come *religion* also more fully conscious of itself, made aware of its proper and inexorable human dimension. (Again we think, for instance, of Dietrich Bonhoeffer, whose Christianity finds itself only in the center of life and not at its periphery or in another world.) In the tension of their difference – neither an ontological difference nor the differential play of signs – manifest in the ethical-exegetical exigencies to which this difference gives rise, together humanity and religion would rise to their proper height. In such a perspective, neither religion nor humanism can do without one another, since neither one nor the other would fully be itself without fully engaging the other – for at bottom they would be inseparable, one. The stakes raised by the question of the meaning and status of humanism are indeed high.

Of course, it is not only the Talmud, such as Levinas reads it, which raises and suggests these themes. They are central to civilization and hence have been raised in many different contexts in many different ways. This in no way involves a diminution or rejection of philosophy, science, and knowledge, per se, except when and insofar as cognition asserts its exclusivity, its hegemony, putting reason before and above revelation, knowledge before and above trust, truth before and above morality, and hence immanence before and impervious to transcendence. Reason is required by ethics, but in the service of ethics. Or, alternatively, if reason is challenged not on ethical but on aesthetic grounds, its abstract exclusivity is merely replaced by another perhaps even more seductive authority, by the shining glory of Homer, by fate and fortune, undermining the difficult freedom demanded of a being created in the "image and likeness of God" with the glory, however reverential, of fame and success. Who, after all, speaks for be-ing? One wonders, then, whether Heidegger has really criticized the Bible, whether he has understood its deepest message, when he criticizes self-glorification. Perhaps he has only found a new mask for self-glorification. Or, returning to religious fundamentalists, have they really grasped the provocative transcendence proper to religion, proper to God, when they denounce the humanism launched and sustained by the very Bible they claim to be defending?

Levinas's writings and readings show a deeper meaning at work in the reasonableness of reason than the ontological disclosure of what is revealed in truth or the imposition of a being in being. Revelation ethically revealed, continually revealed across the chasm of responsibility separating and joining one and another, "I" and "you" and "he" (others), opens up the humanity of the human. In so doing, revelation is at work underlying and guaranteeing the veracity of truth.

"Ashes," so Levinas teaches in a Talmudic Reading entitled "Who is One-Self?,"[96] are neither spirit nor matter, but the humility of an Abraham – "I, ashes and dust" – who in the deepest recesses of his being, deeper than his being-for-himself, denucleating being itself, to the point of selflessness, responds and is response to the demands of the other. Homo Sapiens may have walked the earth tens of millions of years ago, Adam may be the first human, and Noah our ancestor, but Abraham remains "our father," the father of humanity, for he has shown a humanity whose dignity, whose "as-for-me," is already "for-the-other," the neighbor. Such is *wisdom*, reason wedded to virtue, far surpassing the narrow but imperial confines of rationality.

---

[96] Levinas, *New Talmudic Readings*, pp. 109–126.

# CHAPTER 8

# *What good is the Holocaust? On suffering and evil*

The Nazis are resorting to systematic atrocities on a gigantic scale. In Odessa 25,000 Jews were massacred in cold blood; in Kiev "after the Nazi occupation, 52,000 Jewish men, women and children were systematically put to death amidst scenes of undescribable horror."

*Jewish Standard*, 28 November 1941[1]

Can I see another's woe,
And not be in sorrow too?
Can I see another's grief,
And not seek for kind relief?

William Blake, "On Another's Sorrow," *Songs of Innocence* (1789)

## INTRODUCTION: GOD AND EVIL?

*What about evil?* If the genuine self is supposed to be – "ought" to be – for-the-other, how about the countervailing weight of being, being-for-itself, selfishness, refusal of the other, the "as for me"? Even if we cannot have a good conscience, after all the horrors of the twentieth century, are we really expected to continue to take any ethico-religious tradition seriously? After all, did not the Holocaust take place in the most Christian part of the world? And even if, to explain the failure of Christians and Christian Churches, one were to offer explanations based on contingent events, on fear, Nazi power, intimidation, would one not, with the best of good wills, still be trapped by a theo-logic incapable of accounting for

---

[1] Quoted in I. Rennap, *Anti-Semitism and the Jewish Question*, with an Introduction by William Gallacher, M.P. (London: Lawrence & Whishart Ltd., July, 1942; reprinted September, 1942; January, 1943; August, 1943), p. 62.

evil, and then – built on this incapacity, and worse – also incapable of standing up to evil?

The theological explanation for evil, theodicy, is that evil is willed by God, willed by an absolute God, an absolutely benevolent God. The logic may be painful, in the sense that it outrages moral reason, but it remains logical for all that. Since God wills all things, God willed the Holocaust. Because all things willed by God are good, the Holocaust too was good. Not just that good comes from the Holocaust, but that the Holocaust itself was good, as repentance, sacrifice, purification, sign, redemption, punishment, perhaps all of these, but ultimately good in itself. Not only do such scandalous conclusions necessarily follow from the logic of a philosophical God, from an absolute omnipotence, omniscience, omnipresence, and benevolence, but even more painfully and intimately, they follow from the personal God of Abraham, Isaac, and Jacob, from His special covenant with the Jews, and in our day with "Israel, in its Passion under Adolph Hitler."[2] Part of holy history (*Heilsgeschichte*), the Holocaust above all – where the Jews once again take center stage, not only in the locale of the Middle East, or of Europe, but globally – would have been willed by God, and thus would be good. It would have to be good, or it would be meaningless, and the Jews forsaken. As we know, this very line of thought, enunciated in 1961 by a leading German cleric whose moral heroism had earlier been proven saving Jews during the Nazi period, so shocked Richard Rubenstein that he rejected altogether any belief in the special election of Israel.[3] As we know, too, in the name of this same logic certain Jewish "pietists" have blamed the German Jewish reformers, Zionists, anti-Zionists, et al., and in so many contradictory ways have tried to "explain" the Holocaust as the will of God.[4] Levinas too is shocked by this sound

---

[2] "The passion of Israel in the sense in which one speaks of the passion of Christ – is the moment humanity begins to bleed from the wounds of Israel." "Emmanuel Levinas se souvient . . ." in *Les nouveaux cahiers: Emmanuel Levinas*, no. 82, Fall 1985, p. 35. Cf. Franklin H. Littell, *The Crucifixion of the Jews: The Failure of Christians to Understand the Jewish Experience* (Macon, GA: Mercer University Press, 1986; originally published by Harper & Row, 1975).

[3] Richard L. Rubenstein, *After Auschwitz: Radical Theology and Contemporary Judaism* (Indianapolis: Bobbs-Merrill, 1966).

[4] For these and more Jewish "explanations" of the Holocaust, see Dan Cohn-Sherbok, *Holocaust Theology* (London: Marshall Morgan and Scott, 1989).

but appalling logic. Like Rubenstein, he too rejects theodicy, the
vindication of evil in terms of divine justice. But he does not, in
contrast, reject God or the idea of Jewish election.

How can one affirm God, Israel's election, and ethics after the
Holocaust?[5] We are driven to ask anew what sense, if any, religion
and morality have if human affairs are divorced from divine
transcendence and divine justice. Is a God who hides His face,[6] or
is eclipsed, any different than no God at all? Are religious persons
expected to become like those "agnostics" whose mendaciousness
Nietzsche derides because "they now worship the *question mark itself*
as God"?[7] If the rejection of theodicy leaves those for whom God is
still meaningful with the numbing astonishment of a *tremendum*,[8] is
this really something more than a clouding of consciousness, an
elliptical but false gesture, or a brave but empty stubbornness?
Levinas answers in the negative. After the Holocaust, to be sure,
he rejects theodicy. But for Levinas the "meaning" – or meaninglessness – of the Holocaust is to be found neither in a deviously
disguised agnosticism or atheism nor in the fetishization of dumb
astonishment. Rather, it is found precisely in the "end of
theodicy." "The most revolutionary fact of our twentieth century," Levinas writes, "is that of the destruction of all balance
between . . . theodicy . . . and the forms which suffering and evil
take." (US, 161) "The Holocaust of the Jewish people," he con-

---

5 This chapter was first presented as a paper at a conference entitled "Ethics After the
  Holocaust," held at the University of Oregon, 5–8 May 1996.
6 Psalm 44:25: "Why dost thou hide thy face, and forget our affliction and our oppression?"
  See also Deuteronomy 2:17–18. Eliezer Berkovits, in *Faith After the Holocaust* (New York:
  KTAV, 1973), relies on this notion, that God hides His face, to explain His "absence," or,
  positively, to explain the presence of human freedom, and hence human evil, during the
  Holocaust.
7 Friedrich Nietzsche, *On the Genealogy of Morals*, III, 25, trans. Walter Kaufmann and R. J.
  Hollingdale, in Friedrich Nietzsche, *On the Genealogy of Morals and Ecce Homo* (New York:
  Random House, 1967), p. 162.
8 For Arthur A. Cohen, in *The Tremendum* (New York: Crosswords, 1981), the unique
  *tremendum* that is the Holocaust should force Judaism to rethink and revise the meaning of
  the *Mysterium Tremendum* that is God Himself, or more precisely, it should force Judaism to
  rethink God's relation to history and the role of human will in that history. Levinas would
  agree with this, and the point of this chapter is to show in what way. But for Levinas, as we
  will see, in this new conception God is not, as he is for Cohen, "detached" from history,
  but is precisely involved in history inasmuch as humans are moral and just. Levinas will
  also suggest – through exegesis – that to think God this way, while certainly critical of
  some Jewish thinkers, does not require a radical break with certain other Jewish concep-
  tions of God and Holy History.

tinues, is the "paradigm of gratuitous human suffering, where evil appears in all its horror." (US, 162) "Auschwitz:" he writes, "the radical rupture between evil and mercy, between evil and sense." (CA, 16) The negative lesson of the Holocaust, then, is precisely the end of theodicy. And its positive meaning? It would have to do with suffering.

To approach this positive meaning we must return to the question of evil. (For above all, the Holocaust was an evil, whether the greatest evil or a very great evil, that is not the issue; the issue is the question of evil.) This most questionable question, older than Job, is in fact newly deepened, newly sharpened, radicalized by the Holocaust. Levinas faces the question squarely; he does not shirk from asking: What can suffering mean when suffering is rendered so obviously "useless" (*inutile*), useless to its core? What can suffering mean when it is "for nothing," when it heralds and leads only to death and is intended only for obliteration? Jews were tortured and murdered for no other reason than that they were born Jewish – how else "explain" the torture and murder of one million Jewish babies and small children? What had they done? What can suffering possibly mean, what sense can it make, when it is rendered meaningless?

Friedrich Nietzsche was also troubled by "the meaninglessness of suffering."[9] Like Levinas, but of course decades before the Holocaust, he too rejects as false and self-deceptive all the justifications of suffering provided by theodicy, for example, punishment for sin, or a necessary piece of a hidden but divinely ordained whole. But with the same stroke, with the same hammer blow, Nietzsche rejects all interpretations whatsoever for suffering. "'Why so hard?' the charcoal once said to the diamond; 'for are we not close relations?' 'Why so soft?'" Nietzsche has the diamond answer, "for are you not – my brothers?"[10] Nietzsche's readers are acutely aware of the provocation concluding the third book of *On the Genealogy of Morals*, where after having masterfully tracked down and categorically rejected the self-deceptions of the "ascetic ideal," including theodicy in all its multifarious forms, both gross and

9 Nietzsche, *On the Genealogy of Morals*, III, 28, p. 162.
10 Friedrich Nietzsche, *Twilight of the Idols*, trans. R. J. Hollingdale (Harmondsworth: Penguin Books, 1968), p. 112.

subtle, Nietzsche challenges himself and his readers with the regretful admission that fundamentally no other interpretation of suffering has existed hitherto: "It was the only meaning offered so far."[11] For himself, Nietzsche answers with a brave but empty and fantastic heralding of the heralding of yet another messiah: Zarathustra heralding the Overman. In agreement with the rejection of theodicy, Levinas takes up Nietzsche's challenge, the stigma of the meaninglessness of suffering, but he articulates another response, where suffering and evil, without losing and without denying their essentially useless character, nonetheless retain a meaning – "the only meaning" (Levinas's expression![12]) – for religion and morality.

Levinas takes up the interwoven topics of evil and suffering, the end of theodicy, and a "new modality of faith today,"[13] that is to say, the topic of ethics after the Holocaust, in three short articles, comprising twenty-four pages in all, published at four-year intervals, in 1978, 1982, and 1986. The first is entitled "Transcendence and Evil" ("*Transcendence et Mal*").[14] It is a creative review of Philippe Nemo's book *Job and the Excess of Evil*, also published in 1978.[15] The second article, entitled "Useless Suffering" ('*La Souffrance inutile*"),[16] and the third, under the heading "The Scandal of Evil" ("*Le Scandale du mal*"),[17] invoke the Holocaust and Emil Fackenheim's book, *God's Presence in History*, which appeared in French translation in 1980.[18] The third article concludes, as we will

---

[11] We know, too, that unable to rise to his own challenge, Nietzsche's thought falters in a longing for eternity (perhaps more pathetic than parodic) in its own constructive efforts to situate suffering within a larger justifying whole, even if that whole is now not only quite small but indifferent and God-forsaken, and even if that longing, bravely refusing genuine elevation, is reduced to an elitist and solitary will to eternal recurrence.

[12] Emmanuel, "Useless Suffering," trans. Richard A. Cohen, in R. Bernasconi and D. Woods, eds., *The Provocation of Levinas* (London: Routledge, 1988), p. 159.

[13] Ibid., p. 164 (see n. 16).

[14] Levinas, "Transcendence and Evil," trans. Alphonso Lingis, in Emmanuel Levinas, *Collected Philosophical Papers* (Dordrecht: Martinus Nijhoff, 1987), pp. 175–186.

[15] Philippe Nemo, *Job et l'excès du Mal* (Paris: Grasset, 1978).

[16] Levinas, "Useless Suffering," pp. 156–167.

[17] Under the general heading, "Le scandale du mal: Catastrophes naturelles et crimes de l'homme," in *Les Nouveaux Cahiers*, no. 85, Summer 1986, Levinas contributed an article, pp. 15–17. Henceforth cited as "Scandal of Evil," my translations.

[18] Emil Fackenheim, *God's Presence in History* (New York: New York University Press, 1970); *La Présence de Dieu dans l'histoire*, trans. M. Delmotte and B. Dupey (Lagrass: Verdier, 1980).

later, by referring back to another short article of 1955, entitled "Loving the Torah More than God" (*"Aimer la Thora plus que Dieu"*),[19] comprising Levinas's thoughts on evil and suffering one decade after the Holocaust.

The three articles work as most of Levinas's writings work, by progressively building on original phenomenological and ethical insights, by means of review and elaboration, circling back to retrieve, extrapolate, and amplify earlier thoughts. Each progresses, that is to say, as an ever deepening commentary upon its own insights, like Talmudic exegesis, resaying its own said – like *musar* [ethical self-development] itself, as Rabbi Ira Stone[20] has pointed out. The three articles each develop, in different proportions and depth, three basic components: (1) they begin with a phenomenology of evil and suffering, and then, building on these intuitions and insights, (2) they turn to ethics, negatively to criticize theodicy, as we have already seen, and (3) positively to propose an ethical alternative, which we shall shortly see. In the following, relying on all three articles at once, I will trace this same route, beginning with suffering and evil, and concluding with Levinas's positive religico-ethical alternative to theodicy.

## PHENOMENOLOGY OF SUFFERING AND EVIL

Though, as we have seen, ethics transcends phenomenology, it is phenomenology that it transcends. Thus Levinas brings phenomenology to bear and uncovers two primary and related dimensions to suffering: (1) excess or transcendence, and (2) meaninglessness. These two dimensions are fundamental, and through them Levinas links suffering with evil, both in oneself and in the other.

---

[19] Levinas, "Loving the Torah More Than God," in Emmanuel Levinas, *Difficult Freedom*, trans. Séan Hand (Baltimore: Johns Hopkins University Press, 1990), pp. 142–145. This article also appears in two short volumes pertinent to the themes of this chapter, the first written by an American Jesuit priest and professor, and the second edited by an American Jewish author: Franz Jozef van Beeck, S. J., *Loving the Torah More than God?: Towards a Catholic Appreciation of Judaism* (Chicago: Loyola University Press, 1989); Zvi Kolitz, *Yossel Rakover Speaks to God: Holocaust Challenges to Religious Faith* (Hoboken: KTAV, 1995).

[20] See Ira F. Stone, "Emmanuel Levinas, The Musar Movement and the Future of Jewish Ethical Living," unpublished paper given at the University of Oregon, "Ethics After the Holocaust" conference, 6 May 1996.

Suffering appears in and as an "extreme passivity,"[21] a passivity "more passive than receptivity,"[22] "an ordeal more passive than experience."[23] The passivity of suffering is extreme or excessive because of its quality of "unassumability,"[24] "non-integratability."[25] This quality of "excess"[26] or "transcendence,"[27] which makes up its essence, cannot be understood quantitatively. Little and great suffering are both suffering. The "too much" of pain is its very essence, "manner," or "quiddity."[28] Suffering, that is to say, is not only a suffering from something, as Husserl's commitment to intentional analysis would suggest, but also at the same time it is a suffering from suffering itself, a redoubling of suffering. Thus all suffering, regardless of its quantitative measure, and regardless of whether it is endured voluntarily or not, is unwanted, insupportable, unbearable of itself. Just as a bodily being enjoys enjoying,[29] it suffers suffering. The unwanted and at the same time inescapable character of pained corporeal reflexivity is what distinguishes the phenomenon of suffering: one suffers from suffering itself. If one wishes, one can turn to an abundant autobiographical literature of the Holocaust for corroborating testimonies.

It is interesting to note that shortly after the Holocaust, in 1947, and thus also shortly after his own wartime internment in Germany, Levinas had already described the over-determination of suffering in *Time and the Other*. There, describing "the pain lightly called physical,"[30] – which he distinguishes from "moral pain" in which "one can preserve an attitude of dignity and compunction"[31] – he writes:

Physical suffering in all its degrees entails the impossibility of detaching oneself from the instant of existence. It is the very irremissibility of being. The content of suffering merges with the impossibility of detaching oneself from suffering. And this is not to define suffering by suffering, but to insist on the *sui generis* implication that constitutes its essence. In

[21] Levinas, "Scandal of Evil," p. 15.
[22] Levinas, "Useless Suffering," p. 157.    [23] Ibid.    [24] Ibid., p. 15.
[25] Levinas, "Transcendence and Evil," p. 180.
[26] Ibid., pp. 179–181; Levinas, "Useless Suffering," p. 156.
[27] Levinas, " Transcendence and Evil," p. 181.    [28] Ibid., p. 180.
[29] See Emmanuel Levinas, *Totality and Infinity*, trans. Alphonso Lingis (Pittsburgh: Duquesne University Press, 1969), pp. 110–121.
[30] Emmanuel Levinas, *Time and the Other*, trans. Richard A. Cohen (Pittsburgh: Duquesne University Press, 1987), p. 69.    [31] Ibid.

suffering there is an absence of all refuge. It is the fact of being directly exposed to being. It is made up of the impossibility of fleeing or retreating. The whole acuity of suffering lies in the impossibility of retreat. It is the fact of being backed up against life and being. In this sense suffering is the impossibility of nothingness.[32]

Thus the notion that suffering involves an inescapable suffering from suffering itself is a relatively early notion in Levinas's thought.

From the inherent excess of suffering comes its second characteristic and its link to evil: meaninglessness. Despite a variety of *post facto* explanations or finalities – for example, that pain serves as a biological warning, or is the price of spiritual refinement, or of social or political regeneration,[33] etc. – the "non-sense of pain . . . pierces beneath reasonable forms."[34] Levinas writes of suffering: "[I]n its own phenomenality, intrinsically, it is useless, 'for nothing'."[35] As such it is "monstrosity,"[36] "non-sense *par excellence*,"[37] the "absurd,"[38] "basic senselessness,"[39] the "disturbing and foreign of itself."[40] "The evil of pain, the harm itself, is the explosion and most profound articulation of absurdity."[41] "The break with the normal and the normative, with order, with synthesis, with the world, already constitutes its qualitative essence."[42] Jean Amery, writing from his own experience of having been hung by his hands by the Nazis, writes in confirmation: "The tortured person never ceases to be amazed that all those things one may, according to inclination, call his soul, or his mind, or his consciousness, or his identity, are destroyed when there is that cracking and splintering in the shoulder joints."[43]

Unbearable and useless, in this way suffering is evil. Suffering is evil; evil is suffering. Together they constitute an irreducible zero point of significance, an *Ursignificance*, as it were, "where the

---

[32] Ibid.     [33] Levinas, "Useless Suffering," p. 159.     [34] Ibid., p. 160.

[35] Ibid., pp. 157–158.     [36] Levinas, "Transcendence and Evil," p. 180.

[37] Levinas, "Scandal of Evil," p. 15.

[38] Levinas, "Useless Suffering," p. 157; Levinas, "Scandal of Evil," p. 15.

[39] Levinas, "Useless Suffering," p. 158.     [40] Levinas, "Transcendence and Evil," p. 181.

[41] Levinas, "Useless Suffering," p. 157.     [42] Levinas, "Transcendence and Evil," p. 180.

[43] Jean Amery, *At the Mind's Limits*, trans. Sidney Rosenfeld and Stella P. Rosenfeld (New York: Schocken Books, 1986), excerpt in John K. Roth and Michael Berenbaum, eds., *Holocaust: Religious and Philosophical Implications* (New York: Paragon House, 1989), p. 189.

dimensions of the physical and moral are not yet separated."[44] "All evil," Levinas writes, "refers to suffering."[45] It is "not," he continues, "through passivity that evil is described, but through evil that suffering is understood."[46] – "Sickness, evil in living, aging, corruptible flesh, perishing and rotting."[47] In the end suffering and evil are names for the meaningless painfulness of pain which is always, regardless of quantitative considerations, intrinsically excessive, unwanted, not to be accommodated. To make suffer is evil, because to suffer is evil. The original meaning of suffering is evil: it is unwanted, it is meaningless.

From this character of being an unwanted burden, suffering as unwanted burden, comes Levinas's first articulation of an ethical issue: "the fundamental ethical problem which pain poses 'for nothing'."[48] The ethical problem is not the sufferer's, the one subject to the pain of meaningless suffering, but that of the witnesses in relation to the sufferer: "the inevitable and preemptory ethical problem of the medication which is my duty."[49] In the other's suffering, then, Levinas sees an "original call for aid,"[50] an original call "for curative help"[51] – "where the primordial, irreducible, and ethical, anthropological category of the medical comes to impose itself – across a demand for analgesia."[52]

Earlier, in 1961, in *Totality and Infinity*, Levinas had already written: "The doctor is an a priori principle of human mortality."[53] There he contested one of the central claims of Heidegger's *Being and Time*, that dying or being-toward-death (*Sein-zum-tode*) isolates and individualizes human subjectivity. For Levinas, in contrast to Heidegger, "[a] social conjunction is maintained in this menace"[54] of death, which "renders possible an appeal to the Other, to his friendship and his medication."[55] The evil of suffering, then, meaningless for the sufferer, would at once be an appeal to the other, "a demand for analgesia." Suffering – mortality – is already an appeal to the other. Again the testimony of Jean

---

[44] Levinas, "Scandal of Evil," p. 15.
[45] Levinas, "Useless Suffering," p. 157. In Latin *malus*, "bad," and *male*, "ill," both derive from *mel*, "bad." In biblical Hebrew *mameer*, "malignant," "evil," (e.g., Leviticus 13:51), suggests *to cause pain*.   [46] Levinas, "Useless Suffering," p. 157.
[47] Levinas, "Transcendence and Evil," p. 179.   [48] Levinas, "Useless Suffering," p. 158.
[49] Ibid.   [50] Ibid.   [51] Ibid.   [52] Ibid.
[53] Levinas, *Totality and Infinity*, p. 234.   [54] Ibid.   [55] Ibid.

Amery: "Pain, we said, is the most extreme intensification imaginable of our bodily being. But maybe it is even more, that is: death."[56]

These are Levinas's first and fundamental ethical elaborations of suffering: suffering as a call to help, as my obligation to help. But what if the other's call is silenced?

## HOLOCAUST: THE END OF THEODICY

The phenomenal or intrinsic meaninglessness of suffering and evil render them resistant to all theodicy. The enormity of the Holocaust would be the unforgettable and irrefutable historical proof, and henceforth a paradigmatic proof, prospectively and retroactively, of the essential disproportion between suffering and explanation. But Levinas goes one step further. After Auschwitz theodicy itself becomes immorality. The idea of theodicy may remain a consolation or a moral challenge for the sufferer, but as an interpretation coming *from me*, it is my flight, rationalization, imposition, as if the other's suffering, meaningless to the sufferer, were meaningful to me. Thus there are two sorts of evil: the intrinsic evil of suffering for the sufferer, and the evil of one rationalizing the other's suffering. Levinas will call the latter, because it is the most radical form of a refusal of the alterity of the other, "the source of all immorality." "For an ethical sensibility," Levinas writes, "confirming itself, in the inhumanity of our time, against this inhumanity – the justification of the neighbor's pain is certainly the source of all immorality."[57] Theodicy is thus one form – the theological form – of the doubling of evil that occurs in every rationalization of the other's suffering. That I can explain someone else's pain, that I can justify it, is to pile evil upon evil.

But how, we must still ask, reflecting on Levinas's words just cited above, is it possible to retain an "ethical sensibility," beyond the nonsense of evil, after the Holocaust? If suffering is intrinsically

---

[56] Ibid., p. 182. We are certainly all of us familiar with the reaction of children to their own illnesses, however minor: they fear they will die. In many films Woody Allen has depicted an almost comical adult version of this fear – "almost" because death does haunt illness.

[57] Levinas, "Useless Suffering," p. 163. Levinas's strong claim finds a fainter echo in the normative Jewish code of Law, *Shulchan Aruch, Choshen Mishpat* 228:4–5.

meaningless, and the Holocaust the unavoidable global proof of
this meaninglessness, the proof of the inapplicability of any explanation, then why and how can we still speak of evil and morality at
all? This remains a fundamental question. How can we retain an
ethical sensibility? Or, as Levinas expresses this in the now famous
opening sentence of *Totality and Infinity*: "Everyone will readily
agree that it is of the highest importance to know whether we are
not duped by morality."[58] Since Kant, if not earlier, philosophy
has known that it is possible to deny the entire realm of morality as
fantasy. Why call a suffering that is meaningless "evil"? Why
blame as "evil" a refusal to attend to the other's suffering as
suffering rather than explaining it away?

Levinas will not flinch from the phenomenological "fact" that
suffering and evil are intrinsically meaningless. The inordinate
suffering and evil of the Holocaust make this evident not only to
diligent students of phenomenology or Nietzsche, but to the whole
world, and to all the religions of the world. "The philosophical
problem," Levinas writes, "which is posed by the useless pain
which appears in its fundamental malignancy across the events of
the twentieth century, concerns the meaning that religiosity and
the human morality of goodness can still retain after the end of
theodicy."[59] Precisely this "philosophical problem" agitates the
various exigencies that drive the imperatives of ethics, the "problem of evil" (that is, its "reality" or ontological status), and the
meaning of religion in our time. What is Levinas's answer?

### SUFFERING FOR THE SUFFERING OF ANOTHER

Deepening his earlier formulations regarding the "category of the
medical," and the "a priori principle" of the doctor, by holding
fast to the phenomenon of suffering itself, Levinas's entire answer
regarding the ethico-religious meaning of suffering can be summed up in a simple but powerful statement. The only sense that
can be made of suffering, that is to say, of evil, is to make one's own
suffering into a suffering for the suffering of others. Or, to put this
in one word: the only ethical meaning of suffering, indeed, "the

---

[58] Levinas, *Totality and Infinity*, p. 21.     [59] Levinas, "Useless Suffering," p. 163.

only meaning to which suffering is susceptible"[60] is *compassion*. In this way meaningless suffering enters into an ethical perspective. The other person suffers – that is evil. There is no moral or religious explanation for it. Indeed, such explanations are themselves immoral, irreligious. Suffering, in short, cannot be made into an object, cannot be externalized. Remember its other characteristic: the compression of suffering, its passivity, suffering as a suffering from suffering. Suffering lacks the distance of objectivity. Any attempt to erase the suffering of the sufferer by inserting an explanatory distance between the sufferer and his/her suffering, in whatever exalted name, is not only a sham and hence futile, it is immorality itself. But I am a being who suffers too. What Levinas is proposing, then, without any "mystical" implications, is a kind of holy, almost sublime, contagion of suffering.[61] He is proposing that morality and religion can still make sense, indeed can only make sense – after the Holocaust – in "suffering elevated or deepened to a suffering-for-the-suffering-of-another-person."[62] The fundamental philosophical problem of suffering, its evil despite its meaninglessness, its malignancy, would then become the "problem of the relationship between the suffering of the self and the suffering that a self can experience over the suffering of the other person."[63]

It is this empathy, this compassion, which would be the "new modality of faith today"[64]: "that in the evil that pursues me the evil suffered by the other man affects me, that it touches me."[65] To take on, in and as one's own affliction, the affliction of the other, is not simply a feeling, however, nor is it a mystical or vicarious action at a distance. Rather, it is a being *responsible* for the other, the self-as-responsibility, the self as "ashes and dust," as Abraham

---

[60] Ibid., p. 159.
[61] Recently, from within an explicitly Christian standpoint, and primarily regarding the suffering of children with terminal illnesses, Stanley Houerwas, in *God, Medicine, and Suffering* (Grand Rapids: William B. Eerdmans Publishing Co., 1990), touchingly recognizes many of the themes we have found in Levinas: that suffering has "no point" (pp. 78–79), the link between suffering and medicine, the crucial difference between other's suffering and "my suffering as service" (p. 89), and the wrong committed when forcing the other's suffering into an explanation, including traditional theodicy.
[62] Levinas, *Scandal of Evil*, p. 16.      [63] Levinas, "Transcendence and Evil," p. 184.
[64] Levinas, "Useless Suffering," p. 164.
[65] Levinas, "Transcendence and Evil," p. 185.

said.[66] Morality and humanity, in other words, arise in the humility of a painful solidarity. The humanity of the human would arise
– it is an elevation, an "election" – across the narrow bridge of
compassion, a bridge which despite its narrowness is linked to all
and everything. "[T]he humanity of man," Levinas writes, "is
fraternally solidary," solidary not only with all humans, but even
more, it is "fraternally solidary with creation."[67] This is not, then,
the human defined by spiritualization or, conversely, by absorption into nature, whether nature be spirit or mother. Rather it is
nature uplifted to creation, where across human responsibility –
"responsibility for everything and for all"[68] – no one, not the
greatest and not the least, no creature whatsoever, whether animal, vegetable or mineral, is left out.[69] Levinas will call this vast
empathy, this vast compassion, this vast responsibility:
"theophany" and "revelation."[70] Beyond theodicy, it is compassion without concern for reward, recompense, remuneration. It is
solar love. Putting the other above oneself, converting one's own
suffering into a suffering for the other's suffering, has "no other
recompense than this very elevation."[71]

   This "new devotion"[72] after the Holocaust, then, would be the
"ultimate vocation of our people,"[73] and hence the ultimate vocation of and for humanity: "to give rather than receive, to love
and make love, rather than be loved."[74] Such, again, would be

---

[66] Genesis 18:27. See Levinas's Talmudic Reading on this topic, "Who is One-Self?" in
   Emmanuel Levinas, *New Talmudic Readings*, trans. Richard A. Cohen (Pittsburgh:
   Duquesne University Press, 1999).      [67] Levinas, "Transcendence and Evil," p. 185.
[68] Ibid., p. 184.
[69] Here, in the solidarity of suffering, in compassion, lies the path to the ethical theory of
   "animal rights" that certain commentators (e.g., John Llewelyn, "Am I Obsessed by
   Bobby?" in Robert Berasconi and Simon Critcley, eds., *Re-Reading Levinas*, Bloomington:
   Indiana University Press, 1991, pp. 234–245) have found lacking in Levinas's thought.
   More broadly, it opens the path to the entire dimension of an ethical rather than a
   naturalistic environmentalism. Alphonso Lingis, for instance, writes: "But to turn away
   from the intrinsic importance of the fragile and endangered earth, the air, the skies, the
   lakes and the mountains, and flood plains of rivers and the rain forests, the insects and
   the fish is also an injustice done to human voices." Lingis, "Practical Necessity," in
   *Graduate Faculty Philosophy Journal*, vol. 20, no. 2–vol. 21, no. 1, special issue on "Levinas's
   Contribution to Contemporary Philosophy," p. 82.
[70] Levinas, "Transcendence and Evil," p. 185.      [71] Ibid.
[72] Levinas, "Scandal of Evil," p. 17.      [73] Ibid.
[74] Ibid. Regarding the moral conflict between humanity's desire to receive and its desire to
   give, from a perspective of Kabbalah that is also close to Levinas, see Rabbi Yeheda
   Ashlag, *Kabbalah: A Gift of the Bible*, trans. Samuel R. Anteby (Jerusalem: Research Center
   of Kabbalah Books Edition, 1984).

Israel and humanity and, conceding nothing to Caesar,[75] it would be the "u-topian" imperative Levinas sees required of the State of Israel *and of all the nations of the earth.* In demanding that after the Holocaust Jews remain faithful to the uttermost depths or heights of Judaism, in a unique particularity which always refers to the universal without ever giving up its particularity, Levinas several times invokes the demand of Emil Fackenheim that now more than ever Jews (and in this sense everyone is a Jew[76]) must deny Hitler a posthumous victory.[77] Jews must remain Jews. After the Holocaust, in other words, humans must remain human. We must be "servants," Levinas writes, citing the Talmudic tractate *Pirke Avos,* I:3, "who serve without regard to recompense."[78] And this, he continues – circling back to his article of 1955 – this new devotion and ultimate vocation of Israel after the Holocaust, is nothing other and no less than "loving Torah more than God."[79]

## CONCLUSION: LOVING TORAH MORE THAN GOD[80]

In conclusion, then, let us turn to the vista opened up by Levinas's conclusion. In 1955, Levinas had already written of suffering, God's absence, and the Holocaust. "What," he asked then, "can this suffering of the innocent mean?"[81] The answer is powerful and magnificent, and true. I will cite it at length:

The God who hides his face is not, I believe, a theological abstraction or a poetic image. It is the moment in which the just individual can find no help.[82] No institution will protect him. The consolation of divine pres-

---

[75] See Levinas, "The State of Caesar and the State of David," in Emmanuel Levinas, *The Levinas Reader,* ed. by Séan Hand (Oxford: Blackwell, 1989), pp. 268–277.

[76] Levinas writes: "The authentically human is the being-Jewish in all men (may you not be shocked by this!) and its reflection in the singular and the particular." "Judaism and Christianity," in Emmanuel Levinas, *In the Time of the Nations,* trans. Michael B. Smith (Bloomington: Indiana University Press, 1994), p. 164.

[77] See Emil Fackenheim, *The Jewish Return into History: Relections in the Age of Auschwitz and a New Jerusalem* (New York: Schocken Books, 1978).

[78] Levinas, "Scandal of Evil," p. 17.     [79] Ibid.

[80] Cf. *Jerusalem Talmud,* tractate *Hagigah* 1:7, commenting on Jeremiah 16:11: "Better that they [Israel] abandon Me [God] and continue to observe My laws."

[81] Levinas, *Difficult Freedom,* p. 143.

[82] I permit myself to interject the following citation, again from Jean Amery: "In almost all situations in life where there is bodily injury there is also the expectation of help; the former is compensated by the latter. But with the first blow from a policeman's fist,

ence to be found in infantile religious feeling is equally denied him, and the individual can prevail only through his conscience,[83] which necessarily involves suffering. This is the specifically Jewish sense of suffering that at no stage assumes the value of a mystical atonement for the sins of the world. The condition of the victims in a disordered world – that is to say, in a world where good does not triumph – is that of suffering. This condition reveals a God Who renounces all aids to manifestation, and appeals instead to the full maturity of the responsible person.[84]

"The suffering of the just person for a justice that has no triumph," Levinas continues, "is physically lived out as Judaism. The historical and physical Israel becomes once again a religious category."[85] It is through the Torah, then, *through* law dedicated to justice, and justice bound to morality, and morality emerging out of compassion, that is to say, through a life edified continually through education in the moral instruction Judaism calls "Torah" – where "education in Torah" is understood like justice and compassion as yet another form of responsibility to others – that we discover "the link between God and man."[86] Such, then, in contrast to an "infantile religious feeling," would be a mature ethics and a mature religion, inextricably linked, as one person is linked to another in the humanity of the human. "[O]nly the man who has recognized the hidden God," Levinas concludes, "can demand that He show Himself."[87]

"Loving Torah more than God" would thus have two senses. Nothing would be more serious than the play between them. It would mean, first of all, loving God's commands, His law, loving the redemptive work of institutionalizing justice, the u-topos of the "State of Israel" (hence of all states), which depends on the work of loving one's neighbor, on moral relations between humans, and loving all of these moral and juridical tasks more than one's own unmediated personal relationship with God. This is Buber's rejoinder to Kierkegaard: marrying Regina, sanctifying God

against which there can be no defense and which no helping hand will ward off, a part of our life ends." Amery, *At the Mind's Limits*, quoted in Roth and Berenbaum, eds., *Holocaust*, p. 178.

[83] In the discussion period following the presentation of this paper in Oregon, Professor Sandor Goodhart quite rightly pointed out that the French term *conscience*, here translated "conscience," can also mean "consciousness," since for Levinas consciousness itself, and not only an explicitly moral conscience, is a vigilance awakened by the other.

[84] Levinas, *Difficult Freedom*, p. 143.    [85] Ibid., p. 144.    [86] Ibid.    [87] Ibid., p. 145.

through the world, are not flight from purity, flight from God, but rather the very work God demands of humans. Morality would be revelation; justice would be redemption; redemption would be the spread of revelation.

But "loving Torah more than God" would also have a second sense, unavoidable after the Holocaust. It would mean humans must love the work of morality and justice more, apparently, than does God Himself. It would mean that even if God seems to have let humanity down, having hidden His face or having been eclipsed, as our twentieth century seems to teach again and again, that now *all the more* must we, we humans, love the Torah, that is to say, "do justice and love mercy." The prophet Isaiah taught the lofty lesson that God Himself was "afflicted by her [Israel's] afflictions" (Isaiah 63:9).[88] After the Holocaust, Levinas is urging that we must take this burden upon ourselves, joining Yom Kippur[89] to Purim.[90] Regardless of God's silence or absence, indeed inspired by the responsibilities which devolve upon us through this silence and absence, we must be moved in our afflictions by the afflictions of our fellow humans. Perhaps only in this way, finally, without making any demands, without expecting any rewards,[91]

---

[88] Isaiah 63:9: "In all their affliction He was afflicted, and the angel of His presence saved them: in His love and in His pity He redeemed them; and He bore them, and carried them all the days of old." Of course, long before Isaiah, the Jews already understood God to be "compassionate" (רחום, *rachoum*) and "long-suffering" (ארך אפים, *erek apayim*), see Exodus 34:6–7.

[89] Cf. Chapter XII, "The Day of Atonement," in Hermann Cohen, *Religion of Reason: Out of the Sources of Judaism*, trans. Simon Kaplan (Atlanta: Scholars Press, 1995), pp. 216–235. Originally published in 1919, in *Religion of Reason* Cohen also rejects interpreting another's suffering (p. 226), "unless the sufferer is considered as suffering for the sake of others" (p. 227), which compassion is a "means" toward redemption, for "redemption is also liberation from suffering" (p. 230). All this, encapsulated in Cohen's formula: "Without suffering – no redemption," invites comparison with Levinas on suffering and evil.

[90] In stark contrast to the inaugural story of the Jewish nation leaving Egypt for Israel in Exodus, the story of Esther in Persia, told on Purim, contains no overt miracles or divine interventions. Jewish sages have often noted that in this biblical text, unlike any other, the name of God does not appear. Precisely for this reason, too, it is said (e.g., Midrash to Proverbs 9) that when in the messianic era all the other holidays become outmoded, only Purim – a "minor" holiday today – will remain. But was there no miracle – precisely the "miracle" of ethical suffering – in the three-day fast of Esther, Mordechai, and the Jews of ancient Shushan?

[91] For a comparison of morality without compensation in Levinas and Spinoza, see my article, "To Love God for Nothing: Levinas and Spinoza," in *Graduate Faculty Philosophy Journal*, vol. 20, no. 2–vol. 21, no. 1, Spring 1998, pp. 339–352.

without reservation or reserve,[92] without miracles, can each of us for the first time as adults "walk humbly with your God."

[92] On the notion of an "economy without reserve," see the very suggestive paper of Robert Doran, "Speaking After the Holocaust: Infinity, the Sublime, and Economy in Bataille and Levinas," presented at the University of Oregon, 8 May 1996.

# CHAPTER 9

# *Ricoeur and the lure of self-esteem*

I have much admiration, as you know, for Paul Ricoeur. In all of contemporary philosophy, he is a spirit of both audacity and perfect honesty. But there is a small disagreement between us regarding good relations with the other.

Emmanuel Levinas, interview, 1992[1]

## INTRODUCTION

The pull of immanence is powerful. Given its title and subject matter, it is no surprise that Paul Ricoeur's recent work, *Oneself as Another (Soi-même comme un autre[2])*, based on his 1986 Gifford Lectures, concludes with three discussions of the work of Emmanuel Levinas. No one more than Levinas has made the relation of self to other, as ethics, more central to philosophy. And now in *Oneself as Another* Ricoeur, too, wants to highlight the ethical character of selfhood and its intimate relation to the alterity of other persons. That the confrontation with Levinas strikes close to Ricoeur's efforts is underscored by the fact that his confrontation with Levinas appears at the two culminating moments of *Oneself as Another*: at the beginning (chapter seven) and at the end (chapter ten) of its fourth and concluding part on the moral and ontological character of the self. Furthermore, since its last chapter, chapter ten, was developed two years after the rest of the work, for the Cericy Decade of 1988, it represents not only two more years of reflection on all the themes presented in 1986, but especially, as the

---

[1] "Le Quotidien de Paris," Monday, 10 February 1992.
[2] Paul Ricoeur, *Oneself as Another*, trans. Kathleen Blamey (Chicago: University of Chicago Press, 1992) (*Soi-même comme un autre* [Paris: Éditions du Seuil, 1990]) (henceforth: *OA*).

text bears out, two more years of reflection on the criticisms of Levinas initiated in chapter seven. Furthermore, seven years after the publication of *Oneself as Another*, in 1997 Ricoeur published a small volume, *Autrement*[3] (*Otherwise*), devoted entirely to his critical engagement with the thought of Levinas. The object of this chapter is to show how and why Ricoeur criticizes Levinas in *Oneself as Another*, and how and why these criticisms miss their mark.[4]

Before turning to this confrontation, however, a few remarks about the striking parallels in the intellectual careers of Levinas and Ricoeur are in order. While Ricoeur was born in France, in 1913, and Levinas, born in 1906, came to France from Lithuania, in 1923, the fact that in predominantly Roman Catholic France Ricoeur was a Protestant and Levinas was a Jew already links them in their distance from mainstream French culture. Both were prisoners-of-war during World War II. Both translated Husserl. Both were at the University of Strasbourg (Ricoeur as a Professor from 1947 to 1957; Levinas as a student in the 1930s). Both lived in (or near) Paris. Both were Professors of Philosophy at the University of Paris-Nanterre (Levinas from 1967[5] to 1972; Ricoeur from 1966 to 1970, and then from 1973 onwards), and at the University of Paris-Sorbonne (Ricoeur from 1957 to 1966; Levinas from 1972 to 1976). But their links are far more profound. Before (and after) the war both thinkers were influenced by Gabriel Marcel, through personal contact, to be sure, but also and particularly by his notion of "incarnate existence."[6] Like Levinas, who found ontological and ethical meaning in the very sensing of sensations, Ricoeur, very early in his career (though later than Levinas), in several

---

3 Paul Ricoeur, *Autrement: Lecture d'Autrement qu'être ou au-delà de l'essence d'Emmanuel Levinas* (Paris: Presses Universitaires de France, 1997).

4 I am focusing on *Oneself as Another* rather than *Autrement* because the latter volume repeats the criticisms of the former, and the former is a more extended presentation of Ricoeur's own thought.

5 Marie-Anne Lescourret, in her biography of Levinas, *Emmanuel Levinas* (France [no city named]: Flammarion, 1994), writes that "Dufrenne, Ricoeur were counted among the architects of his entry into university life. Thus it is more than forty years that he kept close to Ricoeur at phenomenology conferences" (p. 240).

6 For an interesting discussion of the Levinas–Marcel relation, including extended citations from Levinas on Marcel, as well as relevant texts cited from Marcel, see Robert Gibbs, *Correlations in Rosenzweig and Levinas* (Princeton: Princeton University Press, 1992), chapter nine, "Substitution: Marcel and Levinas," pp. 192–228. Ricoeur's first book was entitled *Gabriel Marcel et Karl Jaspers* (Paris: Temps présent, 1947).

volumes, such as *Freedom and Nature* (1950), *Fallible Man* (1960) and *The Symbolism of Evil* (1960), found in incarnation a conjunction of the ontological and the ethical. But most striking and most important is their mutual attachment to and mutual exceeding of phenomenology. This link, with its double edge, has been mentioned at the start of chapter 2, where we briefly reviewed the deep involvement with phenomenology that joins such diverse thinkers as Heidegger, Sartre, Merleau-Ponty, Levinas, Ricoeur, and Derrida. Ricoeur and Levinas were not only influenced by Husserlian phenomenology, they were both important expositors and commentators upon it. More importantly, they both broke from phenomenology – exceeded phenomenology – in the direction of exegesis, a divergence already in evidence in Ricoeur's early work *The Symbolism of Evil.* While Ricoeur's dissatisfaction with phenomenology led him primarily toward linguistics, and Levinas's led him toward ethics (or was led by ethics), both thinkers profoundly appreciated the role of ethical subjectivity in the constitution of meaning. And this is why, beyond the accidental convergences of their personal histories, in the confrontation we are about to examine in *Oneself as Another,* both thinkers are on the same turf, as it were, launched from phenomenology to ethics and ethical subjectivity, and appreciative of the ruses of language, the significance of saying,[7] and the philosophical necessity of exegesis.

*Oneself as Another* is a dense, layered, complicated, and nuanced text. Ricoeur's overall critical intention is one shared by Levinas and by most contemporary thinkers, namely, to challenge the modern philosophical conception of selfhood determined as posited ego. In challenging selfhood *qua* posited ego, Ricoeur and Levinas share a further aim, but one that this time separates them from many of their philosophical contemporaries. Aiming to obviate the Cartesian "thesis of the indecomposable simplicity of the cogito," they aim also to avoid the antipodal thesis, the "Nietzschean deconstruction" or "vertigo," as Ricoeur expresses it, "of

---

[7] There is a close parallel though not a complete equivalence between Ricoeur's distinction between "discourse" as "event" and "meaning" as "system" (see, e.g., Paul Ricoeur, *Interpretation Theory: Discourse and the Surplus of Meaning;* Fort Worth: Texas Christian University Press, 1976), and Levinas's distinction between saying and the said.

the disintegration of the self".[8] To elaborate an alternative conception of selfhood than that of a posited ego, *Oneself as Another* is split into four related parts, based on four levels of meaning essential to selfhood: discursive (chapters one and two); practical (chapters three and four); narrative (chapters five and six); and prescriptive (chapters seven through ten). Each dimension of the self is approached from two points of view: the analytical and the hermeneutical. No wonder, then, that Ricoeur invokes and criticizes Levinas in part four, when he treats the prescriptive dimension of selfhood.

### CHAPTER SEVEN: "THE SELF AND THE ETHICAL AIM"

Ricoeur's first discussion of Levinas, whose thought centers on selfhood, alterity, and the ethical, occurs when Ricoeur first considers the moral dimensions of selfhood, beginning in chapter seven, entitled "The Self and the Ethical Aim." Chapter seven is split into three subsections, based respectively on the three components of Ricoeur's "definition" of "ethical intention." "Ethical intention" is the cornerstone of moral selfhood, and hence the pinnacle of the entire conception of selfhood in *Oneself as Another*. "Let us define 'ethical intention,'" Ricoeur writes, "as *aiming at the 'good life' with and for others, in just institutions*."[9] These three clauses: (1) "aiming at the *good life*"; (2) "with and for others"; (3) "in just institutions," provide the topics of the three subsections of chapter seven. The number, relation, and movement between them is basically "Hegelian": starting with the self as moral character, one then moves to the alterity of moral sociality, to finally return to the reconciliation of the moral self and the other as justice. The discussion of Levinas in chapter seven quite naturally occurs in its second subsection, on moral sociality.

The first of the three components of "ethical intention," "aiming at the good life," which I will call "moral character" for short, has the status of *primus inter pares*. Its primacy appears first in the fact that the other two components of moral life, moral sociality and justice, are part of *its* definition. Its primacy appears second and

---

[8] *OA*, p. 19.    [9] Ibid., p. 172.

more deeply in the fact that establishing the primacy of moral character over moral sociality is the specific aim of chapter seven, and the basic reason Ricoeur criticizes Levinas, who in sharp contrast gives primacy to sociality. The primacy of moral character in ethics is reflectively grasped as the primacy of what Ricoeur calls "self-esteem." Ricoeur's argument is that the second component of moral life, moral sociality, only makes sense as "the articulation of this aim" – self-esteem – "in norms."[10] "Self-respect," the reflective grasp of this second component, is thus a development of, and as such remains dependent upon, "self-esteem."

The differences separating Ricoeur and Levinas are sharp. First, Ricoeur's hierarchy of self and other is exactly the reverse of Levinas's, for whom moral sociality precedes moral character. Second, Ricoeur equates moral sociality with *normativity*. For Levinas, in contrast, moral sociality does not by itself, or does not at first, manifest itself as normativity. Normativity, for Levinas, is a conditioned development which appears later or consequently at the level of justice. The initial morality Levinas discerns emerging with sociality is "purer" or more stringent than normativity, if one can say this, commanding prior to and without commandments. To be sure, laws are a part of a developed morality, but they are not its initial moment. Levinas's antinomianism, though restricted, separates him from Ricoeur, and from Kant. The different way these two thinkers part company from Kant is instructive. Ricoeur gives precedence to moral character over moral sociality, and hence rejects Levinas, precisely because Ricoeur also insists, following Kant, but contra Levinas, on binding the moral sociality he puts second, to normativity. Ricoeur and Levinas agree, in other words, that norms are not the ground zero of morality; they part company over whether norms are or are not synonymous with moral sociality.

In the first subsection of chapter seven, on "aiming at the 'good life'," Ricoeur examines Aristotle's account of virtue, friendship, and *phronesis*, in the *Nicomachean Ethics*. The analyses are complex and nuanced. What Ricoeur takes from them, however, to apply in the second subsection of chapter seven, ". . . with and for

---

[10] Ibid., p. 170.

Others," where Levinas appears, is less so. "From Aristotle," Ricoeur writes, "I should like to retain only the ethics of reciprocity, of sharing, of living together"[11] – in a word, of *mutuality*. Mutuality serves as a bridge from the first subsection on moral character to the second subsection on moral sociality because the mutuality of genuine friendship, as Ricoeur understands Aristotle, comes from two persons each aiming at the same good life, united by the same aim. The genuine friend, then, is in this respect actually "another self [*allos autos*]."[12] Thus conceived, mutuality is not an affirmation of the alterity of the other person, as it is in Buber, but rather a social or shared confirmation of the primacy of each person's correct aim or moral character.

In the second subsection of chapter seven, without altering its function as a bridge, Ricoeur shifts from Aristotle's notion of mutuality to his own more "inclusive concept of solicitude," as the basic meaning of the moral self in its ethical intention toward another. Constructively specifying the "equality" which informs Aristotelian friendship, Ricoeur conceives the sociality of solicitude on an economic model, based "principally," as he writes, "on the exchange between *giving* and *receiving*."[13] Even without the Kantian practical rule of non-contradiction, we can see why, following Aristotle's notion of equality or mutuality, Ricoeur equates social morality and normativity: norms regulate judgments regarding equality. Good solicitude, then, means equal exchange. Bad solicitude means unequal exchange. Proper solicitude, upon which the reflective concept of self-respect is based, is thus "a fragile balance in which giving and receiving are equal, hypothetically." In contrast, if "in the initiative of exchange"[14] one or the other pole predominates, if the self's solicitous relation to the other is not mutual, reciprocal, or equal, to that extent moral sociality fails, and to that extent the self loses its self-respect.

It is precisely at this point, when speaking of bad solicitude as an imbalance between giving and receiving, that Ricoeur invokes Levinas. Levinas represents a radical imbalance: the extremity of all initiative coming from the other, the extremity whereby all is received and nothing is given. "Levinas's entire philosophy rests

[11] Ibid., p. 187.    [12] Ibid., p. 185.    [13] Ibid., p. 188.    [14] Ibid.

on the initiative of the other in the intersubjective relation."[15]
Having situated Levinas thus, Ricoeur's argument is transparent:
because Levinas has made extremity rather than mutuality the
basis of ethics, his is surely a false and perhaps even an evil path.
Even worse, Levinas's privileging of the other is so unbalanced, so
extreme, as to be more than a moral impediment: it is a philosophical impossibility; it establishes no link at all.

So, first of all, Levinas mistakenly gives priority to moral sociality over moral character. Second, within the social domain,
Levinas mistakenly exaggerates the initiative of the other, hence
mistakenly gives priority to an unbalanced alterity over the balance of good solicitude. The impossibility of Levinas's position
hinges on Ricoeur's unswerving allegiance to a Parmidean-
Hegelian conception of the nature and limits of relationality and
transcendence. Levinas's fundamental error is to attempt, per
impossibile, to think what Hegel called "external relation," when
in truth such an alleged relation is no relation at all, an "irrelation", as Ricoeur calls it.[16] Although Levinas seems to be in the
good company of Kant and Plato on this point, for Ricoeur, as for
Hegel, genuine philosophy must be limited to "internal" or "dialectical" relations, that is to say, relations whose terms do not in
any irreducible sense exceed their relationality.

In the wrong on all three of the above requirements – begin with
the self, link sociality and normativity, stay within internal relations – it follows that Levinas's essentially futile effort to upset the
apple-cart of solicitude results in a number of more specific but
interrelated problems. Ricoeur isolates three, all having to do with
excess: (1) The other person's exteriority is so excessive he/she is
out of contact; (2) The separation of the self is so excessive, so
passive, that it is inviolate, that is to say, again, out of relation; and
finally, (3) Reviving Derrida's 1964 criticism, violence and war, not
morality, remain as Levinas's only avenues to breach the "irrelation" between self and other. The following citations from chapter
seven articulate these three lines of criticism:

This [Levinas's unbalanced] initiative establishes no relation at all, to the
extent that the other represents absolute exteriority with respect to an ego

defined by the condition of separation. The other, in this sense, absolves himself of any relation. This irrelation defines exteriority as such. The summons to responsibility has opposite it simply the passivity of an "I" who has been called upon . . . Taken literally, a dissymmetry left uncompensated would break off the exchange of giving and receiving and would exclude any instruction by the face within the field of solicitude. This is why the Other . . . has to storm the defenses of a separate "I."[17]

Such is Ricoeur's rejection of Levinas in chapter seven.

But far from deviating from or capitulating to the hegemony of the Parmidean-Hegelian heritage of philosophy, Levinas's thought intends to directly challenge it. This challenge, as Ricoeur obviously recognizes, strikes at the heart of the meaning of self-hood. It is not at all likely, then, that Ricoeur's appeal to the logic of Parmenidean-Hegelian philosophy will carry much weight with a philosophy deliberately and conscientiously set upon casting aside the gravity of this heritage. For Levinas the uniqueness of the ethical relation, and its importance for philosophy, is precisely that its terms, self and other, are both out of relation and in relation. Their "dephasing" or "diachrony" is the very force of ethics, not merely contrasting with but contesting the priorities of epistemology and ontology, determined as they are, and as Ricoeur would have all domains determined, by an attachment to internal and dialectical relations.

Levinas raises the priority of the encounter with the alterity of the other, ethical priority, to the status of the very humanity of the human. Humanity arises in moral responsibility. Moral responsibility, for its part, is inaugurated by overturning *conatus*, "perseverance in being," natural indifference to alterity. Radical alterity, far from leaving the self unmoved, as Ricoeur suggests (relying on the circular or self-defensive requirements of *epistemology*), radically moves the self, "reconditions," "transubstantiates" its naturally selfish inclinations and auto-nomous syntheses into moral responsibility for the other. Levinas's responsive *"Me voici," "Here I am,"*[18] formula for the moral self, is not undercut by an allegedly

---

[17] Ibid., pp. 188–190.

[18] Though Ricoeur acknowledges "borrow[ing] an expression dear to Levinas" (22), Kathleen Blamey translates *"Me voici"* as "It's me here," instead of the standard for Levinas translations, "Here I am." *Me voici* is a French translation of the biblical Hebrew הנני, *hineni*; see Genesis 22:1, 22:7, 22:11, and Isaiah 6:8.

deeper "Here I stand" (*"Ici je me tiens"*[19]), Ricoeur's counter-formula, but rather arises as morality arises: as a displacement, a hollowing out, a being-for-the-other, a "despite-oneself" (*malgré-soi*), to invoke several of Levinas's formulae for the moral self.

In contrast, the moral self in society is for Ricoeur not a hollowing out, but rather the tragic[20] taking of a stand in the face of compossible moral alternatives. The tragic character of Ricoeur's moral self in society is not our primary concern, however. What is important is to note that for Ricoeur social alterity stimulates an *already* morally inclined solicitude, drawing out moral character by drawing upon what Ricoeur calls its *"benevolent spontaneity."*[21] This move is perplexing, however, and not only from a Levinasian point of view. We must ask a hard question: independent of sociality and the complexities of choice introduced therein, from whence is selfhood inclined to benevolence? With the notion of "benevolent spontaneity," do we not see Ricoeur succumbing, in company with such English moralists as Shaftesbury and Hutcheson before him, to an unwarranted moral *optimism*, to what Freud called "wishful thinking"? Ricoeur posits what he cannot prove. No wonder he will later, in chapter ten, rely on the moralistic language of "conscience," "attestation," and "conviction." No evidence supports his optimism, or, rather, equal evidence opposes it. Only a transcendental argument (such as that which motivates Kant's *third Critique*), which Ricoeur disclaims, could postulate the goodness of natural being as an explanation for morality. Levinas, in contrast, does not equivocate on this point: "No one is good voluntarily." Only the unassumable alterity of the other person has the moral force – though not the necessity – to convert, to shame the natural self into moral being.

As for Ricoeur's related equation of social morality with a normative economic model, and the criticisms of Levinas which follow from this equation, it smacks of the procrustean bed – for Levinas, and for Ricoeur. Because he rejects external relation a priori and gives priority to character, Ricoeur argues: "On the basis of this benevolent spontaneity, receiving is on an equal footing with the summons to responsibility." "This is why," he

---

[19] *OA*, p. 339.  [20] Cf. ibid., pp. 241–249.  [21] Ibid., p. 190.

continues, "it is so important to us to give solicitude a more fundamental status than obedience to duty."[22] But why in the first place does Ricoeur limit the question of social morality to a choice between solicitude and norms? Levinas would argue, in contrast, that the moral status of both norms and solicitude depends on a prior opposition between natural indifference or perseverance (*conatus*) in being and moral responsiveness, between the for-itself and the for-others. *Conatus* plays a completely different role in Ricoeur's thought. Far from representing a morally reprehensible indifference to alterity, for Ricoeur *conatus* has only an epistemological function: the "priority of the *conatus* in relation to consciousness . . . imposes on adequate self-consciousness" the "very long detour"[23] of analysis and hermeneutics – in other words, Ricoeur's program.

What is procrustean, then, for both Levinas and Ricoeur is the latter's supposition that giving priority to moral sociality means giving priority to moral norms, hence reducing alterity to moral law, and moral selfhood to obedience to duty. This fundamental misrepresentation is summed up in Ricoeur's reduction of the Levinasian other to a "master of justice."[24] We have seen Ricoeur's alternative economic model, but we must insist on our question regarding how the authority of the "good life" inclines solicitude. In contrast to the empty abstraction which allegedly results from Levinasian excess, Ricoeur's "benevolent spontaneity" is said to be concretely disciplined by means of "the self's recognition of the superiority of the authority enjoining it to act in accordance with justice."[25] That is to say, Ricoeur's concept of moral sociality requires that the self recognize the legitimate superiority, the authority, of what Gadamer calls "the legitimacy of prejudices."[26] What Ricoeur refuses to accept is that without resorting to norms the authority of alterity in Levinas operates at an altogether different level than does Gadamerian authority. Gadamerian authority is epistemological. To cite from the page in *Truth and Method* to which Ricoeur refers, the other's "authority has nothing to do with obedience, but rather with knowledge"; the

[22] Ibid.   [23] Ibid., p. 317.   [24] Ibid., p. 189.   [25] Ibid., p. 190.
[26] Hans Georg Gadamer, *Truth and Method* (New York: Crossroad, 1982), p. 246. Ricoeur refers to Gadamer in *OA*, p. 190, n. 27.

agent's recognition of the other's superiority is "an act of freedom and reason, which fundamentally acknowledges the authority of a superior because he has a wider view of things or is better informed, i.e., once again, because he has superior knowledge."[27] Levinas's objection (made years earlier to the entire ecstatic apparatus of Heideggerian fore-structure [*Vor-Struktur*]), is that the moral dimension of social encounter cannot be preserved against a critique of representational consciousness by *deepening* the meaning of knowing, *incarnating* knowing. Rather, the moral dimension of social encounter operates beneath and sustains all levels of understanding, precisely because – contra the Parmidean-Hegelian heritage – it is an encounter with alterity as such.

For Levinas, as I have indicated, humanity and moral humanity arise together. Morality is neither a prior constituent nor a gloss added to an already constituted humanity. Rather, the other *qua* other and moral alterity emerge together: the only genuine other is the commanding-obliging other, the moral other. This level, Levinas would argue, must be presupposed by any analysis or hermeneutics of moral life. Without it one could not even begin to speak of such things as the *goodness* of the "good life," or the *benevolence* of spontaneity. Spontaneity, unless it is already socially conditioned, is neither benevolent nor malevolent but amoral – hence malevolent. The superiority of the other in an exchange of giving and receiving, even if based on the most careful epistemological assessment of the other's attributes, cannot be called moral, rather than simply economic, unless the moral dimension as such is already operative through a prior encounter with alterity as such.

It is because he misunderstands the *level* or significance of the alterity of the other in Levinas that Ricoeur misunderstands, in addition, the passivity of the self that responds to alterity. The Levinasian self is not so separate as to be inviolate, simply passive, or, as Ricoeur would have it, the (im)possible object of violence and war. Rather, it is, as Levinas writes, "more passive than any receptivity," "more passive than any passivity." These superlative expressions do not refer to an inertia, since for Levinas the inertia

[27] Gadamer, *Truth and Method*, p. 248.

of the self is its natural *conatus*. Rather they refer to the moral self's irreplaceability, its non-substitutability, and to its inexhaustibility. The moral self arises as pure subjection to the other, as a subjectivity irreplaceably subject, hence as "elected" by the other. While the *conatus* is *soi-même*, it-self, one-self, the moral self is *malgré-soi*, despite-itself, despite-oneself. In the face of the other, "I" am responsible – no one but myself, no one but me ("*moi*"). Not only is this fixing of the moral self, its irreplaceability, extraordinary, but so too is its sufficiency. Just as the alterity of the other is irreducible and unassumable, so too the hollowing out of the moral self – its desire for goodness – is endless. What this means, concretely, is that the moral reserves of the self are in principle inextinguishable. Beyond giving or attempting to give food, shelter, clothing, employment, etc. – that is, beyond giving *things* – and beyond the kind word, warm hand, or even silent company – that is to say, beyond any giving *of* the self – the responsibility of the self exceeds the very limits of finitude. The oneself of response goes all the way to giving the very self of the self, all the way to death, the ultimate self-sacrifice. One can be for-the-other all the way: one can die for another – such is the ultimate structure of morality, of the "unrelating relation,"[28] as Levinas calls it, at the heart neither of knowledge nor being, but better, more demanding, of morality.

CHAPTER TEN: "WHAT ONTOLOGY IN VIEW?"

In chapter ten, more specifically in its second subsection, entitled "The Otherness of Other People," we find the central and most extended critical discussion of Levinas in *Oneself as Another*.[29] In addition to reasons already noted above, Levinas's prominence in this chapter is due to its level, approach, issue, and chief figure. The level is ontological. The approach is a "second-order discourse," utilizing the "metacategories," as Ricoeur writes, of "the 'great kinds'; akin to the Platonic Same and Other." The issue – "by far the most complex and most inclusive, as it involves the very title of this work" – "concerns the specific dialectical structure of the relation between selfhood and otherness."[30] The chief figure is

---

[28] Emmanuel Levinas, *Totality and Infinity*, trans. Alphonso Lingis (Pittsburgh: Duquesne University Press, 1969), p. 295.　　[29] *OA*, pp. 335–341.　　[30] Ibid., p. 298.

Martin Heidegger, the *Dasein-analytic* of *Being and Time*, more specifically, the nature and role of conscience (*Gewissen*).

Regarding the latter, an important way to grasp the difference separating Ricoeur and Levinas is in terms of their fundamentally different responses to Heidegger. First some similarities. Both thinkers acknowledge Heidegger's tremendous and inescapable contribution to philosophy, especially the brilliant phenomenological analyses of *Being and Time*. And neither thinker is a Heideggerian in any simple or straightforward sense, although Ricoeur is by far closer to Heidegger, as we shall see, than Levinas, who is not a Heideggerian at all. In criticizing Heidegger, too, Ricoeur and Levinas share a bond. Both find his thought *morally deficient*, especially his conception of the self. Rectifying this deficiency is the work of the third and concluding subsection of chapter ten, entitled simply "Conscience," where Ricoeur will a second and final time engage Levinas critically.[31] Despite their many agreements regarding Heidegger, it is precisely in their critical relation to his thought that Ricoeur and Levinas radically part company.

Though more intimate, Ricoeur's critical relation to Heidegger is on a par with his relations to other major figures in the history of philosophy. As one sees at each step of the way through *Oneself as Another*, Ricoeur takes up texts – of "Plato, Aristotle, Descartes, Spinoza, Leibniz, and so on" – close to his position, in order to critically and creatively rework them to suit his own vision. We have witnessed this approach very briefly in relation to Aristotle's conception of virtue and friendship in the *Nicomachean Ethics*. Ricoeur gives credit for his "reinterpretations and reappropriations, thanks to a meaning potential left unexploited."[32] It is here precisely that we see Ricoeur's special *methodological* intimacy with Heidegger. His reconstructive approach to the history of philosophy, his revisionary manner of philosophizing, exploiting "meaning potential left unexploited," is precisely the approach taken by Heidegger, especially in his many works after *Being and Time*. So, while Ricoeur does indeed criticize Heidegger's results, specifically the moral deficiency of Dasein in *Being and Time*, he will

---

[31] Ibid., pp. 341–355.     [32] Ibid., p. 298.

do so in a Heideggerian manner. We shall have to see to what extent this deforms Ricoeur's alleged independence.

Levinas, in contrast, opposes both Heidegger's results *and* Heidegger's manner of thinking. Levinas does not tease out or put in "a meaning potential left unexploited" in Heidegger's *Dasein-analytic*, at the price of leaving its overall structure or issue intact, as does Ricoeur. Rather, he offers a radical alternative, and thereby criticizes Heidegger through and through. Displacing and recontextualizing all meanings to his own bent – which is another way of saying that Levinas's is a truly original thought – it follows that they are stripped of a Heideggerian sense. This difference is one between critique, an internal variation, and criticism, an external alternative. This difference explains why, despite Ricoeur's concluding moral reconstruction of Dasein's conscience, *Oneself as Another* ends where Heidegger's work ends, in ontology. In contrast, Levinas's work begins and ends elsewhere, in ethics. Ricoeur's moral criticism of Heidegger aims not to overthrow Heidegger's conception of Dasein but to fix it – in a word, to *moralize* Dasein. Levinas's moral criticism of Heidegger, in contrast, intends not to fix Heidegger's conception of Dasein, but to oppose it – in the name of morality. Thus Ricoeur, while standing within Heideggerian ontology, supplements and corrects it with morality, while Levinas, standing in an ethics outside Heideggerian ontology, uses morality to overthrow it. Obviously, then, Levinas's criticism of Heidegger is more radical than Ricoeur's critique. And yet, it is *precisely for this greater radicality* that Ricoeur takes Levinas to task, going so far as to deny the very possibility of Levinas's criticism.

Before turning to a detailed reckoning with Ricoeur's criticism of Levinas, a preliminary but disturbing perplexity must first be assuaged. Ricoeur begins his discussion of Levinas in chapter ten by stating that "we have reserved until this moment the encounter with the work of Emmanuel Levinas."[33] But obviously, as we have seen, this is not true. Ricoeur has already "encountered" the work of Emmanuel Levinas in chapter seven, and encountered it critically. An even greater perplexity with Ricoeur's statement

---

[33] Ibid., p. 335.

emerges insofar as in chapter ten Ricoeur reactivates several of the earlier criticisms found in chapter seven. What then has Ricoeur "reserved until this moment"? While only close examination of the criticisms proper can answer this question fully, two preliminary remarks help pave the way.

One answer, not especially deep, but worth noting, is that the repetition might simply result from the fact that chapter ten was given as a free-standing lecture at Cericy-la-Salle in 1988, two years, that is to say, after chapter seven had been given as part of the Gifford Lectures in Edinburgh. Inasmuch as criticism of Levinas is the culminating critical moment of the Gifford Lectures, and hence also of chapters one through nine of *Oneself as Another*, there need be no surprise, really, that it is repeated and incorporated into the later ontological resurrection of the lectures. This reiteration would mark the importance of Levinas for Ricoeur.

A second deeper reason has to do with the significance Ricoeur gives to his own work, the significance, that is to say, of doing ontology, and hence of chapter ten and *Oneself as Another* as a whole. I have already noted this significance but want to underline that it is *Ricoeur's*. Shifting from the "first-order" discourse of chapters one through nine, to the "second-order" ontological discourse of chapter ten, does not simply mean that the latter is *about* the former. Ricoeur puts much more stock in his method of "reinterpretations and reappropriations." The difference is between the old and the new. Chapter ten, in other words, represents an "innovation"[34] – much like the Hegelian *Aufgeheben*, uplifting sublation – relative to the earlier first-order discourse, and indeed *to all prior discourse*, Levinas's included. The aim and result of *Oneself as Another*'s many "reinterpretations and reappropriations" of the history of philosophy is thus neither a dry "repetition" nor an "aimless wandering,"[35] but rather a creative development in the history of thought. Although I have characterized Ricoeur's relation to Heidegger as one of revision, rectification from within, Ricoeur sees his own reconstructions more grandly as fundamental innovations, indeed as fundamentally original thinking. Thus Ricoeur's perplexing statement about reserving his encounter with

---

[34] Ibid., p. 299.    [35] Ibid.

Levinas for chapter ten would mean, in this perspective, that here in this chapter Ricoeur sees *himself* opposing Levinas – opposing Levinas, that is, with *Ricoeur's* own distinctive or original thought.

For this reason, in addition to reviewing and challenging two explicit criticisms of Levinas found in subsection two, where (a) the charge of irrelation is renewed and (b) a new charge of hyperbole is introduced, the following will review and challenge (c) the critical force of the positive alternative conception of selfhood as "being-enjoined," which Ricoeur develops in subsection three by creative supplementation of Heidegger's conception of conscience, and the explicit criticisms of Levinas found there, on the very last pages of *Oneself as Another.*[36]

### Irrelation

Ricoeur's first and most fundamental criticism is familiar to us from chapter seven. It derives from what I have been calling the "Parmidean-Hegelian" heritage of philosophy to which Ricoeur subscribes. The argument is that Levinas's account of the self and intersubjectivity is flawed, indeed impossible, because it makes the unforgivable error of trying to overstep the bounds of relationality *per se.* Levinas is guilty of the ultimate non-starter in philosophy: treating a non-relation as a relation. "No middle ground," Ricoeur writes, "no between, is secured to lessen the utter dissymmetry between the Same and the Other."[37] Here, as earlier, Ricoeur specifies this broad criticism in terms appropriate to his topic, namely, self and other. Because the Levinasian self is too separate, the other is taken to be too other, hence they cannot be put into relation. "Because the Same signifies totalization and separation, the exteriority of the Other can no longer be expressed in the language of relation."[38]

What the above citation makes clear is that for Ricoeur the basic flaw of Levinas's account is to have overly insularized, overly isolated, overly separated the self. The real truth, so Ricoeur argues, is that in order to receive the other, as the self surely does, the self must first have its own prior moral *capacity* of reception, its

---

[36] Ibid., pp. 354–355.    [37] Ibid., p. 338.    [38] Ibid., p. 336.

own prior moral self-subsistence. Such a prior capacity, as we have seen, is the key to Ricoeur's alternative conception of moral selfhood, and indeed of selfhood altogether. Although, in proleptic response, Levinas time and again refers to the self in terms of a passivity deeper than receptivity, there is an entire alternative avenue of response, having to do with eros, and more specifically with familiality.

This first answer, regarding the familial dimension of selfhood, an answer that stands in obvious and ready opposition to Ricoeur's depiction of Levinasian selfhood and the critical charges built on that depiction, is one that has been entirely ignored by Ricoeur, for whatever reasons. Ricoeur is thus tilting at a straw man. He nowhere touches upon Levinas's very fine analyses of the self's capacity of reception found in Part Four of *Totality and Infinity*. There the separated self – the self susceptible to moral relations – is determined as capable of moral encounter precisely because of its *created* rather than its *caused* or *posited* being. This distinction, and Levinas's account of selfhood starting with created being, are of the utmost importance. Levinas's point is that the self is first the product of familial relations, is conditioned by birth, filiality (pater-nity, maternity), and fraternity. The self is susceptible to radical alterity because it is a being that is *born*, born from and into a web of familial relations.[39] These analyses are not only original, then, but "solve" the basic charge regarding a lack of receptivity that Ricoeur lays against Levinas. Levinas is quite explicit on this point, even to the extent of anticipating a criticism such as Ricoeur's, as the following citation from *Totality and Infinity* bears witness:

The acuity of the problem lies in the necessity of maintaining the I in the transcendence with which it hitherto seemed incompatible. Is the subject only a subject of knowings and powers? Does it not present itself as a subject in another sense? The relation sought, which qua subject it supports, and which at the same time satisfies these contradictory exigen-cies, seemed to us to be inscribed in the erotic relation.[40]

Unfortunately, Ricoeur nowhere refers to these all-important

---

[39] Levinas, *Totality and Infinity*, pp. 254–285; also see chapter 9, "The Metaphysics of Gender," in Richard A. Cohen, *Elevations: The Height of the Good in Rosenzweig and Levinas* (Chicago: University of Chicago Press, 1994), pp. 195–219.

[40] Levinas, *Totality and Infinity*, p. 276.

analyses of the erotic relation, of the self as born, the self as a child of parents, as a sibling, and so on, which for Levinas are in no way to be understood as merely psychological or sociological attributes. Rather, Levinas presents them as part of "a new ontological principle"[41]: "Sexuality is in us neither knowledge nor power, but the very plurality of our existing." . . . "Fecundity is to be set up as an ontological category"[42] At this level they represent Levinas's answer to the problem Ricoeur repeatedly harps upon and takes to be insoluble, namely, establishing a selfhood capable of receiving transcendent alterity without at all diminishing the radical transcendence of that alterity. "[B]ecause the son owes his unicity," Levinas writes, "to the paternal election he can be brought up, be commanded, and can obey, and the strange conjunction of the family is possible"[43] Too many pages would be necessary to fully explicate this dimension of the Levinasian conception of selfhood; I have attended to this topic briefly in my introduction and, more extensively, elsewhere (see footnote 39, p. 299). Having noted the existence and importance of the erotic and familial dimension of selfhood in Levinas, and that in this dimension lies the basic answer to Ricoeur's criticism, and without diminishing the importance of this answer (as a response to Ricoeur and as an original account of selfhood in its own right), we will move on and respond to Ricoeur's criticism without tapping these Levinasian resources that Ricoeur has ignored.

Ricoeur's criticism is even more specific: in addition to lacking the basic capacity of reception, Ricoeur argues that Levinas's separated self also lacks the requisite capacities of discrimination and recognition. "[A]wakening a responsible response to the other's call," Ricoeur writes, cannot work "except by presupposing a capacity of reception, of discrimination, and of recognition."[44] We will look in turn at these three necessary characteristics of selfhood – reception, discrimination, and recognition – that Ricoeur finds lacking in Levinas.

First, reception: "If interiority were indeed determined solely by the desire for retreat and closure," Ricoeur writes, renewing the argument of chapter seven against the irrelation of a monadic self,

---

[41] Ibid.   [42] Ibid., p. 277.   [43] Ibid., p. 270.   [44] *OA*, p. 339.

"how could it ever hear a word addressed to it, which would seem so foreign to it that this word would be a nothing for an isolated existence?" Ricoeur is claiming, of course, that the Levinasian self has fallen into the solipsistic abyss from which the Cartesian ego emerges only with divine help. To remedy such an isolated insularity, Ricoeur writes: "One has to grant a capacity of reception to the self that is the result of a reflexive structure, better defined by its power of reconsidering preexisting objectifications than by an initial separation."[45] The latter, "separation," refers to Levinas's position, the former, "reconsidering preexisting objectifications," is Ricoeur's. By "reconsidering preexisting objectifications" Ricoeur means his own union of analysis and hermeneutics, which both uncovers and reflects a self always only partially known to itself. Such a self has not just "fallen" (*verfallen*), to use Heidegger's terminology, into the inauthentic superficiality of the concerns of the "they" (*das Mann*), but is also never fully able to recover itself even when authentically focused upon itself. As such it is ontologically "in debt," "guilty," *schuldig*. It is the later term, Dasein's guilt (like "mutuality" in Aristotle), that holds Ricoeur's attention, and which will, later in *Oneself as Another*, be subject to reinterpretation. In any event, an unending spiraling self-illumination is the only avenue of self-understanding that obviates the aporias which inevitably arise, or so Ricoeur believes, from an account like Levinas's which is not at bottom ontological, not oriented by the question of being or essence – that is to say, not hermeneutical.

One answer to this charge, Ricoeur acknowledges, is to aver that Levinas's account of the self's encounter with the other works "at a level of radicality where the distinction I [Ricoeur] propose between two sorts of identity . . . cannot be taken into account."[46] Although Ricoeur clearly intends this comment as a criticism, as if Levinas had missed a crucial distinction, the truth of the matter is that Levinas's account *does* operate at a level more radical than Ricoeur's. This difference of level, which is also a difference in aim, makes all the difference in distinguishing between their accounts. Levinas's account aims to grasp a more radical aspect of the self–other encounter than does Ricoeur's, namely, encounter

---

[45] Ibid.    [46] Ibid., p. 335.

with alterity as such. Taken up in this problematic, Levinas is indeed in a more Cartesian mold, as it were, than is Ricoeur. But by being so he is able to break it up more radically than Ricoeur by shattering the basic commitment to epistemology upon which all Cartesianism is constructed. Thus, while Ricoeur rejects Cartesian epistemology for the foundation of his thought, Levinas rejects epistemology as the foundation of thought altogether. It does no good, then, for Ricoeur to criticize Levinas for missing out on the advantages of a hermeneutic-analytic epistemology over an obsolete Cartesian-representational epistemology – because Levinas rejects both.

For all that, Levinas does not give up philosophy. Rather, he reorients or disorients philosophy from its usual epistemological base to an even more exacting ethical height. This does not mean, less we misinterpret the consequences of such a radical shift, that Levinas gives up epistemology in a Nietzschean frenzy. Rather, he reorients it to the essential disorientation effected by ethical exigencies. Levinas articulates the priority of prescription over description or denotation. After acknowledging in his own way and for his own purposes their differences in level, Ricoeur writes: "[I]n Levinas, the identity of the Same is bound up with an ontology of totality that my own investigation has never assumed or even come across."[47] And this is precisely right. It is precisely right because concerned as Levinas is to account for a more originary encounter with alterity, the emergence of alterity as such, it follows that the appropriate conceptual alternative must be totality. Because Ricoeur never accounts for the emergence of alterity as such, he never comes across, as he says, "an ontology of totality." Their difference, then, comes down to asking different questions and thus exposing different answers. The Levinasian rebuttal, then, is to point out that this difference cannot authorize Ricoeur, or anyone else at a conditioned level, in this instance a level of inquiry that takes radical alterity for granted, to criticize its own conditioning level, where alterity first takes shape.

Let us recall that in chapter seven, where Ricoeur defended the priority of the self-directed orientation of self-esteem over the

[47] Ibid.

other-directed orientation of self-respect, the self's autochthonous *capacity* to receive the other, its "solicitude," was characterized as "benevolent spontaneity." We questioned – and, outside of certain logical and epistemological considerations, could not find – his grounds for introducing the term "benevolence" to characterize the self's spontaneity independent of or prior to its response to the other. At the conclusion of chapter ten Ricoeur addresses this question anew by means of a positive account of moral selfhood developed by means of "reinterpretations and reappropriations" of the Heideggerian notion of conscience (*Gewissen*). We will turn to this shortly. In subsection two of chapter ten Ricoeur is once again relying on a logical and epistemological argument, compelling within the Parmenidean-Hegelian (and, let us add, Heideggerian) horizon of philosophy, to renew his charge that Levinas has failed to establish a relation between self and other. But what Levinas wants to account for, as has been indicated, is not the relation *between* self and other, but the encounter with *alterity* as *transcendence*, as the outside, the other. And he does so not by a "pretension"[48] – Ricoeur's word – greater than Fichte's, but by recognizing the inadequacy of the entire epistemological framework that makes even Fichte's account of the transcendence of the non-I inadequately transcendent. We are able, then, to ask a new question: If the being of the self includes a "benevolence," as Ricoeur believes, then what role could the moral other play in the moral constitution of the self? Even if one answers "norms," as Ricoeur does, we must still wonder from whence norms gain their *moral* sense. Norms could be generated like other "objectivities" from rational calculation. "Truth" and "beauty" could also provide norms, that is, socially codifiable prescriptions, imperatives ("tell the truth," "seek the truth," "create beauty," and so on) no less than "moral goodness" ("be good," "do the good"). If one resorts to the self's alleged benevolent spontaneity for an answer, social morality would still be something of a luxury, a graciousness or charity, hardly worth fussing about so much as to risk one's equilibrium or social position, and certainly not one's life. At worst, social morality taken on in this way could just as easily slip

[48] Ibid.

into becoming an art – the art, say, of grand politics. I am not suggesting that the latter eventuality is Ricoeur's intent, conscious or otherwise, but it remains nonetheless a horizon of his thought.

In addition to receptivity, two additional capacities of the self are also said to be lacking their proper priority in Levinas: discrimination, also called "discernment,"[49] and recognition of superiority. Here in chapter ten, the latter, recognition of superiority, is once again, as in chapter seven, treated in Gadamerian fashion, as recognition of the other's superior wisdom. The other's superiority is a function of knowledge, in the self and in the other, even if that knowledge is not wholly representational or self-transparent. Thus an imperative such as "thou shalt not kill" – which for Levinas is at once the moral significance of the "face" and the initial impact of the alterity of the other – would not come to the self by reversing the natural order, reversing, that is to say, the self-aggrandizing thrust of a desire to persevere in being. Rather, it would presuppose a prior capacity in the self able to recognize the other's superiority, a capacity embedded, incarnate in the self, which under the force of sociality would become "conviction." Ricoeur writes: "As for the master who teaches, does he not ask to be recognized in his very superiority? In other words, must not the voice of the Other who says to me: 'Thou shalt not kill,' become my own, to the point of becoming my conviction, a conviction to equal the accusative of 'It's me here!' ["*me voici!*"] with the nominative 'Here I stand'?"[50] To see how Ricoeur's rhetorical question is a real one, and to answer it in the negative, we must again note a difference in level. What Ricoeur takes to be prior is a capacity to recognize an alterity as superior in one way or another, that is, the superiority of moral attributes, attributes recognized as and by personal wisdom. Levinas, in contrast, takes the impact of the alterity of the other to occur as moral transformation, the implosion and precedence of moral exigency on the self's otherwise self-serving interests. One would not first sovereignly recognize moral attributes, rather one undergoes them, suffers morally. But following an existentialized version of philosophy's transcendental route, for Ricoeur, in contrast, there must

---

[49] Ibid., p. 339.   [50] Ibid.

always first be self-reflexivity, a capacity in the sense of a base, ground, or zero-point, from which and out of which and into which otherness is *correlated*. For Levinas, in contrast, such an insistence on recognition, or on recognizing the priority of recognition, misses accounting for the prior impact which is at once the impact of alterity as such and moral obligation.

No matter what it may and should become in addition or subsequently, for Levinas encounter with alterity is not *from the first* a matter of attributes and recognition. It is a matter of transcendence, of "contact" with alterity as such. For Ricoeur, following Heidegger and much of the Western philosophical tradition, transcendence is modulated and muted by the priority of thought and its dialectic, in this case articulated as receptivity. That is to say, for reasons compelling to a logic unable or unwilling to see limitations in its own circularity, and in Heidegger's case exalting such circularity into the rarified and exclusive atmosphere of "authentic" "thinking" (*Denken*), transcendence is only transcendental, the external only immanent. In this way thought never exceeds its own reach, and makes of its self-fulfillment a virtue and standard. To perform this reduction and at the same time to overlook its reductiveness, Ricoeur relies on Heidegger's concept of fore-structure, in this case fore-knowledge. As part of his critical effort to moralize Dasein, Ricoeur will reinterpret fore-knowledge as "attestation" and "conviction," striving at this price to avoid an unwonted amorality, the amorality of "resolution" (*Entschluss*) as Heidegger conceives it. Still, conviction remains for Ricoeur (as resolution remains for Heidegger) an epistemological capacity, the accumulated result, as it were, of recognition of the other's superior wisdom, knowledge, teaching, mastery, and the like.

For Levinas, in contrast to Ricoeur, as we have seen, recognition of the other as superior – *morally* superior – is recognition of alterity as such. Alterity, in other words, in the most radical sense possible, that is, as unassimilated transcendence, can only "appear" to the self as moral alterity, the alterity of moral command. It is hence a puncturing of the self's capacities of self-identification all the way, a puncturing of the self's synthesizing powers, whether active or passive, hence a "recognition" mediated neither as knowledge nor as fore-knowledge. The self is "more passive" in relation to such moral transcendence "than the passivity of receptivity," as Levinas has repeatedly written. This does not, however, make the encounter with the alterity of the other a stupidity or ignorance, as Ricoeur critically suggests. Nor is it fair to suggest, as Ricoeur does by misreading a citation from *Totality and Infinity*,[51] that for Levinas the self's separation is an ignorance. Actually, it is neither the case that the self alone is ignorant nor that the encounter with the other is a knowledge. Rather, to express the matter directly, encounter with alterity precedes and conditions knowledge. What is prior to knowing is not ignorance but the *priority* of moral priority. What has priority over knowing and conditions knowing is subjectivity as moral responsiveness, subjectivity as subjection to the other in a humbling of powers and capacities, a reorientation of the self's natural for-oneself – its *conatus* – into a for-the-other. Contra Ricoeur, neither spontaneous benevolence nor conviction can be at the origin of morality, since to recognize and then internalize moral superiority one would first of all have to encounter and engage the moral. Levinas's reply to Ricoeur, then, is to appeal to an aboriginal priority.

Ricoeur's critique continues: not only can the Levinasian self not recognize superiority, it cannot distinguish or discriminate one other from another. "[I]t is in each case for the first time that the Other, a particular Other, says to me: 'Thou shalt not kill'."[52] Ricoeur obviously misconstrues the radical alterity of each concrete other in Levinas, taking it to mean a reduction of all others, all persons, to the same pure alterity and to nothing but that pure alterity. A strange faceless world that would be indeed. An adequate Levinasian reply would follow the same line as we have already seen above regarding the recognition of superiority. That is to say, Ricoeur's strange picture of Levinas comes from promoting a category mistake, actually a conflation, into a criticism. But Ricoeur goes a step farther with the lack of discrimination charge than with the charge of lack of recognition. He argues that not only is there a lack, but that in addition it represents an internal flaw because Levinas's own works present multiple figures of the

[51] See ibid., p. 337.    [52] Ibid., p. 336.

other. Levinas would thus be preempted, his answer – the plurality of others – being taken as more evidence for the problem. "Who will be able to distinguish," Ricoeur asks rhetorically, "the master from the executioner, the master who calls for a disciple from the master who requires a slave?"[53] In addition to inventing figures of his own, Ricoeur names several different figures that appear in Levinas's texts. Especially emphasized, however, is the difference between the positive figure of the so-called "master of justice" found in *Totality and Infinity* and the more radical and negative figure of "the offender"[54] found in *Otherwise than Being or Beyond Essence*. What is alleged to follow is that in addition to not being able to distinguish between various good figures, all of whom forbid murder, according to Ricoeur's reading Levinas's self cannot distinguish good from bad figures, or even bad from worse figures such as the offender, the executioner, and the master who enslaves. Leaving aside a point that might have been used to strengthen his contention, namely, that even "Thou shalt not kill" has various levels of meaning,[55] Ricoeur discerns in Levinas's alleged failure to provide the self with a capacity to discriminate a fatal "reversal."

It is because of the self's inability to discriminate that Ricoeur detects in the difference between *Totality and Infinity* and *Otherwise than Being or Beyond Essence* a "strange reversal." "I perceive," he writes, "a sort of reversal of the reversal performed in *Totality and Infinity*."[56] The self assigned to be responsible, thereby reversed of its natural being by morality in *Totality and Infinity*, by being reversed once again in *Otherwise than Being or Beyond Essence*, so Ricoeur contends, is thereby returned, contra Levinas's own intent, to its original position. Levinas thereby undoes his own efforts, or circles back to his starting point. I cite Ricoeur:

The assignment of responsibility, stemming from the summons by the Other and interpreted in terms of the most total passivity, is reversed in a

53  Ibid., p. 339.       54  Ibid., p. 338.

55  In Judaism, for instance, the prohibition against murder applies to killing one's fellows, to be sure, but it is at work, too, in prohibiting one person from greatly embarrassing another, or denying food and security to travelers, or taking away someone's job, or making a rash halakhic ruling, or withholding halakhic expertise. These actions strike so deeply against the other that they are "tantamount" to murder, though of course they are not "literally" murder.       56  *OA*, p. 340.

show of abnegation in which the self attests to itself by the very movement with which it removes itself.[57]

It is true that for Levinas the passivity of the moral self of *Totality and Infinity*, having initially reversed its power, having had its for-itself converted into responsiveness to and for the other, becomes in *Otherwise than Being or Beyond Essence* a self "substituting" itself for the other, a for-the-other's for-itself. Thus one might say along with Ricoeur that its first reversal into responsive passivity is reversed again into a substituting activity. Ricoeur invokes Levinas's term "testimony," from *Otherwise than Being or Beyond Essence*, where the moral self in its encounter with the other is said to *testify* to that other, in order to suggest critically that Levinas has reverted to what Ricoeur, without the unnecessary detour of a reversed reversal, calls "attestation." "Is this [Levinas's] testimony so far removed," he asks, "from what we have constantly called attestation?"[58]

In his very next sentence, however, Ricoeur answers his own criticism and exposes his own rhetoric: "To be sure," he writes, "Levinas never speaks of the attestation *of self*, the very expression being suspected of leading back to the 'certainty of the ego.' " This difference, emphasized by italics, is precisely to the point, precisely Levinas's resounding answer. To be for-the-other all the way to taking responsibility for the other's for-itself is still to be for-the-other. One is testifying *not to oneself but for the other*, washing the other's hands not one's own. Levinas has said:

Ethical testimony is a revelation which is not a knowledge. Must one still say that in this mode one only "testifies" to the Infinite, to God, about which no presence or actuality is *capable* of testifying. The philosophers said there is no present infinite. What may pass for a "fault" of the infinite is to the contrary a positive characteristic of it – its very infinity.[59]

Testimony, radical as it can become, up to the point of substitution, stepping in for-the-other, is testimony *of* and *for* the other's moral height, the other's alterity. In contrast, Ricoeur's attestation always remains self-attestation, attestation of and to the *self*'s moral

[57] Ibid.        [58] Ibid.
[59] Emmanuel Levinas, *Ethics and Infinity*, trans. Richard A. Cohen (Pittsburgh: Duquesne University Press, 1985), p. 108.

righteousness, of and to the *self*'s part in the play that reflection, at a distance, recognizes as moral encounter.

Thus there is no surreptitious reversal of reversal in Levinas's account, but the intensification of an original reversal. Levinas's account is not a reflection at-a-distance on-the-distance of an already given morality, a reflection compressing its distances, to be sure, by means of hermeneutical circling, reducing the other to the self, to the oneself *as* another, as in Ricoeur's title. Rather Levinas's ethics aims to go closer to morality than hermeneutics dares to go or can go. It aims to give voice not to the hermeneutical "this *as* that," but to what makes the *as* structure possible, the unlikeness at the root of likeness, the uniqueness at the root of similarity. The emergence of transcendence "*as*" morality is at once the emergence of transcendence and the emergence of morality, in a contact "closer to the self than the ego," as Levinas expresses it. "The self, a hostage," Levinas writes, "is already substituted for the others. 'I am an other,' but this is not the alienation Rimbaud refers to. I am outside of any place, in myself, on the hither side of the autonomy of auto-affection and identity resting on itself." Or, as if once again in direct response to Ricoeur: "The ego is not an entity 'capable' of expiating for the others: it is this original expiation." "In this sense the self is goodness, or under the exigency for an abandonment of all having, of all *one's own* and all *for oneself*, to the point of substitution."[60] Ricoeur will have none of *this* compression. When Ricoeur remarks that "[i]t remains that, through the form of the accusative, the first person is indirectly involved and that the accusative cannot remain 'nonassumable,'"[61] he has only projected a development onto its condition, that is, projected the self-reflective self proper to his own account onto Levinas's more radical account.

This sort of reductive projection, reflection reflecting itself, with its insistence on erasing residues, has had a long history in philosophy, and is perhaps its most consistent patrimony. Ricoeur's is but the latest instance of a long bottom line of "transcendental conditions," from Kant's "I think" to Husserl's "I represent" to

[60] Emmanuel Levinas, *Otherwise than Being or Beyond Essence*, trans. Alphonso Lingis (The Hague: Martinus Nijhoff, 1981), p. 118.   [61] *OA*, p. 340.

Heidegger's "issue of being," all insisting on their rights and authority. All owe their allegiances and alleged necessity, however, to the internal and circular requirements of a transcendental epistemology – precisely the "totality that," as Ricoeur has written, "my own investigation has never assumed or even come across."[62] Ricoeur can never come across *this* totality precisely because all his investigations operate within it, unwittingly conforming to its contours. Levinas's thought, in contrast, articulates this totality by exceeding and rupturing it – from a moral angle, a height.

## *Hyperbole*

Of course, Ricoeur is well aware that the central movement of Levinas's philosophy is a rupture, breach, or break with totality. Because this break is indeed impossible within the parameters – being and non-being – of the Parmenidean-Hegelian heritage, it is all the more of a breach, if one can qualify an absolute breach in this manner. Though Levinas speaks of a "more" in a "less," he is certainly not limiting himself to a mathematical or quantitative model. The appearance of language such as this, and other peculiar formulations and grammatical deformations, imposing what Levinas himself often calls an "abuse of language," are no accident. For what can it possibly mean to be outside the all? To be otherwise than being? Beyond essence? The entire thrust of Levinas's thought is precisely to articulate the sense of such exteriority, an exteriority "impossible" from within that which it exceeds. The sense or *significance* of such an exteriority only comes, so Levinas contends, from ethics, that is, from appreciating rupture as *moral impingement*, moral command, "received" by a self overwhelmed and transformed – reversed – by moral obligation, charged and overcharged with moral responsibility for-the-other. The only irreducible alterity, irreducible to the self, is moral transcendence.

Now for Ricoeur the same matter, breaking with totality, obviously has quite a different look. Standing within a seamless totality,

[62] Ibid., p. 335.

the problem with Levinas's thought is precisely its excess. For Ricoeur this excess is reflected in a language of exaggeration, indeed, of hyperbole. Because it is empty, however, speculative in the Kantian sense, it is sustained only by that language – mere words, "sound and fury." Now the way hyperbole sustains itself is to always outdo the force of its own expressions in a linguistic self-overcoming which by its own logic extends to the point of the "scandalous."[63] The scandal originates, however, in three related errors (whose basic contours were first articulated in chapter seven). First error: exaggerating the sameness of the same. Or, in the register appropriate to the present inquiry: exaggerating the separation of the self. Second error, which follows from the first: exaggerating the alterity of the other. Third error, following from both: exaggerating the difference separating same and other, self and other person. These three errors are responsible for twisting Levinas's language, and Levinas's language is nothing but twisted. To repeat a citation given above regarding "irrelation": "Because the Same signifies totalization and separation, the exteriority of the Other can no longer be expressed in the language of relation."[64] We know Ricoeur's objection because we have already encountered it. Not only reality but (if one can separate these two) language also, and the requirements of meaningful communication (if one can separate these three), will not allow any radical breach: "[M]ust not language contribute its resources of communication, hence of reciprocity . . .?" "In short," he continues, "is it not necessary that a dialogue superpose a relation on the supposedly absolute distance between the separate I and the teaching Other?"[65] The requirements of language and communication, so Ricoeur contends, should force Levinas to abandon his impossible philosophy, just as they force him to unwittingly reverse himself while enunciating it, and force him to end in scandal. But they don't.

What on earth, then, is Levinas up to? Insofar as language and communication, like being, require relation and reciprocity, and no meaning can make sense outside of language and communication, are not Levinas's writings simply babble, meaningless noise, ranting? How can he write book after book, article after article? From whence does Levinas's work derive its force of persuasion for an impossibility, for an impossible break? Ricoeur's answer is direct. What Levinas is up to is "the systematic practice of *excess* in philosophical argumentation." In a word, his writings and their central "break effect," are a product of *hyperbole.*[66] The whole force of Levinas's impossible philosophy comes from the strategic use of hyperbole. I will cite Ricoeur at some length:

It appears to me that the break effect related to this thought of absolute otherness stems from the use of *hyperbole,* one worthy of Cartesian hyperbolic doubt . . . By hyperbole, it must be strongly underscored, we are not to understand a figure of style, a literary trope, but the systematic practice of *excess* in philosophical argumentation. Hyperbole appears in this context as the strategy suited to producing the effect of a break with regard to the idea of exteriority in the sense of absolute otherness.[67]

Levinas's entire philosophy, then, is but an "effect," the product of clever staging, an elaborate show, display, or mask. To take it seriously would be to be duped. Of course Ricoeur's criticism recalls Hegel's 1807 polemic, entitled *"Faith and Knowledge,"* against Jacobi (and Kant and Fichte) whom he accuses of "empty shouting," of wanting "to replace philosophical Ideas with *expressions and words* which are not supposed to give knowledge or understanding."[68] They recall also Parmenides' theogony, his warning against taking the path of non-being: "a way wholly unknowable. For you could not know what is not – that is impossible – nor could you express it."[69] Levinas's talk of the self's extreme passivity, the other's extreme exteriority, and the extreme exigency of their ethical bridge, are hyperboles masquerading as truth, a "strategy suited to producing the effect of a break," but only an *effect,* like a stage effect, one must suppose, since such a break is impossible a priori.

The first and primary hyperbole is that of the radically separ-

---

[66] Ibid., p. 337.    [67] Ibid.
[68] G. W. F. Hegel, *Faith and Knowledge,* trans. Walter Cerf and H. S. Harris (Albany: State University of New York Press, 1977), pp. 119–120.
[69] Translated by John Mansley Robinson, in John Mansley Robinson, *An Introduction to Early Greek Philosophy* (Boston: Houghton Mifflin Co., 1968), p. 110.

ated self. The second and conditioned hyperbole is that of the radically exterior other. "To the hyperbole of separation, on the side of the Same," Ricoeur writes, "replies the hyperbole of epiphany on the side of the Other."[70] The logical motif from chapter seven is here transposed to the level of rhetoric: "Separation has made interiority sterile . . . since the initiative belongs wholly to the Other . . . Hyperbole, in *Totality and Infinity*, culminates in the affirmation that the teaching of the face reestablishes no primacy of relation with respect to the terms."[71] Having begun with a hyperbolic rhetoric masking an impossible irrelation in *Totality and Infinity*, there is nothing to stop, and everything to encourage, an even more excessive, even more hyperbolic rhetoric in *Otherwise than Being or Beyond Essence*. Indeed, since the entire force of Levinas's thought is said to derive from the strategic deployment of excessive language, and since such a deployment would suffer, as does all figurative rhetoric, from diminishing returns over time (analogous to the phenomenon of sensory fatigue), the rhetorical ante must be constantly increased.

"Levinas's *Otherwise than Being*," Ricoeur writes, "employs even greater hyperbole, to the point of paroxysm." The "reversal of the reversal" noted earlier regarding the difference between *Totality and Infinity* and *Otherwise than Being or Beyond Essence*, according to which an initial responsibility extends so far as to become a withdrawal or retraction into the self, is in fact no reversal at all but rather a collapse, exhaustion, or "paroxysm" resulting from over-exaggeration. "As retraction," Ricoeur writes, "the assignment of responsibility adopts the figure of hyperbole, in a range of excess never before attained."[72] Two instances of such excess, carved out of Levinas's complex analyses, are paraded for quick view. Ricoeur points first to the Levinasian self's temporality, its "past more ancient than any past of memory," and second to the excessive imposition of responsibility, "that is justified by no prior commitment."[73] Tempting and instructive as it would be to respond to these particular instances by recontextualizing them, we will instead hold our sights on the broader criticism which makes

[70] *OA*, p. 337.   [71] Ibid., pp. 337–338.   [72] Ibid., p. 338.
[73] Ibid.; Levinas, *Otherwise than Being or Beyond Essence*, p. 102.

them possible.[74] Commenting on the excess of *Otherwise than Being or Beyond Essence*, and linked to the earlier criticism regarding discrimination, Ricoeur continues:

After this, the language becomes more and more excessive: "obsession of the Other," "persecution by the Other," and finally, and especially, "substitution of the I for the Other." Here, the work reaches its paroxysm: "Under accusation by everyone, the responsibility for everyone goes to the point of substitution. A subject is a hostage" (*Otherwise than Being or Beyond Essence*, p. 112). This expression, the most excessive of all, is thrown out here in order to prevent the insidious return of the self-affirmation of some "clandestine and hidden freedom" maintained even within the passivity of the self summoned to responsibility. The paroxysm of the hyperbole seems to me to result from the extreme – even scandalous – hypothesis that the Other is no longer the master of justice here, as is the case in *Totality and Infinity*, but the offender, who, as an offender, no less requires the gesture of pardon and expiation.[75]

Levinas's attempt to exceed the limits of philosophy thus ends in scandal, in the "scandalous hypothesis" of the indistinction of teacher and offender, of good and evil, both taken up by a responsibility so exaggerated that it is no less responsible for the one than for the other, indeed, a responsibility never responsible enough for either. How to respond?

It is obvious that Ricoeur neglects to acknowledge the clear distinction Levinas draws between the morality of the face-to-face, with its excessive obligation and responsibility, and the normative demands of justice, where offenders are punished and teachers rewarded. Without excusing or justifying the distortion of Levinas's thought that this neglect produces, we might say that it is due to Ricoeur's overly narrow focus on Levinas's account of the morality of the face-to-face relation (which in Levinas precedes but also requires justice). But even at the level of morality, without invoking the distinction between morality and justice, the Levinasian response to Ricoeur's charge of verbal excess must be to *affirm* the excessiveness of morality itself while denying its merely

---

[74] For an account of Levinas's theory of time and intersubjectivity, see my *Elevations*, chapter 6, "On Temporality and Time" (pp. 133–161), and chapter 4, "Rosenzweig contra Buber: Personal Pronouns" (pp. 90–111); for an account of the relation of morality to contracts, see chapter 8, "G-d in Levinas: The Justification of Justice and Philosophy" (pp. 173–194).    [75] *OA*, p. 338.

rhetorical or calculative status. That is to say, the Levinasian answer is to reaffirm the deeper significance of what appears to be merely an abuse of language. Shouting, after all, is not always empty for being shouting. When the wounded cry out, are we not there to help them, because their cries are cries of pain?

The excess of morality is no less moral for being excessive. Indeed, the opposite is true: because of its excess morality is moral. The very sign, as it were, of morality is its excess, the surplus of goodness over being, or, from another angle, the deficiency of being in relation to the good. It is to Levinas's credit, then, that his thought does not shrink from this excess, lets no one off this hook. Because the alterity of the other cannot be encompassed by the self, because there is no set of all sets, as it were, no totalization of the infinite, the self cannot – should not – rest in the complacency of self-esteem. Bad conscience, Levinas will say, is better than good conscience. Good conscience is not good enough. One never has done enough, and never will, unto death. "Responsibilities increase," Levinas wrote in *Totality and Infinity*, "to the measure that they are taken on." They *increase*, but they are never finished, never done. Corresponding, as it were, to the excess of morality is the excessive language of ethics.

In discussing the proper function of exaggeration in rhetoric, Richard Weaver in *The Ethics of Rhetoric* (1953) distinguishes between exaggeration as caricature and exaggeration as prophecy. The former, which is disreputable, "mere wantonness," "seizes upon any trait or aspect which could produce titillation and exploits this without conscience."[76] Levinas as much as Ricoeur would disparage such an abuse of language. But there is a proper use of exaggeration, used by the biblical prophets, and used by the true rhetorician, that is, the rhetorician who couples persuasion with truth (the truth which requires persuasion). "The exaggeration which this rhetorician employs," Weaver writes, "is not caricature but prophecy; and it would be a fair formulation to say that true rhetoric is concerned with the potency of things."[77] Although Levinas does not use the Aristotelian language of potency and actuality to express the relation of morality to being, the

[76] Richard Weaver, *The Ethics of Rhetoric* (South Bend, IN: Regnery/Gateway Inc., 1953), p. 19.  [77] Ibid., pp. 19–20.

parallel is clear. The exaggeration Ricoeur points to in Levinas's writings is not, as he would have us believe, empty caricature, mere effect, the result of mistaking the impossible for the possible. It is rather the language proper to ethics, not equivalent to morality or to prophecy, but close to them in wanting to give a genuine account of the imperative exhortative force of the priority of the "ought" over the "is." With Ricoeur's criticism in mind (and without reducing it to a caricature), I will cite one more passage from Weaver:

What he [the literalist] fails to appreciate is that potentiality is a mode of existence, and that all prophecy is about the tendency of things. The discourse of the noble rhetorician, accordingly, will be about real potentiality or possible actuality, whereas that of the mere exaggerator is about unreal potentiality.[78]

Levinas, then, is attempting to articulate neither being nor non-being, nor becoming, but rather a "real potentiality or possible actuality," the priority of goodness over being, and the insatiable desire of the self that responds to this call. To do so he must be a "noble rhetorician," not because moral exigency, and the exhortative language it puts into play, is a gloss on being, a decoration or luxury, but because morality makes greater demands than being, cuts deeper than being.

The whole greatness of Levinas's ethics – and the "glory" of morality itself – is to have put no stop to morality. The human is *not* the measure, but is measured by morality. So what if humanity proves again and again that it is insufficient to the demands of morality, is that the "fault" of morality or of us ourselves? Are we to revise morality to suit our need for satisfaction, for self-satisfaction, for the benefit and consolation of what Ricoeur calls "the good life"? Would that be *truthful*? Who is really more philosophical, more the philosopher: the one who measures morality by the truth of an unsurpassable reflexivity, or the one who measures truth by the radical transcendence of morality? Which moral philosophy is more correct, the one that ends with balanced accounts, with the satisfaction of knowing, with firmness of conviction, or the one that ends in infinite debt, required to give all while more still is demanded, agitated by bad conscience? Ricoeur answers with the former, Levinas with the latter.

To bridge this portion of our exposition, confined to the second subsection of chapter ten, and the next portion, which turns to the third subsection, where Ricoeur's basic effort is to remoralize Heideggerian *Gewissen*, let us note an oddity. At the start of the third subsection Ricoeur excuses and even condones *with regard to Hegel* the "excesses, transgressions, and hyperboles" that just three pages earlier we have seen him condemning with regard to Levinas. Ricoeur acknowledges that in his quarrel with Kant's moral philosophy, Hegel resorts to an "artifice," a "strategy" that "misrepresents Kant," attacking Kant for a non-Kantian " 'postulate' wholly invented" by Hegel.[79] Admitting this, Ricoeur then writes:

> The artifice of the Hegelian construction is not, however, to be deplored; as an artifice it takes its place among the excesses, transgressions, and hyperboles of all sorts that nourish moral reflection, and perhaps, philosophical reflection in general. Moreover, the fact that this is a vision *of the world* that is mobilized by moralism is of the greatest importance.[80]

How peculiar. The very thing for which Levinas is taken to task, namely excess and a strategy of hyperbole, when set in motion by Hegelian moral thought, are all of a sudden the very stuff by which "moral reflection, and perhaps, philosophical reflection in general" are nourished! It seems that Ricoeur thus admits, along with Richard Weaver, precisely what we have been insisting upon in Levinas's defense. It seems that Ricoeur here agrees, contra his own criticism of Levinas, that rhetorical exaggeration is neither camouflage nor adornment, but required by "moral reflection" and "philosophical reflection in general." So be it.

### Conscience

The first pages of the third subsection of chapter ten are given over to a reinterpretation and reappropriation of Hegel's critique of Kantian morality, and Nietzsche's critique of the moral order more generally. Without entering into his argumentation, the

[79] *OA*, p. 343.    [80] Ibid.

innovative outcome of both examinations for Ricoeur is to "to step outside the poisoned circle of 'good' and 'bad' conscience."[81] Heidegger, to whom Ricoeur devotes the remaining pages of his book, is enlisted for the same service. But there is more to Heidegger. In line with the previous analyses of Hegel and Nietzsche, Ricoeur first shows that Heidegger's ontological account of Dasein's conscience also demoralizes conscience. Dasein's authentic self-appropriation guided by conscience is neither "good" nor "bad" in a moral sense. The "voice of conscience" is simply a call from Dasein to itself. It is a call at once "from" Dasein and "above" Dasein insofar as Dasein calls itself to more fully be its own being, to be its own being from the top down, or from the bottom up. While Ricoeur eagerly takes over Heidegger's ontology he is dissatisfied with his demoralization of conscience. To rectify the latter, he assimilates the onto-logical movement of Dasein, *attested* to by conscience, to his own notion of the moral self moved by the desire to live well ("aiming at the 'good life' "). In the following I will review these developments in greater detail before turning to Levinas's role and response.

In its movement to be itself, Dasein cannot be its own basis. This failure results not simply, as has been indicated, because Dasein sporadically "falls" away from its own proper task of being itself into the anonymity of a "they-self" (*das Mann-selbst*), but, more deeply, because even when it strives resolutely to be itself fully, its oncoming death, coupled with its engagement in the larger con-text of a historical being that is always already ongoing, make its task of being itself essentially impossible to complete. Dasein is always too late to fully be itself, even if its highest calling is nonetheless to make the attempt. Heidegger uses the term "guilt" (*Schuld*), as we have seen, to characterize this fundamental failure in Dasein, its inability to be the basis it nonetheless must strive to be. The first point of Ricoeur's *explication de texte*, then, is to show that for Heidegger Dasein's "guilt" is ontological rather than moral.

Ricoeur's second point is to argue, against Heidegger, that having grounded Dasein in the ontological *in this way*, he is incapable of showing how in the depths of its being Dasein *can* be a moral being. The question or "issue" that Dasein is, that to which the "voice" of its conscience calls it, is an exigency to be, not an exigency to be good. "Ontology stands guard on the threshold of ethics . . . Unfortunately," Ricoeur writes, "Heidegger does not show how one could travel the opposite path – from ontology toward ethics."[82]

Before moving to Ricoeur's positive solution to this latter problem, let us remark in passing something nowhere mentioned in chapter ten, namely, that both of Ricoeur's points regarding Heidegger are Levinas's too, and that they were articulated and emphasized by Levinas long before the appearance of *Oneself as Another*. The first point, regarding the amorality of Dasein, is one upon which Ricoeur, Levinas, *and Heidegger* agree. Of course Ricoeur and Levinas evaluate it critically, in contrast to Heidegger, who in the name of ontology (the "ontological difference") insists upon and celebrates the amorality of Dasein's conscience and guilt. Morality is ontic, Heidegger's interest – the interest of "thinking" – is ontological.[83] Regarding Ricoeur's second point, that starting in ontology one cannot get to ethics, this too has been Levinas's longstanding criticism of Heidegger, and more broadly his criticism of the entire Parmidean-Hegelian tradition of philosophy. Despite this double agreement, in his discussion of Heidegger it is only when Ricoeur turns to his own positive alternative, which is at the same time the culmination of *Oneself as Another*, that he invokes Levinas for criticism. I am drawing attention to Ricoeur's unacknowledged adherence to Levinas's reading of Heidegger both to contextualize Ricoeur's criticism of Levinas, and to emphasize one last time the almost inestimable importance Levinas's thought of alterity has for Ricoeur.

Moving to the positive, the following citation succinctly encapsulates what Ricoeur takes to be the innovative outcome and the culminating contribution of his critical reinterpretation and reappropriation of the ontologized conscience of Heideggerian Dasein.

---

[82] Ibid., p. 349.
[83] That the shift from the ontic to the ontological *does* have a moral dimension has been noted by several commentators. See, e.g., Richard A. Cohen, "Dasein's Responsibility for Being," in *Philosophy Today*, vol. 27, no. 4, Winter 1983, pp. 317–325.

To this demoralization of conscience, I would oppose a conception that closely associates the phenomenon of *injunction* to that of *attestation*. Being-enjoined would then constitute the moment of otherness proper to the phenomenon of conscience, in accordance with the metaphor of the voice. Listening to the voice of conscience would signify being-enjoined by the Other. In this way, the rightful place of the notion of *debt* would be acknowledged, a notion that was too hastily ontologized by Heidegger at the expense of the ethical dimension of indebtedness.[84]

Conscience, then, instead of being a listening to the voice of being, is a listening to the voice of the other. In the face of Levinas's thought, this innovation is hardly earth-shattering. Ricoeur's earlier definition of "ethical intention" in chapter seven (*"aiming at the 'good life' with and for others, in just institutions,"*[85]) returns now rewoven into the very fabric of selfhood. "Benevolent spontaneity" is now *attestation*. The social dimension of morality, for which the self's receptivity prepares, is now characterized as *conscience enjoined by the injunction of others* to produce a self with *conviction*. These three terms, attestation, conscience, and conviction, summarize what we earlier called the "Hegelian" movement of Ricoeur's account of moral selfhood: starting with an already moral self, attesting to itself (self-esteem), one then turns to moral injunction as the impact of alterity, as conscience enjoined by others (self-respect), which results in a self holding its moral charge as conviction (justice). Such is the overall result of Ricoeur's studies, and his picture of moral selfhood. With regard, more specifically, to Heidegger's voice of conscience, Ricoeur's innovation, as we see in the citation above, is fairly obvious: the voice of conscience, its injunction, comes not from Dasein but from others. It is here, at such close quarters, as it were, that Ricoeur wants to distance himself from Levinas.

On the last pages of *Oneself as Another* Ricoeur argues against Levinas in two ways. First, it is because Levinas fails to understand social morality within the larger context of attestation-conscience-conviction that he has obscured the proper role of conscience and thus, owing to this obfuscation, mistaken it for the hyperbolic and violent voice of the "master of justice." Ricoeur asks rhetorically: "Is it not because the state of [social] morality has been dissociated

[84] *OA*, p. 351.    [85] Ibid., p. 172.

from the triad . . . then hypostatized because of this dissociation, that the phenomenon of conscience has been correlatively impoverished and that the revealing metaphor of the voice has been eclipsed by the stifling voice of the court?"[86] At bottom, this criticism is but a final restatement, now from the perspective of Ricoeur's conclusions, of his earlier criticism (in the second subsection of both chapters ten and seven) that having exaggerated the initial separation of the self, Levinas has so amplified the alterity of the other, and its moral force, that he has drowned out any appreciation for the self's prior moral capacity to receive moral alterity. By exaggerating the isolation of the self and the alterity of the other, or, to say this in another way, by not recognizing Ricoeur's triad of attestation-conscience-conviction, Levinas has both "impoverished" and "eclipsed" the conscience, and concomitantly turned the other's injunction into a "stifling voice of the court." We have already responded to the basic ground upon which this criticism rests.

Explaining Levinas's alleged error, Ricoeur reinforces his criticism by supplementing it with an aspect borrowed from Jacques Derrida's well-known critical essay of 1964 on Levinas: "Violence and Metaphysics: An Essay on the Thought of Emmanuel Levinas."[87] Following Derrida, Ricoeur attributes the alleged Levinasian "reduction of the voice of conscience to the verdict of the court" to the *violence* inherent in all interactions.

It is because violence taints all the relations of interaction, because of the power-over exerted by an agent on the patient of the action, that the commandment becomes law, and the law, prohibition: "Thou shalt not kill." It is at this point that the sort of short-circuit between conscience and obligation takes place, from which results the reduction of the voice of conscience to the verdict of the court.[88]

Curiously, even ironically, Ricoeur chooses at precisely this juncture to enlist one of Levinas's spiritual teachers, Franz Rosenzweig, using the centerpiece of his *Star of Redemption*, the non-legal non-prohibitory commandment to love, against Levinas, to indicate that commandment need *not* be interpreted

---

[86] Ibid., p. 352.
[87] Jacques Derrida, *Writing and Difference*, trans. Alan Bass (Chicago: University of Chicago Press, 1978), pp. 79–153.    [88] *OA*, p. 351.

as law and prohibition. The irony is that this is exactly Levinas's point, indeed the point we raised against Ricoeur's earlier insistence on the normative character of social morality.

Because the face of the other is for Levinas command without law he opposes Kant, and hence opposes Ricoeur's earlier efforts, in chapter seven, to conflate alterity and normativity. Here, at the end of chapter ten, at the conclusion of *Oneself as Another*, it is again exactly because the face of the other commands ("Thou shalt not kill") *without* making this command a law, that Levinas argues for the priority of obligation over what Ricoeur now identifies as conscience. There is thus no "short-circuit between conscience and obligation," as Ricoeur suggests, but rather an absolute priority given to an obligating other who evinces responsibilities in the self, indeed, who evinces a responsible self. And it is because the self made responsible can never be responsive enough, as we have seen, that Levinas will not hesitate to support "bad" conscience (the conscience that has never done enough) over the complacency of "good" conscience.[89] The latter, which Levinas opposes, is precisely what Ricoeur supports in giving primacy to self-esteem and "the optative of living well."[90] This is why Levinas and Ricoeur are so far apart when it comes to the fundamentals of their respective ethical theories. Violence does not reduce Levinasian command to law. Indeed, the break which the alterity of the other effects upon the self is only violent from the point of view of the refusal of a *conatus* absorbed with itself, with its own possibilities, however historically rooted. For the moral self, opened up for-the-other, such a break and its "violence" is precisely a *pacific* call to responsibility from an unsurpassable height. If this is violence (which it is not) it is certainly not violation. It is, in any event, preferable to the indifference of complacency.

Unlike the first criticism in subsection three, Ricoeur's second and final criticism, found on the very last pages of *Oneself as Another*, is new – but at the same time it seems surprisingly weak. Levinas is accused of having reduced the multiple senses Ricoeur gives to conscience as the "voice of the other" to one sense: the otherness

[89] See Emmanuel Levinas, "Bad Conscience and the Inexorable," trans. Richard A. Cohen, in Richard A. Cohen, ed., *Face to Face with Levinas* (Albany: State University of New York Press, 1986), pp. 35–40.     [90] *OA*, p. 352.

of other persons. Ricoeur first criticizes Freud for reducing conscience by means of an "internalization of ancestral voices." He
then criticizes Levinas, on the other hand, for an externalization of
conscience, for a "reduction, which seems to me to result," he
writes, "from the work of Emmanuel Levinas as a whole, of the
otherness of conscience to the otherness of other people."[91] "The
model of all otherness is the other person" – such is Ricoeur's final
criticism of Levinas.

Though Ricoeur's "advance" over Heidegger was to treat the
voice of conscience not as Dasein's own voice but as the voice of
the other, in apparent contrast to Levinas, he insists upon "a
certain equivocalness" regarding the alterity of the other persons
who are the source of the injunction of conscience. "The ultimate
equivocalness with respect to the status of the Other in the phenomenon of conscience," Ricoeur writes, "is perhaps what needs
to be preserved in the final analysis." First there is a large equivocation between an "anthropological reading" and a "theological
reading."[92] Second, in addition to preserving the larger equivocation between anthropological and theological readings of conscience, Ricoeur wants also to preserve equivocations within each
category. On the side of the anthropological, Ricoeur points to the
difference between grasping the voice of conscience as "parental
and ancestral figures,"[93] in one's head, as it were, and "another
person whom I can look in the face or who can stare at me,"[94] in
the flesh. On the side of the theological, he points to the difference
between "God – living God, absent God – or an empty place," as
sources of injunction.[95] Levinas's fault, then, is to have made the
living person in the flesh, within the anthropological reading,
"[t]he model of all otherness."

For Levinas, however, it is not a matter of reducing different
figures of alterity to one figure. Rather, to say it again, the issue is
to grasp the alterity that makes any and all figures of alterity other.
And here Levinas would insist upon the priority of the alterity and
injunctive force of the flesh and blood other. A "sculpted arm by
Rodin," as Levinas puts it, can inspire the self to its moral obligations, true, but it can do so only because of the originary priority of

---

[91] Ibid., p. 354.    [92] Ibid., p. 353.    [93] Ibid.    [94] Ibid., p. 355.    [95] Ibid.

the flesh and blood other.[96] Regarding the anthropological read-ings, then, it seems that there can be no question that unless one is to sink into infinite regress (an error, by the way, for which Ricoeur faults Freud), then the injunctive force of "parental and ancestral figures" must of necessity be modeled on the injunctive force of the alterity of living persons "whom I can look in the face or who can stare at me," as Ricoeur puts it. All internalized exterior figures, that is to say, were once – whether developmentally or historically, whether fully or partially – *external* exterior figures. An internalized parental or ancestral figure carries injunctive force, furthermore, precisely because one knows of the injunctive force of real living parents and progenitors, or, more broadly, of real living others. Here again we wonder why Ricoeur neglects part four of *Totality and Infinity*. Regarding equivocations within a "theological read-ing," the injunctive force of God, or "the absent God – or an empty place," Ricoeur is right: Levinas does indeed insist that for an "adult religion" relationship with God occurs *through* moral relations with others. Not only the desire for goodness elicited by the other, but the demand for justice elicited by others, are mani-festations of God's presence – and absence – in history. "[T]he universality of the Divine," Levinas writes, "exists only in the form in which it is fulfilled in relations between humans."[97] The moral reconditioning of the self, leading to the demand for redemptive justice for all humankind, is the way, as Levinas expresses this movement, "God comes to the idea." Doctrinal positions within theological disputes have no dogmatic authority when it comes to God's injunctive force. "There can be no 'knowledge' of God," Levinas writes, "separated from the relationship with men."[98] It can be said unequivocally, regarding the larger distinction be-tween the theological and the anthropological, that Levinas's thought has no room for moral injunctions coming to conscience

---

[96] Emmanuel Levinas, *Entre Nous*, trans. Michael B. Smith and Barbara Harshav (New York: Columbia University Press, 1998), p. 232. Levinas also writes: "There are different ways of being a face. Without mouth, eyes or nose, an arm or a hand by Rodin is already a face." Emmanuel Levinas, "On Obliteration," trans. Richard A. Cohen, in *Art & Text* 33 (Winter 1989), p. 38.

[97] Levinas, *Difficult Freedom*, trans. Séan Hand (Baltimore: Johns Hopkins University Press, 1990), p. 137.

[98] Levinas, *Totality and Infinity*, p. 79.

directly from God, unmediated by a human and humane sociality. To require such mediation does not, however, reduce God to humanity: "The Other is not the incarnation of God, but precisely by his face, in which he is disincarnate, is the manifestation of the height in which God is revealed."[99]

If Ricoeur's stand regarding the relation between self and God is otherwise, and it is not at all certain in *Oneself as Another* where Ricoeur stands on his own concluding challenge to Levinas,[100] then Levinas's response would be to unequivocally reject that stand as idolatry. He would point to all the horrors of Western history, especially in the twentieth century, that stem from a faith alleged to be directly and unilaterally ordered by God. "The comprehension of God taken as a participation in his sacred life, an allegedly direct comprehension," Levinas will insist, "is impossible, because participation is a denial of the divine, and because nothing is more direct than the face to face, which is straightforwardness itself."[101] What, then, of the God who exceeds morality, Kierkegaard's God who "suspends the ethical"? Levinas rejects Kierkegaard's famous and influential interpretation of the story of Abraham's near sacrifice of Isaac. "Perhaps," Levinas responds, "Abraham's ear for hearing the voice that brought him back to the ethical order was the highest moment of this drama."[102]

[99] Ibid.
[100] In the final section of the introductory chapter of *Oneself as Another* (pp. 23–25), Ricoeur explains why he refrains from including his two concluding Gifford Lectures in the book: "I have presented to my readers arguments alone, which do not assume any commitment from the reader to reject, accept, or suspend anything with regard to biblical faith. It will be observed that this asceticism of the argument . . . leads to a type of philosophy from which the actual mention of God is absent and in which the question of God, as a philosophical question, itself remains in a suspension that could be called agnostic, as the final lines of the tenth study will attest" (p. 24). In contrast, the unity of Levinas's philosophy, which includes God, disputes the necessity for Ricoeur's asceticism and agnosticism.
[101] Levinas, *Totality and Infinity*, p. 78.
[102] Levinas, "Kierkegaard: Existence and Ethics," in Emmanuel Levinas, *Proper Names*, trans. Michael B. Smith (Stanford: Stanford University Press, 1996), p. 74.

# *In-conclusion*

The task is not yours to complete; neither are you free to leave it off.

Rabbi Tarfon, *Wisdom of the Fathers (Tractate Pirke Avot)*,

ch. 2, v. 21

The word by way of preface which seeks to break through the screen stretched between the author and the reader by the book itself does not give itself out as a word of honor. But it belongs to the very essence of language, which consists in continually undoing its phrase by the foreword or the exegesis, in unsaying the said, in attempting to restate without ceremonies what has already been ill understood in the inevitable ceremonial in which the said delights.

Levinas, "Preface," *Totality and Infinity*

Because philosophy – like life – must be exegetical and ethical does not mean that it is not also critical, argumentative, analytical, logical, and reflective. Rather, it means that these approaches, all crucial to philosophical thought concerned with truth, find their ultimate context – their ultimate significance – in the unsurpassable yet non-encompassable encounter of one human being with another, and with all others, and hence in the overriding exigencies of kindness and fairness. This does not, as I have argued in all the chapters of this book, mean that philosophy is reduced to the relativism of psychology, sociology or history, or to that of decisionism, will to power or the play of semantic polysemy. Rather and precisely, it means that thinking – insight, illumination, vision, intuition – serves a transcendence whose significance is from the first ethical and as such escapes a pure epistemology.

That thought does not contain itself even thinking can recognize. But that the excess of this non-containment is the very surplus of ethics, the overwhelming immediacy and height of obligations and responsibilities, this thinking has always found difficult to acknowledge. Thinking, however, is not its own end, and neither is its lack of end an end in itself. Rather, thinking always already serves humankind. To be sure, its service can be destruction, as when wrapped up in itself it forgets or refuses, and defaces the face of the other. But it can also be beneficent, constructive, when it recognizes its seeking as part of a larger impetus serving others, alleviating suffering, and in this way facing up to mortality, not its own but the other's.

### ALTERITY IS NOT ABSTRACT

In articles and conversations, and at philosophy conferences, I have often heard Levinas's notion of "otherness" characterized as and derided for being abstract and hence empty. If "one does not know the color of the other's eyes," so it is said, then in what sense is the alterity of the other a face? If the alterity of the face is not visible, says another critic, then what is it? Of course academic philosophers are rightly trained to be critical – but not facile. This line of thinking, too clever by far, then leads to the elaboration of various logical permutations typical of a purely discursive philosophy more sophisticated than genuine. To respect the absoluteness of the alterity central to Levinas's thought, so it goes, one must disagree with him. Hence one must be non-Levinasian. Hence one must not be ethical. Levinas as authority for evil! Such a manner of thinking, silly and deliberately lost, so it seems, in the realm of the mind, reminds us more of Sextus Empiricus or Nietzsche than of philosophy, the love of wisdom. Having found Nietzsche, one must indeed lose him – because Nietzschean thought is a thought beholden to the will, hence beholden to domination, either master or slave, and master only when solitary. Or critics will somehow – how? – strip Levinasian alterity of its ethical character. Deprived in this way, it becomes a pure excess, so pure as to authorize any and all intellectual play, whether semantic, structural or I know not what, in a frenzy of nothingness, all sound and fury. Such

abstract freedom authorizes anything – anything *except* the
obligations and responsibilities of ethics. Perhaps such intellectual
lucubration is liberating or fun, or draws attention, but it is
anything but Levinas.

The truth is otherwise. The truth is that nothing is more concrete in Levinas's thought than its central and metaphysical notion
of alterity. The excess that cannot be contained by thought is the
moral alterity of the other person, an alterity constituted by
the mortality of the other. But it is not simply "constituted" by the
other's mortality. Ethical alterity, as Levinas understands it, is
concretized in the other's mortality. That is to say, it is concretized, first, by the inexorable fact that the other faces death,
and hence is subject to suffering, and, second, by the shameful
possibility that I am able, that I have a power that can murder the
other. It is thus that the alterity of the other is an excess that
imposes itself on the self – on me – as moral obligation and
responsibility, that is to say, as moral imperative. Alterity, mortality, and morality therefore all arise together. To strip off one
dimension or another is to have misunderstood Levinas. Alterity
"*par excellence*," as Levinas might say, is nothing other than moral
imposition in the face of the other's mortality. That the other dies,
that the other's death, including the other's suffering, concerns
me, that it concerns me more than my own concerns with myself,
my own powers, and my own mortality – this lies at the heart of
Levinasian thought and is the determinate sense of an alterity that
might otherwise, mistakenly, be interpreted as an abstract otherness. Indeed, nothing is less abstract. Or, to say this positively,
nothing is more concrete, more immediate, more pressing, more
urgent. It is this precisely that is Levinas's double point: ethics
is more urgent than ontology, and nothing is more urgent
than ethics. As we saw in chapters 6 and 7, it is precisely under
the moral pressure or imperative of this most concrete and
pressing alterity that the human psyche is constituted, in its very
sensibility, as singular, irreplaceable, "maternal," the one-for-the-
other. In the same way, under the same pressure, but including all
others, the humanity or the humanism of the human, the one-for-
all-others, is constituted. This is not, to be sure, a Husserlian
constitution. It is not the constitution of sense by consciousness,

but the disruption – for better – of self-constituting consciousness by the other.

In this regard, we recall Levinas's promise very early in the development of his own thought, on the opening page of *Time and the Other*: "to deepen the notion of solitude and to consider the opportunities that time offers to solitude."[1] The deeper the solitude, the deeper the isolation, the greater the transcendence. Atheism as a condition for religion! Because time is the very structure of subjectivity, because the time of "dia-chrony" disrupts the inner-time of temporality, this is another way of seeing that nothing is deeper, nothing more self, as it were, than the self commanded by the other. I am my brother's keeper – this is who or what the I is, responsibility to its core. The alterity of the other, in other words, is an opportunity to be oneself truly – that is to say, an opportunity to act morally in view of the other's suffering and mortality, and hence for the sake of the other's material and spiritual requirements prior to one's own. It is feeding the other "bread from my own mouth," for bread is always from my own mouth, because I, too, am hungry, and I, too, enjoy bread.

Why is the priority of the other a scandal for thought? Of course, thought would rather think itself, just as instinct and will would rather serve and preserve themselves. Whatever "I will," it is always the "I" that wills, always "I" who will. Is this not precisely also the celebrated structure of idealist thought: whatever "I think," it is always the "I" – whether transcendental and absolute or personal and relative – that thinks? One thinks of Husserl's claim that all consciousness is intentional. Of course, too, thought finds all "immediacy" intolerable, but it conflates all "givens" into the epistemological immediacy against which it rightly rebels. The very structure of thought appears as a refusal to be compelled by anything other than thought – this is the lesson of Hegel's philosophy. Schopenhauer and Nietzsche understood this lesson so well that they conflated thinking with willing. But the alterity of the other is not an epistemological compulsion. Rather, it is moral imperative, the call to be kind and to be fair, the twin calls of

---

[1] Levinas, *Time and the Other* [*and Additional Essays*], trans. Richard A. Cohen (Pittsburgh: Duquesne University Press, 1987), p. 39.

morality and justice. Not a scandal for thought, but rather a higher vocation. Perhaps it is this higher vocation that Hans Jonas has sought, in his book *The Imperative of Responsibility: In Search of an Ethics for the Technological Age*,[2] when he writes that science must be tempered by a new sense of responsibility whose "heart is the veneration for the image of man, turning into trembling concern for its vulnerability."[3]

## MORE THAN SCIENCE

But might not one be tempted to say that genuine science – modern science in contrast to philosophical idealism – has already understood all this?[4] And if it has, why make such an extended philosophical fuss about alterity when everything Levinas proposes already appears within science? Is it not the case, contrary to Levinas, that modern science, because it is a doubting and self-correcting intellectual enterprise, is already fully cognizant of the "disorder" that Levinas insists on naming "ethics"? Does not science already contain within itself, with no prodding from an "otherwise than being or beyond essence," a sufficiently ethical dimension? Thus science, properly understood, would have no need for a Levinasian "critique" or a transcendental[5] supplement. Levinas, according to this view, is blind to this possibility because his account of science is artificial and abstract, a tilting at windmills. Science is already sufficiently aware of internal difficulties and disturbances, indeed haunted with doubt about truth.

[2] Hans Jonas, *The Imperative of Responsibility: In Search of an Ethics for the Technological Age*, trans. Hans Jonas (Chicago: University of Chicago Press, 1984).   [3] Ibid., p. 201.

[4] Much of the present section was stimulated by the critical charges against Levinas made in the name of science by Professor Steven Fleishman (George Washington University, Washington, DC), at a session of the American Philosophical Association meeting held in Chicago on 7 May 1998, devoted to my earlier book, *Elevations*. The next section, too, on religion, was in some part stimulated by the more positive comments made by Professor James B. Sauer (St. Mary's University, San Antonio, Texas) at the same session. Their comments and my response can be found in *Philosophy in the Contemporary World*, vol. 4, no. 4, Winter 1998, pp. 1–25.

[5] I use the term "transcendental" here in the sense developed by Theodore De Boer in his superb book on Levinas, *The Rationality of Transcendence: Studies in the Philosophy of Emmanuel Levinas* (Amsterdam: J. C. Gieben, 1997). In chapter one (pp. 1–32), entitled "An Ethical Transcendental Philosophy," De Boer writes: "Dialogue is the transcendental framework for the intentional relation to the world" (p. 2). (This chapter also appeared in Richard A. Cohen, ed., *Face to Face with Levinas* (Albany: State University of New York Press, 1986), pp. 83–115.)

Here the defender of science points to "the timidity, hesitancy, anxiety, doubt, self-depreciation, cyncism, irony, suffering, yearning for love which are all also part of the Greek view."[6] Levinasian thought would have misunderstood the fact that for science, far from being the defender of totality, "[e]verything is subject to doubt." Science and its assumptions "are subject to constant criticism, to revision, to the call for more or better justification." My answer to this line of thought is that these criticisms have themselves missed the entire point of the Levinasian critique.

Levinas is quite aware of the self-corrective character of modern science. He is acutely aware that for modern science "everything is subject to doubt" – words almost precisely spoken by Rosenzweig. But Levinas's critique is not simply epistemological. It is ethical. Unlike previous philosophical criticisms of epistemology – that is to say, criticisms that remain within science but want to improve science through a "call for more or better justification" – Levinas is arguing that epistemology as such, in its entirety, including its inherent problems, difficulties, disturbances, anomalies, and so on, including its need for constant revision, including especially its doubts, is transcended by ethics. While within science "everything is subject to doubt," science as a whole is – and "ought" to be – guided by an ethical dimension that exceeds, in a manner unacknowledged by scientism, the "everything" of science. For instance (which is in truth not simply an "instance"), the ethical command "Thou shalt not murder" is not subject to doubt. Whether this or that particular deed qualifies as an instance of murder or, say, is an instance of self-defense or killing sanctioned by war, must indeed be debated. But that murder is evil, that murder is forbidden – this is not subject to doubt. Or, rather, if it is subject to doubt then all of ethics is subject to doubt. To point to this sort of indubitability, one that is not a function of theory, is to indicate the depth of the struggle between science (and aesthetics) and ethics, a struggle for priority. As we saw in chapter 4, science (or ontology) and ethics approach reality from entirely different angles. To subject everything to doubt is not at all the same thing, then, as breaching the totality of science. It is rather and precisely to reinforce it.

---

[6] All non-referenced citations are from Fleishman's comments, cited in n. 4 above.

The disturbances that are legitimized by the ongoing activity of science, and which are cited as evidence for an already operative Levinasian type of ethics, are in truth manifestations of epistemological rather than ethical challenges. Levinas's whole point, however, is that despite being self-corrective, and despite being self-reflectively aware of being self-corrective, science is not by itself the only account of the whole. The good cannot be reduced to the true, to knowledge. Nor can it be reduced to an epistemological "problem," that is, a problem for epistemology to solve. What Levinas has shown is that the good – goodness, kindness, compassion – is more immediate, more important, more pressing, a greater exigency, than knowledge. So, too, justice is a far greater demand than the demand for epistemological justification. Goodness commands humanity otherwise than do the linked ontological and epistemological stringencies of scientific inquiry, difficult and admirable though that may be, including its many and continuing epistemological challenges. The basic distinction upon which philosophy – search for truth, love of wisdom – hinges is not between appearance and reality, as the philosophy of science has hitherto argued, but rather between sincerity and lie, the face-to-face relation between self and other which "is" the non-encompassable, non-thematizable, ethical non-context of all thought and all action. Ethics is the "set of all sets," as it were, which is not and cannot be contained within itself. It is not that Levinas wants science to be good, as if this involved the sacrifice of truth. Science demands objectivity. It is rather that for science to be science, for objectivity to be objective, an unacknowledged reliance on the ethics and justice constitutive of inter-subjective relations is already at work. Science presupposes the good, even if it does not always acknowledge this presupposition, even if in its hubris it proposes to oppose this presupposition or pretend to eliminate it. Levinasian thought, however, points to the ethical inspiration – the ethical transcendence – at the root of all human endeavors, including science.

What transcends thought, Levinas teaches, is not thought, or more thought, but goodness. Whether one accepts Hegel's awkward formulations or those of other more modest philosophers of science, it is clear that thought by itself never transcends thought, even if thought remains forever incomplete and self-correcting (or, as one often hears today, incomplete and self-destroying), an unending progressive (or deconstructive) task.

But the case must not be overstated. It seems to me that the epistemological difficulties invoked above do reveal traces of the fundamentally ethical inter-subjectivity that exceeds and sustains science. Scientific objectivity is not a robotics. Creativity, for instance, is not a "science," cannot be manufactured. And verification, at the heart of objectivity, requires a community of trustworthy inquirers. To say that science relies upon and is sustained by an ethical dimension, as I am saying, in no way reduces science to a mere subjectivism. Here I refer to Levinas's analogical ("as if") argument in chapter five of *Otherwise than Being or Beyond Essence*, in the penultimate concluding section entitled "Skepticism and Reason."[7] Levinas does not argue that skepticism refutes science. Science refutes skepticism. Nor does he argue that science incorporates skepticism. Science would not be possible if skepticism were true (the latter idea: "if skepticism were true," is already self-refuting). Rather, he argues that the irrepressibility of skepticism, its ever renewed challenge to the ever proven universal authority of science, "signifies" the irrepressibility of an ethical humanity, the individual in his or her unique singularity, outside the system, one person – the one and only person – responsible for another. Skepticism is not and cannot be true, of course, but its protest reveals a human dimension to thought. Levinas writes: "It is as though skepticism were sensitive to the difference between my exposure without reserve to the other, which is saying [i.e., ethics], and the exposition or statement of the said in its equilibrium and justice."[8]

I think, too, regarding the inner workings of science, that the peculiarities that have always haunted the notion of "infinity," from Zeno onwards, even in its most mathematical formulations,

---

[7] Emmanuel Levinas, *Otherwise than Being or Beyond Essence*, trans. Alphonso Lingis (The Hague: Martinus Nijhoff, 1981), pp. 165–171. For an interesting reading of this section, see also Robert Bernasconi's article, "Skepticism in the Face of Philosophy," in *Re-Reading Levinas*, pp. 149–161. Bernasconi sees in Levinas's text the argument that it is Derrida's deconstruction – which must also be a deconstruction of deconstruction – that is a (self-refuting) skepticism, an "argument" to which Derrida has never responded.

[8] Levinas, *Otherwise than Being or Beyond Essence*, p. 168.

indicate another tracing of the ethical dimension bursting through a pretended scientific totality.[9] Infinity, even in its most mathematical formulations, even confined to a calculus, resists containment. Of course skepticism cannot and should not overthrow knowledge. But the inner impulse of knowledge to totality, its *conatus essendi*, is not properly tempered by its own self-correction, or the admission of doubt – these are its own techniques, its own game, as it were. Rather, what tempers knowledge, or what *should* temper knowledge, giving it its *raison d'être*, is the commanding height of the face of the other, the imposition of an ethical demand more demanding than the demands of knowledge, and a justice more stringent than epistemological justification.

It is important to note that Levinasian thought is not against science. Quite the reverse is true. Though it is neither equivalent to science nor reducible to the ongoing refinements of science, ethics not only provides a reason and justification for science, but because it does provide a reason and justification it also *requires* science. Unlike Heidegger who, in his attack on "technology" as the closure of the revelation of being, seems to find no positive place for science, Levinas not only finds a place for science, but argues that ethics both justifies and demands science. As I argued in chapter eight of *Elevations*,[10] one of the great virtues of Levinasian thought is that it provides a justification for science and philosophy. This was the final question whose answer eluded Nietzsche: Why knowledge?

The exigencies of ethics, the non-encompassable face-to-face relation, the priority of the other, of "saying" over the "said," are both more important than the exigencies of knowledge and are required for knowledge to be knowledge. Ethics is the "ground," as it were, for the constitution of that community and those

---

[9] In a thought-provoking exposition, Norbert Samuelson, in his *An Introduction to Modern Jewish Philosophy* (Albany: State University of New York Press, 1989), pp. 162–176, will argue something similar regarding Hermann Cohen's mathematical defense of the "infinitesimal" to explain differential calculus, against Karl Weierstrass's alternative explanation. Samuelson also shows how, via the idea of an asymptote (the moral idea *as* an asymptote), Cohen's defense of the infinitesimal plays a central role in his ethical-philosophical thought.

[10] Cohen, "God in Levinas: The Justification of Justice and Philosophy," in Richard A. Cohen, *Elevations: The Height of the Good in Rosenzweig and Levinas* (Chicago: University of Chicago Press, 1994), pp. 173–194.

communications of knowers that put the imprimatur of truth on possible knowledge. But there is another aspect to the relation between ethics and science. Morality, by itself, is itself inadequate, ethically inadequate, for a moral humanity. The other the moral agent faces is also other to others not faced. Because of these others, whom Levinas will call "the third," the asymmetry or inequality of morality, the priority of the other over the self, gives rise to the new demand for justice, for the equal treatment of all. But the equality required by justice, in turn, is not possible without measure and calculation – that is to say, without the thematic rationality proper to science and technology, or to philosophy as epistemology. These are required to produce the goods to feed, clothe, and shelter the destitute, as well as to distribute those goods fairly and equitably. In falling short of morality, Nietzsche correctly saw that he must also fall short of knowledge, insofar as truth and lie could no longer be distinguished. Levinas, in contrast, who makes no such radical break with morality and moral tradition, is able to ground science's claim to truth in the deeper claims of morality, and then, derived from the exigencies of morality itself, to uncover the links binding knowledge to morality and justice.

Levinas's criticism of science is only – but this is a very great thing – a criticism of its tendency toward self-absorption, toward scientism, toward science taking itself, including its difficulties, to be the whole story, the only truth, the be-all and end-all. It is the hubris of science and not science that Levinas attacks. In this he is radically anti-Spinozist. Truth and meaning are inextricably linked; the "said" is not only first a "saying," saying comes first; the said derives its *raison d'être* from saying. Thus, to invoke scientific doubts in no way undermines scientific hubris. Quite the reverse: self-correcting science is far more hegemonic and far more potentially close-minded in its alleged open-mindedness than a static and therefore brittle science could ever be. For this reason, too, the science of phenomenology, because its range is so broad, indeed because it pretends to comprehensiveness, contains an even more powerful impulse to close-mindedness in its alleged open-mindedness. It is not odd, then, or paradoxical, that those who claim to be the most open-minded, the most "enlightened," are all too often the most close-minded. To limit humanity to the truths of a scientific openness upon the true is to take the very humanity out of the human. The "philosophy of mind," for instance, with its concern to *prove* the existence of other minds, for all its subtlety, indeed in large measure because of its subtlety, can never figure out what ethics knows from the very start. Not only are there others, who in their mortality are far more than just minds, but they come first. The mind can perhaps prove the existence of other minds, but humans are constituted in their humanity, in their mortality, in their flesh and blood, in their letters and spirit, across the excessive elevation of an ethical transcendence. Not "other minds," mind you, but the "face" of the other, and the faces of all others.

### ETHICS, RELIGION, AND EXEGESIS

In conclusion I would like to return again to the question of religion, the religious dimension of Levinas's ethical-exegetical metaphysics. In the second subsection of *Totality and Infinity*, Levinas proposed "to call 'religion' the bond that is established between the same and the other without constituting a totality."[11] In the present book we have presented this "bond" as the priority and imperative ethical force of the face-to-face relation, paying special care to show that the philosophical manner in which a proper appreciation for this morally imperative priority is accomplished is through ethical exegesis – commentary upon commentary. Through exegesis a care is taken for both semiotic and semantic dimensions of intelligibility without sacrificing the more serious and underlying moral and juridical sources of these significations. In *Otherwise than Being or Beyond Essence* and in his later writings, Levinas came to understand God in terms of the human demand for justice, a demand that "thanks to God" includes me as well as all others. Nevertheless, in all of these readings Levinas inextricably links religion and justice by invoking the ab-soluteness of an imperative transcendence. But, let us ask, has he thereby reduced religion to ethics? Is his yet another voice in the modern rationalist and reformist Enlightenment of Judaism? I think not.

[11] Emmanuel Levinas, *Totality and Infinity*, trans. Alphonso Lingis (Pittsburgh: Duquesne University Press, 1964), p. 40.

The issue I am raising here, then, must deal with the significance of religion as personal and social prayer, and as personal and social ritual. In the early Enlightenment period reformers considered these dimensions – prayer and ritual – as merely parochial, historical or "positive" forms, and rejected them in favor of purely rational, "natural" (in the sense that reason was considered natural) and universal forms of religion. The former could not enter into a universal discourse without violence, and hence were rejected as roadblocks to the universal peace and justice – good will to all – whose promotion was said to be the inner truth, indeed the "messianic" truth of Judaism. Of course, such an Enlightenment approach, even when it was sympathetic with religion (and it often was not), was unable to rationally defend an adherent's loyalty to his or her particular religious tradition. This was especially problematic for Judaism insofar as Christianity claimed to be the universal fulfillment of Judaism's narrowly particular and nationalist limitations.

It is true that Levinas for the most part eschews invoking the name of God, or speaking about God directly. He certainly never relies on the Bible or any sacred literature as "proof" text. Exegesis is not authoritarianism. This is so because when he speaks about ethics and justice he *is* speaking about God. Morality and justice are the passage of a divine transcendence through the world. Levinas will even call this passage "holiness" or "sanctity." But this use of religious language is precisely what provokes our question. Levinas was not only, in his personal life, a practicing traditional Jew ("keeping Shabbat," adhering to kosher dietary rules, saying the required daily prayers, etc.), but in his writings – both philosophical and "confessional," though I have throughout been making the case that this "distinction" is not a separation – he has only had the most positive things to say about all the most particular dimensions of Judaism, that is to say, about prayer and ritual. The central thesis of the present book – that the priority of ethics over ontology is manifest in a philosophic understanding best characterized as ethical exegesis rather than by an objectivist or critical science or a subjectivist or playful relativism – is yet another way of endorsing what the Enlightenment rejected. Exegesis embraces all that the Enlightenment rejected under the label

"positive," without, for all that, embracing all that the Enlightenment rejected as "superstition," or embracing anything of what
Levinas calls "mythology." But does exegesis accomplish its inclus-
iveness at the cost of bad faith, using religious language and
referring to religious behaviors only to reduce them to morality
and justice? Is religion, then, but an expendable stage prop for
Levinas, as it certainly was for Spinoza?

Let us pursue this question by insisting on asking about the
status of "God talk." What is the proper role or meaning of
personal prayer? What is the proper role or meaning of religious
rituals? By "proper" I mean that which would be consistent with
the high demands of Levinas's ethical metaphysics, and at the
same time retain a "residue" of sense, as it were, an inherent and
irreducible integrity. Surely, at least at first glance, prayer and
ritual are not components of a moral relation to the other who
faces, a moral relation to those flesh and blood persons who suffer
and die. One saves a drowning person, not a drowning Jew,
Muslim, Hindu or Christian. And one saves that person as a
person, again, not as a Jew, Muslim, Hindu or Christian. But at
the same time, the drowning person and the one who rescues is no
less a Jew, Muslim, Hindu or Christian, at the very same time! Are
prayer and rituals, then, and all the particularities that distinguish
one positive religion from another, nothing more than a distrac-
tion and occultation of the naked directness of the face-to-face
relation, diverting the human from its proper humanism? Of
course, the central thesis of the present book has been precisely to
argue that ethical exegesis – as practiced by Levinas, and as
practiced by the rabbis of the Talmud, according to Levinas's
vision – is precisely the middle path avoiding the *fronte praecipitium*
of an abstract universalism, the critical rationalization of religion,
and the *tergo lui* of an opaque particularism, the closed cult.[12]

Levinas's position regarding the opacity of myth is perfectly

---

[12] This is also the position of the nineteenth-century rabbi and kabbalist of Livorno, Italy,
Elijah Benamozegh, who has been mentioned earlier in the present work, as articulated
in his important *opus*, *Israel and Humanity*, trans. Maxwell Luria (New York: Paulist Press,
1994), a book I cannot recommend too highly. This book is another extended instance of
the exegesis that Levinas practices. It reveals a universal human significance in the most
particularist Jewish practices. Though Benamozegh was in fact quite influential, his
name is still almost unknown.

clear, as we have shown in chapter 7 of this book. Philosophy as wisdom and Judaism as ethical monotheism both oppose myth. Both oppose myth by loving truth associated with virtue, by articulating and supporting a sober mentality, a clearheadedness, an ethical alertness anathema to any submergence, participation, or intoxication in mythic consciousness. In contrast to the high demands of philosophy and Judaism, the allure of myth represents a violence, the return to an animal vitality that violates the moral stature, the humanity of the human, the moral "election" of the singular one. In a word, myth is irresponsible. But religion, in contrast to philosophy, also supports prayer and ritual. Indeed, the world's religions are far more easily distinguished from one another in terms of their differences in prayer and ritual than regarding differences in basic moral tenets (e.g., no murder, lying, stealing, coveting). Be that as it may, philosophy, struggling against the violence and mendacity promoted by opinion and myth, proposed an alternative mode of life in the mind's lucidity, in a life of questioning, in knowledge and rationality, in self-justifying thought. Levinas, in the name of philosophy, insists that the source of such lucidity is found in the wakefulness, sobriety, and vigilance of ethics. The source of philosophy would be found in the obligations and responsibilities of the face-to-face relation and in the call to justice that arises as a further demand of this very relation. But religion, beyond philosophy, also insists on putting the individual in a prayerful and ritual relationship with God. Its proper dimension is the holy, and not only the ethical, or knowledge bound by virtue, or, far less, knowledge infatuated with itself.

Why, then, since he in no way rejects "positive" religion, does Levinas focus so exclusively on the ethical when he speaks of religion? This question does not challenge the ethical significance of ritual and prayer, but wonders about residues, about the dimension of religion that seems to exceed ethical exposition. Despite his clear critique of mythology, is Levinas perhaps fearful that the demands of the holy might exceed those of the ethical? Is he not concerned with, or at least aware of, what struck Kierkegaard as so central to becoming a religious person – which he explained at great length in a book he so appropriately entitled *Fear and Trembling* – namely, that the demands of holiness might actually require

unethical behavior, including murder, from the individual? For
Levinas such a thought would indeed invoke a fear and trembling,
but not of the kind envisioned by Kierkegaard. For Levinas the
fear would be precisely to succumb to such excess, and in this way
to *lose* one's religious way.

No doubt the demands of holiness are not equivalent to the
demands of morality and justice, or else one could speak sufficiently of a "secular" rather than a "biblical" humanism. But can the
demands of holiness override morality and justice? Could the holy
be holy if it were immoral? Levinas will categorically reject this
possibility, and his exegesis is often designed to show why his
rejection lies in the mainstream of rabbinical thought too. It is
fascinating, it seems to me, that the one time Levinas speaks of the
awe-inspiring story of Abraham's near sacrifice of Isaac[13] – the
story central to Kierkegaard's interpretation of faith and religion
in *Fear and Trembling* – it is not Abraham's willingness to sacrifice
Isaac that holds Levinas's attention. We really do not know, after
all, whether Abraham was or was not prepared *in the final account* to
slaughter his beloved son Isaac. For who knows the innermost
intentions of a man or a woman before he or she has acted, other
than God? What holds Levinas's attention, rather, and what he
claims to be the "essence" and "highest point" of this overcharged
story, is not Abraham's alleged willingness to exceed morality, to
murder his son, but rather, in his words, "Abraham's attentiveness
to the voice that led him back to the ethical other." Central to
Levinas's exegesis is Abraham's obedience to the voice of an Angel
of God, the voice that calls out to him *not* to sacrifice Isaac. Thus
for Levinas the lesson of the Binding of Isaac is exactly the reverse
of what Kierkegaard learned. God does not demand the supra-
ethical. God does not demand the immoral. Holiness does not
require that one exceed ethics. While much of traditional Jewish
exegesis bravely stares evil in the eyes, without flinching, calling
evil evil, many other pages are spent "explaining away" the
manifestly immoral actions that appear in the Bible (e.g., David's
treatment of Uriah). Exegesis, never forgetful of the ultimate moral
underpinning of the real, and never forgetful of the imperfect or

[13] Levinas, "A Propos of 'Kierkegaard vivant'," in Emmanuel Levinas, *Proper Names*, trans.
Michael B. Smith (Stanford: Stanford University Press, 1996), pp. 75–79.

"unredeemed" moral character of the reality we live concretely, can show the good in an apparent evil as well as it can show the evil in an apparent good. And it does this without the least hint of sophistry, knowing well the difference between good and evil. Holiness is found in the "Thou shalt not murder" – this is the living word of the living God, inscribed on the face of every other who faces. This is Levinas's teaching. This is why he roots himself in religion – but not in the "God talk" of a self-confident faith, nor in the fearful and trembling faith of a Kierkegaard, a faith whose potential immorality is more fearsome than fearful, more terrifying than trembling.[14] In the same article, Levinas will wonder why Kierkegaard, in his long reflection on Abraham, nowhere considers or even mentions Abraham's glorious defense of the few righteous individuals who might have been present even in Sodom and Gomorrah. We have already remarked on the superiority of Abraham over Noah: when the world is threatened Noah accepts his own and his own family's salvation, while Abraham pleads for his fellow humans.

I would like to suggest an answer to the question why Levinas did not speak or write directly of "personal religious experience," and rarely spoke or wrote directly of the "faith" of inner relation to God, prayer and ritual. And in this answer I see yet another way to appreciate the value of exegesis as a philosophical "method" and as a form of religion, as the bridge linking the divine and the human. My answer can be stated briefly as follows: God's public face, as it were, is morality and justice – ethics. His private face, in contrast, is the inner relation of prayer and ritual – the faith of "positive" religion. To write philosophically, that is to say, publicly, about the faith of prayer and ritual, is to skirt falling into the trap of personal witness. By the "trap of personal witness," I mean a discourse that really only makes sense to the one who enunciates it. I do not mean that it makes no sense at all (i.e., is an impossible because contradictory "private language," pure gibberish, sounds or scrawls on paper, "talking in tongues"). Not at all. I am not at all suggesting that prayer and ritual make no sense. The question is not whether they make sense, it is rather what sense they do make.

[14] The recent American movie *The Apostle* (1999) vividly portrays a faith that commits murder but remains complacent in its alleged faithfulness to God.

The discourse that reveals the inner meaning or faith of prayer and ritual, both in their doing and in a testimony about them, necessarily remains personal, necessarily lacks the compelling hold on the consent or dissent of others that universal discourse commands.

Prayer and ritual are peculiar, then, in that the sense they make is not exhausted by a sense that can be communicated universally. In this they resemble song, whose sense is not exhausted by the discursive meaning of the sentences enunciated, but also involves such non-linguistic dimensions as melody, harmony, intonation, and rhyme. The faith of prayer and ritual, in a word, represents the private side of religion. One can speak of them, to be sure, and in them one speaks, too, but they have to do, in their depths, with individual personal relationship with God (even and also when they are manifest in a communal setting). Like the bonds of marriage, in other words, they have an *inwardness* essentially resilient to public scrutiny. Morality and justice, in contrast, are the public side of religion, the public face of God, as it were. Unlike prayer and ritual, they do command universally. Prayer and ritual cannot contradict ethics, but neither are they exhausted by it. For ethical discourse, which articulates the incomparable "impact" of a non-encompassable transcendence, rises to the sobriety of the universal. Such is exegesis. Exegesis is "testimony," to be sure, involves the exegete existentially, as we saw in chapter 7, but its involvement is fundamentally an ethical involvement. Its involvement is not unfaithful to its faith, but neither is it a pure expression of faith.

To attempt to make the private or faithful side of religion public is necessarily to succumb to "fundamentalism" (or what recent philosophers have castigated under the label "foundationalism") of one sort or another. I may choose to share, as best I can, the meaning of my personal "experience" of God in prayer and ritual with select friends, presumably with close friends. But when I make this meaning public, when I communicate to each other and to all others – that is to say, when I enter into public discourse – then the particularities of my discourse can have no verifiable or ethical claim whatsoever on those others. Others may judge me, to be sure, but never will the self be able to make manifest its unique relationship – as unique – to God as expressed in prayer and ritual. This was, I think, Schleiermacher's basic insight: that each individual must experience God individually, and that means in a way that precisely cannot be either fully understood by the individual or directly communicated to others. Kierkegaard, too, with his various *noms de plume*, struggled with this same dilemma: communicating a faith that is meaningful but essentially incommunicable. Nonetheless, let me add, and as Schleiermacher also recognized, it is interesting, though difficult to explain, that individuals who have in their unique individuality experienced God through prayer and ritual seem to have more in common with one another, even if no universal discourse can capture that commonality – which after all is not the commonality of essence – than those individuals who have never had such personal "experience" of God. Such commonality, with nothing in common, is no doubt at the root of the formation of "positive" religions: communions of the incommunicable. The route from personal "experience" to public discourse, that is to say, to philosophy, is rather found through the testimony of exegesis, at once personal (existential), public and ethical.

Piety, then, delineates our private sphere with God, an irreducible aspect of the holy. Morality, justice, and ethics – however little they are in evidence in our world – are not independent of piety, but rather represent the public or universal manifestation of God, what Levinas calls "holy history." The proper "philosophical" mode of both ethics and religion, then, would be exegesis. Ethics as exegesis and exegesis as ethics would thus be a bridge joining the private and the public, the holy and the true, being and transcendence. When, on the contrary, the private faith of piety attempts to usurp the public place of ethics, ostensively bypassing universal discourse for "religious witness," what results is not piety but "fundamentalism" and fanaticism, having very little to do with genuine religion. And when, for its part, ethics attempts to usurp the place of piety, when it forgets its biblical and revelatory beginning, when it turns its back on all transcendence except its own self-transcendence, then political fundamentalism and political fanaticism result. Piety, then, is the hidden, personal, or inward face of ethics – its ethical name is "conscience" – just as ethics is the public face of piety.

What this means, assuming that public and private are not mistakenly reified and treated as two separate ontological regions, is that Levinasian thought, with its overriding concern for morality and justice, is not at all another case of reductive universalism, or of secular humanism. Rather, Levinasian thought – exegesis – is precisely the humanism of religious humanism, the only humanism worthy of its name. For only this sort of humanism respects both the public and private dimensions of humanity, as it respects both the public and private faces of God. And it does not do so abstractly, as a theory or thesis. Rather, exegesis speaks to each person in his or her unique singularity, across the unity and diversity of social nearness and distance, from the situation of one's own self, in solitude, to one's family, friends, neighbors, community, nation, country, all the way to one's bond with humanity as a whole. And that whole is not the reductive whole of commonality, of species being, but the prospective whole of peace, *shalom*, where each is beholden to the other and all others, "and I," as Dostoyevsky wrote, "before all others."

# Index

345